In Colonial New Guinea

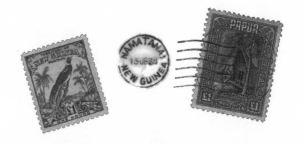

ASAO Monograph Series

Andrew Strathern, General Editor
Pamela J. Stewart, Associate Editor

In Colonial New Guinea:
Anthropological Perspectives

Edited by Naomi McPherson

University of Pittsburgh Press

ASAO Monograph Series no. 19

Published by the University of Pittsburgh Press, Pittsburgh, Pa., 15261, by arrangement with the Association for Social Anthropology in Oceania

LIBRARY OF CONGRESS CATALOGING-IN-PUBLICATION DATA

In Colonial New guinea: anthropological perspectives / edited by Naomi McPherson.
      p. cm. — (ASAO monograph; no. 19)
Includes bibliographical references and index.
    ISBN 0-8229-5751-5 (pbk. : alk. paper)
1. Ethnology—Papua New Guinea. 2. Papua New Guinea—History. 3. Papua New Guinea—Colonial influence. I. McPherson, Naomi M. II. Title. III. Series.
   GN671.N5 C64 2001
   305.8'009953—dc21   2001002662

In Colonial New Guinea is designed by Todd Duren of Firefly Design. The text is set in Filosophia and the titles in Gill Sans.

For Lawrence

Contents

Acknowledgments   ix

ASAO Editors' Note   xi

Notes on Contributors   xiii

Chapter One · **Introduction**   1
Naomi M. McPherson

Chapter Two · **Colonial New Guinea** · The Historical Context   15
Paula Brown

Chapter Three · **Conceiving New Guinea** · Ethnography as a
Phenomenon of Contact   27
Sjoerd R. Jaarsma

Chapter Four · **Anthropology and Administration** · Colonial
Ethnography in the Papua New Guinea Eastern Highlands   45
George Westermark

Chapter Five · **Unvarnished Truths** · Maslyn Williams and
Australian Government Film in Papua and New Guinea   64
Robert J. Foster

Chapter Six · **"Wanted: Young Man, Must Like
Adventure"** · Ian McCallum Mack, Patrol Officer   82
Naomi M. McPherson

Chapter Seven · **Paternalism, Progress, Paranoia** · Patrol
Reports and Colonial History in South Bougainville   111
Jill Nash

Chapter Eight · **The Queen of Sudest** · White Women and
Colonial Cultures in British New Guinea and Papua   125
Maria Lepowsky

Chapter Nine · **Juxtaposed Narratives** · A New Guinea
Big Man Encounters the Colonial Process   151
Richard Scaglion

Chapter Ten · **Three-Day Visitors** · The Samo Response to
Colonialism in Western Province, Papua New Guinea   171
R. Daniel Shaw

Chapter Eleven · **Afterword** · An Anthropology of Colonialism
Out of the "Last Unknown"   174
Eugene Ogan

Notes   201
References   221
Index   243

Acknowledgments

The idea for this volume originated in 1993 while I was interviewing retired patrol officers and their wives, nurses and medical officers, and agricultural officers about their experiences as part of the Australian administration in the Territory of New Guinea. The annual meeting of the Association for Social Anthropology in Oceania provided an ideal venue for the exploration of the topic of colonialism in Papua and New Guinea, and I am grateful to Okanagan University College for the financial support that permitted me to attend the ASAO meetings. My thanks also to those many Pacific scholars who participated in our seminars at the meetings and contributed their ideas and experiences to our discussions, thereby enriching all the papers presented here. I wish to express my gratitude to the contributors to this collection, who waited patiently for the outcome of their efforts in the publication of this volume. I am most indebted to the ASAO Monograph Series Editors, Andrew J. Strathern and Pamela J. Stewart, who stuck with me and provided moral support and editorial leadership without which this book would not have been possible. Finally, I wish to thank my husband and in-house computer expert, Lawrence McPherson, who saved me innumerable hours and days by converting all the different word-processing programs used by the contributors; reformatting all text, bibliographies, and notes; and fixing computer crashes and glitches.

ASAO Editors' Note

Andrew Strathern and Pamela J. Stewart

Studies of colonialism and its aftermaths in the *longue durée* have acquired importance in anthropological analyses in step with a general turn in anthropology to the writing of history. Among Pacific scholars, this overall shift in focus has by now produced a long list of innovative works, many of them cited by the authors in this volume. It is worthwhile to note here that, as with all things, this turn to history did not suddenly emerge out of a vacuum. Historical dimensions formed a part of earlier traditions of writing, for example, under the rubric of acculturation in American cultural anthropology and in Britain with works by anthropologists such as M. G. Smith on West Africa and the Caribbean and Isaac Schapera on South Africa, both scholars who brought their biographical experience to these topics in the early 1960s. The present volume therefore has benefited from both the more recent proliferation of writings on history in general and the longer traditions of work in the field, as Eugene Ogan notes in his concluding observations.

In keeping with the contemporary emphasis on multiplicity and critical reflection, the authors of the essays collected here look at the colonial experience through a diversity of eyewitnesses, sources, and viewpoints, including those of indigenous leaders, Australian government officers, prominent women, a filmmaker and his sponsors on patrol, and a Summer Institute of Linguistics linguist and anthropologist, who shares an unusual set of reflections on his role and that of his family. These narratives give us a rich and nuanced set of testimonies and observations, enabling the volume as a whole successfully to highlight the diversity of historical personae involved in the colonial area. Equally, these case studies aptly convey the point, known also from popular accounts, that colonial rule by no means implied unanimity or harmony among the missionaries, traders, and government officers who formed the bulk of the colonial agents. This collection of papers is an important contribution to the ongoing and ever shifting debate on the topic of the colonial experience as seen from various perspectives. The contributing scholars have each uniquely addressed colonial impacts from their own point of view as specialists who work in New Guinea. The book will undoubtedly appeal to a wide audience, especially to those interested in history, and will complement the contemporary work of others who have used the historical approach (for example, Strathern and Stewart 2000) as well as research that has utilized biographical materials from Pacific Islanders (for example, Strathern and Stewart 1999 and Stewart and Strathern 2000). New Guinea is a place that captures the imagination, owing in part to its great linguistic, cultural, and environmental diversity. Much of the historical complexity of human experience in this island is revealed by the contributions herein. Naomi McPherson has done a splendid job bringing these papers together and shepherding them along through the three-year ASAO cycle in which papers are presented and discussed annually until they are ready for final presentation. The job of the session coordinator and volume editor is a difficult one that requires patience and intellectual strength. We are very pleased to see this collection published at the beginning of the new millennium and are confident that instructors will seek to use this text as they introduce their students to the colonial experience.

March 22, 2000—Pittsburgh, PA. USA

References

Stewart, Pamela J., and Andrew J. Strathern, eds. 2000. *Identity Work: Constructing Pacific Lives.* ASAO (Association for Social Anthropology in Oceania) Monograph Series No. 18. Pittsburgh: University of Pittsburgh Press.

Strathern, Andrew, and Pamela J. Stewart. 1999. *Collaborations and Conflicts: A Leader through Time.* Fort Worth: Harcourt Brace College Publishers.

———. 2000. *Arrow Talk: Transaction, Transition, and Contradiction in New Guinea Highlands History.* Kent, Ohio: Kent State University Press.

Notes on Contributors

Paula Brown received her Ph.D. from the University of London in 1950. She was a Fellow at Australian National University from 1958 to 1965 and is currently Professor Emerita State University of New York, Stony Brook. She conducted fieldwork among the Chimbu (Simbu Province) in Papua New Guinea (1958–1987) and in the New Hebrides (Vanuatu, 1964–1965). Her interests include social anthropology, agriculture, social change, history, multiethnic relations, and politics. Her recent publications are *Beyond a Mountain Valley: The Simbu of Papua New Guinea* (1995); "Introduction to Change and Conflict in Papua New Guinea Land and Resource Rights," *Anthropological Forum* (1997); and "Simbu Property," in *Property in Economic Context* (1997), ed. R. C. Hunt and A. Gilman.

Robert Foster teaches anthropology at the University of Rochester, Rochester, New York. He is the author of *Social Reproduction and History in Melanesia* (1995) and the editor of *Nation Making: Emergent Identities in Postcolonial Melanesia* (1995). His current research interests include globalization, nationalism, mass consumption, and comparative modernities.

Sjoerd R. Jaarsma is a graduate of Utrecht University (1982) and obtained his Ph.D. at the Catholic University of Nijmegen (1990). An anthropologist by training, he specializes in the history of anthropology and comparative ethnography of New Guinea. His present interests include the repatriation of ethnographic knowledge and field data, on which he is preparing an edited volume. He is the author of "An Ethnographer's Tale: Ethnographic Research in Netherlands New Guinea (1950–1962)," *Oceania* (1991), and "Your Work Is of No Use to Us: Administrative Interests in Ethnographic Research (West New Guinea, 1950–1962)," *The Journal of Pacific History* (1994). He co-edited, with Marta A. Rohatynskyj, *Ethnographic Artifacts: Challenges to a Reflexive Anthropology* (2000). At present he is attached to the Centre for Pacific and Asian Studies, University of Nijmegen.

Maria Lepowsky is Professor of Anthropology at the University of Wisconsin, Madison. She received her BA, MA, and Ph.D. in anthropology from the University of California, Berkeley. She is the author of *Fruit of the Motherland: Gender in an Egalitarian Society* (1993), and her current research interests focus on the gendered histories of intercultural relations in frontier and colonial New Guinea and California.

Naomi M. McPherson received her Ph.D. in cultural anthropology from McMaster University (1985). Currently she teaches at Okanagan University College, Kelowna, British Columbia, where she is Chair of the Department of Anthropology. She has spent two years living and working with the Kabana of West New Britain, Papua New Guinea, and has written on a variety of topics, including primogeniture (1985); myth, belief systems, and cosmology (*Pacific Studies*, 1994); gender relations and ethno-obstetrics

(*Urban Anthropology*, 1994); and the concept of culture shock (A. Thakur and G. Tunnell 1999). Among other projects, she is currently working on oral histories of the women and men who were members of the Australian administration and lived and worked in the Territory of New Guinea from 1939 to 1975.

Jill Nash was educated at the University of Minnesota and Harvard University. She is currently Professor and Chair, Department of Anthropology, Buffalo State College, Buffalo, NY. She has written and published on a variety of topics concerning the Nagovisi of North Solomons Province, Papua New Guinea, including music and archaeology. Her primary writings have concerned kinship, gender, and ethnicity.

Eugene Ogan is Professor Emeritus of Anthropology, University of Minnesota. He received his Ph.D. in anthropology from Harvard University. Intermittently from 1962 to 1978, he carried out ethnographic research among Nasioi speakers in North Solomons Province, PNG, publishing on topics ranging from pottery making to childbirth and alcohol use to modern political movements. He is presently based in Honolulu, where he continues his research and writing about the history and ethnology of the Pacific Islands.

Richard Scaglion is Professor and Chair of Anthropology at the University of Pittsburgh (where he also received his Ph.D.). His primary interests are Melanesia, comparative Austronesia, and the anthropology of law. Dr. Scaglion has conducted ethnographic field research among the Abelam people of New Guinea since 1974. He is the former Director of Customary Law Development for the Law Reform Commission of Papua New Guinea and has been a Visiting Fellow at the Australian National University, The University of Hawaii, and the East-West Center. He is editor of *Homicide Compensation in Papua New Guinea* and *Customary Law in Papua New Guinea*, and author or editor of numerous books and articles about Pacific cultures.

R. Daniel Shaw is Professor of Anthropology and Translation at Fuller Seminary in Pasadena, California. His publications, based on twelve years of living among the Samo, include *Kandila: Samo Ceremonialism and Interpersonal Relationships* (1990) and *From Longhouse to Village: Samo Social Change* (1996).

George Westermark is Associate Professor of Anthropology at Santa Clara University in California, where he is Section Head of the anthropology program. He received his Ph.D. at the University of Washington in 1981. His research work has centered on the topics of law and colonialism, with primary emphasis on the Papua New Guinea Highlands. His publications have dealt with conflict resolution and the courts. Currently, his research is focused on the colonial period on Guam. Recent publications include "Clan Claims: Land, Law, and Violence in the Papua New Guinea Eastern Highlands" (*Oceania* 1997) and "History, Opposition, and Salvation in Agarabi Adventism" (*Pacific Studies* (1998).

In Colonial New Guinea

One

Introduction

Naomi M. McPherson

> By endowing nations, societies, or cultures with the qualities of inter-
> nally homogenous and externally distinctive and bounded objects, we
> create a model of the world as a global pool hall in which the entities
> spin off each other like so many hard and round billiard balls.
>
> (WOLF 1982)

Wolf's billiard-ball metaphor is apposite to a reified concept of European colonialism as a self-contained, monolithic, and integrated causal force that
careened into or rolled smoothly over indigenous cultures and societies. The
reification of colonialism as a homogeneous entity is a legacy of the ahistoricism of
functionalist theory in anthropology, which assumed that non-Western cultures
were somehow poised in evolutionary stasis until "impacted" by incursions of European imperialism. Such incursions sent these societies hurtling toward the contemporary modernity of the relative century. We have "taken colonialism and its
European agents as an abstract force, as a *structure* imposed on local *practice* ..."
(Stoler 1989:135; original emphasis). Rather than defining "colonialism" as a
single structured experience that can be neatly labeled, recent studies of colonial
processes in Pacific societies assume that a much more complex multiplicity of
historical and cultural contingencies, events, and imaginings created a mosaic of
colonial experiences.[1]

Stoler argues that colonizers lived in "imagined communities" that were "con-
sciously created and fashioned to overcome the economic and social disparities
that would in other contexts separate and often set their members in conflict"
(1989:137). These disparities include differences of class, religion, ethnic origin,
and sex (Lepowsky, Chap. 8 herein), as well as ideas about the "native question."
Although colonials surely shared a sense of "being in this together," Lewis (1996)
provides a masterful analysis of the nightmare that was "the plantation dream" in
colonial Papua, showing that such "imagined communities" did not always rise
above their disparities. Fissures occurred among Papuan settlers along lines of

social class, job status, country of birth (Australia, England, Ireland, Scotland), and religious affiliation (ibid.:89). Planters, settlers, capitalist consortia, and governments were locked in bitter dispute about the *raison d'être* of the Papuan colony, their role in the colonization process, and, more specifically, their relationship to the Papuan people themselves. More imagining is going on here: not only did the colonizers imagine themselves, their communities, and the various colonial projects in which they were engaged, they also imagined the native communities into whose midst they had transplanted themselves. The situation is further complicated by the fact that the indigenes were also imagining the colonists among them. As Brown (1995) notes, the "white man" was a favorite interview topic with Simbu elders.

Having admitted the complexity of colonialism, we cannot possibly maintain a simplistic Cartesian dualism of us/them, colonizer/colonized, victimizer/victim or perceive a situation of one-sided influences implied by the unequal relations of power inherent in colonizations. Rather, we must acknowledge the differential relations of power and recognize that "arrows of influence may be drawn from the colonized to the colonizers. . . . [Thus] . . . individuals and local groups resist, subvert, accommodate, embrace, transform, or transcend the discourse, policies, and practices from the centre" (C. Shaw 1995:23). In this sense, "colonial projects" are "transformative endeavors" (Thomas 1994:106) that affect everyone involved, not just the subjugated peoples. Each of the original contributions contained herein explores specific events, experiences, personalities, and perceptions that constituted the transformative nature of Australia's colonial projects in Papua New Guinea. The locus of analysis is not just between colonizer and colonized, but on the way in which colonialism is experienced by individual actors and agents, for it is out of such interaction that colonial cultures are created (C. Shaw 1995). The chapters that follow provide a spectrum of historical and ethnological background to the colonial projects in New Guinea and Papua and look more closely at individual experiences and perspectives, drawing on the archival record, patrol reports, interviews, autobiography, oral history, and, not least, on ethnography.

In Chapter 2, Paula Brown provides an important historical overview of the incursions into Western Melanesia, over the last one hundred years or so, by foreign powers—which included Germany, the Netherlands, Britain, and Australia—represented by a miscellany of adventurers, administrators, travelers, traders, planters, miners, missionaries, and anthropologists. Brown also traces the development of the Australian administration from first-contact situations to an established colonial presence.

Australian interest in New Guinea grew out of a perceived need by the British Crown colony of Queensland to create a buffer zone between itself and the encroaching imperial powers of Europe as France, Germany, the Netherlands, and Britain busily established colonial outposts in the South Pacific. Given Britain's continued implacability to Australian concerns, particularly about German expansionism into the Pacific, the Colony of Queensland had dispatched in 1833 the Resident Magistrate of Thursday Island, Henry M. Chester, to take possession of eastern New Guinea and adjacent islands. Her Majesty's government was not amused. The message sent to the Colony of Queensland read, in part: "It is well understood that the officers of a Colonial government have no power or authority to act beyond the limits of their Colony, and if this constitutional principle is not carefully observed serious difficulties and complications might arise" (quoted in van der Veur 1966:15). This unsubtle slap on the wrist was followed by a critique of Queensland's concerns about then current geopolitics:

> The apprehension entertained by Australia that some foreign Power was about to establish itself on the shores of New Guinea appears to have been altogether indefinite and unfounded, and the inquiries which have been made by Her Majesty's Government have given them the strongest reason for believing that no such step has been contemplated (ibid.).

Britain ignored Captain John Moresby's annexation of New Guinea in 1873 and Queensland's involvement in the lucrative *bêche-de-mer* and pearling industries; however, an awareness of the strategic and commercial navigational importance of the Torres Strait led the Queensland government continually to pressure Britain to annex New Guinea. In the meantime, Germany had established commercial interests in the Pacific, founded the Neuguinea Kompanie, and, in September 1884, dispatched Dr. Otto Finsch from Sydney, New South Wales, to explore "the unknown or little known coasts of New Britain as well as the north coast of New Guinea to the 141st meridian in order to discover harbours, to establish friendly relations with the natives, and *to acquire as much territory as possible*" (ibid.:16; original emphasis).

By 1886, New Guinea and adjacent islands had been divided among the Netherlands (see Jaarsma, Chap. 3 herein), Britain, and Germany. Events in the last decade of the nineteenth century—including fears "of German aggression in New Guinea, of the French in the New Hebrides or, more vaguely, of Russian and American economic imperialism in the Pacific" (Clark 1987:184); a long history of intercolony rivalry in Australia and a burgeoning chauvinism cum nationalism; and the economic collapse of the 1890s and the subsequent depression—culminated in 1900 in the federation of the Commonwealth of Australia. On August 5, 1914, Australia awakened to find itself at war; a few short months later Australia had captured Rabaul in New Britain, the center of German colonial administration in New Guinea. With the New Guinea Act, effected in 1921, the German colonies in northeastern New Guinea and the Bismarck Archipelago became a League of Nations Mandated Territory under Australian administration.[2] On the island's southwestern coast, British New Guinea became the Territory of Papua in 1906, administered by Australia. The two territories continued to be administered separately until

1942, when, as Papua and New Guinea, they came under a single Australian administration. In 1975 Papua New Guinea became an independent nation-state.

It is important to note that the Australian colonial presence in New Guinea and later in Papua and New Guinea was a recent phenomenon and, compared to the history of European imperialism elsewhere in the world (e.g., the Americas, India, Africa, and Asia), was relatively short-lived and in many respects quite different. New Guinea was acquired for strategic purposes rather than in the quest for material riches (although certainly there were riches to be found), and its colonization was authorized and monitored not by a sovereign imperial power, but by the newly formed League of Nations, which played watchdog to the Australian administration of that mandate. This had an immense impact on Australian governmentality in New Guinea and on New Guinea's eventual independence. Contrary to other imperialist presences in the Pacific, the colonial presence in New Guinea was itself a colonized people: "Australia herself was still a colonial federation, still evolving through a piecemeal process of changing relations with her own metropolitan power, Britain" (Hudson 1971:2). New Guinea was never intended to be a "settler colony" like Australia; it was always assumed that, eventually, the expatriate Australians would repatriate to Australia, albeit not as soon as they in fact did leave. These differences affected the colonial project in New Guinea.

Taking a wider historical perspective, Sjoerd Jaarsma explores the relationship between contact situations and ethnography, both as a contact phenomenon and as a source of knowledge and understanding of the contact situation. Starting with a comparative overview of colonial and academic anthropological endeavors at ethnography in both New Guinea and West Papua (Irian Jaya), Jaarsma explores the relationship between different "stages in the contact process" that may double as a frame of reference for and as a representation of the ethnographic process. He perceives contact as gradually increasing in complexity, provisionally divided—by looking at the indigenous reactions to contact—into five consecutive stages: (1) first contact, (2) the early contact period of pacification and proselytization, (3) a stage of development and reaction that culminates in (4) decolonization, and, finally, (5) emancipation. The practice of (colonial) ethnography can then be envisaged in terms of the margins of interaction that the development of contact allows for. Each of the five stages of contact creates a frame of reference that both demands and allows certain ethnological questions to be asked and answered that the previous stage did not. The kinds of ethnographic questions raised and the data gathered change accordingly as local people become familiarized with the contact situation and more self-reflexive and responsive to the ethnographer's project, if only to try and figure out what is happening to them. Similarly, the ethnographer becomes increasingly familiar with the people, language, and environment under study, and this familiarity creates a framework for representation. Over time, as contact increases, so too do the possibilities for increasingly sophisticated ethnographic data gathering. But as Jaarsma points out, we need to "go beyond mere representation" of the contact situation in order to discover "why contact resulted in certain kinds of representation."

Several contributors to this volume take excellent advantage of a type of representation contained in patrol reports, the official record of the administration's colonial projects.[3] These written representations nicely complement those of indigenous oral history and ethnography. Compiled by the administration's man in the field, the patrol officer, or *kiap*, patrol reports were intended to keep the various levels of the colonial administration informed about the native situation. The reports were also an official record of the administration's "progress." At their inception, patrol reports, much like early ethnography, were highly descriptive and multifaceted, which makes them invaluable as ethnographic documentation. It was only after 1946, during the immediate postwar period when civilians began to return to New Guinea, that patrol reports took on a uniformity in terms of their format and style of reportage. In addition to reporting on village cleanliness, disputes, taxation, and the like, each patrol report included a title page, a daily diary, maps, census charts, and a report on members of the native constabulary who accompanied the patrol. Patrol officers reported on all those social and cultural topics so familiar to ethnographers; in many respects their reports constituted the administrative equivalent of the anthropological *Notes and Queries*. As reports were read and passed up the administrative hierarchy, items of importance to various governmental agencies were noted and forwarded to the relevant department for action.

Patrol reports included census data that, in addition to counting people, also counted houses, pigs, coconut palms, gardens plots, crops, and the like. The census was a standard ritual of the administrative presence that not only structured patrol officers' visits but also provided a primary reason for return visits on a six-month or annual basis (e.g., Sinclair 1984:50–53). When the *kiap* arrived (or even in expectation of his arrival), villagers lined up to be counted as the *kiap* required, usually in nuclear family units. The census was a critical part of the administrative intention to create a "population" that was bounded, countable, and connected to a particular geographic place. Through censuses, the administration imagined linguistically and culturally diverse indigenous peoples as a unified population.

Regardless of cultural, linguistic, or regional differences, the census reduced groups of people to units of enumeration, units perceived as structurally homogeneous, hence interchangeable. All natives were the same, subject to the same rules of administration; differences were only perceived in degree of progress (see Nash, Chap. 7 herein). Control required that people and places be accessible to government representatives; thus, semi-nomadic people were enjoined to become sedentary (see Shaw, Chap. 10 herein) and, in places like northwest New Britain, many hinterland settlements were relocated to the coast.

Censuses enumerated people according to place, sex, age, marital status, births, and deaths and were updated with each visit from the patrol officer. The information was scrutinized for public-health problems such as standards of hygiene (e.g., the outhouse issue in Shaw, Chap. 10 herein), diseases, and epidemics (e.g., the 1926 influenza epidemic in eastern New Britain investigated by Ian Mack, discussed in McPherson, Chap. 6 herein). Patrol officers looked carefully at disease types and rates and at the causes of death, and this information was abstracted out of the reports and forwarded to the medical officer (who would make his own medical patrol) and then to the Ministry of Health.

Jill Nash (Chap. 7 herein) analyzes the concept of "progress" in terms of economic development, the engagement in a cash economy, or even the ability for the indigenes to grasp European intent. The census, particularly birth/death rates, and its relation to public-health issues were implicit in the concept of "progress" as economic development. Thus, PO Dwyer (1954) notes that "control of malaria is essential if the natives are to benefit from the various copra and trochus shell projects in the area. . . . Any attempt to spray the malarious areas with suitable chemicals would help the immediate needs of the situation."[4] Good hygiene and health were valued in their own right by the administration, but a demographic transition from infectious to noninfectious disease was associated with the economic development or "progress" of a population.

The census was also critical to administrative efforts in the acquisition and recruitment of labor for commercial interests (plantations, mines, missions, and so on). The *kiap*'s census enumerated an available labor pool by counting the number of men between the ages of 15 (later dropped to 12 years) and 45. This number provided a basis from which, according to labor ordinances, one-third of the eligible male population was available to be recruited for the labor market. The ritual of the census permitted patrol officers to monitor the activities of recruiters in the area and to ensure that laborer quotas were observed. *Kiaps* were responsible for signing local men on and off their labor contracts and for making sure laborers received their payment settlements. Patrol officers frequently shut down areas to recruiters who had abused their licenses or where over-recruitment had occurred. In my reading of the patrol reports from West New Britain, much musing and complaining about the relative "backwardness" and "progress" of various groups is attributed to the desire, or lack of it, on the part of New Guineans to engage in what the colonizers defined as appropriate work. In a European worldview, work is redemptive spiritually and socioeconomically. In the colonial project, work was thus a crucial means through which the local people were inculcated with the desired ends of the civilizing process.

Besides census information, patrol reports also contained ethnographic and linguistic data gathered by the *kiaps*. In 1925, a system for training cadet patrol officers (CPOs) was implemented to provide cadets with training in anthropological concepts, notably the functionalist anthropology of A. R. Radcliffe-Brown, who was then building a department of anthropology at the University of Sydney (Campbell 1998). In his analysis of Eastern Highlands patrol reports over a thirty-year period,

6

George Westermark (Chap. 4 herein) focuses on the relationship between anthropology as an emerging profession and the evolving colonial administration. He is especially concerned to explore how anthropology "influenced the construction of cultural knowledge." At the Australian School of Pacific Administration (ASOPA), patrol officers received training in anthropology as well as "geography, government, health and first aid, history, law and map reading." Accordingly, anthropological concepts were deemed useful in dispelling ethnocentrisms, for instilling an appreciation for cultures as integrated systems, and in providing a methodology of inquiry into native life.

In the period from 1945 to 1973, Westermark identifies four distinct phases of reportage in the patrol reports, each lasting about six years. In the Eastern Highlands reports of the late 1950s and 1960s, global movements for decolonization and anticolonial sentiment accompany changes in reportage. In the late 1960s, reportage shifts again as pressure from the United Nations for Papua and New Guinea independence turns administrative attention to speeding up the civilizing process by creating local councils as a precursor to independent self-governance. Consequently, the range and detail of ethnographic data decreased, and as more and more New Guineans entered the patrol system in the late 1960s and beyond, anthropology as a subsection disappeared entirely from the patrol reports. Indeed, with independence, the patrol report as colonial text ceases to exist.

Westermark's identification of the changes in the patrol reports as colonial discourse applies equally to the patrol reports for West New Britain, with which I am familiar. The changing discourse styles he observes infuse all patrol reports, because the reports represent the changing politics of colonialism. In 1946, the newly returned civil administration was faced with post–World War II reconstruction and reparation (patrols were undertaken specifically to make war compensation payments to individuals and villages that had suffered losses in the war). This was a tense time as old hands and newcomers clashed pragmatically and ideologically (cf. Bulbeck 1992). Also, 1951 was the beginning of the Paul (later Sir Paul) Hasluck era (see Foster, Chap. 5 herein), which initiated a total alteration of the administrative system. A sense of promoting appropriate change (see Nash, Chap. 7 herein) accompanied a general decline in ethnographic reportage. What comes more to the fore in the reports is what can be called a constructivist reportage dealing with political and economic infrastructures such as roads, plantations, education facilities, government councils, elections, and so forth. This really was *A Time for Building*, as the title of Paul Hasluck's (1976) work suggests. The near "total absence of anthropological reporting" in patrol reports from the late 1960s on, as observed by Westermark, also correlates, interestingly, with the indigenization of the service. However, the decline of ethnographic data in patrol reports is compensated by an influx of professional anthropologists. "Between 1950 and 1955 a veritable 'wave' of anthropologists conducted sustained, intensive fieldwork" (Hays 1992:ix–x), and a second wave (which included Paula Brown, author of Chap. 2 of this volume; see Brown 1995) went into the highlands in the late 1950s and the 1960s.

Although patrol officers and their reports were the basis of the local administration in the Territory of New Guinea, the relationship between Territorians (expatriate Australians) and the federal government in Australia was fractious at best. Furthermore, Australians at home either did not know or did not care about the mandate in New Guinea. This lack of awareness of the Territory of New Guinea in Australia generally had much to do with the fact that the Territory was to be economically self-sufficient and not subsidized by Australian taxes. Because of this intended self-sufficiency, the local territorial administration was mostly unsuccessful when it did solicit the Federal Treasury for funds (see Downs 1980).

In 1951, Paul Hasluck was assigned the first portfolio as Minister of Territories, a position that Hasluck saw would be the end of his political career (which turned out to be correct). He was determined to "extend Australian knowledge of and interest in the Territory [of New Guinea]" in order to gain the political (and financial) support he needed to put various programs (e.g., health, education, economic development) in place (Hasluck 1976:218). He reasoned that, in order for his policies to work, he needed political support from the Australian people. One way he chose to solicit their political goodwill was to commission the production of a series of films that would inform Australians (and the United Nations) about Australia's role in Papua and New Guinea. He selected Maslyn Williams to create these films.

Robert Foster (Chap. 5 herein) presents a fascinating analysis of the relationship between Hasluck and Williams and provides insight into how "the government films made by Maslyn Williams in and about the Territory ought to be seen as potent projections of an Australian national identity." Hasluck's objective was to inform the United Nations (the watchdog) of the various problems and issues Australia faced and to demonstrate the work already accomplished in Papua and New Guinea in fulfillment of the United Nations Trusteeship Agreement of 1946 (cf. Hudson 1974). Williams's films also constitute another form of colonial project. Besides showing the United Nations the administration's progress in the Territory and the distance yet to be covered, the films were designed to attract recruits to the civil service in the Territory, which was always severely understaffed (see McPherson, Chap. 6 herein). The films played on the taming of a wilderness, with the local inhabitants—as icons of "natural man"—represented as one more aspect of the wild and perilous landscape to be tamed. Colonialism was always a masculine (heroic) undertaking (see Lepowsky, Chap. 8 herein), and themes of masculinity and mateship permeate the films.

With this as political background, Foster's focus is on the experiences of Maslyn Williams as a filmmaker and on the constraints under which he worked to produce the films. Foster explores the "ethic of constrained authenticity" under which Williams worked in an effort to produce a film in his own way. Williams's agency, his "circumstantial capacity to act autonomously," is compromised in the production process, as the films were never entirely his own design or under his control.

Williams was always subject to Hasluck's agenda, which, as Foster points out, is a "set of circumstances . . . generally familiar to both individual colonizers and colonized alike." Williams reclaims his creative agency by shifting from filmmaking to fiction writing, through which, ironically, he "freed himself to make things up" and to represent New Guinea on his own terms, honestly and believably.

Naomi McPherson's chapter returns to the business of "fielding the mandate" in the Territory at the beginning of the New Guinea Mandate period with a focus on a particular patrol officer, Ian MacCallum Mack, who patrolled New Britain from 1926 to 1933. It was always difficult to recruit field officers, but Mack recruited himself. His motivation seems to be a complex admixture of duty to King and country, a desire to compensate for being too young to serve in World War I, and an ineffable stubbornness and sense of adventure. Mack's patrol reports describe the conditions and day-to-day grind of patrolling, the dangers and challenges met, as well as the small personal victories. His reports also document events going on at the time—the complex circumstances preceding the slaying of several miners; intergroup disputes and murders among the local population; punitive expeditions—and his growing knowledge of the country and genuine affection for the people. As was the case during the early years of the Mandate, Mack's reports include lengthy ethnographic descriptions, detailed linguistic data, and insights into administrative attitudes.

The key to the colonial administration's presence and purpose was the patrol officer. To the colonized, these men represented a foreign presence and will and were exemplars of a particular type of European culture and society. *Kiaps* were pivotal in interpreting and carrying the colonial message to the indigenous people with whom they came in contact and, conversely, in interpreting the villagers to the colonial administration through their firsthand experiences and written reports. Rather than see Ian Mack as an exemplar of colonialism or a patrol officer writ large, McPherson's objective is to show him to be a complex and complicated individual. Roger Keesing and Margaret Jolly (1992:234) suggest that recapturing experience from archival material, such as patrol reports, requires more than just reading the text; it requires an attempt to hear silent voices, submerged perspectives, and actions through the text. This is clearly another form of imagining. McPherson sketches a sociohistorical context against which to ponder one *kiap*'s experiences of New Guinea across the gulf of time, age, and gender. Newspaper clippings, patrol reports, and personal details about Mack and his family background generously provided by Mack's sister, Miss Margaret Mack, and his nephew, Richard Mack, allow glimpses of Ian Mack and the colonial project within which he lived and for which he died.

Jill Nash injects a much-needed subaltern point of view by combining official depictions of Mesiamo, a Nagovisi big man, with her own understanding of Mesiamo gained during her fieldwork in Nagovisi. Patrol reports from the postwar period to independence are the basis of Nash's discussion of the themes of

paternalism, progress, and paranoia, which, to some degree or another, characterize the colonial period not just in Bougainville but throughout Papua and New
Guinea. From the Nagovisi reports, Nash examines the intentions of the colonial
government and the factors involved in the "creation of an official record through
the writing of patrol reports." At a grand level, the whole concept of colonialism is
paternalistic, based on masculine authority, hierarchy, and power differentials. In
the Nagovisi reports, this finds expression in the sentiment that native leaders,
such as Mesiamo, should allow themselves to be led by the administration rather
than show their own initiative, and they should never challenge the administration.
These attitudes are also expressed within the hierarchy of the service itself: young
patrol officers should not challenge their senior officers either through their own
knowledge and experiences in the field or through offering opinion and interpretation of the situations they encounter in the field. Implicit in the concept of paternalism are issues of progress, development, and advancement—all ideas associated with theories of evolutionary progress and the ranking of peoples and
cultures as more or less civilized.

That colonized people are "backward" and in need of direction and guidance to
advance is an attitude that underwrote and validated colonial incursions. Indeed,
paternalism and progress are major rationales for colonization as expressed in the
League of Nations Mandate and, later, the United Nations Trusteeship. Within the
Covenant of the League of Nations, colonized peoples, by definition, are backward
and "not yet able to stand by themselves under the strenuous conditions of the
modern world . . . [consequently] . . . the tutelage of such persons should be en-
trusted to advanced nations . . . [and] the well-being and development of such
peoples form a sacred trust of civilisation" (Covenant, cited in Hudson 1974:179).
The UN Trusteeship declared that member states have a responsibility to assist
these peoples "in the *progressive development* of their free political institutions, according to the particular circumstances of each territory and its peoples and their
varying stages of development" (ibid.:181; emphasis added). As Nash and others in
this volume point out, local peoples are compared to one another as more or less
backward relative to their acceptance or rejection of administrative (and missionary) advice, effort, and direction. Individuals or groups who appear resistant to
authority (either passively or aggressively) and whose social and political movements threaten the status quo were defined as anti-white and anti-administrative
by worried patrol officers and administrators. The rise and fall of Mesiamo's reputation with the administration highlights issues of paternalism, progress, and paranoia so prevalent at the time.

Indeed, Lepowsky argues here that scholars have assigned a "disproportionate
historical weight" to accounts and memoirs created by "government officials and
missionaries who lived in New Guinea." The official administrative presence was
the patrol officer in the field, but the number of officers on the ground was extremely thin, and *kiaps* patrolled only once or twice a year in areas where there

were no patrol posts with resident patrol officers. Thus it was the "unofficial" whites—missionaries, planters, miners, traders—that the local people interacted with on an ongoing, long-term basis. These "unofficial" whites—who also included various sojourners such as traders, pearlers, publicans, and women—are submerged or ignored in the "official" historical record. Rarely did these people keep or publish accounts of their lives, and retrieving their experiences from the historical record is a difficult undertaking. Lepowsky is concerned here to recover the voices of white women who came to New Guinea and to Papua.[5]

Mrs. Elizabeth Mahoney became a part of Lepowsky's own fieldwork experience when the Vanatinai assumed Lepowsky to be the incarnation of this intrepid colonial woman. For two decades, the widow Elizabeth Mahoney ran her plantation and reared her large family alone. Lepowsky attributes the key to Mahoney's success, aside from her almost larger-than-life personality and presence, to her awareness that "the best incentive for securing gold and labor" was to engage in exchanging these commodities for the desired local valuables: "shell disc necklaces." Clearly, Mrs. Mahoney was not duping the locals, for, as Lepowsky points out, the islanders themselves "socialized local European traders" by withholding their labor and the products of their labor, such as gold dust and pearls, "unless compensated with their own valuables" and with new valuables such as tobacco, calico, machetes, and the like. Through their interactions, Mrs. Mahoney and the islanders transformed the indigenous system of exchange.

Richard Scaglion's juxtaposition of indigenous biography and a personal history of contact to the public histories generated by Euro-Australian colonists and Japanese soldiers in New Guinea during World War II provides another much-needed perspective, not only in this volume but within analyses of colonialism generally. By representing and highlighting the agency of New Guineans during this colonial era, Scaglion portrays the invasive Other from a New Guinean perspective. In particular, we are introduced to Moll, an Abelam big man, whose autobiographical account of his experiences during various colonial projects in the Sepik foothills turns our attention to two theories of time that "result in quite different historical orientations." Euro-Australians perceive time as a linear phenomenon, an epistemology from which notions of progress, advancement, and development follow logically. The Abelam concept of time is processual; change usually involves repetition and replacement, but sometimes time is episodic and cataclysmic, resulting in a complete restructuring of reality (see also Thurston 1994).

Scaglion injects an important cautionary note into an anthropology of colonialism. In our rush to condemn colonialism, he asserts, we must not lose sight of the fact that "essentializing the colonizers as victimizers in a hegemonic global ideology trivializes the field of action of the colonized." Moll's perspectives on, opinions of, and experiences with Euro-Australians as a cargo carrier, plantation laborer, and domestic worker at a Sepik patrol post and, later, his experiences with the Japanese during World War II are, in terms of governmentality, an unofficial history of major events in New Guinea's colonial era. Moll's voice and his autobiographical accounts of these events thus "act as a corrective to the more structural and monocultural versions of the historical process."

Daniel Shaw's chapter presents yet another perspective on relations between colonizers and indigenous peoples based on his long association with the Samo in the Southern Highlands. Shaw's relationship with the Samo is based on his dual role as an anthropologist and as a Bible translator for the Summer Institute of Linguistics (SIL), which, he acknowledges, might appear to some as "self-contradictory." No doubt other contributors to this volume (indeed, most anthropologists) have explained their presence and motives to the Papua New Guineans with whom they lived and worked by carefully differentiating themselves from missionaries, government officers, and other intrusive foreigners. Thus, Jan Pouwer (quoted in Jaarsma, Chap. 3 herein) relates the process of translating and being translated in the presentation of self and his efforts to disassociate himself from missionaries, government officers, traders, and other types of foreigners with whom the Mimika were already familiar—all of whom "exerted some form of foreign power" that might have affected his own objectives as an anthropologist. Yet, as becomes abundantly clear, Pouwer the anthropologist was a bit of all those Others: he took censuses (*kiap*), he was interested in Mimika beliefs (missionary), he wrote incessantly (clerk), obviously due to a bad memory. And Pouwer (indeed, all anthropologists) *does* exert a form of foreign power—both beneficial and potentially dangerous—the power of the written word to capture knowledge and the power of ethnography to represent the Other in a world system of "incommensurate differences" (Gewertz and Errington 1991:14–22).

From his perspective, Shaw sees his dual role not as self-contradictory but as complementary, emphasizing that his "sole reason for being involved with the people is to do linguistic and cultural research which can be applied to doing Bible translation." Although not a missionary—indeed, their translators are expressly forbidden by SIL rules to actively proselytize or preach—and often in conflict with other resident Christian missions in Samo territory, he is committed to bringing the Christian "word" to the Samo through biblical translation and exegesis. Thus, while he cannot exclude himself from membership among those "outside agents of change" about whom he writes, Shaw does believe that, by having "the Bible available," the Samo are better prepared to respond to the changing circumstances wrought by those outsiders.

The Samo were first contacted in 1953, but they didn't have a close look at the strangers until an extensive patrol came through the area in 1959. The first census was done in 1966. A series of biologists, botanists, and doctors went through the area in 1973, taking various specimens and tests. In the 1970s, a series of religious missions were set up but then disappeared over several years. Strangers came and went. Nobody seemed to stay long until Shaw and his family arrived and stayed among the Samo for a twelve-year period, a length of time that few anthropologists (and no colonial administrators) are able to accomplish.

Shaw chronicles the various patrols through the area during which the patrol officers were intent on reducing killings, tribal fighting, and cannibalism. Initially, the Samo understood little about the reasons behind the strangers' demands on them, but they accommodated themselves to the various intentions of a series of patrol officers. The Samo welcomed the cessation of local hostilities, Shaw tells us, because of the toll on human life. With the end of raiding, the rationale for isolated longhouses also ceased and, coinciding with patrol officers' decisions to set up patrol rest houses throughout the area, social organization shifted to nucleated villages established around government sites. Other officials, such as agricultural officers, came to the area, and gradually the Samo reduced their forest foraging to cultivate small fenced gardens. In order to construct gardens near their settlements, the Samo cut the forest back from habitation sites, thus moving the evil forest spirits farther away from humans. More people came to Samo: teachers, medical assistants, and others whose intention was development and progress.

Eventually, as national independence came closer, expatriate *kiap*s were replaced by indigenous *kiap*s. These new administrators were equally "foreign" to the Samo. Shaw makes an important point here when he observes that "national teachers, medical personnel and others" who replaced their expatriate counterparts "did not understand such a 'primitive context' and they sought to remove the Samo from it with haste." Like their predecessors, these dark-skinned Others also exhibit "paternalism" and are concerned with "progress" in their dealings with the Samo. Shaw is both chronicler and culture broker as the Samo respond to change. He is also philosopher-mentor, contemplating with the Samo the intricacies and intentions of Christian cosmology that have always been deeply embedded in Western colonialism.

The essays gathered here contribute novel perspectives on colonialism in Papua New Guinea expressed through a number of thematic issues. The colonial period was not homogeneous but rather a mass of contradictions and tensions located in the experiences of the colonizers, and we have tried to capture some of that diversity here. We have also tried to bring other voices to the fore by looking at particular individuals who were either marginalized or obliterated from the "official" histories of this period: Moll of Abelam and Mesiamo of Nagovisi; Mrs. Mahoney and other "unofficial whites"; Ian Mack, *kiap;* Williams, filmmaker; and, not least, anthropologists who stay longer than three days. We have looked at how a foreign minority imposed itself on a population and at the power differentials upon which their relationships were based. We have implicitly or explicitly touched on concepts of agency and intentionality on the part of both colonized and colonizer in the context of the sociohistorical background of a mandate developed as a consequence of two global conflicts and the shifting geopolitics of the late nineteenth and the twentieth centuries. Besides delving into the archival record, we have drawn on our own experiences during anthropological fieldwork in Papua New Guinea and on the experiences of our Papua New Guinean hosts through their oral history, biography, and autobiography, thus combining "fine-grained microethnography with holistic analysis" (Gordon and Meggitt 1985:41) to capture something of the heterogeneity of events, experiences, and perspectives that constituted Papua New Guinea's colonial era.

A great deal of work in this vein remains to be done. Scholars of Papua New Guinea have not focused overly much on patrol officers and not at all on other administrative officials who have been relegated to obscurity, for example, nurses (but see Kettle 1979), medical officers and medical assistants, and agricultural officers. Also, as Eugene Ogan points out in his afterword, there has been little anthropological analysis of the various commercial interests in Papua and New Guinea (but see Lewis 1996 for a historical account of plantation culture in colonial Papua). We hope the essays gathered here will stimulate further understanding of colonial projects in Papua New Guinea and beyond by "bringing concepts and techniques of anthropology to bear on colonial situations" (Ogan, Chap. 11 herein).

Two

Colonial New Guinea
The Historical Context

Paula Brown

This chapter provides a historical context for the chapters that follow, whose subject is the course of the colonial project (Thomas 1994) as it involved the people of New Guinea and foreigners—officials of the colonial governments, settlers, traders, missionaries, and others. Histories of colonialism in West Irian and in the territories of Papua and New Guinea are already published and others will follow. Here, I review and summarize the history of contact between newcomers and the indigenous people of the eastern half of New Guinea. Although a general process can be traced from first contact through missionization and government control to the colonial state and (in Papua New Guinea) independence, individual experiences and local conditions show a great deal of variation.

First Outside Contacts

Western Melanesia, including the island of New Guinea and the many offshore islands and archipelagoes, has been inhabited for many thousands of years. It was probably settled in two main waves: first, the Papuan or non-Austronesian, and, later, the Austronesian, which was part of a larger movement that reached islands of the central and eastern Pacific. Likewise, trade with Indonesia and Asia to the west is well documented (Swadling 1997) for the region over a comparable historical period. Before there were colonies or claims by Holland, Britain, or Germany, a steady stream of visitors and settlers, including naturalists and collectors, traders, missionaries, miners and prospectors, frequented the area. Plantations were established and labor recruiters took Melanesians to work in Fiji, Samoa, and Queensland (Denoon 1997).

Missionaries arrived on the scene in the Pacific early on, as seventeenth- and eighteenth-century Christian European explorers communicated their concern about heathens to their homelands. However, the early missions did not succeed in New Guinea as they had in Polynesia. Marist missionaries first attempted a station at Woodlark Island in 1847, but it survived only eight years. Dutch Protestants began mission work at Dorei Bay in 1855, but again met with little success. The

London Missionary Society, which had great success in Polynesia, expanded mission work into southern New Guinea in 1871. Mission stations were established by Rev. William Lawes at Port Moresby in 1874, Rev. James Chalmers on the south coast of New Guinea in 1878 (Lovett 1903), and Rev. C. W. Abel at Kwato in Milne Bay in 1891 (Wetherell 1982). Between 1871 and 1890, over 190 South Sea islanders, mainly Cook Islanders, Rarotongans, and Samoans, entered southern New Guinea as employees of the London Missionary Society. In the Bismarck Archipelago, George Brown, a Methodist missionary, set up a mission in 1875. Several Catholic missions were established in German New Guinea before 1914, and German Neuendettelsau missionaries began in Finschafen with Johann Flierl in 1886. Many others followed (Biskup, Jinks, and Nelson 1968).

In some parts of New Guinea, mission settlements preceded by many years the establishment of permanent government posts and towns. In coastal areas, Pacific islanders settled in villages as teachers and missionaries, becoming the key "foreign" contacts long before Europeans or Australians were known. The mission settlement and personnel exerted influence and aimed to attract parishioners from nearby communities with schools and health facilities as well as church services. Mission staff also served as interpreters and intermediaries between the villagers and government officers, visitors, and others.

Early contact also included explorers and naturalists. Nikolai Mikloucho-Maclay made three visits to Astrolabe Bay beginning in 1871. He settled in the area, traded with local inhabitants for his needs, and collected specimens (Mikloucho-Maclay 1975; Webster 1984). In the 1870s, Luigi D'Albertis traveled in Papua, up the Fly River, and in the islands of Torres Strait observing wildlife and collecting plants and animals (D'Albertis 1881). Settlers, plantation owners, traders, and labor recruiters preceded colonial government representatives in many coastal and island areas.

Miners and prospectors, mainly in search of gold, began to work claims at Laloki in 1878, Sudest in 1888, Misima in 1889, Woodlark in 1895, and Yodda in 1899. Most missionaries, settlers, miners, and labor recruiters made their first contacts on outlying islands and coastal areas and only penetrated inland for some specific reason, as when mineral deposits were found.

Historical Overview of Colonial Administrations

Colonialism is created by the competitive relations of the great powers with one another, as it is a means of gaining power and economic benefits. Colonialism includes the establishment of settlements, investment in plantations, trade with ships for supplies and export of produce, use of native labor, and exploitation of resources—plants, animals, and minerals from sea and land (Lagerberg 1979). In the colonization of eastern New Guinea, "at no time were the indigenous inhabitants of Papua or New Guinea consulted about the various dispositions by Germany, Britain and Australia of their ancestral lands" (Parker 1995). The same can be said of western New Guinea.

Germans in New Guinea

Germans established plantations and trade in northeast New Guinea, mostly on the coasts of mainland Kaiser Wilhelmsland, the Bismarck Archipelago, and the Gazelle Peninsula. The coastal areas were controlled by the Neuguinea Kompanie and then by the German Imperial Government, whose main mode of travel was by sea, as there were no roads at first; thus, they had a profound impact on some coastal areas but little penetration inland. Their primary concern was development of European enterprise, especially by establishing plantations using local labor. In the process, they appropriated land of the Tolai people of New Britain for their plantations and for government use. The Parkinson plantation was established in 1882, a German settlement was founded by Godefroy in 1873, and in 1884 the Neuguinea Kompanie began developing primary resources and broader trade. Native police were used as an armed military service to work on government stations, to protect settlers, and to stop tribal fights. They conducted punitive expeditions, especially where the local inhabitants threatened German enterprise. The Germans appointed *luluai* (native officials) as village chiefs, held courts, and required natives to cultivate foods and coconut to sell to traders (Firth 1982).

The northeast section of the island was German New Guinea from 1883 to 1914. Dr. Albert Hahl was the governor from 1896 to 1914, although his administration had its greatest impact on the development of communications in the Gazelle Peninsula, where he spent most of his time.

British New Guinea

In 1884, southeast New Guinea was declared a British protectorate, and in 1888 British New Guinea became a Crown possession. Dr. William MacGregor was appointed administrator in 1888 and served as lieutenant governor from 1895 to 1898. MacGregor is best known for his contributions to exploration, institutional development, education, and pacification. In these early years in British New Guinea and Papua, a major responsibility of government administrators was to secure the safety of Europeans; indigenous murderers were arrested and punished (see Monkton 1921; Mayo 1973). MacGregor did not like to use physical force (Joyce 1971) but would resort to it if he deemed it necessary, up to and including the dispatching of punitive expeditions (see Schieffelin and Crittenden 1991:22). Early contact was often peaceful; however,

> the most violent encounters between villagers and foreigners in British
> New Guinea took place in the Northern Division. Every year between 1895
> and 1910 some community in the Northern Division or along the Waria

fought with foreigners. . . . Government officers, sometimes following and sometimes in advance of the miners, used the language of war. (Nelson 1976:172)

After MacGregor left in 1898 there were brief administrations of George LeHunt, C. S. Robinson, and F. R. Barton. In 1904, Hubert (later Sir Hubert) Murray, then chief judicial official in the protectorate, gave evidence that saw Barton dismissed and sent to a remote outpost in East Africa.

Australia in Papua

The British passed the administration of Papua to Australia with the Papua Act in 1905, and Australia appointed Hubert Murray to serve as lieutenant governor of Papua (Biskup, Jinks, and Nelson 1968). Murray set policy for the Papuan administration and set up his center of operations in Port Moresby (see Lattas 1996; West 1968b). He was opposed to violence, took a moral and humanitarian viewpoint, and would make colonialism a philanthropic project. Murray disliked the Australian legacy of power and violence in Queensland and the Northern Territory. For Papuans, his goal was not assimilation (which was an Australian goal for Aborigines), but association, preserving the individuality of native races while maintaining the equality and unity of the human race. He opposed the punitive expeditions that were a feature of German New Guinea and favored the British practice of Indirect Rule: "Murray saw his government's task as policing the violent excesses of power of white entrepreneurs, missionaries and government officers" (Lattas 1996:144). He would have only peaceful penetration in Papua, but this approach was not always followed by his officers, who had to stop cannibalism and killings and execute the law. In Papua most of the foreigners' contact was with the coastal and island people, so when the "Outside Men"—exemplified by Jack Hides and Ivan Champion, who had grown up in Papua—penetrated into unknown inland territory, they encountered people with no experience of colonial administration (Sinclair 1969, 1988). Hides and James O'Malley, with inadequate supplies and unsuitable trade goods, had a difficult time during their Strickland-Purari Patrol (Hides 1935; Schieffelin & Crittenden 1991). Murray's administration continued to encourage European enterprise, although Murray himself gradually began to support native enterprise as well. He believed that the established law must be based on the European model and often visited Papua posts to review the decisions of magistrates. Murray's paternalistic Papuan administration lasted until the beginning of World War II and was generally carried out separately from the larger and more populous New Guinea administration headquartered at Rabaul (Griffin, Nelson, and Firth 1979).

Australian New Guinea

The First World War was a turning point for New Guinea. Following Germany's defeat in the war, German New Guinea came under Australian military government

THE HISTORICAL CONTEXT

until 1921, after which it became a League of Nations Mandate until 1945. German properties were reviewed by the Australian Expropriation Board, which then auctioned moveable property and paid Germans for their possessions. Australians, primarily returned service men, subsequently took over German plantations and lands (Cahill 1997). Australia appointed an administrator, whose center operated from the capital, Rabaul, on New Britain. The new Australian administration brought contact and control inland from the coast (see McPherson, Chap. 6), but many German procedures, such as the form of census and village books and the appointment of *luluais* and *tultuls* (native village officials), continued under the Mandate.

The Germans had barely penetrated inland New Guinea, but Australian exploration proceeded in the 1920s and 1930s with missionaries, miners, and administration officials (Griffin, Nelson, and Firth 1979). Discoveries of gold sparked highland prospecting and exploration, and the large highland populations attracted mission development. Two large exploratory expeditions in the 1930s, the Mt. Hagen Patrol and the Hagen-Sepik Patrol, made first contact with the inland area, mapped it, and laid the foundations for further administrative contact as well as for the introduction of trade, missions, and prospecting. Here, too, highlanders and other inland peoples might have their first or most significant encounter with intruding missionaries, miners, or government officers and police, with distinctively different consequences (Taylor 1933, 1939; O'Neill 1979; Nilles 1987; Radford 1987; Leahy 1991; Gammage 1998; Kituai 1998; Bergmann n.d.).

World War II and After

The war period from 1941 to 1945 disrupted the administration of Papua and New Guinea. The civil administration throughout the Territory was replaced by the military administration of the Australian New Guinea Administrative Unit (ANGAU), which employed many Papuans and New Guineans as laborers, aides, and carriers in the war effort. Some areas were occupied by Japanese military units, and the local people saw fighting and foreign soldiers at close range. The war had profound effects on the communities closest to military action and on people working in war activities. Reestablishment of civil administration following the war involved new officers, new duties, and, after the transfer to the United Nations, a drive for education and economic and political development never contemplated in the prewar administration.

After World War II, the mandated territory became a United Nations Trusteeship, Papua and New Guinea were joined for administrative purposes, and colonial officers were reassigned. A much-expanded body of officers was developed, and new departments were created for specialists in agriculture, economic and political development, education, and medicine. The administration trained Papua New Guinean teachers, medical workers, and field officers in government, agriculture, and economic development. New political institutions—local government councils, a Legislative Council, an elected House of Assembly—were established and preparations were begun for independence, which would require an elected parliament and Papua New Guinean people trained for administrative and technical positions. This period was dominated by Paul (later Sir Paul) Hasluck's administration (Hasluck 1976; Ward et al. 1979) and those of his successors, Charles Edward Barnes and Andrew Peacock (see Downs 1980). From 1953 until his retirement in 1967, Donald (later Sir Donald) Cleland was administrator of Papua and New Guinea. During this time, several United Nations visiting missions reviewed the Territory's progress as well as any publicity and information produced about Papua and New Guinea (see Foster, Chap. 5). These administrative and educational developments set the stage for self-government and the rise of Papua New Guinea's political parties. Independence in 1975 brought new and different relations between Papua New Guinea and outsiders.

Colonialism and the Indigenous Population

> Colonialism . . . was . . . a cultural project of control. . . . Cultural forms in newly classified "traditional" societies were reconstructed and transformed by and through colonial technologies of conquest and rule, which created new categories and oppositions between colonizers and colonized, European and Asian, modern and traditional, West and East, even male and female. (Dirks 1992b:3)

The great eighteenth-century period of European exploration and trade expansion began a new era in the movement of people, the spread of goods in trade, labor recruitment, mineral prospecting, foreign settlement, the development of plantations, missionization, colonization, and colonial administration in the region that finally culminated in the inclusion of West New Guinea in Indonesia in 1965 and the independence of Papua New Guinea in 1975. The peoples of New Guinea and the islands met with these visitors and colonizers at different times and in different circumstances, and early contact took many forms, from kidnapping men in the Louisiades to work on Queensland sugar fields in 1884 (Nelson 1976:7) to peaceful penetration of the Southern Highlands by Australian patrol officers in the 1950s (Sinclair 1984). Each community, and sometimes each person in the community, had a distinct early-contact experience that might include Polynesian or Scottish missionaries and teachers, New Zealand and Australian goldminers and prospectors, German coconut plantation managers, Chinese traders, European labor recruiters, Australian colonial officers, Papua New Guinean police, or American anthropologists (Hays 1996). The chapters that follow show some of this diversity; however, we are only beginning to recognize the importance of New Guinean police (Gammage 1996a, 1996b; Kituai 1998), evangelists in isolated posts, and South Sea missionaries in intercultural relations (Bromilow 1929), and of the relations between Indonesians and New Guineans in the western part of the island.

Many of the accounts of early contact (e.g., Humphries 1923; Lett 1935) show that the villagers' immediate reaction to the intruders was hostility: "Go away" is frequently quoted. The community men met the intruders armed and often barred their entry into the village. In the 1930s, the discovery of large native populations in what was then called the central highlands (as well as in the less-populated interior mountain area) began with gold and oil prospecting, mission exploration and establishment, and exploratory government patrols. A patrol required supplies for the leaders, a police force, and a body of carriers. Usually, police supervised the carriers, checking their loads and arranging their work, food, and sleeping places. Local people who acted as guides and interpreters as well as carriers might join the patrol.

Many instances of resistance, refusal to trade, and violence against the intruding newcomers are recorded (Hides 1935; Schieffelin and Crittenden 1991). Most patrols depended upon friendly trade with village communities for food, since the food they carried was intended for emergencies or for travel to areas with either no population or hostile people. The larger the patrol group of police, officers, and carriers, the greater the demand upon local people for food supplies. Patrol camps required firewood, tent poles, and other materials that were taken from the locality, often without recompense to the local inhabitants. Metal and shell became the favored trade goods in the highlands. When trade was denied or local people fled, the patrol "foraged" for food in gardens and left some trade goods for the garden owners. When the large Hagen-Sepik Patrol was unable to obtain food by trade, they made sago from native stands of palms.

Whether it took place as an encounter with a ship on the coast or an island in the nineteenth century or as an exploratory patrol into a remote inland village in the mid–twentieth century, first contact was a surprise to the local community. Native people who resisted or attacked were shot and killed by explorers, prospectors, and armed government police and officers. These first encounters must surely have been remembered when later patrols demanded pacification and arrested resisters, and they may have been responsible for further resistance or fear of arrests, and for acceptance of mission and government intervention. Reactions ranged from refusal and attempts to have the newcomers leave immediately (see Shaw, Chap. 10; Hays 1996) to enthusiastic acceptance and obvious strong desire to obtain the goods offered (Sinclair 1988; Brown 1995; A. Strathern 1996). In some other early encounters, local people found that providing food to visitors brought payment in shells, steel, cloth, and other valued goods (see M. Strathern 1992). Sometimes, as in the case of small shells given to helpers and suppliers in the highlands, an item of very small cost to the explorers or missionaries would bring a great quantity of food or pigs. In his discussion of highland patrols, Ian Downs notes that the amount of shell or other goods given for food needed care to avoid inflation, and that "interpreters had to be prevented from taking initiatives that would misrepresent us and frighten the people" (1986:114).

The earliest encounters could take many forms, but the gap in understanding and expectations was always very great. There are numerous examples of what I have called "no dialogue" contacts (Brown 1990; see also Schieffelin & Crittenden 1991; Fajans 1997; Shaw, Chap. 10). Everywhere, first contact and trade was followed sooner or later by the entry of missionaries, settlers (see Lepowsky, Chap. 8), and government officers. Local plantations as well as the sugar fields in Fiji and Queensland required labor, and men were recruited for this work. Recruitment as contract laborers gave New Guinea villagers experience of a world of control and technology never imagined at home. As time and exploration continued, first contact might be preceded by the tales and travels of New Guinea people who had already encountered Europeans (cf. Humphries 1923).

The Process of Colonial Administration

The early purpose of colonial administration was to protect European, and some Asian, settlers, miners, and traders and to stop thefts and raids. Foreigners entered the Territory to explore, seeking exploitable resources. The indigenous people were a resource as laborers. When preparing for or protecting European settlement and the exploitation of resources, colonial officers acted to stop raids and fights and to arrest murderers; punitive expeditions were at times considered necessary. As these goals were pursued, colonialism became defined as conquest, domination, pacification. It has also been characterized as governmentality (Pels 1997). Control was established by administrative action to stop raids and attacks on foreigners and to enforce pacification of neighboring warring communities.

> Those who hold that we should have left the primitive mountain tribes of New Guinea to their innocent, idyllic existence would possibly change their views had they have been able to see the fear, superstition and pain that dominated the lives of these people before the government stopped tribal fighting, bound their wounds and broke open the prison of their fearful isolation. (Sinclair 1984:89)

Pacification had two aspects: (1) to stop native tribal warfare and killing and (2) to stop rebellion and resistance to government control. Thus, pacification entailed disarmament and curtailment of the power of the native—both against neighbors and enemies, and against colonists and *kiaps*. In Australian New Guinea, there were stages of colonial projects. The administration would first define an area as "uncontrolled," meaning that the communities were known and may have been visited by an exploratory patrol. Second, areas "under government influence" meant that pacification was an important activity and an officer could enter the community to make an arrest. Finally, areas "under administrative control" were those where the people of the community had a census and a headman or *luluai*, were subject to Native Regulations, and could be punished for homicide, theft, or fighting, according to the law and order defined by the government.

Later, structured patrol officer visits were set up for village census taking, which involved lining up and viewing the whole population, and these occasions were often the only encounters villagers had with the bureaucracy. The census makes people quantifiable; births and deaths are recorded, needs for education and health provisions are assessed, and opportunities for labor recruitment are evaluated. The village book thus created a named unit—a tribe, village, or clan. Enumeration stabilizes and differentiates, fixes membership in a unit, and creates a collective identity.

From the beginning, Western intrusions demonstrated contrasts in relationships between the colonialists and the Melanesians. When police posts were placed in newly contacted areas, the first dialogue was between local people and the Australian-trained police from areas in Papua and New Guinea with longer contact. Supervision of police by officers could not always be close, and instances of coercion, taking of food, killing of pigs and of people, and taking of women may have been common (see Kituai 1998).

What we know of the Papuan and New Guinean views of the foreign intrusion and early contact is never a statement from the specific time and place,[1] although the moment of first contact may be recaptured, as in Connolly and Anderson (1987) and Schieffelin and Crittenden (1991). After some experience with government patrols or other outsiders, some sort of communication may be possible with the community members, as mediated by a police interpreter. When the first encounter is not a hostile one, and the community accepts the visitor's offer of trade goods for food, the welcome can become a demand for axes, knives, cloth, or other goods such as shell or beads.

Police from many districts served in newly contacted areas. Youths from villages along the route accompanied James Taylor's exploratory patrols. These youths learned Tok Pisin, the *lingua franca*, quickly and became interpreters in their communities and in places speaking related languages. Many later took official positions as police and interpreters, becoming significant intermediaries between these recently contacted communities and colonial administrators. Taylor established police posts throughout the highlands, where a single isolated policeman was the main contact for local people. Remote communities were considered "under government influence" when patrols and police succeeded in reducing tribal fighting and arresting murderers.

In the 1920s and 1930s, important new first contacts occurred between native inhabitants and Australian explorers, prospectors, patrol officers, and missionaries penetrating inland areas, especially the Sepik, then part of Morobe District, New Guinea, and the highlands of Papua (Taylor 1933, 1939). Pacification was the first endeavor (Knauft 1999), and discovery was followed by patrols to stop tribal fighting. Officers and police raided villages at night, took captives, sought and arrested murderers. Prisoners were employed as laborers and carriers, and after a term that included schooling in the new requirements of Australian colonial rule, they were returned home to be headmen, *luluais*, and *tultuls* appointed by the administrators as their representatives in local communities. In this collection, McPherson, Nash, Scaglion, and Westermark all describe *kiaps* (government officers) and local people in what we may term the high period of Papua New Guinea colonialism. Nash's apt terms *paternalism, progress,* and *paranoia* may have a far wider application than she makes for Bougainville.[2]

After the administrative posts were established, interpreters, police of the language group, headmen, and other representatives of the local people developed relationships that took a mediating and interpreting role between the *kiaps*, police, and other government officers and the villagers. Police had direct contact with local communities, especially on patrols and at police posts, but their exploitation of local people was rarely apparent to officers (Townsend 1968; Downs 1986; Gammage 1996a) and the full appreciation of the power and importance of policemen in colonial contact is only now being understood (Gammage 1996b; Kituai 1998). The government-trained medical-aid-post orderlies and teachers were also potential influences.

In the early days of contact, and even later when the local people had little experience of foreigners, stereotyping was common. If missionaries came first, all Europeans might be called "Padre," or if government officers were known, every newcomer might be *"kiap."* For example, since white women were only known in association with the mission in the area near Mingende in 1958, I was greeted with "God bless" for some time, but later was distinguished as Missis Paula or, more locally, as "Mintimamam" (mother of Mintima in Kuman Chimbu).[3] Soon after the Chimbu post was established, government officers remarked that the Chimbu did not yet recognize the difference between mission personnel and government personnel. It was only after some time with the same white person that individual names were used.

The same stereotyping is evident in the reports of officers on patrol and in memoirs. For example, J. Keith McCarthy (1963), George W. L. Townsend (1968), and Ian Downs (1986) usually name their fellow officers and other white men, and sometimes even their dogs and horses; they occasionally name Papua New Guinean police officers and personal servants, but rarely do they name local people. (See Scaglion, Chap. 9 of this volume, for a comparative discussion of information from government records and informants' stories.) The memoirs and books intended for a general audience are most often patronizing of Papua New Guineans, and frequently discuss the local people as undifferentiated categories of primitives, head hunters, cannibals, or, at best, villagers (cf. Williams 1964; Rowley 1966).

Local community members were more likely to have contact with Papua New Guinean police, interpreters, and government aides than with white officers, and

THE HISTORICAL CONTEXT

their understanding was guided by these contacts. The missions trained helpers and evangelists who became their most important contacts and interpreters in the local communities. The early contact period, whether the first view of the white man or a more protracted period in which a trader, mission, or government post was established in the area, was a time when the *kiap*, padre, or settler had a colonialist's idea of the purpose of contact and its requirements. However, the local people had their traditional views about strangers, their new knowledge of the white man's trade goods, and an evolving realization of the power of these new-comers and the danger of the weapons they used to stop attacks and tribal fights. When opportunities for employment as carriers, servants, or interpreters became available, some men (very rarely women) found the relationship rewarding both in learning the white man's ways and expectations and in the goods paid as wages. Men recruited for labor outside the area would have important tales to tell on their return. These people became the media for information and for ways to adapt to the new demands and expectations of the foreigners. Interpreters from local com-munities and police from other areas were also important intermediaries.

Since the 1920s, government anthropologists in both Papua and New Guinea conducted studies in local communities, usually to investigate specific problems or troublesome situations during a short stay. F. E. Williams carried out anthropologi-cal studies that have become classics; studies by E. W. P. Chinnery and Charles Julius are mainly in government reports. The course of study for patrol officers included instruction in anthropology at the University of Sydney, and later at ASOPA, the Australian School of Pacific Administration (Campbell 1998; see also Westermark, Chap. 4.).

When anthropologists set up residence in communities, their relations with the people took on a different character. In our 1959–1960 field visit, Harold Brookfield and I were able to attend pig feasts at a number of Chimbu ceremonial grounds. At a Siku ground, a few miles from our base at Mintima, we were welcome visitors and given a small portion of pork. The leading spokesman said, "Now when I visit you at Mintima you will have to give me what I ask for." Over the period from 1958 to 1965, Harold and I made many revisits to the Mintima area of Chimbu, where the Australian National University had built a house for research workers in the area. On each return visit we recorded population, land, and residential changes, marriages, births, and deaths; Harold's maps noted house locations, settlements, fencing, land tenure, and land use. Our friends would come to see us and update us on changes and events since our last visit. Then in 1967 Ben and Ruth Finney were assigned to occupy the house to begin a study of entrepreneurship. Our friends duly appeared and told them of the happenings since our last visit, as evidently Harold and I had trained them well. But the Finneys had other interests and found the Mintima people not readily retrainable to answer different questions. They removed to Goroka town and conducted their well-known study (Finney 1973) from there. As Sjoerd Jaarsma observes (Chap. 3), anthropologists are actors in the culture of contact, and our relations with the local population are structured by the culture of contact at that time. In this instance, the culture included our specific research interests and typical questions. The difference between the interests and resulting research publications of Finney, Brookfield, and myself demonstrates the point made by Jaarsma that the scholar's particular interests (and we might also include their style of personal relations with members of the community) create the context of contact culture.

European missionaries settled into a community and acquired land for their houses, churches, schools, clinics, and gardens. They formed close ties with the host community, often learning the language, and these establishments are often long-lasting. Schools and training programs prepared local people for service roles in their communities, and many became intermediaries and interpreters between the mission organization and local people.

In these ways, cultures of contact develop in specific contexts of village people and the different newcomers who represent official government, trade, plantations, missions, and so on. Differentials of power also vary, as the newcomers may be employers, priests, anthropologists, nurses, district officers, or teachers. There is no single culture of colonialism or form of colonial domination. The experience of colonialism involves a revision of behavior toward others, whether it occurs at the beginning of contact with traders, during the imposition of law and order by officers of the colonial government, or with acceptance of a foreign missionary in the village.

Three

Conceiving New Guinea
Ethnography as a Phenomenon of Contact

Sjoerd R. Jaarsma

As Naomi McPherson points out in her introduction to this volume, the concept of a single unified colonial experience is increasingly challenged these days. The result is the acknowledgment of a "complexity of colonialisms" in which it becomes impossible to "perceive a situation of one-sided influences implied by the unequal relations of power inherent in colonizations" (McPherson, Chap. 1). The ethnographic discourses of the period, as well as past and present uses of ethnographic knowledge, are equally subject to challenge in this respect. Although it may be more or less obvious to acknowledge the colonial character of ethnography, the less-than-monolithic nature of the colonial context of ethnographic writing usually remains unappreciated. It is my intention to show here that in appreciating ethnography we should go beyond its basis in anthropological method and theory, and look at the colonial context of its construction and consumption, as well as the indigenous appreciation of the colonial curiosity it stood for.

Though we need not share Talal Asad's (1973) monolithic qualification of anthropology as colonialism's handmaiden, it is useful to remind ourselves that anthropology's institutional history is strongly intertwined with colonialism. Anthropology's role is not necessarily that of an apologist of European expansionism, but it is an institutionalization of the need to describe and account for what happens as a result of such expansionism into other cultures. In the specific context of colonial contact, anthropologists focused on this encounter from a very specific position as members of a colonizing society and of necessity studied it only from the inside out.

Once we realize that what we study is determined by the nature of contact, it becomes obvious that our representation of contact cannot be unbiased. The essence of what we studied was determined by inequality, empowering one side of the contact equation and disempowering the other (see, for instance, Thomas 1991:84). We might surmise, then, that when the relations between the parties involved become more and more equal, contact itself would change in nature and become the direct exchange of goods, services, and information.[1] In fact, this element of delimitation extends to the way we study (and are able to study) processes of contact. We are, in a sense, as determined by what we study as by what we try to represent of the people we study. The early ethnographers had little if any concern for the people they studied. They were usually accompanied or preceded into the field by administrative personnel as a guarantee of both safety and cooperation (see George Westermark, Chap. 4).[2] Even when, after successful pacification of a certain area, such measures were no longer deemed necessary, the initial uncertainty about the identity of the researcher, usually confused with administrative officers or missionaries, effected similar cautions on the part of the people studied (see Shaw, Chap. 10).[3] Nowadays, our activities in the field are heavily proscribed both by a set of self-imposed ethical rules and—certainly in Papua New Guinea—by a system of permissions intended to increase local input into our research activities. In essence, we can say that where the emancipation and political empowerment of the people studied (or their advocates) has progressed enough for them to negotiate purpose and means of research on an equal footing, research is no longer part of a contact situation and ethnography no longer implicitly portrays the contact that engendered it.

What we know, then, of a culture of colonialism inevitably mirrors this inequality at specific stages; it is a representation of what we want to know at any one time. Dealing from this position of inequality, ethnographers have never felt the need to represent the situation studied as one of contact. We may either represent the people we study as being in contact with the larger-scale colonial society, or not. Ahistorical approaches to the description of culture and society, such as functionalism, have made the single-minded focus on culture in its own terms very much part of the development of ethnographic description. Whole bookcases full of ethnographies have been produced in which the process of contact is marginalized, categorized in terms of "elements of change" due to the "incursion of European imperialism," as McPherson so neatly phrases it in her introduction to this book. A representational ideal, the traditional society, is created that—though slowly being eaten away by (often unspecified) change coming from the outside—is taken as the focus of ethnographic description. That in itself becomes an anachronism if we start to take it too seriously, for any ethnography—anthropological, amateur, or otherwise—is an attempt to translate relative to our own culture a way of life that is beyond our immediate and commonsense understanding. Better put, it is an attempt to phrase questions and answers in a way that is relevant to our own understanding. The fact that we are there to describe or analyze a culture is an indication that there is contact, and hence change. We need to realize that not only the presence of the ethnographer, but the expansionism s/he stands for (or has stood for in the past) is interpreted and appreciated both in producing and consuming ethnography. There is always a two-way exchange of information, even though its tale is not always told.

Borrowing Insights

To illustrate both the relativity of contact and the problems facing the anthropologist in colonial times, I can do no better than borrow a lengthy anecdote from a Dutch anthropologist, Jan Pouwer, who worked among the Mimika or Kamoro of the south coast of Irian Jaya in the early 1950s. The quote is taken from *Translation at Sight*,[4] a lecture that aimed to provide its audience of graduate students and fellow academics with some measure of the theoretical and practical obstacles facing the anthropologist trying to "translate" the meaning of the concepts of one culture into those of another. While my excising of its central anecdote does no justice to Pouwer's theoretical argument, it provides me with a good sketch of an anthropologist's first plunge into the field, but more importantly, some measure of the indigenous appreciation of his presence:

> It will be clear by now that translation at sight is an intricate affair, where objects and subjects merge or at least intermingle. Moreover, this represents only one side of the picture. The other side is equally important: the research worker acting as a translator is being translated himself by his informants. This translation affects his translation considerably, and adds to the complications.
>
> Let me elucidate the process of translating and being translated by reviving my first and rather traumatic experience as a fieldworker in a New Guinea society, namely Mimika. In 1952 when I arrived in this swampy, coastal, somewhat isolated district of former Dutch New Guinea, the population had witnessed for about 25 years the presence and activities of two categories of foreigners: Roman Catholic Missionaries and Administration Officers. These agencies were assisted by Indonesian teachers on one hand and Indonesian administrative personnel on the other. A third category, namely Chinese traders, had preceded the two other ones by about 10 years. These traders set the pace even to such an extent that the Mimika term for foreigners in general is *Tèna-Wé*, that is, literally, China-people. I did not belong and did not wish to belong to one of these three categories because all of them exerted some form of foreign power, which might easily have had an adverse effect on my relations with the people. When I arrived in Kaokonao, the administrative centre of Mimika, it so happened that most of the village chiefs—occupying positions created by the Dutch Government—had been summoned to Kaokonao to attend a meeting arranged by the District Officer. I took this opportunity to deliver an address. I tried to drive home the point that I was neither a District Officer nor a missionary, nor a trader. To them I must have looked like a foreign no-man, for the position of anthropologist was as unknown to them as it is to large numbers of

civilised people. I translated my speech from Dutch into Malayan, the lingua franca of West New Guinea. In his turn the District Officer, an East-Indonesian Ambonese, translated the speech into a simpler version of Moluccan Malayan. His Mimika interpreter then proceeded to translate both translations into the Mimika language. Finally, it was up to the chiefs and their followers to render the address, considerably watered down and distorted by three translations, into their classification of foreigners. They then provided the fourth translation in succession. Small wonder their response to my presence could be best described as follows: "Let us be polite, but not commit ourselves. Wait and see."

What *did* they see? A puzzling jack-of-all-trades, who did not substantiate his claim to be a mile apart from the categories of foreigners experienced by them. Let me render their observations in their own words as follows: "Who is this man? He joins government officers on short trips and assists them in taking a census, an activity typical of a District Officer. After giving his attention to men, women, born and unborn children alike, he together with the District Officer turns to the job of vaccinating hens. It is true that after one or two months of co-operation with the District Officer, he now mainly travels on his own. But like a prospective District Officer he visits every village in the district and takes a census everywhere. He even asks for far more details than the present District Officer does. He takes down the name of your parents and grandparents. He is anxious to know to which kin group you belong. This is a rather embarrassing question, for you may not be quite sure. He inquires after your exchange-partners in marriage transactions. He is interested in the relation between the people living together in your home. He even tries to find out whether your children have changed teeth in order to estimate their age. In short he wants to pin you down. If you can avoid it, you had better not mention your name. Why take the risk of being jailed?" (Here I might add, it was not accidental that names were often supplied by the government-sponsored village chiefs rather than by the persons directly involved.) Census means foreign power. You are required to attend it. And foreign power is potentially dangerous. Census also means tax for the tax-roll is based on it.

"It is quite probable that the new Red-Man (Mìra-Mìra Wé), that is a white man turned into a Redskin by the sun, will replace our present District Officer. Haven't there been persistent rumours that our present District Officer will be transferred?" The translator translated. End of First Act.

"However, there are certain inconsistencies in the behaviour of the newcomer. Just like some Roman Catholic missionaries, he seems to be deeply interested in our sacred stories and our rituals. The District Officer is not really. So the prospective District Officer could equally be a priest. But then how to account for a married priest?" (Please remember, it was then 1952 and not 1968!) There are two possible answers: "Either he is a married ex-priest, or he is a priest turned into a Protestant exactly because he wished to marry. After all the ancestor of the Protestants, Luther, broke away from the Roman Catholic Church for the same reason, as some of our Indonesian teachers make us believe." The translator translated. End of Second Act.

"But whoever he is, he always carries with him a pencil and sheets of paper, piles of paper. Even when he strides behind the mortal remains of one of our beloved singers and drummers he inquires about the names of those who carry the coffin and takes them down in a notebook. Unlike us Mimika people, this man has a poor memory. We store our knowledge in our heads, but he stores it in his papers. He is Tuan Tõrati," that is, Mr. Paper, Mr. Letter (Tõrati is the Mimika equivalent of the Malayan word Surat = letter). "His letters, although dangerous, can be beneficial too. If we want to safeguard the ownership and content of our traditional lore so that a story-teller from another village can no longer steal the show or modify its content, we can have our stories fixated for ever, by the priest or by the Letter-Man." The translator translated. End of Final Act. The fieldworker impersonates a solicitor, a glorified clerk. (Pouwer 1968:11–14)

Representing New Guinea

Prior to dealing more extensively with the relation between contact and ethnographic description, we need to consider the diversity of contexts across the island that provide a setting for New Guinea ethnography.[5] My focus is limited here to the postwar colonial situation, as my own research material largely relates to that period. Though I consider differences between Papua and New Guinea and West New Guinea, I gloss over the earlier divisions in what was initially Papua and German New Guinea, then later Papua and the Mandated Territory of New Guinea. It is not my intention to be exhaustive here, merely to indicate the differential development of research attention against colonial contact as a frame of reference and representation. Also, we should keep in mind that the vast majority of ethnographic research has been done in the postwar period. Prior to the Pacific War, long-term ethnographic or linguistic research was occasionally done by missionaries and a handful of academic researchers. At the time, most of the ethnographic knowledge, whether on Papua, the Mandated Territory, or West New Guinea, was based on incidental writings by administrators, missionaries, travelers, traders, and explorers.

Whereas the actual contacting of peoples and the first clashes between colonial and other cultures can be placed both before and after the Pacific War, the attempts to develop the area (and subsequent obstacles to this) are a postwar phenomenon. In fact, the Pacific War can in some respects be regarded as a watershed, as it implied a number of very important changes. First, both West New Guinea and Papua and New Guinea suffered considerable setbacks owing to the Pacific War, not only in a material sense, but more importantly in administrative and missionary infrastructures. In both areas, along the north coast and in the interior, recently contacted groups had resumed precontact patterns of warfare. Also, mainly along the northern coast, cargo movements had sprung up. These movements relate both to the breakdown of administrative and missionary control and to the large influx of military goods and personnel resulting from the war effort.

Before the war, the administrations of Papua, the Mandated Territory, and West New Guinea had involved themselves mainly with maintaining control with a minimum of personnel, but in the first five years after the war, the purpose, scale, and setup of the colonial administration changed considerably. The purpose of administration now began to extend to development. Both Australia and the Netherlands, as members of the United Nations, were forced to abide by the stipulations in the UN charter on non-self-governing and mandated territories. The political reality of this was that economic and, in its wake, political development became priority issues. Both West New Guinea and Papua and New Guinea maintained the colonial status quo until after the main wave of decolonizations in the late 1940s through early 1960s had ebbed away. The fears of violent decolonizations like those in Africa and of the rise of communism in Asia were, however, consistent factors in the colonial policies of both Australia and the Netherlands.

By the early 1950s both the Dutch and the Australian administrations had been reorganized. In line with the wartime administration under the Australian New Guinea Administrative Unit (ANGAU), the Australian government had decided to unite both Papua and the Mandated Territory under one administration. The Dutch—retaining only West New Guinea after Indonesia's independence—had had to restructure their New Guinea administration entirely, increasing its scale and complexity. The combination of reorganization, enlargement, and new tasks meant that new personnel were drawn in. Contrary to the situation before the war, this new generation of administrative personnel by and large had no colonial background. Only the higher echelons of the administration remained intact. This meant that opinions toward the indigenous population began to shift, as some writers indicate, though this should be considered a very gradual process, as the "old hands" who did return after the war moved up in the administrative hierarchy.[6] This way their attitudes kept on influencing both administrative policies and junior officers responsible for implementing these policies (see Westermark, Chap. 4; Fenbury 1978).[7]

With the enlarged scale of administration and its new tasks, information on the population became more important and was gathered at an increasing rate. Prior to the war, both Papua and the Mandated Territory had a government anthropologist. This position still existed after the war, but apparently became less important.[8] A similar position did not exist for West New Guinea before the war, but one was created as a special research office (Kantoor voor Bevolkingszaken) in 1951. In the 1950s, the situation on both halves of the island developed differently. The Dutch administration retained most of the responsibility for research, using people from its various administrative departments. This was possible in part because the Dutch administration had a large core of academically trained staff and could employ them on assignments that demanded specific expertise if necessary. The Australian administration, with its largely professional but not academically trained staff, lacked these possibilities. Somewhere along the line the decision was made to use Australian universities as resources for expertise and to employ academic researchers in specific research institutions run by the administration.

Nevertheless, in the 1940s and 1950s the bulk of ethnographic information—both in Papua New Guinea and West New Guinea—was still gathered by the administration and missions, largely by amateur or untrained observers. The influence of these observers differs. In the Papua New Guinea administration, the names of the two 1930s government anthropologists, E. W. P. Chinnery and F. E. Williams, are still remembered.[9] Considerably more names are linked to the Dutch administration, mainly during the 1950s. Of these academically trained anthropologists, many went on to academic careers as anthropologists, development experts, and such. The missions in both parts of New Guinea show less contrast. The larger missions usually had one or more ethnographers, either of amateur status or academically trained, active at any one time. Additionally, a considerable amount of linguistic research was (and still is) done by the missions.[10]

The developmental influence of commercial interests is limited largely to Papua New Guinea. Although plantations existed in West New Guinea prior to the Pacific War, there was little further development during the 1950s. Large-scale enterprises (oil, mining, and lumber) did not really take off in West New Guinea due to the tense political relations between the Netherlands and Indonesia. Both in Papua New Guinea and West New Guinea these industries engendered some ethnographic research, however.[11] Ethnic Chinese played a leading role in small commerce both in West New Guinea and in the Mandated Territory of New Guinea. Additionally, large contingents of Indonesians and Indo-Europeans occupied commercial and clerical functions in West New Guinea. Consequently, small commercial enterprise was less of an option for indigenous entrepreneurs in West New Guinea/Irian Jaya than it was in Papua New Guinea (see Jaarsma n.d.b). In both areas some research was done—mainly following requests by the administration—into the development of small-scale enterprise in urban environments.[12] Additionally, the New Guinea Research Unit effected research into indigenous entrepreneurship in the highland and coastal regions.

Academic anthropologists were still rare in the early 1950s, though overall more numerous in Papua New Guinea than in West New Guinea. For the first time in the history of the discipline anthropologists were among the first to contact certain populations. This created a new problem, as there was little in the way of examples for comparison. Consequently, the frames of reference used to analyze the available material relate more to the background of the discipline than to New Guinea itself. While Papua New Guinea material was placed against African ethnography,[13] West New Guinea ethnographic data were interpreted in terms of what one knew of Eastern Indonesia. This difference gradually cleared as, in the late 1950s and early 1960s, enough ethnographic material became available to use New Guinea itself as a basis for comparison and analysis. Nevertheless, as indicated earlier, the distinction between the eastern and western side of the island that was introduced in this early period of large-scale academic attention remained of basic importance.

From the early 1960s onward, the number of academic researchers active in New Guinea began to increase.[14] Initially, most of the researchers active in Papua New Guinea worked from Australian universities, mainly the Australian National University and Sydney University, but in the late 1960s an increasing number of United States–based researchers became involved. Similar developments occurred too late for a stable academic base to develop on West New Guinea/ Irian Jaya at Dutch universities, and this had to wait until the late 1980s and early 1990s. It is hard to say what would have happened in Irian Jaya if it had remained accessible for academic research.[15] In Papua New Guinea, however, the spectacular increase in academic researchers outstripped most of the administrative research effort and confined most of the missionary ethnographers to an institutional discourse.[16] The number of administrative and missionary contributions in the larger anthropological journals and in journals dedicated to New Guinea gradually decreases after the 1960s. Also, most of the journals dedicated to a mixed popular, professional, and academic audience on Papua New Guinea and West New Guinea stopped appearing during the 1960s and 1970s.

Compared to the situation of the late 1940s and early 1950s, much of the diversity in ethnographic representation has now disappeared, effecting probably an unforeseen increase in the inequality of relations between researchers and people studied. Previously, at least some of the ethnographic description was produced to satisfy a local missionary and administrative audience. Presently, most of the ethnographic representation of New Guinea is done as the result of academic anthropological research. By and large academic institutions and non-governmental agencies sponsor this effort. In consequence, ethnographic knowledge on the area is considered to be an academic domain. The audience addressed is equally academic; an audience among the people being studied is only starting to develop and cannot make a stand as yet for its rights to be kept informed.

Dimensions and Representations of Contact

As indicated above, I see colonial contact primarily as a background against which we can see develop both the people we study and the way we describe them. Colonial contact, however, is far from a constant and consistent phenomenon. I analytically discern a number of different settings in the contact process, each of which might to some extent be taken as a specific context for ethnographic information, specifying needs for information and allowing certain types of information to be gathered. These settings are first contact, early contact (pacification and proselytization), development and reaction, decolonization, and emancipation.[17] It is hard to avoid the suggestion that there is a linear progression in the nature of contact between these settings. In general, we find the first three settings concentrated in the 1960s and 1950s, extending back to the beginning of the exploration of New Guinea. The final two settings are largely found in the 1960s and increasingly in the 1970s and beyond. Keeping this "line of progression" in mind, we still find different settings existing concurrently at any one time. Contact not only occurred at different moments across the island, but often at a vastly different pace if we compare one place to another. Essential to note here is that the increasing sophistication of contact engenders, on the one hand, new questions for ethnographers to answer. On the other hand, it allows ethnographers to gain more information from their fieldwork, in both a qualitative and a quantitative sense, as the people studied become increasingly used to the contact situation, more self-reflexive, and hence responsive to research.[18]

So-called first contact is the best-known stage. Archetypal for the description of this stage of contact are the diaries of explorers like Michael Leahy, reports of both private and administrative expeditions entering and occasionally crossing the interior of New Guinea, and the writings of very early ethnographers like Mikloucho-Maclay and Richard Thurnwald. All these writings have in common that the fieldwork on which they are based is explorative, that is, there is no preset purpose or aim except to open up new areas, locate new resources, and such. The study of people met along the way in the course of the expedition was usually of very limited duration, unless the people in question happened to be located near one of the more permanent camps used by the expedition or explorer. The extent and nature of the information gathered was very much determined by the kind of expedition or purpose of the exploration.

Keith McRae, in "*Kiaps*, Missionaries, and Highlanders" (1974:17), can still state that his article "attempts to add some depth to the sparse treatment of early contact history in the New Guinea Highlands." Since then a lot of historical and ethnographic material has been added to what we know of those early explorations and the kind of contact they established. Edward L. Schieffelin and Robert Crittenden, for instance, working from the concept of "structure of conjuncture" developed by Marshall Sahlins (1985), distinguish several aspects to first contact that may lead to cultural revaluations as a result of contact (Schieffelin and Crittenden 1991:283, 292; Schieffelin 1995). In fact, Schieffelin and Crittenden extend Sahlins's conception, as they consider contact to be not only a "structure of conjuncture" but also a possible "structure of *mis*juncture." They distinguish three aspects as influencing the impact of first contact.

First is the ability of the people contacted to evaluate the events of first contact in terms of their cosmological knowledge, thus providing a frame for conjecture upon contact. Even if such a frame for conjecture is present, the actual nature of conjecture and understanding is subject to subsequent historical events: "It may also happen that subsequent historical events are so constituted that they disrupt or displace this understanding, or reframe it under another set of ideas" (Schieffelin and Crittenden 1991:286). The incorporation of the arrival of newcomers into the local cosmological framework would, of course, be all the more strengthened if and when it triggered an important scenario, such as a ritual sequence.

A second point (ibid.:288) specifically addresses the long-range implications of first contact and the possibilities for retrieval of information on first contact: The temporal continuity of events and more importantly the way these are retained in the local memory influence how contact is perceived and especially who is seen to have effected it.[19]

The last factor that Schieffelin and Crittenden mention is what they call "the integrity of the social distribution of knowledge" (ibid.:289). They point out that the sense of shared history is for some groups expressed in shared overlapping biography. If and when such groups become dispersed, their shared memory may very well fragment into "individualistic biographies scattered across the countryside" (ibid.).

As Schieffelin and Crittenden's evaluations of first-contact events are dedicated to the Strickland-Purari Patrol of 1935, the researchers can to a large extent ignore the aspect of precontact knowledge. Given the existence of trade contacts and the like stretching into noncontacted areas, the knowledge of outsiders may very well predate any actual European attempts at contacting.[20] McRae summarizes Leahy's progress through the highlands as follows: "The further south they moved the more reluctant the people were to exchange food, and they were certainly less aware of the potentialities of steel. Leahy felt that some people, then living in caves near Lemaki, were 'too stupid to sell a pig for a tomahawk, asking instead for tambu shell'" (McRae 1974:17).

The demand for and appreciation of iron is a good way to evaluate the amount of preexisting knowledge; it is in many respects the most "revolutionary" innovation linked to first contact. Thus McRae's summary describes Leahy's gradual move out of areas that had any conception of what was to come. In this sense, Schieffelin and Crittenden's first three points on the nature of contact retention can be extended to allow for indigenous evaluations of contacts with whites prior to the actual event. "Decisions" to integrate such events into existing cosmological events, such as to take them as precursors of ritual sequences, were then not made "on the spot," but were already well rehearsed. Also the possibility to react to unforeseen events—as indicated in Schieffelin and Crittenden's second point—was enhanced.

Pacification is usually dealt with as the "inevitable" outcome of colonial contact, and in a sense it is, because of the vast difference in scale and resources of the colonized and colonizing society. Still, opinions differ as to what pacification entails. In a symposium on the pacification of Melanesia, the following very general definition of the process was coined: "a sequence of linked events that follows from direct or indirect contact between native peoples and a colonial or neocolonial power" (Ploeg 1979:161). Anton Ploeg, commenting on this definition, adds that it sets pacification apart from a wider process of encapsulation and that it ignores a radical change in the use of violence that he considers central to the phenomenon. He then rephrases the definition as follows: "that part of the process of encapsulation of a native people which entails the restriction of its use according to the wishes, or presumed wishes, of the encapsulating power" (ibid.). Though this definition is appropriate to Ploeg's purposes as he recounts the introduction of the Pax Neêrlandica in the Bokondini area, it still only describes part of what actually happens. We must not only take into account changes in the use of violence, but also changes in patterns of trade, the safety and extent of movement, and so on. More important is that the "encapsulation" involves a radical change in the scale of society and the subsequent need for infrastructure: economical, political, and otherwise. Pacification can in that respect also be defined as "the phenomenon whereby a central intertribal or interregional institution imposes on a relatively autonomous population a form of societal organization and order suited to controlling multiple groups, thereby for the first time adding this previously relatively autonomous group permanently to a larger political unity" (Miedema 1984:21; translation SRJ).

An interesting aspect of Jelle Miedema's definition is that we need not automatically assume that the intertribal or interregional institution we are speaking of is the colonial administration. It can equally well describe the activities of missionary institutions, which is why I have previously placed pacification and proselytization in the same category (Jaarsma 1997:70). Until the Pacific War, the pattern in West New Guinea was usually one of the missions preceding the Dutch administration and forcing official acknowledgment of the territory thus gained (Verschueren MSC 1953–1954). Similar developments can be seen on the Papuan coast and the islands of New Britain and Bougainville.[21]

The role of commercial interests as pacifying agents is harder to assess (see Maria Lepowski, Chap. 8). The establishment of plantations certainly had the effect of pacifying the immediate surrounding areas, usually in cooperation with the administration. Similarly, the recruitment of labor has had the effect of pacification in the sense of creating dependencies and breaking down precontact patterns of subsistence (Panoff 1979, 1990). It is doubtful, however, that it created a lasting larger political unity among the people contacted. This is essentially why not all first-contact efforts can automatically be qualified as effecting pacification. As I pointed out above, not all cases involved a "temporal continuity of events"; rather, some groups were subsequently left to fend for themselves again, sometimes for as long as a generation.

To curb the rampant growth in exploration and to limit its negative effects, the Australian administration in 1935 imposed a ban on access to uncontrolled areas and restricted the movements of those people already present in the highlands.[22] Connolly and Anderson (1987:216) indicate the deaths of two Catholic missionaries and the resultant concern with the protection of Europeans as an immediate cause (see Brown 1995:88–89). Indigenous reactions to the presence of Europeans had gradually become more belligerent, especially where the impact of first contact had receded and contact had increased. The increase in violence toward Europeans is usually represented as the result of disappointment and frustration. A pattern of expectations had been created by the contact with the whites, but very few means had become available to fulfill these expectations. All administrations gradually enforced an increasing number of stipulations to regulate the developing contact process. These concerned not only the access to uncontrolled areas, but also the use of indigenous labor.

The representation of pacification and proselytization is, apart from some retrospective studies, a very one-sided affair. We know very little of the indigenous reactions, barring the often near-mythical representations of the first missionaries and *kiaps*.[23] The attention given in many ethnographic representations to the unaffected, precontact situation usually precludes the extensive analysis of change. Our knowledge, historical or otherwise, only begins to improve once the concerted efforts to develop the indigenous population gain momentum. Then, too, an increasing number of—often equally concerted—reactions from the indigenous population can be discerned. We can in fact look at the contact process here through different glasses, using two distinct types of representation: first, the evaluations of development efforts, often focusing on economic aspects as well as indigenous health, social welfare, and the like; and second, representations of indigenous reactions to change, ranging from straightforward descriptions of social disturbance to attempts at unraveling the "logic" of an unforeseen backlash. Both types of representation—in many respects artificially—create bodies of ethnographic description that differ in purpose and nature (see Jaarsma 1997). Taking a purely Eurocentric point of view, we can easily distinguish these efforts in terms of the investments made in education, economic assistance, and religious morality by administrations, missions, and other developing agencies. Initially, analyses of cults followed this straightforward ethnocentric judgment in using negative terms like "short-circuit reactions" (i.e., van Baal 1953–1954:247). In later years, the method followed became more sophisticated, focusing on indigenous intellectual attempts to find answers to problems raised by contact (Jaarsma 1997). Neither method adequately explains what happens, they just make "common sense" of what we see and provide us with instruments for its description.

We cannot automatically assume that there are actually two different reactions to describe. Although descriptions of acculturative movements seem to have diverged from those of "desirable" economic, social, and religious development, it is hard to say whether we actually study or merely represent divergent developments. Nancy McDowell puts this very clearly:

> What I want to suggest here is that . . . cargo cults do not exist, or at least their symptoms vanish when we start to doubt that we can arbitrarily extract a few features from context and label them an institution. For that is what many anthropologists have been doing: isolating and classifying these phenomena as if they constituted an objective separate institution, category or class of events. (1988:121–122)

She suggests that we change the semantic field and relate the cult in our analysis to people's ideological or cultural constructions of change. Some ethnographers, of course, have attempted to bridge this representational gap. Ton Otto (1991), in his analysis of the Paliau movement, for instance, begins by analyzing three different frames of power (*kastam, lotu, gavman*) emanating from the contact situation. Only then does he show how Paliau and his followers, manipulating these frames, could build and maintain their movement. There is a limit, however, to what we are shown. Even though Otto provides us with a considerable amount of detail on the contact history that gave rise to the movement, the focus is inward, expounding mainly on local issues.

On the other extreme are statements like that of Pem Davidson Buck, who contends that the entire discourse on cargo cults serves but one purpose, which is to make the simultaneous oppression and protection of Papua New Guineans acceptable in terms of colonial contact:

> This, then, has been the role of cargo-cult discourse. It purports to expound the truth of Papua New Guinean activities, and at times provides worthwhile analysis of cargo thinking itself. But by exaggerating cargo thinking and divorcing it from practical activity which it generally justified and accompanied, it has contributed to a more generalized colonial and neocolonial myth about exploitative relationships between colonized people themselves and about the dependency relationship between "developed" and "underdeveloped" nations. This myth explains domination and exploitation by defining the behavior of the dominated as irrational or self-defeating behavior which thus produces "underdevelopment" despite the best efforts of the colonizers in their use of local labor. It permits the differential suppression and encouragement of activity that has been labeled "cultic"; as a result it has been formative of Papua New Guineans as well as Europeans. (Buck 1988:168)

Here the focus is clearly outward, on more global issues. We are shown that cargo cults are equally a representational must for the colonizing society, serving as an ambiguous category that can be used to encourage or repress as the situation dictates.[24]

In both cases we are shown only partial images of specific efforts to make contact develop into a situation that works for both sides. The partial character works in different directions and is—at least in part—dictated by circumstance. Although both Buck and Otto bridge the "perceived gap" between European and indigenously engendered representations of the changes resulting from colonial contact, neither author would have been able to cover the other's focus without his argument becoming unmanageable. This is, in fact, what we generally see in representations of contact in the setting of development and reaction. Contrary to representations of first and early contact, the former no longer have any overview; now we only see details where before we often lacked the necessary detail on the indigenous appreciation of contact. In this third setting—most noticeably in the ethnographic descriptions of acculturative movements—there is an increasing struggle to make sense of the changes (and representations thereof) relating to contact.[25] The amount of ethnographic data is such that representing it holistically is no longer possible. This affects what we know and especially the way we know.

Contact and Representation

The changes in data gathering involve more, however, than just a change in scale. A definitive change in nature and content also occurs. Researchers who have worked in both first- and early-contact settings and in more sophisticated settings have remarked upon the difference in the ethnographic data they have gathered, both qualitatively and quantitatively. The more contact experience the people studied have, the more easily informants seem to comprehend not only the questions asked but more basically the need for information. A significant quote in this respect comes from James B. Watson:

> No stranger, I had returned to find I could talk readily with the people, elicit once difficult information with unprecedented ease. They for their part knew much more about white men, surely magnifying the acknowledged advantage of the ethnographer's revisit. While the distance had shrunk between the villagers and me, that between some villagers and others had widened. Much had happened to set old and young apart, in a village which, to the best of their effort and insight, had qualified for—and proclaimed—its entry into modernity. Talking to fellow villagers was now in some respects not unlike talking to outsiders. . . . Learning from having to understand their own children, older Agarabi have apparently acquired some facility in understanding strangers. Meeting villagers today, an inquisitive outsider would quite likely feel relatively little frustration. They would probably find his questions comprehensible, even in-

ETHNOGRAPHY AS A PHENOMENON OF CONTACT

teresting. They would grasp at once his lack of background and need of explicitness. If they wanted to, some of them could explain to him the premises he must recognize in order to understand their answers. They could talk to him, and he might therefore never realize what it was like before for them to talk with strangers. (1972:181)

During the ten-year period between Watson's two visits, the Agarabi had not only opened up considerably to the outside world, they had opened up to themselves, become self-reflexive. To consistently answer questions on the nature of culture, the people studied need first to appreciate that there is a question to answer. With the factual growth of the world perceived around them, the Agarabi have also had to come to grips with their own place "within" it (see Shaw, Chap. 10).[26]

These changes in the understanding between researcher and people studied are not merely coincidental, they are structural. J. W. Schoorl, writing on the methodology of short-term ethnographic research by administrative personnel, formulates a number of prerequisites for its successful performance. One of these is a need for a certain openness in the research area for this kind of research or, more to the point, a familiarity with its performance (Schoorl 1967:176–178; cf. Jaarsma 1994:165). Generalizing this to some extent, we can say that the people we study need to be able to represent themselves in order to be represented by ethnographers with any kind of subtlety and sophistication.[27]

What evolves is a balance between the need of the researchers for good and interested informants and the need of the people studied to comprehend what is happening to them. This does not imply that there is actually a situation of reciprocity here.[28] The people studied have little if anything to say about what is being researched or why. They may have made themselves an image of a "European asking questions," but their grasp of what anthropological research is all about still remains limited. Also, they have no access to the ethnography written about them, as literacy remains rare.[29] The researcher, on the other hand, has the means at hand to go beyond a holistic description of the culture, focusing on specific issues that s/he can now describe in depth, study by comparison, and possibly even hypothesize about.

To conclude, let me deal briefly with the final two stages of colonial contact I distinguished, decolonization and emancipation, and their effects on representation. These changes for once do not emanate from the European side of the equation, except with regard to a gradually developing call for a code of ethics among anthropologists. The major changes involved, however, stem from the process of independence in Papua New Guinea, the subsequent development of a nation-state, and the gradually rising resistance among the autochthonous population of Irian Jaya against the increasing marginalization to which it is subjected (Lagerberg 1979; Jaarsma n.d.a). Entreated by the United Nations, the postwar administration in Papua New Guinea and West New Guinea began to introduce the political instruments for indigenous self-determination. In the subsequent years, not only did a system of indigenous political representation emerge, along with the political elite to fill it, but there also emerged a sense of regional, national, and, not to forget, ethnic identity (Griffin et al. 1979; Jaarsma n.d.b). Additionally, both the independence process in Papua New Guinea and the annexation of West New Guinea as a province of the Republic of Indonesia put an end to most indigenous perceptions of Europeans as an ever present source of material certainty. The resultant feelings of insecurity and fear of what was to come probably did much to amalgamate the indigenous peoples into several kinds of supralocal identity.

As indicated at the outset, emancipation might possibly signify an end to the inherent colonialist inequality of ethnographic representation. Three factors occurring in mutual balance can cause a shift in this direction. First is the gradual process of indigenous empowerment, not only on a national but increasingly also on a local level. Second, in Papua New Guinea (less so in Irian Jaya), the gradually increasing stipulations related to research permits have made the preparations for and initial planning of research a more serious investment than it ever was before. In consequence, it becomes increasingly difficult for a researcher to consider his/ her research population in terms of an "easily interchangeable" object. Linked to this is, third, that the process of decolonization itself has given rise to an increasing call for a new identity and ethical consciousness of anthropology as a discipline. These three factors interact to create a new balance in which the relations between ethnographer and people studied gradually become more reciprocal in nature and lose the character of inequality that is basic to colonial contact.

Ethnography in Context

Years ago I read a simile that describes the problem dealt with here very well. It compared man studying man to a gas molecule trying to determine the physical laws of gases. Each time this inquisitive gas molecule tried to observe something about its fellow molecules, it inevitably moved around and equally inevitably became subject to the laws it tried to study. There is a similar circularity to much of the ethnography on New Guinea, written as it has been within the context of colonial contact, within an inevitable setting of inequality, the negative consequences of which all parties involved are trying to resolve or gloss over. It is not enough simply to quote historical facts to support our claim; one can dissemble just as well with the past as one can with statistics (Urry 1997:1–2). To go beyond mere representation, we need to find out not only what contact represented in ethnography, but why contact resulted in certain kinds of representation, what was revealed, and—where possible—what remained hidden from the audience's view.

Placing ethnography within the context in which it is written allows us to highlight the conditions that give rise to specific representations. Ethnography is representation, but as representation, its environment—at least in part—structures it. In focusing on ethnography not only as colonialist representation but also as part of the contact situation, one tries to depict not only the ethnographic statement itself but also the way it is structured by its environment. I showed through-

ETHNOGRAPHY AS A PHENOMENON OF CONTACT

out that, with increasing contact, the possibilities for ethnographic data gathering have increased, and hence the possibilities for an increasingly sophisticated ethnographic argument grow.

While development in the contact situation is by and large proportionate to the investments made by the European colonizers, gathering and interpreting information is dependent on a complex of checks and balances. Each individual research effort is admittedly an idiosyncrasy, but, overall, certain limitations to some extent determine what kind of representation will result at any one time. Each effort, existing against the background of a developing contact situation, consists of three mutually interdependent aspects. The first aspect is the development of the institutional context of the discipline, which gradually moves away from viewing ethnography as an amateur practice or auxiliary skill in a diversity of professions. It is only when the colonial process reaches the late colonial stage, in which development of the indigenous population and a self-sufficient economic and political infrastructure of the colony becomes an issue, that the demand for dedicated specialists to gather and analyze ethnographic information becomes important (Brookfield 1972:18; cf. Campbell 1998). Then, too, a specific demand arises for academic anthropology and for professionals specifically trained in anthropological fieldwork, implicitly creating an enlargement of scale. These developments strengthen and in many cases cause the creation of anthropology as an independent academic discipline, thus enhancing the conditions under which anthropologists question not only how they are making certain representations, but also why. As we have seen earlier, this development progresses until academic anthropology is, if not the sole, certainly the dominant voice on New Guinea ethnography. The downside of this is that ethnographers from other disciplines are increasingly discouraged from adding to the resultant (academic) ethnographic discourse and, in some instances, are forced to create their own discourse.

A second factor of importance is that the creation of economic and political infrastructures in the colony will have brought a larger part of the indigenous population into more intensive contact with colonial culture. As indicated earlier, this increase in contact will have enabled the indigenous population to deal with their colonizers in more sophisticated ways. "Translated" into fieldwork terms: the people we study become able to appreciate anthropologists' need for information and to reciprocate in ways that anthropologists expect of their informants. "Reciprocate" is used here in a considered sense, as most of the people studied still will not be able to appreciate the motives anthropologists and their sponsors have for gathering information. Nevertheless, it is equally doubtful that the anthropologists will always appreciate their informants' motives for cooperating with them. Contact needs to develop in order for these motives to add—other than serendipitously —to the exchange of information and ethnographic representation. By the time this becomes possible, chances are that the people studied have themselves become an audience for the resultant ethnographic reports. Until that stage is reached, the exchange going on is (an opaque) one in which information is exchanged against goods and services, with only one party involved clearly able to realize her/his own purposes.

Related to both these forces is a third one: the development by anthropologists of increasingly sophisticated ways and means of representing the people they study. An increased demand for ethnographic data—if satisfied—produces not only new practitioners but also new quantities of data. In the case of New Guinea, this involved vast new quantities of data, especially during the 1960s and early 1970s when the amount of research done multiplied several times. Paralleling this is an improvement in the quality of the material gathered, in part due to the increase in trained professionals and in part to the increased sophistication of the people studied. The increase in quantitative and qualitative scale enables and encourages anthropologists to challenge and improve upon existing theoretical paradigms in line with the normal dynamics of science.

Also to be expected is that the present ethnographic distinction between the eastern and western parts of New Guinea will increasingly be challenged. However, the fact that at present this distinction still draws only limited attention, and lacks definition as a viable option for study, shows that this is very much interwoven with the way we perceive ourselves as a discipline. What we see and study dictates our identity as much as do our national background and the political implications thereof. In the case of New Guinea, these parameters are interwoven to the extent that simple causality no longer applies. Here, disciplinary specialization divides anthropologists' products into different—in this instance, Papua New Guinea and Irian Jaya—ethnographies. In that respect, anthropology's colonial inheritance is still present even where it is denied. Resolving the differences in "the" ethnographic description of New Guinea is only workable if we can account for the ethnographies' (or ethnographers') past.

Each of these aspects can, of course, be considered (and has been considered) in its own right, but we should not rely only on these partial images; they are—and should be seen as—a balance of forces. In fact, if we look at the three in isolation, we lose the possibility of making sense of New Guinea ethnography as a whole. The present state of New Guinea ethnography divides the island in two halves that have generally been described in different terms, with different depth, and from different focuses. These differences cannot (and should not) be accounted for in terms of what has been described, but in terms of representation. This only makes sense if we take the different aspects described above and see them as an interdependent set of checks and balances on a developing process of ethnographic description. Long-term ethnographic description of any one area consists of the balance of developing insights. It is the attention given to ethnographies as "colonialisms" that allows us to perceive a considerable part of the dynamics involved in this process and its resultant image. We speak here of representation, a metalevel structure that allows us to indicate the added gain in not glossing over the differences in cultural descriptions as dictated by the differential contexts of colonial contact.

Four

Anthropology and Administration
Colonial Ethnography in the Papua New
Guinea Eastern Highlands

George Westermark

The aim of this chapter is to explore the complex social, historic, and intellectual linkages between the discipline of anthropology and the colonial system in Papua New Guinea. I believe that if we are to understand the work of the Australian colonial administration, some recognition must be given to the various ways in which anthropology informed the work by Australian colonial officers, or *kiaps*, in the decades that preceded independence. What makes this subject particularly interesting for an anthropologist are the cultural analyses of the peoples of Papua New Guinea written by the *kiaps* and included in their patrol reports. As I intend to show here, these reports reveal the significance anthropological information had within the system, yet also the transition in interests and reporting that occurred during the colonial era through the phases of postwar reconstruction, economic and political development, and the preparation for independence. Moreover, when viewed as part of the broader transformations that characterized the Australian colonial experience in Papua New Guinea, the reports reflect the heterogeneity that existed within this evolving colonial project.

The research for this paper was based on the Australian Patrol Reports for the Eastern Highlands between 1945 and 1973. From the 18,000 pages of reports for these years available on microfiche from the Papua New Guinea National Archives, I selected three periods from the Goroka and Kainantu Subdistricts, and studied 330 reports. Admittedly, this is just one step toward a comprehensive review of the available material for the province, but by examining the records for these three six-year periods from different decades—the immediate post-World War II years (1946–1952), a decade later (1955–1961), and the years nearing independence (1964–1970)—I believe I have touched on several issues related to the broader examination of the articulation of anthropology with the colonial system.

After briefly reviewing a number of theoretical concerns and examining the development of anthropological training for colonial officers, I organize the material from the reports in five sections. I begin by examining the types of anthropological data that tended to be collected. Recognition of cultural diversity in the Eastern Highlands was included in several ways, and this forms my second section. Next, I describe the types of social changes dealt with in the anthropological work of the reports. I then explore evidence of the anthropological influences on administrative policies. Finally, I note the changes in the nature or extent of anthropological reporting in the patrol reports.

Theoretical Considerations

The conceptual basis of this chapter emerges from diverse themes in the field of historical anthropology. The 1990s saw new interest in examining colonial systems from both anthropologists and historians. At a 1988 interdisciplinary conference, representatives of these disciplines attempted to "rethink what frameworks and themes the anthropology of colonialism should entail" (Cooper and Stoler 1989:609; see also Ohnuki-Tierney 1990; Dirks 1992b; Stoler 1992a). In the course of this reexamination, they moved beyond the simplistic dichotomies of colonizer and colonized to recognize the diverse relationships that exist within these categories. Elsewhere, Stocking (1991:5) has similarly called for a "pluralization of the 'colonial situation' concept" so that a range of colonial contexts would be examined, including the distinct interest groups within those different situations. Similarly, Thomas (1994:8–9) has advocated approaching colonial systems as "a pluralized field of colonial narratives," and as "colonialisms rather than colonialism." Here my aim is to understand the production of colonial cultural knowledge in the Eastern Highlands within a broad context of social and political factors extending well beyond the mountain homes of the highlanders.[1]

Another related theme comes from within the study of the history of anthropology itself. The study of anthropology's ties to various colonial administrations has been a subject of continuing interest and, often, acrimony. Beginning in the 1970s, scholars attacked or defended the discipline's record (e.g., Goddard 1972; Asad 1973; Loizos 1977). Although the critique of anthropology as the "child of colonialism" came to be accepted in various ways among many anthropologists (e.g., Marcus and Fischer 1986:34; Pels 1997; see also Weiner 1987), careful examination of direct linkages has received little support (Kuklick 1978, 1991; Kuper 1983, 1991). It appears that the conclusions of anthropological research were as frequently looked upon with suspicion as they were with comradeship by colonial officers (Kuper 1983:112–113; Kuklick 1991:204, 217; see also Jaarsma 1994; Bashkow 1995). Where anthropologists seem to have had greater success was with their claims for the practical significance of their work, including the training of colonial officers, and these claims did benefit the discipline by expanding funding for programs and research in the 1920s and 1930s (Kuklick 1991:209–213). Thomas reminds us, however, that "if ethnology was in fact often of little practical value for administrators, it can be understood at least to reinforce an imperial sense of epistemic superiority" (1994:7). In this respect, my intention is to contextualize the associations between the growth of Australian anthropology, the anthropological training of *kiaps*, and the conditions of Australian colonial government in Papua New Guinea.

Anthropology and the Australian Administration

The emergence of professional anthropology in Australia was inextricably connected with the needs of colonial administration. As a result, Australian colonial involvement is significant for understanding the tradition of anthropology that developed in that country (Barwick, Beckett, and Reay 1985).[2] Australia's colonial role in Papua and New Guinea began in the first quarter of the twentieth century, and it is at the close of this period that serious attention to anthropology begins. During the 1920s and 1930s, government anthropologists such as Walter Strong, F. E. Williams, and E. W. P. Chinnery were appointed (Williams 1977; Hays 1992:7; Campbell 1998). The establishment of the first chair of anthropology at Sydney University in 1926, funded by money provided by the Rockefeller Foundation and several state governments, required that training for the colonial officers from the New Guinea service be offered (Wise 1985:74; see also McPherson, Chap. 6). The chair's first occupant, A. R. Radcliffe-Brown, argued for additional federal governmental support by comparing the growth of anthropological work in the colonial training of the British, Dutch, and French with the limited role for the discipline in Australian training (Bashkow 1995:4).

At this early stage in the development of Australian anthropology, however, a significant degree of skepticism on the part of colonial administrators was the norm. The attitudes of Sir Hubert Murray, lieutenant governor of Papua, reflect the ambivalence of colonial administrators toward anthropology. Ian Campbell (1998) describes how Murray consistently supported the idea of establishing government anthropologists to aid the administration in its work with native peoples. He wrote long essays urging the Australian government to appoint staff anthropologists "in the interests of sympathetic government and the importance of basing policy and practice on a sound understanding of native culture" (1998:74). Murray consulted with a number of British anthropologists, such as A. C. Haddon and R. R. Marrett, to identify suitable candidates for these positions. Moreover, he generally favored training government officers in anthropology. Although most of the cadet training at Sydney University before World War II was for the New Guinea service, some training was done for Papuan officials. As a result of this experience, Murray did develop some reservations toward the training because of "the preservationist bias of functionalist theory, which seemed to him to suggest that every native custom was indispensable in maintaining social or psychological integration" (Bashkow 1995:3; see also Thompson 1986). Murray surveyed his officers to determine the usefulness of the anthropology course they had taken at Sydney. Using the officers' responses, Murray concluded that, on the whole, the course was a good thing (see also Wright 1966:72–73). With respect to younger, less experienced officers, however, he determined that they should be kept away from Sydney, as the study in anthropology might make them too sympathetic toward the Papuans: "It is their [the officers'] opinion, and mine also, that the effect of the Course might be to turn him from an administrative officer into an anthropologist—which is just what we want to avoid" (Murray, quoted in Bashkow 1995:11). Nevertheless, Murray did encourage senior staff to take leaves to study at Sydney (Campbell 1998:87). Based on Murray's comments, Bashkow suggests that the relationship between anthropology and administration at this point was far more contested than might be assumed today: "In this context, we encounter a striking inversion of present-day expectations concerning the relations between functional anthropology and colonialism. . . . Rather than serving as the handmaiden of colonialism, Murray feared that it [anthropology] might prove a hindrance" (1995:13).

The opinions of cadets and professors also indicate a mixture of positive and negative opinions regarding anthropological training: "Contemporary evaluations suggested that the scheme was successful. The lecturers at Sydney University were unanimously pleased with the cadets and praised their approach to their studies" (Campbell 1998:86). However, one of the early students, Malcolm Wright, recognized the financial benefits for anthropology: "We were welcomed at the university, not because we were rated highly as students or because, from our experience, we could make some valuable contribution in the field of learning, but because our numbers gave the anaemic Department of Anthropology a shot in the arm" (1966:72). Still, the course did prove personally beneficial for this same student: "In spite of our criticism of the academics, we felt that some knowledge of anthropology equipped us better to do a patrol officer's job and we were eager to get on with it" (1966:78; see also Fenbury 1978:15) and "problems that had baffled us became clear. In my own case, a difficulty I had had in a land ownership argument was solved for me. Until I came to the university I had never heard of matrilineal inheritance which applied in the case in question" (Wright 1966:76). Other students also reported to Radcliffe-Brown the positive effects in the field of their anthropological training (Campbell 1998:86). Such training soon began to result in some prewar patrol reports including pages of "general ethnological observations" (see McPherson, Chap. 6).

After World War II, Australia entered into a decidedly new phase of its colonial experience (Mair [1948] 1970; McAuley 1953b; Griffin, Nelson, and Firth 1979; Boutilier 1985; Thompson 1986). Anthropologists such as Camilla Wedgwood and Ian Hogbin played a critical role in shaping new policies through the Australian Army's Directorate of Research (Jinks 1982; Wise 1985:152; Lutkehaus 1986; Wetherell and Carr-Gregg 1990:142). They devised a "New Deal" for Papua New Guinea's people aimed at shifting Australian efforts more toward the benefit of indigenous people rather than the commercial interests (Roe 1971:145; Wise 1985:158; Wetherell and Carr-Gregg 1990:149; Oliver 1991:78). Their work was not without opposition, however, for conservative circles in Australia critiqued their thinking as "long-haired intellectuals indulging in an orgy of anthropological experiment" (Wise 1985:160), as "socialism" (McAuley 1974:171), or as "the creation of leftist politicians and 'whooping' anthropologists'" (Harding 1997). Outside Australia, very different pressures came from the United Nations and the United States to move quickly toward decolonization (Griffin, Nelson, and Firth 1979:104; Downs 1986:275, 287). The dilemmas created by the various external and internal parties seeking to affect the direction of the Australian colonial system did have an impact. Writing in 1958, the Australian anthropologist Ronald Berndt described the situation as follows:

> If we turn to New Guinea, political expediency is . . . a primary influence in native policy . . . the fact that Australia is geographically part of South-East Asia—with the growing awareness that New Guinea is strategically important to the mainland, has far-reaching repercussions on New Guinea native policy. Some of these have been the encouragement, on a limited scale, of European settlers (the growth of Goroka alone in the Eastern Highlands, is a case in point). . . . At the same time, there are indications that Australia is looked upon (especially by members of the Asian Bloc) as "virtually" a colonial power, and there is pressure on Australia to declare just when the peoples of New Guinea will be given their independence. (1958:615)

These dilemmas are indicative of a critical point for understanding both the Australian experience in Papua New Guinea and colonial systems in general: they must be understood within a dynamic historic framework. The 1960s brought a growing anticolonial sentiment that increasingly influenced Australian policy (Rowley 1966:1–9; Wesley-Smith 1994). By 1960, "more than forty new states had joined the United Nations. Mounting anticolonial sentiment was reflected in General Assembly Resolution 1514 (xv) of 1960, which condemned colonialism in no uncertain terms and demanded that immediate steps be taken to eliminate it in both non-self-governing and trust territories" (Wesley-Smith 1994:197). In 1962, the results of a United Nations Trusteeship Council Visiting Mission to New Guinea were published. Known as the Foot Report, after its chairman, Sir Hugh Foot, it called for the speedy development of indigenous participation in government: "Because of the generally heightened interest in the territory since 1960, because this particular United Nations mission was led by an Englishman notably experienced in decolonization and because of other radical proposals . . . , the report's impact in Australia was profound" (Hudson and Daven 1971:161). During the same year, the need for change was heralded dramatically with the end of Dutch colonial rule in New Guinea: "The withdrawal of the Dutch, and the circumstances of that withdrawal, constituted in 1962 a sudden intrusion of anti-colonial politics into the area, a profound and sudden change in a situation long frozen, and a reminder of how quickly political change can occur" (Rowley 1966:25). Whereas just a decade before, it had seemed to Australian administrators that it might be a century before Papua New Guinea would be self-governing (McAuley 1953b:546; Hudson and Daven 1974:155; Wesley-Smith 1994:198), and the Department of Territories published recruiting brochures for the Australian School of Pacific Administration (ASOPA) "with 'Careers with a Future' emblazoned across the front cover" (Jackson 1983:25), the 1960s brought the clear recognition that a "gradualist" approach would no longer be acceptable on the world scene (see also Nash, Chap. 7).

Anthropological Training at ASOPA

It was in the confluence of these contending forces that training in anthropology and other subjects came to be required of the colonial officers through a new school, the Australian School of Pacific Administration (ASOPA). Certainly, ASOPA grew out of the training begun before the war at Sydney University, but, more than that, it was a direct outgrowth of the reformist colonial policy that emerged for Papua New Guinea after World War II. As one of the early instructors at the school described it: "The Australian School of Pacific Administration was the academic part of the program" (McAuley 1974:171).

The time at ASOPA combined short and long courses separated by field experience (Mair [1948] 1970:58; Grosart 1980:51). In a 1960 Cadet Patrol Officers' Course outline, the training combined courses in anthropology with those in geography, government, health and first aid, history, law, map reading, Melanesian Pidgin, and physical anthropology. The anthropology course had five lectures per week versus four or three for the other subjects. In content, the material covered in anthropology included theory, concepts of culture and society, traditional social structure, traditional land-tenure systems, social control, magic and religion, and social change. The topics of the course seem to reflect the social anthropology that came to dominate Australian anthropology after World War II (McCall 1982; Wise 1985:220–224). A 1965 anthropology syllabus for the Patrol Officers' Certificate Course includes articles and books by such well-known anthropologists as A. R. Radcliffe-Brown, J. A. Barnes, Robert Redfield, Raymond Firth, Ward Goodenough, Paula Brown, and Kenneth Read. However, according to one instructor, Peter Lawrence, the general aims of the courses were "to impress on those attending them that they should regard the natives as human beings, respect their customs . . . [and] see these customs as a distinct and organized way of life" (1964b:198; see also Beckett 1989:31). Another anthropology instructor, Camilla Wedgwood, is described as conveying the message of "modified functionalism: she remained very much a disciple of Malinowski" (Wetherell and Carr-Gregg 1990:191). Similarly, an ASOPA government instructor said of anthropological training:

> Its chief value is in the general formation of the administrator's mind. It
> expels, or prevents the growth of, those amateurish unscientific notions
> about the nature of native society which otherwise would have the field to

themselves. . . . It gives him a feeling for the interconnectedness of the aspects of native culture and teaches him a certain caution about monkeying with it. Finally, to the extent that he needs, or may wish, in the course of his work, to investigate aspects of native social life it gives him a method of inquiry. (McAuley 1953a:520)

Kiaps in Colonial Society

Although colonial society in Papua New Guinea has been the subject of several lengthy studies (e.g., Inglis 1975; Nelson [1982] 1990; Bulbeck 1992), less has been written by academics on the work of the *kiaps* (but see McRae 1974, Gordon 1983, Scaglion 1985). Several studies by retired colonial officers, however, point out many of the logistical and social constraints critical for contextualizing the *kiaps'* work and, especially, their application of anthropology in cultural analysis (Sinclair 1984; Downs 1986).

To understand the postwar New Guinea environment of a region like the highlands, one must not isolate it from what occurred prior to the war. A dynamic historical account of a region like this must include the memories and images of violence that set the stage for postwar colonial society. In her recent ethnohistory of the Simbu, Paula Brown makes this point very clear:

> The writings and statements of Leahy and some other white settlers, miners, prospectors, and a few government workers, proclaim the opinion that these newly contacted natives must be shown that the white man and his weapons represent strength, might and right. . . . The power of guns should be demonstrated in action, by shooting pigs and men. . . . Popular reports and memoirs of these incidents by Australians claim that penetration of the highlands was peaceful. . . . This legend of the benign kiap is shared by many Australian writers and Simbu who experienced the impact and hopes of the postwar period from 1945 to 1965. (1995:90)

Thus, while the reality was that the total number of postwar patrol officers was not large, and never great enough to permit very many in any one location, their administration was premised upon the understandings of power established in the prewar period.

Budget shortfalls also kept the administrative service understaffed. Consequently, administrative work was carried out in isolated conditions supported by indigenous police personnel. Because of leaves and reassignments, there were frequent moves in location so that a consistent cultural understanding of any region was difficult to obtain (Sinclair 1984:63). James B. Watson has commented on this aspect of the *kiap*'s work from the perspective of an anthropological observer in the Kainantu Subdistrict: "In any case, in contrast to a missionary like Mr. Flierl, with decades-long experience in the same vicinity, a *kiap*'s knowledge of local peoples, such as it was, was likely to be acquired over a far shorter span of time" (1992:185).

Australian colonial society was not of one mind regarding the new government policies or anthropology; because of their opposition to the "New Deal" approach, merchants and planters frequently caused difficulties for *kiaps* (Fenbury 1978:18; Sinclair 1984:29; Downs 1986:54; Beckett 1989:31). This "Territorian," or "Old Guard" (see Harding 1997), perspective extended to anthropology and anthropologists, since the latter voluntarily crossed the racial chasm that separated whites and blacks in the postwar period (Giddings 1989). Divisions even occurred within the ranks of the *kiaps*, particularly between those of the prewar and postwar service (Fenbury 1978:18; Sinclair 1984:14; Downs 1986:179). With both "green recruits" and "old hands" training at ASOPA, the information of the anthropologist was often less respected than that of the experienced officer (Sinclair 1984:14–15). Ian Downs, who had experience as a *kiap,* notes that when he was sent to ASOPA for a reorientation course in 1947, he was told by his superior to "counteract some of the garbage being fed to cadets about pre-war officers" (1986:179). A former instructor at ASOPA, Kenneth Read, also took note of the questions about anthropology:

> But both before and after the war, the "old hands," whether civilian or government officials, were sometimes disposed to regard anthropologists with suspicion, their attitudes reflecting the common tendency to assume that those who have been there longer necessarily know more than new comers: 'How can they presume to teach us anything when we've lived the better part of a lifetime here and they come in for a year or so, then leave?' (1986:95–96)

The ambivalent relationships between anthropologists and *kiaps* were underlined by another ASOPA instructor, James McAuley, in a 1953 article published in the ASOPA journal, *South Pacific:*

> It is well known that between anthropologists and administrators there is a certain amount of tension, or mutual dissatisfaction. Both groups are concerned with native affairs, but each has its own standpoint and responsibilities and each is tempted to take an unfavourable view of the efficacy of the other's work. . . . Administrative officers tend, I think, to be more severe upon anthropologists than anthropologists are in return. . . . The anthropologist, by casting doubts on the adequacy of his [the *kiap*'s] grasp of native affairs or the reality of his "little father" role, may become a symbol of all those specialisms that have intruded on him in the name of science or efficiency or welfare. (1953a:518)

However, for the relatively new recruit, anthropology might offer valuable insights for understanding the peoples with whom he was to carry out his duties.

Reminiscent of the opinions of Macolm Wright and other prewar *kiap*s on anthropology (see above), one *kiap*, who began his career in the late 1950s, and who studied at ASOPA after a two-year posting on Bougainville, said of anthropology: "I found that the study of anthropology was probably the most important thing that I did [at ASOPA] . . . I didn't have the key to ask the right questions, not until I'd done the ASOPA course, and that really, that gave me the key to understanding society" (Giddings 1989).[3]

Still, McAuley concluded his reflections on the relationship of anthropologist to administrator by suggesting that, even in the early 1950s, there had been "a partial demoralization of the administrators" (1953a:522). He attributes this "erosion of confidence" both to the recognition that colonial regimes were winding up in many parts of the world and to "the relativist mood inculcated by social scientists" (1953a:522). It seems clear that in attempting to understand the *kiap*s' ability and inclination to introduce anthropological approaches into administrative work, we must include these complex, and sometimes contradictory, intellectual, organizational, and social influences in our consideration, for, whatever may have been recorded by *kiap*s in their reports, these influences certainly helped shape the context of *kiap* decision making.

Anthropological Data

The texts of most patrol reports from both the late 1940s and the late 1950s follow a similar format. A diary of the day-to-day movements of the patrol was followed by accounts of such topics as the "Native Situation," "Health and Hygiene," "Roads and Bridges," and "Village Officials." These reports indicate the multitude of interests to which the *kiap*s were expected to attend, and which, of course, placed significant limits on their ability to collect much anthropological material. Generally speaking, such data were gathered through pidgin interpreters, and this, too, shaped the nature of the material.[4]

Nevertheless, the earliest reports from the postwar era begin to refer to "Native Customs," though the preferred label soon shifts to "Anthropology" or "Anthropological Information." Clearly, anthropological data collection was an expected part of the patrol, and almost all of the ninety reports from the two regions for the first two periods I studied include such information. For contemporary anthropologists, much of the social, economic, and political information recorded throughout the patrol reports is critically important for helping to understand social change in the colonial system, but here I will be focusing primarily on the information in the reports that was labeled "anthropology." This category in the report was clearly a space that was largely devoted to what was perceived by the administration and the patrol officers to be fitting for elements of the precolonial cultures of the region.[5]

Even though *kiap*s were subject to frequent relocation, there is evidence in the reports that attention was paid to the anthropological record that had developed through previous patrols. Thus, in a 1950s report from Goroka, the following comment opens a section on "Anthropological Data" that describes adoption practices: "Extensive Anthropological research was not carried out by the patrol, however, the following account of the customary adoption procedure may be of some help to future officers who will be patrolling this area" (Johnson 1957–1958a).[6] Based on his 1960s research in the Sepik River area, the anthropologist Donald Tuzin concurs with this point:

> My own experience is that, although the level of interest and ethnographic skill varied among different *kiaps*, there was an impressive consensus regarding the importance of such information collected during routine patrols. The ADC in charge of Maprik Subdistrict (as it then was) was unpretentiously quite knowledgeable about local traditions, both on the basis of his own activities, *and because he studied the patrol reports of his subalterns before sending them up through channels*.[7] (emphasis added)

Kiaps were aware that their brief visits on patrol did not afford the ideal situation in which to conduct research. Their awareness of the inadequacy of the time allowed on a patrol appears in frequent statements such as the following: "Since little time was spent truly amongst the native people and their natural habitat, anthropological information hereunder supplied is no indication of the enormous wealth of knowledge which may be gleaned if one were to remain for a longer period of time at any one social group in the area" (Eisenhauer 1947–1948).[8]

Early anthropological accounts in patrol reports covered a number of topics. In the first 1940s report from the Kainantu Subdistrict, accounts of Gadsup marriage, mourning, land tenure, and sorcery accusations are included (Skinner 1946–1947). Other reports consistently touch on topics like initiation, kinship, marriage, legends, material culture, and sorcery.

Comparisons with reports done during World War II by patrols under the auspices of the Australian military in New Guinea (ANGAU) suggest the practical consequences of anthropological research. According to the Gadsup report cited above (Skinner 1946–1947), the military clearly had been insensitive to the details of naming practices in the area, leading to inaccuracies in the census records. For example, the report states: "There is a practice in this area of giving to a newborn child the name of a lately deceased child of the same parents. Where the difference in age is not great, confusion can be created." An obvious implication here is that the research this *kiap* had done had led to improvements.

Social structural characteristics of the Eastern Highlands peoples were frequently noted in patrol reports. Relationships between groups and subgroups were described using the anthropological vocabulary of descent systems (Johnson 1957–1958a).[9] Marriage practices were outlined in some detail, especially as these were often the source of conflicts brought to the *kiaps* for arbitration (Leabeater 1948–1949). One anomaly identified in the census records of the Goroka area was the absence of girls in the 10–16 age bracket. *Kiaps* were puzzled by this pattern until they recognized that many girls in this age range, who had moved to their future husband's village at betrothal, were not brought to the *kiap*'s village census, since they were not considered part of the new family until the marriage was consummated at a later time (Aitken 1957–1958a and b).[10]

Given the emphasis of the colonial system on establishing control, the reports frequently examine the prevalence and causes of intervillage fighting around Goroka and Kainantu in the 1940s and in the southern reaches of the district in the 1950s. A factor noted in these reports, one that has frequently been associated with Eastern Highlands conflicts in the anthropological literature, is that of sorcery. Thus, one report points to a change in sorcery practice:

> As previous patrols have pointed out, sorcery has vastly increased since fighting has been stopped. . . . It is believed in this area that the sorcerer must obtain an article belonging to his intended victim to practice his craft on. Natives are therefore very careful not to leave clothing, food remnants or even feces where a sorcerer might get hold of them.[11] (Jackson 1947–1948)

In another report from Kainantu in 1949, it is clear that sorcery accusations could still lead to intervillage violence: "The original cause of the trouble in the [X–Y] area was the death of an elderly [X] man, attributed by the [Xs] to sorcery worked by the [Y] people" (Linsley 1948–1949).

Although Sinclair (1984:14) suggests that *kiaps* listened more to their senior colleagues than they did to the suggestions of their anthropological instructors at ASOPA, some *kiaps* in the field continued to be affected by professional anthropology through the articles published in ASOPA's journal, *South Pacific*. A 1957 report comments on the attitude toward independence on the part of the southern Tairora people. The *kiap* cites an article by Ronald Berndt to the effect that, from the Tairora perspective, the control of the Australians was only a temporary difficulty similar to the defeats they may have suffered at the hands of enemies in the past. The officer reaches the following conclusion: "This I think helps to explain the present situation and attitude of the Taiora people" (Wiltshire 1957–1958). In a 1964 patrol report on the Tairora, another *kiap* cites this same patrol report and the Berndt quote, and then says of the quote: "I think this quotation should be reproduced in full here for it is most appropriate to the attitude of the people as found on this and most other patrols" (Parker 1964–1965).

References to the work of other professional anthropologists also appear. In a 1957 report, the linguistic patterns of the Upper Asaro peoples are described according to the work of the anthropologists Kenneth Read and Richard Salisbury. Various local groups are divided into two broad divisions, and the divisions are then linguistically categorized as affiliated with either the Chimbu- or Goroka-area language families. The *kiap* even notes a difference of opinion between Read and Salisbury with respect to these linguistic affiliations, and, based on his own experience, finds evidence in support of Read's analysis (Kent 1956–1957).

Cultural Diversity

The practical orientation of the Australian administration in Papua New Guinea, concentrating as it did in the highlands on establishing control and advancing economic development, may not have encouraged a uniform attention to cultural variation. As Watson has noted, the attitude of the colonial system may have been captured in one *kiap*'s sentiments: "Our policies are uniform. . . . We don't care how different local people may be in their personalities, or even if they really are different" (1992:185).

Nevertheless, a regard for cultural diversity could impact the effectiveness of program implementation, and the Eastern Highlands patrol reports do evidence an awareness of the area's cultural diversity on a variety of levels. From a regional perspective, the eastern Kainantu peoples were differentiated from their Kamano, Fore, and Gimi neighbors to their west and south, and the Anga (then "Kukukuku") to their extreme south. With respect to house types, for example, a 1947 report notes that southern Kamano construction differs from that of the Upper Ramu peoples (Grove 1947–1948).[12] On the topic of cannibalism, the same report makes the following comparison: "No history of cannibalism is admitted to by the main Upper Ramu groups—Agarabi, Gadsup . . . and Taiora, but villages south {Fore} cheerfully admitted to cannibal practices." In describing the Gimi people, another *kiap* offers this contrast:

> The Gimi is a mixture of East and West. It is the most Eastern group of the Highland people who wear the "bilum" or net drape as covering. Beyond the Iani River one finds the genital pouch typical of the Bena and Kainantu areas. From the West has come the pride of their own attire (headdresses, kinas, etc.) and many of their customs and from the East the fear of sorcery has been introduced.[13] (Colman 1956–1957a)

Since language was essential to the process of communicating the new Australian order, significant attention was given to the linguistic variations to be found in the district and on its borders. This was clearly the aim of the linguistic work in the Upper Asaro mentioned in the previous section. Similarly, in a 1956 report, the Lamari are described as follows:

> All people in the villages censused as the South Lamari speak a dialect of the Taiora language and can be understood by a Taiora interpreter. This dialect is also spoken by the people of Baira, Mumbaira and Mei'auna. . . .

The North Lamari is a mixed language group. The main language of the area is Useruba. (Lambden 1956–1957)

Such linguistic descriptions were also found for Gadsup and Awa peoples in Kainantu and for Fore, Chimbu, Kamano, and Ungai in Goroka.[14] Special note was taken of those border villages that were multilingual, as they could be "the focal point for any interpretation within the area" (Colman 1956–1957c). Patrol officers were not reliant only on multilingual interpreters, however, as they actively encouraged the spread of Tok Pisin: "Young boys from all of the above language areas are now at the station learning 'pidgin' and they will eventually be of great assistance to future patrols" (Colman 1956–1957c).

The Australian goals of control and economic development led to frequent comparisons as to the degree of "advancement" found within particular communities or ethnolinguistic groups (see Nash, Chap. 7). On the positive side, by the late 1950s, some of the subdistrict's northern groups were being recommended for the establishment of local government councils.[15] On the negative side, however, one group, the Tairora, had established itself as one of the most recalcitrant in the Eastern Highlands: "It was during this period and soon after, that the passive-resistant and stubborn attitude of these people to the Administration and any change whatsoever, became well known throughout the Eastern Highlands" (Wiltshire 1957–1958).[16]

Change

*Kiap*s were quite aware of the changes rapidly occurring in the district, and they took note of it anthropologically. Peter Lawrence, a former member of the anthropology faculties of both ASOPA and Sydney University, was critical of the ASOPA approach to change, saying that "the training would have been adequate if the duties of a Patrol Officer were still the same as in 1930" (1964b:204). From his perspective, more should have been done in the curriculum to study the rapid changes in the field, and less with traditional aspects of village social structure. However, the reports are filled with references to the efforts to curtail what the Australian administration deemed inappropriate change and to encourage that which the administration admired.

Patrol reports include numerous observations on the changes under way in the district. In the late 1940s, there were shifts in village communities related to the desire for consolidation on the part of the administration and a local desire to take on a more "modern" community appearance with lined "streets" and rectangular house forms (Grove 1947–1948). Marriage customs were being transformed with the introduction of cash and Western products. A 1940s report on the Gadsup notes: "It may be added that the custom of inter-village sister exchange is dying out." Bride-price was increasingly a part of the marriage process: "Especially, this is the case when an ex-labourer returns to his village and seeks a wife. The bride price then asked is usually very high—undoubtedly a measure taken by the elders to ensure their social prestige" (Jackson 1947–1948).[17] In contrast, in the southern parts of the district changes were still limited in the 1950s: "The bride price payments in the South Lamari and southern parts of the North Lamari have not as yet been affected by the introduction of European articles. However, the payments in the Auiana area include items of European manufacture" (Lambden 1956–1957). *Kiaps* also sought to restrict such changes: "The patrol attempted to restore the traditional forms of exchange for the functions mentioned above [i.e., bride-price] in all such arbitration cases heard. Whether any success was obtained is, however, a matter for conjecture" (Johnson 1957–1958a).

The *bête noire* of the first decades of postwar rule was the cargo cult. In the 1940s, the *kiaps* found evidence of activities they categorized as cults, or "Vailala Madness," in the north (Grove 1947–1948). Reports indicate a greater prevalence of the cults, or at least a greater attention to them, in the southern portion of the district in the 1950s. For instance, a 1956 report on the Auyana notes the diffusion of cargo ideas to that region as the result of a village leader's visit to the Aiyura Agricultural Station. Apparently, he met there a disciple of Yali, the Madang cargo leader, who had fled to the highlands after Yali's arrest (see Harding 1997). Men from other parts of Papua New Guinea were implicated in activities at Aiyura, and the report listed names for investigation. Other reports from south of Henganofi in the Kamano region list arrests and prosecution of suspected cult leaders, as well as the diffusion of cults from Papua.[18]

Policy Implications

It is difficult to ascertain from the reports how the collection of anthropological information by *kiaps* may have had an impact on administration policies. Certainly the patrol officer's attitude noted by Watson (see above, e.g., "Our policies are uniform") would be one likely to prevail in the senior ranks of the system. Nevertheless, patrol reports were routed through the system in the following sequence:

> So what happened was that the patrol officer sent his report to the Assistant District Officer in charge of the district . . . then he would comment on it to the District Officer, who was just one rung lower than the District Commissioner. Then he sent that off to the Director of Native Affairs and it generally stayed there. But if for some reason they wanted to brief the Administrator then they would send the correspondence up to the Administrator, but most of it stayed with the Director of Native Affairs. (Giddings 1989)

It is in this movement of reports through the hierarchy of the administrative bureaucracy that we find evidence that this information was taken into consideration at the highest levels of the colonial system in Papua New Guinea.

Primary examples of this come from the comments attached by senior administrators to the reports.

An instance of this practice comes in a comment on a Tairora patrol report in a letter from an Eastern Highlands district officer in Goroka sent to the assistant district officer in charge of the Kainantu Subdistrict. Reports in the 1950s note the problem of land disputes arising in the subdistrict. In part, this was a result of the imposition of the Pax Australiana that had temporarily fixed the boundaries between enemy groups. In light of this issue, the district officer observes:

> It is very doubtful whether permanent individual rights over land ever existed in the Highlands, and a system of usufruct in respect of agricultural land within the clan or subclan, seems to be universal. By and large, there was no shortage of land for agricultural purposes before the white man, and it is only since there has been a demand for land by Europeans and for cash cropping that the notion of individual ownership appeared. The paramount importance of officers collecting and collating as much information as they possibly can about traditional land ownership and rights is again emphasized. (Cleleand 1956–1957)

Embodied in this document are conclusions about kinship, social structure, land tenure, and the sources of culture change seemingly tied to the previous research of *kiaps*, with a clear directive that such research should be carried out in the future. A similar sentiment was voiced by the chief native land commissioner in a letter to the director of Native Affairs, J. K. McCarthy. After reading the anthropological information on "Land Tenure amongst the Kamano" from a Goroka patrol report that McCarthy had forwarded to him, he complimented the *kiap* in the following way: "The description of land tenure compiled by Mr. Johnson is a very valuable contribution. . . . If only other officers would emulate Mr. Johnson we would have a very good coverage to form a basis to make more detailed investigations" (noted in Johnson 1957–1958b). Other reports indicate a concern for anthropological information at even higher levels. One letter from the head of territorial administration, J. K. Murray, to the director of Native Affairs, highlights this point:

> I should be glad to know what is done with the anthropological notes in patrol reports with a view to their becoming available to Anthropologists in the Territory like Mr. Julius of the Education Department and the staff of the School of Anthropology at the School of Pacific Administration [i.e., ASOPA]. Later on, it will be necessary to consider the transmission of anthropological information to the School of Pacific Studies in the National University; it may well be that, when the school is functioning, it will approach the Administrator. (Noted in Leabeater 1949–1950)

In another instance, a *kiap* states that his report on a cargo cult was forwarded all the way to the administrator, Brigadier Donald (later Sir Donald) Cleland (Giddings 1989; see also Cleland 1969). A note in a letter from the 1959 director of Native Affairs, A. H. Roberts, to the district officer of the Eastern Highlands demonstrates the recognition of anthropological analyses of cargo cult: "The commercial attitude of the native people to mission activity is interesting in relation to Dr. Lawrence's Report on Cargo Cult in Madang. I hope to send you a copy as soon as some are received" (quoted in Aitken 1959–1960).

Anthropological information that reached the director of Native Affairs in Port Moresby was, in fact, frequently passed on to the government anthropologist for "collective interpretation of anthropological data and possible reference for research" (noted in Swinton 1957–1958) or, "Anthropological data has been passed on to Mr. Julius who comments as follows: 'Collection of data on kinship and marriage has been well done and should, if possible, be extended later'" (noted in Johnson 1956–1957).[19] Such referrals increased in number from the 1940s to the 1950s, possibly indicating a growing perception of the relevance of anthropology in the latter decade. That such recommendations might lead to further work on a subject is supported by reports that note that the government anthropologist was carrying out research in the district (Colman 1956–1957). In the estimation of one anthropologist familiar with ASOPA and New Guinea, the influence of anthropological knowledge through *kiap* training and government anthropologists was "considerable," though "it seems likely that it has indirectly played an important role" (Berndt 1958:615–616).

Changes in Anthropological Reporting

In her examination of the Simbu colonial experience, Paula Brown (1995) cites the work of Ian Downs (1980:179), who suggests that there were three phases of postwar Australian administrative activity in the highlands: postwar reconstruction (1945–1951), economic and political development (1951–1963), and preparation for independence (1963–1975). Although the dates do not correspond exactly, the three periods of patrol reports reviewed in this paper parallel the shifts outlined by Downs. This is especially true of anthropological information, for the reports in my review move from an early period of minimal reporting (1946–1951), to one of consistent reporting (1956–1959), to, finally, a near total absence of anthropological reporting (1965–1969). Since the previous sections have been based on the first two periods, in this section I will concentrate on the reports of the late 1960s.

At the end of the 1960s, the emphasis in administrative work was clearly on the evolution of political institutions prior to self-government and independence. Patrol reports from the Eastern Highlands for this period, as was probably true elsewhere in the country, are filled with discussions of election education and polling efforts. In reports from 1969 to 1970, the significance of work on government is emphasized in responses from the Division of District Administration: "Please note that political education must be a continuing process in all situations, with the emphasis on the advantages of national unity" (noted in Giddings 1969–1970). It also is a time when the first Papua New Guinean *kiaps* begin their work in the province. Thus, it is clearly a time of transition, of looking forward to what is to be the future of the country, however uncertain that may still have seemed at the end of the decade.

Moreover, it was a time when there was a shift in the style of patrol reports, with a change from the lengthier reports covering numerous topics to reports that were shorter and more focused. For some *kiaps*, it meant that as far as "the standards of patrol reports, well the bottom dropped out . . ." (Giddings 1989). In terms of anthropological reporting, it certainly resulted in the absence of explicit accounts that had previously regularly been included as sections of the reports. As with earlier periods, the reports continued to be filled with much information that any anthropologist interested in the transformation of Papua New Guinean societies would find interesting.

Still, the specific sections dedicated to cultural information that were labeled "Anthropological" were no longer included. For instance, of the 135 reports found for the Goroka and Kainantu areas for 1965–1970, only one referred to anthropological reporting, and that reference was negative: "No anthropological data was collected on this patrol" (Milar 1966–1967). Yet anthropological training was a part of the ASOPA curriculum (Lawrence 1964b), and the relevance of anthropological information was not completely eliminated from the *kiap*'s interests, even if it was no longer a part of the regular reporting format. This is indicated by a recommendation made in a Kainantu report: "In this respect, I feel that studies done in the Highlands by anthropologists from any university should be made available to all district and subdistrict libraries where they have relevance." A response to the report from the assistant district commissioner states: "I concur with your views . . . I will endeavour to obtain through our Department copies of any such studies that are available" (Lyons 1968–1969).

Thus, although the concern for anthropology receives some minimal recognition, the late 1960s reporting clearly reflects Downs's third phase of highland colonial experience. Attentions appear to be directed toward the needs of future self-government rather than continuous colonial rule, and, in that light, anthropological reporting seems to have no longer been part of the regular information gathered. The category of anthropology located in the discourse of "tradition" had little relevance for the primary goals of the time. At this juncture, neither the careers of *kiaps* nor the colonial system had much of a future in Papua New Guinea.

Conclusions

If we are to study the operation of colonial systems, it is essential to heed the call for a pluralization of the colonial situation so that we avoid painting with too broad a brush (Stocking 1991; Thomas 1994). Taking into consideration time, location, populations, and political motivations helps us differentiate, for instance, the Papua New Guinea Highlands case from either their neighbors to the north or south in earlier decades, or from the colonial situations drawing to a close in other countries while those in the highlands were just beginning. Although it certainly is appropriate to critique past colonial systems (e.g., A. Strathern 1992:261), it is important, too, to note the presence of variation within the attitudes and actions of actors within any given colonial system, as urged by Cooper and Stoler (1989), which only highlights the relevance of studying both the interactions and the unique influences experienced by any particular colonial group.

In this light, it is important to underline the "New Deal" direction of the postwar Australian administration in Papua New Guinea, and the role that anthropologists played in its origination, even as we examine the pressures of commercial goals and racist attitudes that permeated colonial society. Moreover, the transformation of colonial practice over the three decades of postwar Australian rule must also be considered for what it reveals of the varied external influences shaping this colonial system. The transition from postwar reconstruction to economic and political development and, finally, to the preparation for independence resulted from the varied regional and global pressures brought to bear on this unique situation, one that began in the highlands after World War II in the shadow of the death of colonialism elsewhere in the world. Given the vocal anticolonial sentiment of the postwar era, the highlands experience appears to have been a very "self-conscious" colonialism.

Clearly, the training and practice of anthropology within the Australian colonial enterprise was filled with contradictions. It included anthropological policymakers contributing to a "New Deal" and cadets who saw it as a "key" to understanding their duties; yet it also encompassed "Territorians" who viewed the discipline as the handmaiden not of colonialism but of socialism, and the "old hands" among the *kiaps* who favored their firsthand experience over academic concepts. Opinions regarding the utility of anthropology ranged, therefore, from the positive to the negative. The specter of the end of colonialism had, even by the 1950s, begun to lead to an "erosion of confidence" in the colonial project, but so too had "the relativist mood inculcated by social scientists" (McAuley 1953a:522).

Still, the fact that the training occurred and that consistent attention was addressed to the anthropological information collected by *kiaps* suggests that its role was significant in certain respects. The range of topics and their association with practical administrative concerns does point to the potential use of the anthropological information. Evidence certainly exists that individual *kiaps* used the training they received in anthropology to implement administrative policy (e.g., census work, conflict resolution, and land tenure). At the least, when treated as colonial texts, the patrol reports do reveal how anthropology influenced the construction of cultural knowledge that *kiaps* used to interpret their diverse experiences. Whether or not anthropology was used in the structuring of colonial policy or in its imple-

ANTHROPOLOGY AND ADMINISTRATION

mentation, it still embodied an "epistemic superiority" (Thomas 1994:7), reflecting, thereby, the scientific orientation of the postwar colonial powers seeking to justify their rule to a critical international community. In this light, the decline of anthropological reporting in the last period of Australian rule seems to neatly parallel the progression toward independence that would soon end the colonial era in Papua New Guinea.

Five

Unvarnished Truths
Maslyn Williams and Australian
Government Film in Papua and New Guinea

Robert J. Foster

Propaganda and Trusteeship

In his book *Propaganda and Empire*, John MacKenzie suggests that the preoccupation of many imperial historians with "the radiation of influences *from* Britain *into* its wider hinterland" has led to a view of the British public as largely indifferent to Empire (1984:2; emphasis added). MacKenzie argues that by attending to radiations in the opposite direction—that is, by studying imperialism as part of British social history—it becomes more apparent how Empire contributed to "a world view which was central to their [the British] perceptions of themselves" (ibid.). This worldview, which MacKenzie calls "imperial nationalism," was never communicated through an extensive program of government propaganda mainly because nongovernmental propagandist agencies—from missionary societies to commercial advertisers—made such dissemination unnecessary.[1]

MacKenzie's historiographic argument focuses attention on the blind spots that result from the division of labor between scholars of imperial history and scholars of national history. I found precisely such a blind spot in the historical literature I have consulted on Australian documentary film, especially government film.[2] Although much of this literature naturally recognizes and even critically assesses the place of government film in promoting an Australian national identity, the work done by the government film unit in the Territory of Papua and New Guinea hardly receives mention. This omission might seem particularly surprising inasmuch as the government's project in the Territory was headed by Maslyn Williams, whose other documentary work is routinely discussed. Indeed, Williams's prize-winning Neorealist film *Mike and Stefani* (1952), the story of a displaced Ukrainian couple who emigrate to Australia after World War II, is often hailed as a major innovative achievement (see, e.g., Moran 1991:46–48).[3]

I attribute this omission to two related causes, one general, the other specific. First, critical histories of nationalist ideology, like nationalist ideology itself, frequently do not look beyond the territorial borders of the nation-state; that is, they frequently fail to grasp the construction of national identity as a relational process. This shortsightedness is especially pronounced when the relational Other in question is a colony, a criticism leveled by Segal and Handler (1992; see also Handler and Segal 1993) against much Eurocentric theorizing about the origins of nationalism. Thus, while recognition has been granted to the discursive role played by Aborigines and immigrants in the formation of Australian national identity (see, for example, McMurchy 1994; Greenwood 1995), little recognition has been granted to the discursive role played by Papuans and New Guineans.

Second, consciousness of the Territory of Papua and New Guinea as an Australian *colony* rather than, say, a United Nations Trust Territory seems never to have been strongly developed among Australians (at least or especially among southern Australians as opposed to Queenslanders). The Territory was not imagined as somehow *connected* to the Australian metropole and, consequently, easily disappeared from discussions of Australian national identity.

I therefore propose to demonstrate how the government films made by Maslyn Williams in and about the Territory ought to be seen as potent projections of an Australian national identity. To this end, I talk about the ways in which the films were commissioned, and the initial film, *Papua and New Guinea*, produced and distributed. I also briefly discuss the narrative content of one elaborate film, *New Guinea Patrol*, perhaps the most famous of the lot. This demonstration entails first describing the official record of Paul (later Sir Paul) Hasluck's involvement in the production of the Commonwealth Film Unit (CFU) films. Hasluck was, of course, minister for Territories when the films were made; he had served as the head of the Australian Mission to the United Nations from 1946 to 1947 and later served as governor-general of Australia from 1969 to 1974. I next consider Maslyn Williams's reports of his own motivations and intentions in making the films. I focus in particular on how Williams thought about his own creative role in making state propaganda, that is, how he reconciled his own agency—his circumstantial capacity to act autonomously—with that of Hasluck.

My aim is not to show that Williams's purposes as a government filmmaker were at odds with Hasluck's, or that Williams's agency consisted in the subversion of Hasluck's agenda. On the contrary, I am convinced that Williams—at least in the beginning—would have agreed with Hasluck's assertion that "what we do as a nation in the development of this Territory is something we do in order to live up to our own standards, and in order to live up to our own ideals of national responsibility" (Hasluck 1976:215, from a 1954 speech). Instead, I want to show how Williams defined his own agency within a particular colonial project that he explicitly understood as neither entirely of his own design nor entirely under his own control, but as a set of circumstances, in other words, generally familiar to both individual colonizers and colonizeds alike. I conclude by suggesting how Williams sought to renegotiate the terms of his agency in representing trusteeship by moving from filmmaking to writing, first nonfiction and then fiction. For Williams, it was in the end only through the novel—neither documentary film nor memoir—

that he could represent trusteeship honestly and truthfully. Put differently, it was only in fiction writing that Williams was able to achieve for himself what Chinua Achebe, in his essay "The Truth of Fiction," called "imaginative identification"— a self-encounter that enables us "to recreate in ourselves the thoughts that must go on in the minds of others, especially those we dispossess" (1988:149).

Hasluck's Cinematic Vision

In May of 1955, J. C. Archer, first assistant secretary to the minister for territories, Paul Hasluck, met with Kevin Murphy, director of the Australian News and Information Bureau (NIB), and Stanley Hawes, producer-in-chief of the Film Division (renamed the Commonwealth Film Unit [CFU] in 1956, and then Film Australia in 1973). Archer, according to his minutes of the meeting, told Murphy and Hawes that the minister

> wished to have made on Papua and New Guinea, a series of documentary films designed to tell in an interesting way, the story of the work being done in that Territory. The films would serve several purposes. Notably as an illustration to the UN of the progressive methods and the positive and beneficial results of the Australian Administration, as a vehicle for attracting recruits and as a means of creating a greater awareness of the Territory in the minds of people generally. (Australian Archives: Series A518/1 Item U141/3/1)

A tentative proposal for six films was presented, covering such topics as medical services, agricultural resources, and native administration. Archer declared that

> it was a prerequisite that the script would be prepared in consultation with the appropriate Department in the Territory with final editing in Australia, as the Minister would be the ultimate authority. On the latter point, Messrs. Murphy and Hawes said that the Bureau took its policy direction from the authority requiring the films and simply advised and worked technically and professionally towards achievement of that authority's objective at the highest standard. (Australian Archives: Series A518/1 Item U141/3/1)

On October 14, 1955, Ronald Maslyn Williams, who had been appointed to prepare scripts for the minister's approval, was taken to meet Hasluck. Williams had been involved in making government films since World War II, when he was "offered the job of being the writer and director of the film unit that the government sent away to the Middle East to cover the War for the Australian people" (272[1]-4, Hazel de Berg Recordings, National Library of Australia).[4] He worked there with his friend Damien Parer, the famous Australian war cameraman, whose use of film and photography as means to communicate things of real importance Williams both admired and emulated. By the time Williams, at the age of 44, undertook the job of filming in Papua and New Guinea, he had accumulated years of experience working in a film unit heavily influenced by the didactic philosophy of moral improvement associated with the British proselytizer of documentary film, John Grierson.[5] Grierson, notes MacKenzie (1984:85), "wished to dignify the labour and lives of common people while educating them for democracy, as he rather patronisingly put it." For Williams, Grierson's philosophy also meant the independence of the filmmaker from the government that employed him, that is, the possibility of a film unit with its own charter. In the 1950s, however, the Commonwealth Film Unit was under official scrutiny for suspected left-wing activities.[6] The opportunity to film in Papua and New Guinea thus appealed to Williams as "an escapist thing," both personally and professionally, which he likened to his earlier filming of *Mike and Stefani* in postwar Germany for the Australian Department of Immigration (Pike and Fitzpatrick 1977, Tape 9).

Williams's escape from the day-to-day hassles of the CFU ran right through the office of Paul Hasluck. The official records of Hasluck's first meeting with Williams and Hasluck's subsequent criticisms of Williams's proposals accord with Williams's own claim that Hasluck "made it clear that he had no high opinion of the kind of work that I was doing. . . . He believed that the greatest weakness in my kind of work was its dishonesty" (1964:xvi). Hasluck told Williams exactly what objectives he, Hasluck, had in mind in making these documentary films. According to the notes of D. McCarthy, Hasluck had three main objectives (Australian Archives: Series A518/1 Item U141/3/1):

> (1) to inform interested Australians, and Australians generally, as widely as possible, of the Australian problems, policies and work relating to Papua and New Guinea;
>
> 2) to make pictures which could be used to inform young people who might be interested in making careers in Papua and New Guinea and to stimulate interest on the part of suitable young people so that they could wish to make careers in New Guinea [on the question of recruiting, see Westermark (Chap. 4) and McPherson (Chap. 6)];
>
> (3) to provide a means through which the United Nations and other international organisations could be informed of Australian problems, policies and work in Papua and New Guinea.

McCarthy's notes outline Hasluck's other concerns, emphasizing:

> (b) that he was not interested in publicising Papua and New Guinea overseas, as a matter of mere publicity; in fact he was actively adverse to doing so since he could see nothing to be gained by this; it was no part of

his present plans, for example, to direct tourists and novelty seekers to Papua and New Guinea;

(c) that what he wanted was a series of pictures which would not manifest any of the "commercial slickness" of most of the commercial documentaries that were made, but would tell in a plain unvarnished way of the country, the people and the work. It was no part of his policy to pander to those seeking sensations or pure entertainment. He said that he realised, of course, that some regard would need to be had to the entertainment aspect to make the pictures acceptable to the widest public but he believed that the very nature of the country and the work and the events would fundamentally achieve this. (Ibid.)

Hasluck also informed Williams that he believed the work of the missions to be of vital importance and that it was "desirable," even "logical," that the natives become Christians. The minister also stressed that "there be no suggestion in the pictures that the great changes which the Administration was in the process of bringing about and guiding could come rapidly. The lifting of the native people out of their present levels was inevitably a slow and time-consuming process" (Australian Archives: Series A518/1 Item U141/3/1).

This last comment suggests the minister's awareness of criticisms from abroad, which multiplied at the UN in the late 1950s, that the decolonization process in the Territory was moving too slowly. Set against Hasluck's other objectives, the comment points to a contradiction in representing trusteeship that the CFU project constantly negotiated. On the one hand, the films needed to depict the success and progress of Australian initiatives in civilizing and modernizing the natives; on the other hand, the films needed to depict the Territory and its inhabitants as occupying a stage of development far too primitive and backward to contemplate political independence in the near future. This contradiction accounts for the narrative strategies of some individual films as well as, in part, the structure of the films as a corpus. In short, different regions of the Territory were identified as occupying different stages or levels of development, ranging from the backward Sepik areas through the developing highlands to the highly developed areas around Port Moresby and Rabaul (see Nash, Chap. 7).

Williams traveled widely around the Territory, though mostly in New Guinea, in order to do research for the scripts. He returned on December 14, 1955, and submitted his report to Hasluck's acting assistant secretary, Dudley McCarthy, in late January 1956. The report contained a proposal for five major films (including "a film of one or two reels telling the story of an Administration patrol into new territory" [Australian Archives: Series A518/1 Item U141/3/1]) and miscellaneous newsreel and television programs, as well as a draft script for the first film—a survey or overview of the Territory. McCarthy passed the report on to Hasluck, with suggestions about how topics ought to be allocated among five (rather than the originally proposed six) films.[7] Hasluck approved McCarthy's suggestions and added the following comments:

> One point to be borne in mind in all these films and particularly in Film 1 is that the responsibility in this Territory falls on the Australian nation and that the work—every bit of it—is being done by direction of the Australian Government and in accordance with the policies it lays down on behalf of the Australian nation. There is too much of a tendency to regard the "administration" as something that exists separately on its own. It is in fact the servant of the Australian Government. For the sake of the Territory, for the interest of the Australian people and for better understanding overseas, we have to end this separateness between Government and Administration. It is not a question of giving credit to this or that Government or this or that individual but of emphasising the truth that what is being done in the Territory is being done by Australia. I do not think it would be a wrong emphasis to have Film 1 begin and also end with something that happens in the Commonwealth Parliament at Canberra. We certainly have to overcome the tendency unconsciously revealed in Mr. Williams's notes to regard the Administration as something that has its own objectives and its own original impetus and also remove the tendency to regard the Territory as something entirely on its own.
>
> This is the Australian nation—accent on Australia—doing one of the many jobs that belong to Australia. Don't make the Territory so remote and so separate. (Australian Archives: Series A518/1 Item U141/3/1)

Hasluck's words make my point about the perceived lack of "connection" between the colony and the metropole, even if the minister was referring here to the bureaucratic relationship between the administration of the Territory and the Department of Territories. Indeed, Hasluck imagined the films as being mainly for Australians and mainly about Australians. Accordingly, he showed no interest in the suggestion by the administrator (Donald [later Sir Donald] Cleland) that films be made for training natives—a suggestion apparently discussed by the administrator and Williams in Port Moresby; and he responded harshly to being sent the notes of a meeting with Williams—notes taken by Williams himself—in which he is described as agreeing in principle to making a version of the first film for showing to native audiences. Hasluck also insisted that his wish that the first film begin in Canberra be carried out, despite Williams's objections to the idea: "I should like a further attempt to be made to devise an opening scene which links the Territory more closely with the national capital" (Australian Archives: Series A518/1 Item U141/3/1). In the end, Williams arranged to stage the visit of a small group of students from the Territory—flown to Canberra from Queensland boarding schools expressly for this purpose—to an exhibition about the Territory in the foyer of the parliament building.[8]

Hasluck gave close personal attention to the film project, at least in the beginning, going so far as to edit Williams's draft script for the first film. These emendations speak volumes about how Hasluck directed Williams to represent Australia through Papua and New Guinea. For example, the minister urged that the phrase "law and order" be substituted for "pacification," and he specifically banned mentioning the political distinction between the Australian Territory of Papua and the Trust Territory of New Guinea; "Territory of Papua and New Guinea"—that is, the administrative union—was to be used instead. He also objected to Williams's description of government patrols spreading "ideas of peace and mutual progress": "I wonder what the officers in charge of the sort of patrol depicted would think of 'ideas of peace and mutual progress'? These patrols have precise tasks. They don't wander down the ravine scattering handfuls of abstract nouns" (Australian Archives: Series A518/1 Item U141/3/1). Any flourishes of poetic license on Williams's part were suppressed in deference to "the plain unvarnished way of the country" (ibid.). The country in question was, naturally, Australia, imagined in conventional terms as a nation of honest and simple rural people.

Hasluck saw the first film in Sydney on May 24, 1957. He wrote in a memo that "it appears to me to be a very satisfactory film and meets our needs exactly" (Australian Archives: Series A518/1 Item U141/3/1). He also expressed his wish that the film be titled *Papua and New Guinea* rather than *Papua and New Guinea Today*. Finally, he approved the plan for distribution of the film drawn up by Murphy at the NIB. This plan included theatrical release for the film in Australia and New Zealand and television screenings in North America and the United Kingdom. *Papua and New Guinea* began its run through the Hoyts circuit at the Esquire Theatre, Sydney, in late December, "linked with the feature film, *The Brave One*, . . . [and] timed to take utmost advantage of the increased theatre traffic which always occurs over the holiday season" (Australian Archives: Series A518/1 Item U141/3/1). Hasluck requested that the first screening in the United States be at a reception that the minister for external affairs was to hold for invited guests during a session of the General Assembly of the UN. In addition, 16mm prints were made for overseas posts of the NIB throughout North America and Europe. Prints were also made for distribution within Australia to the National Library Film Division for lending to various public bodies, and to each of the six State Film Centres for use in both state and denominational schools. The Department of Territories itself requested five copies of the film: two for the administration in the Territory, one for recruitment, one for the Information Section, and one for use at ASOPA, the school where both cadet and veteran patrol officers were trained (in part by anthropologists; see Westermark, Chap. 4). In this fashion, a wide and farflung audience of viewers was given access to the Australian government's representation of its trusteeship in Papua and New Guinea (see also Hasluck 1976, chap. 19).

Although the arrangements for screening *Papua and New Guinea* at the Minister's reception in New York eventually fell through, several of Williams's other films were screened at the UN itself. For example, in May 1960, three short films on economic, social, and political development were shown to "an influential audience of more than 60 people, mostly delegates to the current sittings of the Trusteeship Council and the United Nations' Press Gallery." The director of the NIB in New York claimed in a memo to Kevin Murphy that "the audience included some delegates who have been quite critical of some aspects of Australia's administration of New Guinea and we were fortunate in being able to arrange the screening at a most important stage of the debate on New Guinea." He continued:

> At the afternoon session of the Council, the delegate from the United Arab Republic, a constant critic of Australia, began his remarks by offering his congratulations on the films and said that they effectively showed the many problems facing the Australian Administration, especially with regard to the difficult terrain and diversified tribes of the area.
>
> The films were well received at the screening and there were many comments on their straight-forward presentation, objectivity, and sincerity.
>
> It was the honesty of these films that won them the rare privilege of a screening in the United Nations building proper, because it is quite unusual for the secretariat to permit such a screening, particularly on a subject currently under review by one of the councils of the United Nations. Normally the best delegations are able to arrange is to show their films at the Carnegie Foundation building on the other side of the United Nations Plaza and sufficiently far from the conference halls to discourage busy delegates from attending.
>
> However, assurances that the films did not take any strong propagandist line won the secretariat. (Australian Archives: Series A452/1 Item 1959/3484)

NIB officials thus expressed pleasure with themselves that they had satisfied Hasluck's demand for the plain, unvarnished truth.

New Guinea Patrol and Australian National Identity

New Guinea Patrol, the second of the five agreed-upon films, was completed by Williams in 1958. It was shown to the UN Trusteeship Council on January 30, 1959 (and subsequently on television in Australia and the United States, and at the International Film Festival in Florence, where it won the Senate's Gold Medal [*Sydney Morning Herald*, March 26, 1960]). Indeed, Williams remembers that the film was made specifically for this purpose, "as evidence of the difficulty of granting the Territory of PNG immediate elective self-government" (pers. com., January 17, 1996). James Sinclair, the officer who led the patrol in question, remembers the origins of the film in exactly the same way:

> For years, the Russians and Communist bloc countries had been attacking in the United Nations Trusteeship Council the Australian record in Papua New Guinea criticising in particular the rate of political progress, and the delay in bringing the remaining "uncontrolled" areas under full control. . . . Now, as part of a campaign designed to better inform the Australian public, as well as the United Nations, of what was being done in New Guinea, he [Paul Hasluck] directed that a series of films be made. The first would tell the story of a typical exploratory patrol in new country. There would be no faking, no dressing-up. A production unit would accompany the patrol and film its day-to-day activities. Nothing like this had previously been done. It would be a unique record of a fast vanishing aspect of the Australian administration of Papua New Guinea, as well as some answer to the nasty outbursts of the Russians and their friends. (1984:147)

New Guinea Patrol was indeed a unique undertaking and accordingly deserves more discussion and analysis than I can give it here. The bare facts are these: early in 1957, an unusual patrol set off into Duna country beyond Tari in what is now Southern Highlands Province. The patrol line stretched a half mile long, including not only Sinclair (Acting ADO), Neil Grant (Patrol Officer), and Albert Speer (European Medical Assistant), but also the film crew (Williams, Peter Dimond, and John Leake), 16 police (whose names are listed in Appendix A of Sinclair's patrol report), 2 interpreters, 3 medical orderlies, and 125 carriers to handle the massive amount of equipment necessary for the production of an Eastmancolor movie. They were in the field for seventy days, dealing with bad weather and illness. The patrol was resupplied periodically by airdrops of tinned food and fresh film. After one airdrop, the plane, piloted by Helly Tschuchnigg, crashed after engine failure in a swamp near Lake Kopiagu. Tschuchnigg and his four passengers survived with minor injuries. A floatplane retrieved them with the assistance of Sinclair and several police and carriers who had sped to the site on hearing news of the accident.

On the final airdrop, a horrific accident occurred: two of the Duna men who had come with others to visit the patrol's camp were hit and killed instantly by falling cargo. Sinclair notes that "we made an immediate compensation of payment of tomahawks and pearlshell, a payment so generous that the people scrambled to accept and forget about their dead kinsmen, for that was the way of the Huri and Duna" (1984:149–150). Although Sinclair's official patrol report described both incidents in detail, neither the crash of the plane nor the bungled airdrop received mention in *New Guinea Patrol*.

New Guinea Patrol is, in its narrative content and structure, a strong projection of Australian national identity, by which I mean the film condenses prominent themes of official and popular Australian nationalist discourse in the 1940s and 1950s (themes also sounded in patrol reports of the period; see Nash, Chap. 7; see also White 1981 and Moran 1991). Let me briefly identify four of these themes, in no particular order, using, where appropriate, quotations from the script that Williams (1958) himself wrote.

1. *Land, labor, and individual character.* In *Projecting Australia*, Albert Moran (1991:141) notes how the "animating vision" of the 1951 government film *Advance Australia* is of "a people unified by their relationship with the land." The centrality of the land lies in its potential for character building; that is, the Australian character, with its essential qualities of self-reliance and independence, evolves out of the pioneer encounter with a vast land that, although harsh and limited in resources, can be made productive.

The patrol in *New Guinea Patrol* is, from this perspective, the perfect enactment of the first encounter with the land, one in which the character of the patrol officers emerges through their overcoming the difficult terrain—steep mountains, muddy grasslands, and, of course, hostile tribesmen. The officers build bridges over treacherously swollen rivers; erect impressive houses out of bush materials at hand; and deal skillfully—though fairly and even compassionately at times—with the tribesmen (never women) they encounter.

2. *Male mateship/team spirit.* The patrol is composed of self-reliant, virile individuals: "Each man does his own job on the patrol—each in his own sphere." Together, however, they form an organically solidary community, that is, a fraternity. Here is, perhaps, an image of Australian male mateship at once conventional in its depiction of homosocial camaraderie among the patrol members and occasionally unconventional in that it tentatively embraces some black Papuans and New Guineans as well as white Australians. The patrol personnel (excluding the locally recruited carriers) appear to move through the countryside as a discrete national unit differentiated from the surrounding uncivilized tribesmen.

3. *Developmentalism or "starting fresh."* New Guinea Patrol, like the rest of the films commissioned by Hasluck, is about the development of the Territory. But it is specifically about the development of the Territory *by Australia*, and hence about Australia's own development in a period of postwar reconstructionism. In one sense, the film conveys the idea that, like Australia, the Territory is on the threshold of a new age. For Australia, this new modern age entails a greater role in global affairs, a role signaled by the UN Trusteeship itself, and perhaps also an increasing sense of cosmopolitanism stimulated by the arrival of "New Australian" immigrants from eastern and southern Europe. For the Territory, this new age is something more profound still. Thus, as Sinclair scans the Strickland River valley from the edge of a cliff, the film's narrator intones: "Here on this hillside, a new

history begins. A handful of Australian and New Guinea men become the advance guard of changes that will bring these primitive people out of the stone age into the civilization of today." It is as if the first encounter of patrolling Australians with the Strickland recapitulates the first encounter of British settlers with the environs of Sydney.

4. *No heroes/all heroes.* The patrol members are not only self-reliant and independent, but also ordinary men "gaining knowledge that will make it easier for the people higher up to assess the problems and plan to overcome them." The patrol members are not "the experts back at base" to whom they will bring a wealth of useful information. The film depicts the patrol members as simple men at work, thereby participating in a celebration of male labor that manifested itself in other Australian government films in the form of steel workers, sheep ranchers, and lifeguards. These workers are heroic in their antiheroism, everyday men who labor without publicity: "Two months on patrol and another month more. Slow but sure the work goes on. There are no headlines, no heroes. The world outside hears nothing of this little world . . . this little world that is being born again into a new age."

Williams's Propaganda: Compromise and Partial Truths

Given Hasluck's explicit instructions and the sometimes overwrought symbolism of *New Guinea Patrol,* it is not difficult to concur with Connolly and Anderson's (1987:290) claim that the film's objective was "propaganda, not realism." Indeed, their description of this film and other CFU productions is, for all its sarcasm, largely accurate:

> In this film, *New Guinea Patrol,* the shock and wonder of contact is submerged beneath an endless montage of sturdy white men going about their colonial business, shooting at pieces of wood, extracting arrows from grateful bodies; their lap-lapped offsiders blow bugles, raise and lower the Australian flag and scamper after packages dropped from the air.
>
> In other films the progress is shown in more settled regions. Youthful Australian patrol officers explain western law and order to assembled villagers, census the population, tend to the sick. Agricultural officers lecture apparently spellbound highlanders on the care of coffee trees. (1987:290–291)

Yet, oddly, though Connolly and Anderson have no problem seeing through the government propaganda of the CFU films, they nonetheless seem to regard the films as "realistic" representations of the ethos of Australian colonialism. Consider their comments on Williams's 1963 film, *District Commissioner:*

> The "DC" arrives at his district headquarters by chauffeured jeep. Uniformed policemen stiffen in salute as [DC Tom] Ellis stalks to his office

and tells the camera the scope of his kingdom—the Western Highlands. District Commissioner, proconsul of the Wahgi—such was the flavour of postwar colonialism: efficiency, authoritarianism, paternalism. They were earnest men and women, these thousands of Australians, sent north, as they saw it, to civilise New Guinea. Many of them were devoted and dedicated in their desire to impose upon the people the Australian vision of how things should be. (1987:291)

I find this view of "earnest men and women" severely limited, if not wholly simplistic.[9] It erases the moral contradictions and ambiguities involved in doing "colonial business" by portraying Australians in the Territory as either naive zealots on an ethnocentric civilizing mission or, by radical contrast, unscrupulously rational calculators out to exploit the Territory's economic resources, including its people. Neither alternative comes close to describing the way in which someone like Maslyn Williams (or like Ian Mack; see McPherson, Chap. 6) imagined what he was up to in Papua and New Guinea. How indeed, we might ask, did the official producer of Australian state propaganda address the issues of truth and representation—the question of "realism"—in the work of the CFU?

Recall that *New Guinea Patrol* contains no visual or verbal reference to either the crash of the supply plane or the death of the two Duna men. Williams (pers. com., January 17, 1996) explained that it would not have been possible to film the miscalculated airdrop inasmuch as the cargo fell "within a couple of metres of where the camera was set up with a group of the most senior locals gathered around it. The fact that three of these were killed (two instantly) created a dangerous and chaotic situation in which many others, including ourselves, may also have been killed." But when I pressed him in a later interview whether he would have included the botched airdrop if he could have filmed it, Williams answered without hesitation: yes.[10] Williams insisted, however, that it would have ultimately been Hasluck's decision—as the person who was paying for the film—whether to cut the scene.

By his own account, Williams approached his filmmaking with an ethic of constrained authenticity, by which I mean a profound awareness of the constraints under which he worked to produce a film in, as much as possible, his own way. Some of these constraints were technical; for example, the requirement to produce a film precisely one reel in length or—as in filming *New Guinea Patrol*—to shoot only in bright sunlight. Some of these constraints were political; for example, the requirement not to film squalid accommodations provided for native laborers on government stations. In response to both types of constraint, Williams would give a little. He would compromise, but he would not "cheat." By cheating, Williams meant that he would not fabricate scenes to be filmed (in this regard, Williams contrasted himself with Frank Hurley, much like Connolly and Anderson contrasted themselves with Williams). His critical remarks about much of the filming in the Territory prior to 1950 are pertinent in this regard:

> Contrived shots, taken entirely according to the entrepreneurial criteria of photographic quality and "dramatic" action, have been put together without any concern for logical relationships, natural continuity or subject relevance. Seldom has an attempt been made to record accurate factual data such as place, name, time, tribe and "story" background etc., so that much of the early material has lost a great deal of the value it might have had, even as superficial evidence of the local situation at any given time or place. (Williams 1966:6)

But Williams also recognized that the "degree of authenticity" of the CFU films varied according to their individual subjects and circumstances of production, which included the extent to which "indigenous collaboration" was achievable.

Constrained authenticity also ideally required Williams not to film atypical events—such as natives dressed up in their ceremonial best—and present them as though they were typical (although he could and did stage typical activities according to a predetermined script). The goal was, whenever possible, to produce a "balanced" or "averagely objective" picture of things (Williams 1966). In sum, Williams explained, if you are given the opportunity to do something, then do it, but don't cheat. Leaving things out is acceptable; making them up is not. Williams claimed to have followed this rule: if you want to make a good film, then do it your way—as much as they'll let you. Hasluck, for his part, seemed to have recognized Williams's methods, for in a very brief mention of the CFU project in his memoir, he writes: "he [Williams] showed that he could work to our specifications and respond readily to our prescribed requirements and yet could build imaginatively and creatively to give the set task an extra quality of his own" (1976:218).

Williams's ethic of constrained authenticity opened up a space within which he could act as a member of the loyal opposition. He did not agree with Hasluck on all issues concerning the Territory. In particular, he increasingly felt that Hasluck was wrong in thinking that it would be years before Papuans and New Guineans were ready for independence. And Williams felt that the overall CFU project might have benefits that Hasluck himself did not consider, such as altering the racial prejudices of Australian audiences and training indigenous filmmakers in the Territory (and, contra Hasluck, inserting poetry into government films). But Williams was not involved in the work of the CFU to advance his own purpose, which is not to say that he had no purpose in making these films. Rather like the patrol officers he depicted—who Hasluck insisted were patrolling with a purpose—Maslyn Williams the filmmaker imagined himself as a working man with a purpose. He admitted to Albert Moran in an undated interview that in New Guinea "we weren't trying to be great filmmakers. Let's be clear about that." Rather, Williams saw his work as "a tool, an instrument"; or perhaps, as he suggested in an interview with Andrew Pike and Merrilyn Fitzpatrick (1977), as something to be put in the service of moral education (in the fashion of Grierson): "to add another dimension to people's appreciation of what they're about and what life is about in general." Williams told Pike and Fitzpatrick that "I learned a lot about honesty in films. My directors would say 'I want to make the film this way because what you want me to do is the government propaganda line.' And I would listen to it and say 'You're sure you're not making this film because you want to make a big note as a film director? You want to make your film.'" I gather from this statement that Williams was not making his films when he made films for the government; rather, he was devoting himself purposively to a goal that someone else had set. I find this sentiment worth thinking about; it reminds me of Kapferer's (1988) stimulating discussion of an Australian nation that, when called upon, self-sacrificially serves the Australian state. It suggests that what is at stake is not self-expression, but rather a sense of duty—and it is this sense of duty, of commitment, that mattered to Williams in the depiction of both the patrol members in *New Guinea Patrol* and Australia's trusteeship of the Territory on behalf of the UN.

Re-presenting *New Guinea Patrol:* Other Purposes, Other Truths

The ethic of constrained authenticity is thoroughly ambiguous. Is it a form of principled loyalty, unprincipled pragmatism, or plain acquiescence to domination? It strikes me as requiring an extraordinary degree of disciplined self-abnegation to conduct in practice. No wonder Williams's directors protested. The distinction between leaving things out and making things up seems hopelessly arbitrary—especially when the filmmaker is acutely aware that his or her purpose is to represent a point of view that is not the only one possible. And make no mistake, Williams was acutely aware of this possibility. In gauging the ethnographical value of the CFU films, William wrote, "it must be understood that these, too, are 'contrived' documents: that the main purpose of the Producers of these films is to express an official point of view and not to present a balanced assessment of all the facts relevant to a given situation" (1966:7). I therefore suspect that it was the growing strain of managing his ethic of filmmaking that eventually compelled Williams to give it up.

In a 1967 oral-history interview, Williams recalled his departure from the CFU:

> I found, after a time, that I became aware that I was not saying what I thought about Australia and New Guinea, and Australia and Asia, but what the Government thought, and I became aware of this very strongly to a point where I felt that I had to resign from that job, even though at this time I was nearly fifty years of age, and that I had to find myself and try and pick up where I left off when I was about five years old, to being an

individualist and write as I wanted to write, say what I wanted to say. (1967b:272[1]-5)

Williams's first piece of writing after resigning from the CFU was *Stone Age Island* (1964), an account of his travels and observations (but not his filmmaking!) over the previous several years in the Territory. This book records, here and there, some of Williams's doubts about and criticisms of the Australian trusteeship. But these doubts and criticisms are mainly expressed in detached philosophical terms rather than engaged political polemic. For example, as Williams pauses on a hill overlooking a scene of Goilala tribesmen vigorously working on the construction of an airstrip, he asks:

> What did it mean? How do we justify our laboring to lead these people out of their own life-pattern of individually directed violence, conditioned by environment, into our own confusion of impersonal and illogical enmities and hates, and our up-to-date brand of intertribal warfare waged on a scale undreamed of by these simple primitives? Should we, perhaps, be more modest in the assessment of our particular kind of progress? And is the so-called sense of duty which we assumed toward these people genuine and magnanimous, or should we admit that we are simply driven to it by history and pride? (1964:120)

These questions capture well Williams's ambivalence about trusteeship—the same ambivalence that Peter Worsley noted in his harsh but accurate review of *Stone Age Island* in *The Guardian* (October 7, 1964):

> His [Williams's] comments on the social scene rarely move beyond the stock repertory of white man's judgments; he fluctuates between paternalistically deploring the rush to hand over power to peoples whom he often writes of as "miserable savages" little above animal level, and a contradictory relativism which says that their customs "are seldom more curious or less well founded in local logic than our own."

Williams himself seems to admit this ambivalence in his 1967 interview. There he confesses disappointment in the book "because I had not shaken off this long training in seeing things from a certain point of view, an Australian point of view, if not an official point of view. I had still not identified with the people I was writing about. I was writing about them as curiosities or problems rather than as people. I was still writing, as it were, from the point of view of a slightly superior person" (1967b:272[1]-5). *Stone Age Island* thus represented to its author, only three years after its publication, a failure of "imaginative identification." Nevertheless, in conjunction with his numerous documentaries (and programs for Australian television), it sealed Williams's reputation as a public authority on Papua and New Guinea whose opinions about the future of the Territory were aired in Australian newspapers.[11]

Williams's next writing projects focused on his travels to Indonesia and China, but he returned to his experiences in the Territory with the publication in 1967 of a novel, *The Far Side of the Sky*. The novel is an account of a New Guinea patrol through new country that clearly draws on Williams's experience in producing *New Guinea Patrol*. Clearly so, I say, not only because the novel is dedicated to Sinclair, Speer, and Grant, but also because it includes a scene in which two tribesmen are killed when struck by errant cargo dropped from a resupply plane. When I asked Williams how he saw the relationship between his film and his novel—why the fictional but not the documentary account of the patrol made reference to the airdrop—he explained, as above, that it was impossible to film the airdrop. But he also said, "Although the novel drew on the *Patrol* experiences, it had *a quite separate purpose*" (pers. com., January 17, 1996; emphasis added), namely, to comment on the meaning of society and civilization, and on the conflict between two cultures. This was undeniably a different purpose than the one that Hasluck had set for Williams (and not only because it was Williams's own purpose). In this context, then, the airdrop took on a metaphorical meaning that it would not have had if it been included in *New Guinea Patrol*.

The Far Side of the Sky, and writing in general, resolved Williams's personal crisis of representation. It allowed him to assume new and multiple points of view. Referring to the 1956 patrol as a "fundamental experience" in his life, Williams claimed that

> I wondered what in fact it had done to me as a person, going on this long patrol, and what was the justification of it from the government point of view, from the point of view of all of us who went on it. So I wrote a book about this patrol, and in doing so, I began to realize my own feelings and, looking back on incidents, I began to look at it from the point of view of the native people who were on the patrol with us, the native policemen, the native orderlies, the carriers, the wild people we met, and so on. This again has given me another look at myself. (1967b:272[2]-4)

And, in fact, *Far Side of the Sky* does assess critically, through the eyes of its various protagonists (who include different and distinct native characters as well as a missionary and government officers), the "civilization" that the patrol presumed to bring to the Southern Highlands.

There is something unmistakably anthropological in all this exploration of alternative points of view—seeing the world as others see it and in so doing altering the way one sees it. But there is also something unanthropological in it, too, at least in Williams's case. Writing entailed not only a freedom to shift points of view, but also—for Williams—a new ethic of representation: the ethic of unconstrained authenticity. Thus, *Far Side of the Sky* opens with a disclaimer of sorts:

> It is of no real moment whether this tale is taken for truth, or not. It would be as idle to insist that the work is one of pure fiction as to protest that everything that is written here has happened. Marshall is the most shadowy character, perhaps nearest in reality to myself, which is why my sympathies are with him. The others might be recognized, under different names, by anybody who knows New Guinea well. And we are all aware that the priest is dead. His obituary was published in the *South Pacific Times*, together with a picture of the man who killed him. (1967a:10)

Should we read this disclaimer as the prelude to a postmodern ethnography? Or should we perhaps recognize it as marking the contested boundary line between ethnography and fiction? I prefer the latter; for though *Far Side of the Sky* does indeed draw upon Williams's actual experiences on the patrol—such as the airdrop—and it does attempt to imagine the patrol from different points of view, including those of two different highlands men, the effort is nevertheless unconstrained by the dictum of "no cheating." In other words, in his novel, unlike his films, Williams freed himself to make things up, to use the device of alternative and multiple points of view—of characters—as a way of publicizing his own private conversation about the merits of the civilizing mission, of doing "colonial" business. No matter how critical some of these points of view seem to be of the official government perspective, they are all ultimately Williams's ideas and reflections enunciated by characters of his own creation. The novel, unlike a government film or an ethnography, is constrained neither by the efforts of other empirical individuals trying to put their stamp on the final product nor by the obligation of the producer to bear witness to these efforts. The purpose of *Far Side of the Sky* is indeed Williams's own, and so are its truths.

Conclusion: Representing Trusteeship

For Williams, it is clear that the move to writing offered him a chance to escape the constraints of representation imposed by the multi-author process of filmmaking:

> Some people have said that I was foolish and it was wrong of me to give up being a film maker after so many years, to go back to writing, but I'm quite sure in my mind now that it was the right thing to do, because I realize looking back . . . that the film medium is not a good medium for expressing truth or expressing deep feeling. There are far too many people and far too many mechanical processes and far too much money brought to bear from different sources for the cost of making a film, to allow an

UNVARNISHED TRUTHS

individual to give an honest, simple opinion of any thing in a film. The thing is not elastic enough, it doesn't allow you time—you can't control the cameraman and the sound engineer and the writer and the laboratory people and the sponsor, everybody, no individual can do this unless he works entirely alone . . . whereas anybody who can write even badly but has something genuine to say, can sit in front of a typewriter or with a pen in his hand, and say it, and this is what that person honestly thinks and believes. (Williams 1967b:272[2]-6)

It is equally clear that the kind of truth that Williams sought to communicate was not the famous "objective truth"—the one we might think a documentary camera well equipped to capture—but rather what he elsewhere calls "the truth of being," that is, the truth of human existence in a world where increasingly interconnected people face a single collective dilemma over the future of the species. For Williams, the 1956 patrol was good to think about this dilemma.

For myself, however, I prefer to think that Williams's novel is not so much unconstrained as operating under different constraints than those conditioning the multi-author process of film production. These constraints include editorial and commercial considerations, genre conventions, and the demands of intelligibility imposed by an imagined audience. All of our representations of intercultural contact (first or otherwise)—government films, works of fiction, documentary films (like *First Contact*), patrol reports (including Sinclair's report of the 1956 patrol), personal diaries (including Williams's own patrol diary), historical ethnographies (like *People You See in a Dream*)—embody such constraints. My simple point, and what I have tried to demonstrate in this chapter, is that it is necessary to identify and explicate these constraints—to recontextualize representations of trusteeship (and intercultural interactions more generally) in the circumstances of their production—in order to apprehend the effects of the various agents involved in implementing colonial projects (Thomas 1994). Why does this matter? Without such a recovery, both the social complexity and the diversely lived experiences of colonialism are likely to be obscured by a monolithic discourse—whether celebratory or condemnatory—that eclipses its object.

Six

"Wanted: Young Man, Must Like Adventure"
Ian McCallum Mack, Patrol Officer

Naomi M. McPherson

July 13, 1933

Dear Major Marr—

    We would thank you and the Members of the Commonwealth Government for the very kind expression of Sympathy conveyed in your letter of June 23rd. Also I would especially thank you for the wonderful eulogy regarding my son's action—you caused to be printed in the Argus. You cannot think how precious it was to me. Ian was absolutely heartbroken because he could not go to the War. He enlisted on his 18th birthday—which was August 1918—so he could go no further than just into Camp. Forgive me for telling you this but he always felt it such a constant & overpowering sorrow—I had almost said disgrace—that when I read your words I knew at last & forever the stigma was lifted—

    Ian is our second son to lay down his life for the Empire—Our eldest (then only 19) Sub. Lieut. R.A.N.H.M.S. Defense "perished gloriously"—in the Jutland Battle—our third & only remaining son is pioneering in Malaya.

Sincerely Yours,
Margaret R. Mack

    While perusing the Australian Archives for data pertaining to patrols, patrol officers, and the colonial era in northwest New Britain, I came across the above-quoted handwritten, black-bordered letter (Australian Archives:Series A518/1 Item 852/1/334) written by Margaret Rose Mack one month after the death of her son Ian McCallum Mack.[1] My own son was, when I read the letter, the same age as Ian Mack when he died, and I was touched by the anguish of a woman who had lost not one but two sons, and simultaneously appalled by a mother's pride that her sons' lives had been sacrificed on the altar of King and Country. This was a sentiment I could never share, a rationalization I could never make. Nevertheless, my interest in learning about colonial encounters as they occurred in coastal northwest New Britain, particularly in the Bariai District where I have lived and worked with the Kabana while conducting anthropological research,[2] converged at this point with my interest in this young man who could feel "shame" and "disgrace" for being too young to serve unto death in a world gone mad with war. Mack was one of the first colonial officers to patrol many areas of New Britain, and his patrol reports offer a glimpse into his experiences as a patrol officer and his interactions with the peoples and cultures of New Britain from 1926 to 1931.[3] However, he seems better known in the literature of colonial New Guinea for his death than for his life. As the first Australian patrol officer to be "maliciously killed" in the line of duty, Mack's death is described as a "great event that lingered . . . in the European oral tradition" of the Mandated Territory of New Guinea (Radford 1987:4).

It is interesting to peer, as at sepia-colored snapshots, at Patrol Officer Ian McCallum Mack for the light his life sheds on this period in the culture and history of Australia and of New Guinea. A picture of ten-year-old Ian shows an intense lad with a broad forehead, slightly protruding ears, and a direct and solemn gaze. Photographs of the adult Mack in New Guinea in the late 1920s show him to be shorter than his fellow officers and of slim but wiry build; his gaze engaging the camera lens directly. He is described as "a tough man who lived an abstemious and rigorous life" and as a "man of action who wasted little time on patience and tact; he was conscientious and enjoyed a challenge" (Radford 1987:115–116). Although no single individual can stand as the exemplar of an era, generation, or class, the life and death of Ian McCallum Mack, a uniquely talented and, I think, somewhat driven young man, can offer a glimpse into the variety of people, personalities, and politics that constituted colonialism in New Guinea. Mack's experiences in New Guinea are peculiar to him and his background and personality, even though they are framed and constrained by his role as a patrol officer and representative of the Australian colonial government in New Guinea.

In this chapter, I present various perspectives on the colonial enterprise in New Guinea delineated by the life of a single complex individual whose character, motives, and personal monsters are shaped by the era into which he is born, his family, and his personal history. Mack's work in New Guinea, precisely recorded in office memos and patrol reports, depicts the construction of the colonial venture by the administration as a job to be routinely and sensibly accomplished. Newspapers present other colonialisms to the taxpaying public. Journalists soberly exhort the public to engage in Australia's coming-of-age through managing the Mandate in New Guinea, critique the government for the less than ideal working conditions for civil servants in New Guinea, and sensationalize young men in dangerous adventures among cannibals in an inhospitable land.

Australia's official involvement in New Guinea began with the advent of World War I, and, as his mother's letter suggests, the Great War had considerable impact on the young Mack. Much has been written of the Great War, and it is not my purpose here to add to that literature. However, it was veterans of that conflict and young men such as Ian Mack who were the first Australians to administer the mandated Territory of New Guinea. I begin with a brief discussion of the prewar period in the social history of Australia so we may infer something of what might have motivated men like Ian Mack to become patrol officers.

Disaster, Disillusionment, and a Sacred Trust

In turn-of-the century Australia—a British settler colony of convicts, escapees from workhouses or debtors' prisons, and émigrés—the "ideal of respectability . . . [was] the most important cultural baggage brought . . . by immigrants hoping for dignity and prosperity in a new land" (McCalman 1984:20). Respectability meant overcoming the historical stigma of convict antecedents and the economic stigma of being poor or working class to achieve a "self-respecting manly independence [and the] emotional status of being fully adult" (ibid.). Social mobility meant acquiring the values and ideals as well as the material markers of society's upper classes; thus, a "respectable" family could be poor or working class but "just as good as" and have a dignity equal to that of the more affluent members of society.

> Respectability prescribed disciplines in behavior which could alter the conception of the self. In demanding cleanliness, sobriety, extramarital chastity, thrift, time-consciousness, self-reliance, manly independence and self-responsibility, it promoted an ego that was self-regulating, responsible and mature. . . . The self-respect derived from these disciplines could provide working-class people with some sort of psychological defence against the indignities of class stigma and the frustration of political impotence and social insignificance." (Ibid.)

These attributes, attitudes, ideals, and values exerted a powerful influence in the home, schools, and churches. For schoolboys in Australia such as Ian Mack and his brothers,

> learning of goodness and the finding of faith pervaded every part of growing up. . . . Churches sent them out into the world to serve and live for others. But it was not exclusive to church and college people: it was in fact the basic ethic of the times. Working-class children were also brought up to live for others, for if they did not help each other, they could not survive. It was the most powerful and morally significant social ethic of Australian society, taught in homes comfortable and poor and in schools religious and secular. (McCalman 1993:108)

The "catastrophic" collapse of the Australian economy in the 1890s "ushered in more than forty years of stagnation, where the Australian economy was among the most depressed of the developed world" (McCalman 1993:50). In a society "predicated on good character," the economic catastrophe brought shame, disgrace, uncertain futures, and broken dreams. The loss of respectability and "the taint of impropriety could bring about the disintegration of a man's entire personality" (ibid.:53). For many, to be poor, constantly searching for work, and on the move to avoid landlords was an economic as well as a moral disaster.

Born into the new century on August 18, 1900, at Jan Juc, Victoria, Ian McCallum Mack was the third child (second son) of Joseph Gardner Mack (1870–1934) and Margaret Rose "Daisy" McCallum Mack (1874–1949). Between them, Daisy and Joseph could claim a "rich heritage of English Anglicanism and Scottish Presbyterianism" in a genealogy that included two "First Fleeters" who sailed into Sydney Harbour in 1788, as well as "convicts, penal officials, squatters, farm managers/overseers, medical officers and merchants" (R. Mack 1996–1999). Only ten years into Australia's economic collapse, Gardner Mack was employed as a farm manager and, according to Ian Mack's younger sister Margaret (b.1915), the family "lived on a poorish farm 50 miles west of Geelong and Mother was determined there was something a lot better for her children than working and slaving on a farm" (M. Mack 1996–1999).[4] This could explain why, in 1905, Daisy took Ian and his three siblings to England (probably to Bournemouth), where Ian attended a preparatory school. Daisy and the children returned to Australia in 1914, at which time Ian was enrolled at Geelong Grammar School and his elder brother, Joseph, enlisted in the Navy.

The outbreak of world war facilitated the daunting climb up the ladder of social respectability and class mobility for a new generation of Australians. The Great War "was their historical opportunity to recover self-respect after the psychic and financial disasters of the 1890s; and because it was a grand patriotic enterprise, and not a conscripted defence of the homeland, the war offered a path to acceptance" (McCalman 1993:61). In Britain, public schools emphasized militarism and Empire and a curriculum that encouraged leadership and administrative capabilities. Australian public schools, such as Geelong Grammar, "delighted in the great chance for war glory and there was nothing less than a frenzy of blood sacrifice" (ibid.:60). Young men rushed to enlist, forming lengthy queues at recruitment centers, "and strong men choked back their disappointment when rejected as unfit for service" (Macintyre 1986:143). Boys impatiently wished away their days to be old enough to enlist. At sixteen, and too young to enlist, the young Ian Mack no doubt both envied and idolized his elder brother Joseph (b.1896), proudly serving in the Navy. Joseph was killed in action at the Battle of Jutland, 1916, the same year that Ian passed the examination for Naval Paymaster Clerk. In 1917 Ian received his Matriculation from Geelong Grammar and on August 18, 1918, the day after his eighteenth birthday, he enlisted in the Australian Imperial Forces. Armistice was declared before Ian even got to training camp. With the armistice dashing any hope of participating in the war effort, Ian worked with his father and eventually "went jackerooing in Queensland" (M. Mack 1996–1999). In 1921, Daisy, who had a small inheritance from her father, purchased a house in Geelong for herself and the children. Ian continued to work with his father until 1922, when he left to work on a station in Queensland. In 1925 he returned to Geelong to his mother's house, then went on to spend a few months on a station in South Australia. But Ian "wanted something more exciting, so when Australia took on the Mandate . . . he applied for and got the job" (M. Mack 1996–1999).

With the signing of the New Guinea Act (May 9, 1921), the German colonies in eastern New Guinea and the Bismarck Archipelago became the Mandated Territory of New Guinea. It must be recalled that, after the crash of 1890 and the subsequent depression, the full spectrum of classes in Australian society was faced with impoverishment, loss of position and property, and, with the end of the Great War, disillusion and despair. As a country, Australia, too, wanted to be perceived in the eyes of the world (especially British eyes) as "respectable," as having risen above its convict and colonial beginnings. If the Great War had been perceived as a means to redeem individual respectability, national respectability was hitched to Australian governance of the Territory of New Guinea. The Mandate served as a vehicle for mediating Australia's role on the global stage rather than as the object of national activities per se.

Newspapers and politicians alike proclaimed that, by taking on responsibility for the Mandated Territory, Australian "national pride and prestige are at stake [such that] remissness in the discharge of these obligations cannot fail to react to her discredit in the eyes of the world" (*The Sun*, 1929). The press repeatedly congratulated Australia for its "bold essay in altruism" in taking on "a sacred trust of civilization" to oversee the well-being and development of "peoples not yet able by themselves to stand under the strenuous conditions of the modern world" (*The Sun*, 1935). The *Sun* reporter, whose byline is simply "Special Representative," goes on to paraphrase the seven guarantees required of a "country to whose care a backward people was given." The seven guarantees include: no slave trade or forced labor; regulated traffic in arms; no intoxicating drink to be supplied to natives; no military installations to be constructed; no military training for natives except for internal policing and local defense; and, subject to public order and morals, freedom of worship of all kinds. The implicit paternalism (see Nash, Chap. 7) of the Kiplingesque assumption of the "white man's burden" is quite evident in the commonsense notion that "civilized" societies (represented by the League of Nations) could infantilize a society and give it into another's keeping; the latter, by accepting the mantle of the mandate, is then construed as an altruistic keeper of a sacred trust. Barely two decades from being a collection of colonies itself (read: an uncivilized people), and with a population that knew little and cared less about the big island to the north (see Foster, Chap. 5), the newly fledged Commonwealth of Australia assumed responsibility for the peoples encompassed by the Territory of New Guinea.

Fielding the Mandate

Although the war had been over for some years, it wasn't until the New Guinea Act that "the military administrator at Rabaul issued a proclamation that . . . the [Australian] military occupation of New Guinea would cease and a civil administration be established in and over the Territory" (Mackenzie 1987:349). Brigadier-General Evan A. Wisdom became the first administrator of the new Territory and began to implement the Territory's political infrastructure. Stations and base camps had to be established. Officers of the civil service had to be hired and trained to conduct regular patrols to bring the area's inhabitants "under administrative control." Recruitment and training of administrative staff were critical. Wisdom's requirements were for a staff of young men (between 18 and 22 years of age) with "education, tact, personality and physical fitness . . . a strong sense of justice, firmness, patience and knowledge of the native mind" (Campbell 1998:78)—just the kind of young men produced by the public school system of the time.

For the next several years, the Territory administration floundered due to lack of experience in administering a Mandate and a colonized people, and the turnover in public service personnel was astounding. In the seven years from 1922 to 1929, over 400 men passed through the system and, of the 159 officers who staffed the service when it was first classified in 1922, only 54 positions remained filled in 1929 (*The Sun*, April 17, 1929). The *Sun*'s correspondent points out that

> compared to other tropical services, that of New Guinea is certainly very poorly paid and the conditions fall a good deal short . . . judged on any standards, the salaries are by no means over-generous. . . . The very high cost of living—an analysis of the list of 27 essential commodities shows that the percentage of extra cost over Australian prices is just short of 50—makes life no easy matter for the married man who receives less than £500 a year. . . . Taking it by and large, a married man in Australia with two children is much better off with a salary of £300 a year than the same man in the Territory on a salary of £500 per year.

Such a picture is in stark contrast to the "splendor of outposts of a vast and powerful empire" enjoyed in New Guinea by the Germans, who "built homesteads and government offices with an impressive verandahed grace . . . [and] gave themselves the background to a more pretentious and affluent colonial style" (Nelson [1982] 1990:24). Citing the heavy turnover of public service employees, *The Sun* "Special Correspondent" blamed the Commonwealth government's low pay scale and the poor living conditions provided in the Territory for the inability to attract and keep "desirable" officers. It seemed that having acquired the Territory, the administration of New Guinea received very little public interest as Australians recovered from the horrors of the world war and focused on their own internal problems of development. Young men were not flocking to New Guinea, and the continuous turnover in service suggests that those who did go north did not stay long. The allure of adventure and riches no doubt soon gave way to the difficulties of malaria, hard labor, and social isolation.

Ian McCallum Mack was an ideal candidate for the position of *kiap* (Tok Pisin [TP]: government official; patrol officer). He was well educated, unmarried, twenty-five years old, and had eight years' work experience when he penned a letter to the secretary of the Home and Territories Department at Melbourne applying for "the position of patrol officer in Papua, or the Mandated Territories, or failing that, some government position in Papua until there is a vacancy for a Patrol Officer" (Australian Archives: Series A518/1 Item 852/1/534). Mack noted that, as a consequence of his jackerooing experience on the Queensland sheep station, he "gained considerable experience in handling men and was in charge of the 1924 shearing with 65 men in the mess" (ibid.). Mack also pointed out that he was "accustomed to living quite alone for long periods" and had "experience in handling natives and Chinamen" (ibid.). In his letter of recommendation, Mr. Atlee Hunt, the Commonwealth Public Servant Arbitrator, wrote that Mack "appears to me to be of the class that makes good patrol officers" (Hunt to Carrodus 1925, cited in ibid.).[5] In his memorandum of appointment, Territories Clerk J. R. Halligan commented that Mack was "of a good type, and in view of the fact that he has matriculated and is used to country life he should make a suitable Patrol Officer for New Guinea" (ibid.). In February 1926, the administrator at Rabaul recommended Mack's appointment as "patrol officer on probation" and, three months later, Mack was duly appointed to a "position as Patrol Officer at a salary of £342 per annum." Mack could expect annual increments to a ceiling of £438 per annum plus an annual allowance of £3 to replace boots that rotted in the tropics or wore out on patrols. After the requisite medical examination, Mack received a permit to leave Australia and a railway ticket from Melbourne to Sydney, where, on June 5, 1926, he embarked the SS *Mataram* for Rabaul, the Territory's administrative center.[6]

A cadet system had been initiated in 1925 for the training of patrol officers (Campbell 1998). A few years after its implementation, E. W. P. Chinnery (1932–1933), a government anthropologist in the Mandated Territory of New Guinea, reported that the cadet system provided "good grounding" for the field officer by apprenticing him to an experienced officer at the cadet's district posting. Under such experienced tutelage, cadets learned

> general office routine, customs and treasury work, native affairs, legal and court work, lands and survey, medical treatment, native labour, engine running, and other subjects likely to be of use to them in the out-districts. . . . After two years field work they were examined in general knowledge by head-quarters staff . . . sent to the University of Sydney for one

year for a special course of instruction in anthropology, survey work, health and hygiene and legal principles . . . [then] returned to the Territory where they were appointed permanently to the service in the junior rank of the field staff. (Ibid.:155–156)

Probably because of his age and experience, and no doubt because of a desperate need for field staff, Mack was hired not as a trainee cadet but as probationary "Patrol Officer, Class '1' in the Public Service of the Territory of New Guinea" (Australian Archives: Series A518/1 Item 852/1/334).[7] According to J. K. McCarthy, who landed at Rabaul in 1927, one year after Ian Mack,

> there were no formal induction courses for us field staff in those days although Edward Taylor, the District Officer at Rabaul, saw to it that his young men had a detailed knowledge of the Native Regulations and Standing Orders. Standing Orders dealt with every situation—from the issue of rice and trade tobacco to the variations of magnetic north through the Territory. Included was a chapter on hostile tribes and the correct method of bringing the Pax Britannica to them. (1963:15)

Mack's superior, District Officer Edward (Ted) Taylor, was 38 years of age, married, and had five years' experience in the Territory (*Commonwealth of Australia Gazette* No. 59, 1927). Ted Taylor most certainly "believed in practical experience." Eight weeks after he departed Australia, probationary Patrol Officer Ian Mack was assigned his first patrol into northeastern New Britain.

Inaugural Patrol: The Central Bainings

Mack's inaugural patrol lasted twenty-seven days, from August 7 to September 4, 1926. According to the undated cover sheet on his report, the patrol was undertaken for "the purpose of exploring and reporting on the country . . . and bringing the inhabitants of that area under the control of the Government" (Mack 1926–1931). Accompanied by Patrol Officer Ball, Cadet Ross, and five native constables, Mack left Kokopo (East New Britain) administrative headquarters for Vunadidia by car, driven by Cadet Penhalluriack, who returned immediately to Kokopo. A few days later Officer Ball also returned. Eight days into the patrol Mack writes that his interpreter "had been showing signs of nervousness [and] refused to accompany us further . . . so we had to be satisfied with another native who had a very small smattering of Pidgin English [Tok Pisin]" (ibid.). Four days later, Cadet Ross, one native constable, and one native prisoner also headed back to headquarters, leaving Mack to complete the patrol eleven days later, accompanied by his other four native constables and their six prisoners.

As employees of the Public Service, patrol officers were subject to the same hours of work and regulations as any other civil servant. Thus, a patrol officer should begin his day at 8 A.M., work until noon, and, after a two-hour lunch break, work again from 2 P.M. until 4 P.M., except on Saturday, when only a half day until noon was required. No business or work was permitted on Sundays or holidays. Officers who worked or traveled on a Sunday were chastised by their superior officers for setting a bad example to the indigenous population by not observing the Sabbath. Patrol officers, by the very nature of their job requirements, were essentially unsupervised in the performance of their duties. Since their hours of work "could not be accurately determined," *kiaps* on patrol were required to maintain a journal that included shorthand accounts of time and distance traveled, duties performed on an hourly and daily basis, and events encountered during the patrol. The daily logs or diaries, along with maps and census data, were included in the officer's patrol report. *Kiaps* were held responsible for the "careful use and preservation of all Government property in their charge or possession," and many patrol reports give detailed descriptions of the inadvertent loss of supplies and equipment that fell overboard, slid down a ravine, or washed downriver during a patrol.[8]

A standardized patrol report format was not yet in place (see Westermark, Chap. 4), but Mack's first report comprises his daily diary and several pages of general observations of the peoples and customs he encountered in the area. Despite the territory covered, the total population of the ten villages Mack visited numbered only 188. Mack estimated that there were no more than 220 people in the area covered and expressed some concern for "how quickly the people are dying out" (Mack 1926–1931).

> There is ample evidence that even in recent times there was a much greater population, and, in my opinion, the only way to check this rapid decline is to bring the natives together into large well-built villages where there will be less inbreeding and they can be taught to trade and associate with their neighbours. [These five villages] . . . could all be brought together to some site nearer the sea, where the ground is suitable for the cultivation of taro and other native foods.
>
> From enquiries I g[a]thered that their hunting would not be spoilt, nor would their social code be interfered with. This aspect would require closer investigation on the part of the Government Anthropologist [Chinnery], but from enquiries I made this suggestion seems sound in every way." (Mack 1926–1931)[9]

Mack does assume to know what's good for the indigenes, but he also displays a sensibility (that pervades all his reports) for local custom and conditions. Thus, even when he recommended relocation of villages for the convenience of the administration, he attempted to get some opinion from the villagers on how relocation and other upheavals might affect their lives and livelihood. How he managed to access obviously complex opinions with minimal linguistic skills and without translators is anyone's guess. His obvious and continued interest in the people and their languages and cultures is evident in this first report, in which he recorded brief accounts of birth, marriage, and mortuary customs; descent, inheritance, and land tenure; weaponry; foods grown; and so on. The longest entry pertains to local beliefs about souls of the dead, ghosts, and sundry evil bush spirits. His final comment noted that "the natives of LANKA attribute the big sickness of about three years ago [an influenza epidemic that wiped out over half the population] to the ghost of a man who committed suicide, by hanging, in the bush near their old village" (Mack 1926–1931).[10]

Most of New Britain, both the landscape and its inhabitants, was unexplored by the colonists, and thirty days after his first patrol Mack was dispatched on his second patrol with instructions to "explore and report on the unknown country" and "by peaceful means to bring the inhabitants of that area under the control of the Government" (Taylor to Mack, in Mack 1926–1931). The letter of instruction from DO Ted Taylor specified that Mack was to contact as many people as possible in order to estimate the area's population, to stay in each village as long as possible "in order to gain the confidence of the inhabitants," and "to connect" with villages visited by an earlier patrol, especially the village of Mukolkol, which had been "the scene of a brush with a Government party in 1922" (ibid.). Taylor's written instructions to Mack are informative about the required work and the conditions under which *kiaps* worked. Unfamiliar with the area himself, Taylor admonished his novice officer to

> be careful at all times to have a reliable interpreter, preferably one friendly with the people you intend visiting. Vocabularies of the languages spoken by new tribes met with will be compiled where possible. The patrol is fitted out for two months, and you are not bound to time, thus enabling you to do the work thoroughly. Take with you six Native Constables armed each with thirty rounds of ball ammunition. Warn Police frequently regarding interference with native women, and the shooting of natives, and, above all, should you notice any slackness in this respect use the strongest measures to deal with it. The safety of your party and the success of your patrol depend largely on their behaviour.
>
> Should the natives show any armed hostility do not attempt to continue until they have calmed down. Remember that it is only natural for the natives to resent the intrusion of strangers and adopt a menacing attitude until their intentions are known. I might point out that the effective range of a spear or sling (the weapon used in these areas) is under seventy-five yar[d]s. This will give you a good idea as to when drastic measures are necessary. What measures you use, and the method of procedure must be left entirely to your own discretion, and, being on the spot, you must decide there. . . .

Keep in mind during patrol that the policy of the Administration is peaceful penetration and pacification, and you will endeavour by all means in your power to carry out that policy using firearms only if you consider yourself and party in danger, and the measure necessary.

Furnish a report on the completion of the patrol on the work carried out, dealing at length with the new country explored, physical features, natural resources, flora and fauna, and communications, inhabitants, their customs and habits, their villages etc. A report on each member of your Police party is also required. (Ibid.)

Although colonialism is decidedly an act of aggression, field officers such as Mack were constantly enjoined that the object of the exercise was "peaceful penetration and pacification." The indigenes were not an enemy to be conquered but were rather like wayward children to be disciplined into civility.[11] District Officer Taylor attributed the safety of the entire patrol to the *kiap*'s control of the constabulary (who are armed with live ammunition), in particular the behavior of his constables toward the villagers encountered, especially the women. Members of the constabulary, who appeared just as strange and foreign as the *kiaps* to the peoples they encountered, often considered the local population to be *bus kanaka* (TP: uncivilized hillbillies).[12] A *kiap*'s lack of awareness of the interactions and altercations between his police and villagers is critical to the Nakanai incident discussed below. The rationale for restraint, judgment, and control of his own fear when faced with the native's fear expressed as hostility is of interest simply because fear is an acknowledged component of the encounter. *Kiaps* carried the responsibility not only for their own safety, but also for the safety of the entire patrol, whose members were strangers to the local villagers, usually outnumbered, and certainly unfamiliar with the territory. Events that might read as aggressive arrogance on the part of *kiaps* in tight situations may well have been the only way to protect the lives of those in the patrol. Although Taylor was deadly serious in intent, I sense a subtle gallows humor on his part as he gives a rule of thumb for the trajectory of spears and slings for purposes of ascertaining when to take "drastic measures" for protection.

Mack duly sailed from Kokopo—with PO Ball, Cadet PO Ross, six constables and "sufficient supplies for a two months patrol"—to Kolai Plantation, where the *kiaps* were "entertained by Mrs. Parkinson" for two days (Mack 1926–1931). After Australia assumed the Mandate, the resident Germans were expelled from New Britain and their properties expropriated for minimal compensation. Phoebe Parkinson (1863–1944), sister of the infamous Queen Emma, continued to live on Kolai Plantation, one of several plantations she owned in the Gazelle Peninsula.[13] Because of her German connections, the Australian administration eventually expropriated her property and,

when 60 years old, [Phoebe] lost her plantation and her home and for the next 20 years she lived precariously. Her children helped where they could; but she was a woman of fierce independence, and mostly lived her own life. The Tolai natives of the Gazelle Peninsula were her good friends and she lived among them in a little house made of native materials and for years despite her age, she earned an income by recruiting native labour for plantations." (Robson 1971:223)

It makes sense that Mack should visit Phoebe Parkinson, not only because of her renown and glamour, but also because she was knowledgeable of the area and the people. Phoebe "was a woman whom everyone, native and non-native alike, instinctively trusted," and she became the "most successful recruiter and handler of native labour" in the area, intrepidly venturing into the hills looking for new workers (ibid.:168). Like Mrs. Mahoney (Lepowsky, Chap. 8), Mrs. Parkinson seems a tough, resilient woman whose life and times are little known in the early colonial history of New Guinea (but see Mead 1960). Mack could have done much worse than seek her expert advice before setting out on patrol.

For the most part, Mack's patrol is uneventful. Divi, a village headman, "did not seem very pleased to see" the patrol, so Mack camped at his village for a few days, ostensibly to allow village absentees time to return to be censused. While he waited, Mack reports that he "had a long talk with the old men telling them of the aims of the Government." Next morning, Divi "was more friendly" and Mack was able to census the population of "thirty-seven souls" (Mack 1926–1931). Recruiting carriers as he went, Mack's patrol climbed through and over the grueling terrain. Two weeks into the patrol he writes (with a sense of grim humor) that "having obtained sufficient carriers[, we] continued up the banks of the [river] Biag-Biag, crossing and recrossing it seven times then finally leaving it at 3100' at a spot where it is only a torrent about five yards wide; camped at 3800'"(ibid.). Next day the patrol passed an old camp at 4,200 feet and continued its ascent to 5,600 feet before going down to Kiep Plantation, where Mack rested the patrol for a day. Eventually they arrived at a village that Mack describes as "filthy and the houses in a disreputable condition." Worse, from the patrol's perspective, the villagers faced a serious shortage of food "partly owing to a *singsing* [TP: ceremonial feast exchange] having been held recently and partly owing to the depredations of wild pigs on their taro, as they are too indolent to keep their fences in repair" (ibid.). Because of the lack of food, Mack turned back and on November 6, arrived at a coastal village where a native constable awaited him with a week-old memo from Acting DO Calcutt. With a somewhat breathless frisson of danger and excitement, Calcutt writes (ibid.):

> Dear Mack,
>   I have told the police boy not to follow you into the bush, but to send a message by local boys if you are far in. . . . If you have a chance come in by any vessel offering. . . . Much excitement here. About a fortnight ago

Thurston was speared while prospecting in Nakanai with Nickolls [sic] and others. Nickolls made a copper find while patrolling and resigned when he came in, returning almost immediately to Nakanai. He brought Thurston in to Namanula Hospital and later returned to Nakanai. This morning it was rumoured that he and four other whites had been killed, including old Collins. I was told to send [Cadet PO] Ross in a hurry to Nakanai and he will leave in the "Franklin" this afternoon. Mr. Taylor is already in Nakanai, having left for there as soon as possible after Thurston reached Rabaul.

Your fate was to have been first a survey of the road to Taungi and then to Ganna in Nakanai way to open a post, but things are in a whirl and you may be sent elsewhere.

Regards,
B. Calcutt

Mack immediately headed back but, "due to many delays," did not arrive in Kokopo until two weeks later. The Nakanai incidents referred to by ADO Calcutt created a furor that, fueled by lurid accounts of naked savages killing intrepid white men, fired the imagination of the press in Australia.

The Nakanai Incidents

In J. K. McCarthy's account (1963:20–26) of the events in Nakanai, it seems that Taylor's advice that *kiaps* oversee closely the native constables was ignored in this instance. Indeed, McCarthy places responsibility for the "tragedy" at Nakanai on Police Constable Bai, whom he describes as "a man of bad character and evil repute" (ibid.:21). Bai was one of eight constables accompanying Patrol Officer [Ginger] Nicholls into the Central Nakanai mountains. In the village of Silanga, Bai saw two women whom he claimed to be his kinswomen, and he complained to Nicholls that he had not received bridewealth for either woman, one of whom was daughter-in-law to Mosi, the village *luluai*.[14] Bai wanted to reclaim the women and take them back with him to the coast. Refused permission by Nicholls, Bai lagged behind the departing patrol and ordered the women to accompany another constable to the coast. Mosi protested, but Bai was "an armed, unscrupulous native policeman . . . too powerful a being for a primitive *luluai* to argue against and so the women went" (ibid.). When told of the abduction of the women, Nicholls merely reprimanded Bai and, perhaps worse, did not demand return of the women to Silanga. The patrol's "evil reputation" preceded it, and the next village was deserted. Nicholls dispatched Bai and two constables to search out the reluctant villagers. The three constables later reported to Nicholls that they found no one, when in fact they had located "a girl in a hut whom the three policemen had raped!" (ibid.). The constables confessed their crime and, rather than bring them up on charges, Nicholls made them pay fines to the woman's husband and submitted them to an illegal flogging.[15] The patrol moved on to another village, where Bai demanded a pig and, when he didn't get one sufficiently large, threatened to kill the village headman. This did bring forth a large pig that had been designated for a circumcision rite, which was subsequently canceled for lack of an appropriate pig. In yet another village, deserted in anticipation of Nicholls's patrol, Bai and other constables killed and ate a pig, contravening Nicholls's orders. Again, illegally, Nicholls flogged the men for their thieving and disobedience. The "disgraceful patrol" left a "trail of hate and distrust" behind it and, although renegade constable Bai was a target of that fear and anger, Nicholls, Bai, and the other members of the patrol were closely associated in the minds of the villagers (McCarthy 1963:22).

No doubt it was Nicholls's experience with Bai plus the fact that he (Nicholls) was convinced there was gold in the mountains he had just traversed that prompted him, as soon as he returned to Rabaul, to tender his resignation and head back to Silanga.[16] Two other prospectors, Dyson Hore and Jack Thurston, were also in the area. When Nicholls returned with five prospectors to the now deserted Silanga, he was warned that an attack was imminent. Nicholls ignored the advice. In the meantime, Jack Thurston, prospecting on his own, was attacked and speared in the thigh but, helped by his cook, managed to escape with his life. Five days later Nicholls and his group were attacked in Silanga. Three unnamed Nakanai men and four Australians were killed, and two Nakanai men were wounded. Nicholls and Britten escaped (ibid.:23).

On Thursday, November 4, bold headlines in the *Sydney Morning Herald* heralded the story, radioed from Rabaul the previous day:

GOLD SEEKERS
KILLED BY NATIVES
Island Tradgedy

The paper quoted a news release given by the administrator for New Guinea, General Wisdom, which read, in part:

> Following is all known at present: —Three prospectors went inland, leaving one European at an inland base. This man, Thurston, was attacked by natives, and wounded. He is now in hospital. . . . To reinforce the local assistant district officer and his police, I [Wisdom] sent the senior district officer and a special force of twenty police. In the interim, six other Europeans, knowing the conditions, had entered the disturbed area, apparently eager for [gold] claims. . . . Fugitive native servants . . . two of whom were wounded, when interrogated gave the following evidence: —The party were resting prior to a meal, when suddenly, they were attacked. The servants allege that one man, Collins, was killed, also another European

whose name they were unable to ascertain. All this native evidence must be regarded as doubtful. (*Sydney Morning Herald*, November 4, 1926)

The paper goes on to report that a punitive expedition, led by Colonel J. Walstab, was in pursuit of the natives who had "returned to their stockaded villages." A radio dispatch from Rabaul in the same edition of the *Sydney Morning Herald* read:

NATIVE RISING REPORTED

A punitive expedition of about 30 whites and 70 native police has been dispatched to the scene of the tradgedy, armed with rifles and a machine gun.

It is reported that 500 natives have risen.

There was even a suggestion that the punitive expedition should include the military, which could make "a flight over the Nakanai district, as the mere appearance of a flying machine would be likely to have a good moral effect on the natives" (ibid.). Cooler heads obviously prevailed in the politic response of Group-Captain Williams, who readily agreed to make such a flight, provided that "conditions were right," there were "no risks taken," and the "project would not unduly interfere with the valuable survey work" he was currently doing. The flyover never occurred.

The journalistic sensationalism of the "tragedy" of murdered "gold seekers" and punitive expeditions is enhanced further by the last headline in the report, which reads "Cannibalistic Natives" and locates the "scene of the attacks" in the Nakanai region of the Talasea district of New Britain, a "locality seldom visited by whites." The area, classified as contacted but not under administrative control, was, therefore, off-limits to prospectors. The report rationalized the prospectors' entry into the region as a necessary foray into uncontrolled territory to recruit native laborers for their mining operations. The murdered men allegedly encountered five hundred "natives, who are of powerful physique . . . said to be cannibals, and particularly skilful in the use of spear, bow, and arrow."[17]

It seems that the responsibility for restoring law and order was removed from District Officer Taylor and given to the police force headed by District Inspector Colonel Walstab. To apprehend the prospectors' killers, Walstab organized what can only be described as a posse. He "deputized" fifty European civilians as special police, seconded DO Taylor and as many patrol officers as could be spared from duties, and rounded out the expedition with "ninety-eight police and several hundred native prisoners . . . as carriers" (McCarthy 1963:24).

One wonders if Constable Bai was among the seventy native police who accompanied the punitive expedition as it wended its way over the steeply rugged Nakanai mountains past the deserted village of Silanga and camped at Umu village. As the expedition awaited their evening meal, Nakanai spearmen attacked. Within seconds of the alarm being raised, the Nakanai were fired upon again and again by the police, although it is not clear in the report if this fusillade is from the police rifles or the machine gun. Regardless, within minutes, twenty-three Nakanai "were dead and dying across their shields" (ibid.:25). The Nakanai were unsuccessful in their attempt to kill Constable Bai or John Nicholls; the punitive expedition, having accomplished its goal to teach the natives a lesson (any natives would do, it seems), returned "elated" to Rabaul but without the actual culprits, whose apprehension "after all turned out to be a job for the District Officer and his field staff" (ibid.). Back in charge, District Officer Taylor declared the Nakanai area closed to Europeans, opened a patrol post at Malutu in the center of the disturbed area, and calmly organized patrols in search of the murderers. Sixteen Nakanai men were eventually brought to trial for murder, found guilty, and sentenced to death. Despite protests of "mollycoddling" from the Europeans in Rabaul, Chief Judge Wanliss, who considered enough Nakanai had lost their lives for the sake of four white prospectors, commuted the sentences to fifteen years' imprisonment (ibid.).

In the meantime, Ian Mack's parents had read the November 4 newspaper accounts of the killings, and Mack's father, no doubt fearful for his son's well-being, immediately wrote a letter of inquiry to the secretary of Home and Territories in Melbourne:

> Bon Nerrin
> Nerrin Nerrin
> 4.11.26
>
> Dear Sir,
> My son, I. M. Mack, went to New Guinea last April or May as a patrol officer.
> As I have not heard from him since June 12TH last, I wish to know if he is still in your employ or if you can tell me where he is.
> I am Sir,
>
> Yours faithfully,
> J. Gardner Mack

Inquiries were duly made and several days later Wisdom sent a telegram from Rabaul to the ministry, which later confirmed to Mack Sr. that his son was stationed at Rabaul and currently on patrol.

The Nakanai murders were replayed two years later in Australia, when the *Sydney Morning Herald* ran the "Story of a Massacre" based on an address given to the Sydney Legacy Club by Dr. R. Cilento, head of the Public Health Department. Dr. Cilento was making an appeal to the general public "for the development of New Guinea, which, [Cilento] said, was Australia's only war legacy" (*Sydney Morning*

Herald, December 30, 1928). Quoting Dr. Cilento, the newspaper reports that the Nakanai killings should not be construed as a revolt against the administration. Rather, the murders were a consequence of inexperienced patrol officers who lost control of "police boys" who had robbed village gardens and killed pigs when "no other food was available." Clearly, the general public was misled about the "unscrupulous Bai" and the ineffectual and distracted Nicholls, while the murders are presented as an irrational response of savages to petty thievery, since "it was impossible to injure a native more than through his property" (ibid.). Cilento's "graphic description of the manhunt" reprinted in the newspaper is so unlike McCarthy's report (1963) of the incidents that it is worth presenting here. According to Cilento,

> For fifty miles across the country, from range-top to range-top we could see the smoke signals of the natives. . . . They knew we were coming, and they fell back to their closely defended village on the most inaccessible razor-backed ridges. . . . We followed the sound of their drums, and when we eventually located the hostile tribe on a lofty pinnacle, surrounded by spear pits and other defensive works, we called out to them that we wanted only the murderers and that if they were delivered up everything would be alright. Their only reply came as a defiant message, saying: "Come up. We have killed four of your skin, and we will be only too happy to add you to the number!"
>
> Some time later, following further demands for the murderers, two naked savages came to the brow of the pinnacle, and, performing a wild, repulsive dance, made offensive gestures. We turned a machine gun on them, wounding them, and immediately the whole of the tribe, numbering between 200 and 300, left the village and made for the most impenetrable scrub on the other side of the mountain. We established a medical station on the site of the village, and some days afterwards, when the bulk of the tribe realised they were beaten, the natives returned and eventually handed over those concerned in the massacre, who were made prisoners. They realised it was the only thing to do. (*Sydney Morning Herald*, December 30, 1928)

Though all accounts can be only partial accounts, the Nakanai incident generated conflicting stories. Versions by native carriers were to "be regarded as doubtful," in favor of the veracity of the local white establishment, whose version is hearsay at best. McCarthy's account of the unscrupulous Bai and the "trail of hate and distrust" spawned by PO Nicholls's patrol are underplayed or overlooked entirely. Ted Taylor's leadership and understanding of the situation is put aside in favor of a civilian-led punitive expedition. Dr. Cilento's account in the Australian newspapers portrayed the Nakanai as naked, defiant savages, inhabiting a land as inhospitable as they, who performed repulsive dances and were rude and offensive, behavior that no self-respecting, civilized person could countenance. That a spray of bullets from a machine gun, if it actually *was* used, should be deemed by Dr. Cilento an acceptable response to the offensive gestures and savage defiance of men armed only with spears, is nothing short of amazing and totally misrepresents the orders and objectives under which Taylor and his field officers operated. Clearly, in this instance at least, the heavy-handed response to an altercation with the local population was not perpetrated by the administration, but by the settlers and townspeople who, driven by their own fears, were intent on teaching the natives a lesson.

Dr. Cilento's speech is also at odds with the government's 1926–1927 Report to the League of Nations. Always aware of the League of Nations looking over its shoulder, the administration underplayed the whole incident in its annual report, merely noting that "two patrols went out, one to the Northern Bainings [Mack's inaugural patrol] to deal with the epidemic of broncho-pneumonia that occurred in that area, and one to Wide Bay, to investigate conditions in the coastal villages from that locality up to Kokopo." Treated almost as a non-event, the *only* reference to the Nakanai incident in the annual report reads: "The murder of four Europeans in October, 1926, was followed by an expedition of investigation and the opportunity was taken to establish a medical post at Malutu, near Iapogo, in the heart of New Britain" (League of Nations 1926–1927:140–142). The entry is followed by a lengthy report from the medical officer on patrol with DO Taylor to Malutu, where they opened the new station (to which J. K. McCarthy was later assigned). There is no mention of the Nakanai who died in this event.

Ian Mack arrived in Kokopo on November 16, too late to be involved with the Nakanai punitive expedition; but he was not idle for long. On November 18, he was instructed to prepare supplies for three months and to board a schooner for Talasea. At Talasea, ADO Ellis instructed him to cross the Talasea Peninsula to Volupai and embark the M.S. *Elsie* for Iboki Plantation in Kaliai. Here he would begin his patrol into the Kaliai and Bariai subdistricts to apprehend members of a "killing raid" made on a Bariai village.[18] This was Mack's first patrol into northwest New Britain; over the next two years, he made twelve patrols that took him the length and breadth of the island, including the northern offshore islands of Witu, Garove, and Unea (also known as the Bali-Witu Islands).

Judging by the gap in his patrol reports, it appears that Mack returned to Australia on his first long leave for five months from August 1928 to February 1929. Mack's sister Margaret, age 13 at the time, remembers "the excitement of his coming home. . . . He brought home all kinds of artefacts—spears and shields and bows and arrows"—all of which were lost in 1939 when a bush fire consumed their home (M. Mack 1996–1999). Miss Mack also remembers her brother "having bad bouts of malaria. The shivering and shaking was awful to see!" When he returned to duty after his first leave, Mack went to Talasea Station and, when an opportunity arose to go to the Bali-Witu Islands on a plantation schooner, Mack made a hasty decision to take advantage of the passage to conduct a patrol. Some 75 miles north and west of Talasea Station, the highest of these small islands (sometimes referred to as the French Islands) is just visible on the horizon from the coastal villages in Bariai. Besides carrying out a regular patrol of the islands, Mack was to oversee the pay-out and signing-on of native contract laborers on Langu and Ningau Plantations. This routine patrol culminated in a horrifying ordeal for nineteen people.

Return Voyage from Witu Island: Tragedy at Sea

When they had completed the business of the patrol, Mack and eighteen others sailed aboard the plantation schooner *Langu*, headed for Volupai on the west coast of the Willaumez Peninsula. In addition to Mack, six crew members, and the captain, Marehan of Buka, passengers included Mr. Mills of Ningau Plantation; Mr. Saunders, the overseer of Langu Plantation; and nine New Guineans, including Mack's personal orderly, Police Constable Geiti, and his three personal servants: Nali, accompanied by his wife and their infant, and two brothers, Launa and Mataiu.[19] About two hours out in rough but navigable seas, the *Langu* was hit broadside by a wave and capsized. All aboard went into the sea; some scrambled to cling to the keel, but the boat rolled over on its port side and began to sink very quickly. With some difficulty, Mack and Constable Geiti managed to release the 8-foot dinghy, which could barely accommodate Mack, Mills, Saunders (who could not swim), Nali's wife, and Launa. Five of the crew and Mr. Kavulio clung to bits of flotsam and swam toward Witu Island, still visible about 12 miles from the capsized schooner.[20] Four others held on to the edge of the dinghy and, with the oars tied into position with a torn *laplap* (TP: cotton sarong) in lieu of oarlocks, the men in the dinghy rowed toward the island. The dinghy was sitting dangerously low in the water and it was terribly slow going in the heavy seas. When Witu appeared about 6 miles distant, Constable Geiti struck out on his own, with the hatch cover as a floatation device, to send back assistance. He was never seen again. At about ten o'clock that night, within 4 miles of Witu, the survivors were hit by another squall, with the result that dawn saw them even farther from land. Realizing they could not row against the sea to Witu, they hoisted a sail of *laplaps* tied to an oar and let the wind take them east toward Volupai on the Willaumez Peninsula, which now hovered closer on the horizon than Witu.

The makeshift *laplap* sail was torn to shreds and blown away by the wind, but the current continued to carry the dinghy away from Witu and toward the peninsula. The men in the water clinging to the side of the dingy took turns resting in the dinghy, but the bitterly cold winds chilled them and they returned, unrested, to the relative warmth of the sea. When Mack, Mills, or Saunders offered to take their turn in the water, the New Guineans "objected strongly," arguing that their "white skins would probably attract sharks and place them all at risk" (R. Mack 1994:191). Soon, however, exhaustion overcame the men in the sea, and at midday on the second day, Paku collapsed and drowned. Later that night, Marehan, the ship's captain, and Mataiu, one of Mack's personal servants, let go and drowned. At dawn of the fourth day at sea, the peninsula was close enough to see trees on the shoreline, but another wind and rain squall again drove them from the shore. Unable to hang on any longer, Garu slid beneath the sea and drowned; three hours later, an exhausted Tanguri drowned. Only Nali remained in the water, and as the seas calmed and seemed less likely to swamp them, Nali, too, was hauled aboard the dinghy.

The survivors in the dinghy—Mack, Mills, Saunders, Nali, Nali's wife and infant, and Launa—were feeling the effects of four days at sea with no food, water, or sleep. Mills was covered with sores and removed his clothing, which had stuck to and irritated the lesions. On the morning of the fifth day, they came within five miles of the peninsula and, with the last of their strength on the oars, managed to make land safely despite the huge surf that crashed onto the rocky shore. Nali and his wife were the strongest, so they set off in search of local inhabitants. Launa managed to locate some water nearby. Mills and Saunders wandered away in search of a more comfortable place to sleep than was afforded by the rocky beach. When they didn't answer his call, Mack, along with Launa, set out in search of them but, too exhausted for the task, these two soon gave up and slept where they dropped. At dawn they searched for Mills and Saunders again, but instead of finding *them*, they came upon a local man and his wife hunting in the bush near the beach. Clearly startled by the appearance of the strangers, the man shouted at them and ran away. Launa came across some coconut palms and managed to climb one to get drinking coconuts. Later, Mack and Launa heard a woman calling and found Nali's wife, frantic that her husband had collapsed back on the trail. A short while later, the *tultul* of Buli Muri village and several villagers, sent by the man Mack had startled earlier that day, found them and helped them back to the village, a mere half mile away. There was still no trace of Mills and Saunders.

Nearly prostrate with exhaustion and exposure, Mack nevertheless wrote a note to ADO Downing at Talasea informing him of the loss of the *Langu*, the five drownings and the possibility that some survivors made it to land, the condition of the six survivors, and the disappearance of Mills and Saunders. In closing, Mack exhorted Downing to "please send the whaleboat, or better still the Mission pinnace, to Bulu Muri, as soon as possible, and put a fair bit of my food on board. I will tell you all about it, I can't write much yet. Cheerio" (Mack 1926–1931). But rough seas, which had smashed the *Langu*'s dinghy to pieces on the beach, prohibited canoe travel, and the messenger was unable to set out for Talasea that evening. There was still no sign of Mills and Saunders. Mack wrote a second letter to ADO Downing, intending to send both messages overland to Talasea if the sea continued too rough for travel:

> You had better come at once, by road if the sea is too bad for the whaleboat. . . . You had better come as I cannot stand up properly yet, and

won't be able to walk for a few days, but be quick, and make the boys walk all night. Send along my medicine chest, and tell Ranga to pack up a complete outfit of clothes and food, pipe, strop and other things, as all I have is a pair of shorts, a shirt, and the lid of a tobacco tin. . . . Hurry up with things whatever you do. Cheerio.

Next day, the messenger set off overland for Talasea. In the meantime, the villagers organized a search for Mills and Saunders, whom they found late that afternoon and carried to the village. The following dawn, the senior medical assistant at Talasea, Mr. Thomas, and two men from the Lands Department arrived, their motorized canoe severely damaged by rough seas en route from Talasea. ADO Downing arrived soon thereafter aboard the station whaleboat. By the afternoon, everyone was aboard the station whaleboat, and nine hours later they arrived at Talasea Station.

Two days later (February 20, 1930), ADO Downing convened a Coroner's Court for the purpose of examining Patrol Officer Mack on the "reported loss of the Schooner and the death by drowning of a number of free and indentured natives" (R. Mack 1994:189), including those who had struck out on their own but were still missing and presumed drowned. All five survivors, except Nali's wife, were interrogated by the Coroner; the depositions given by Nali and Launa, Mack's personal servants, are included in the record only in English translation. Based on the vari-

Survivors of the wreck of the Langu. *Seated: Mack (with pipe), Mills (l), Saunders (r), and Nali's wife and baby. Standing: Nali (l) and Launa (r). Photograph courtesy Margaret Mack, Personal Collection.*

ous depositions, the schooner was deemed seaworthy. It had not been overloaded; indeed, the hold contained only a few tins of kerosene and some cases of groceries belonging to Mack. However, the relatively empty hold plus the "top hamper" (shade awning built over the deck) made the schooner top-heavy. Mills attested that Marehan, the ship's captain, "was an experienced steersman and seaman" who had once saved Mills's life "by his skilful handling of a whaleboat" (ibid.:193); but, on this occasion, it seemed the captain made an error of judgment and brought the schooner broadside to the sea, where "sea and wind unfortunately acting in unison turned her over" (ibid.:194). Launa, whose brother Mataiu had drowned, related that the captain "seemed very cross at having to go, and said he was "laze finish" [TP: les pinis, or "fed up," "tired of," "annoyed," "bored"] at having to go out in the [Langu] all the time" (ibid.:199). Apparently, Launa overheard Marehan say he would "make the ship jump about plenty" at sea. Nali agreed that, although the captain "was a very good sailor," he was "sure that the whole accident was Marehan's fault, for he was not steering well after we left Witu." Nali, who had been in the water for twenty-four hours before he was rested in the dinghy, testified that "The Masters [TP: white men] in the dinghy did their utmost to help us and worked hard in lifting us in and out of the water" (ibid.:198). Launa also reported that "those in the boat made every effort to save the other natives who were in the water with me. We were each taken into the dinghy in turns, according to our degrees of exhaustion, and rested. This was often done at the risk of capsizing the boat." The Coroner's disposition is not included in the record, which ends on February 20, 1930. On April 15, 1930, in a letter to the Home and Territories Secretary [then Mr. J. R. Halligan], Mack's mother wrote that, although she had "not personally seen the article . . . there was a description in the Sun, of an accident to a boat in which [Ian] was concerned. . . . If possible I would be glad to receive details, or assurance that he is well." Three weeks later, Mrs. Mack is reassured that her son is "in good health."

There follows a gap of five months in Mack's record of patrol reports. Although reports of any patrols he might have made may have been lost, it is equally plausible that Mack remained at Talasea for those months, recuperating from the physical and emotional trauma of the tragic voyage from Witu. Mack's next patrol report is dated July 6, 1930, when he sets out to join PO Penhalluriack in pursuit of attackers who had ambushed Penhalluriack's camp and killed five of his bearers. The steep terrain of the East Nakanai mountains and the ability of the local inhabitants to disappear into the bush before the patrol arrived prevented the kiaps from locating, let alone capturing, the culprits. Dated eleven weeks later, Mack's next patrol is a leisurely nine days by ship along the Nakanai coast for the purpose of collecting the annual Head Taxes. Completing this patrol on October 30, 1930, Mack left soon after for six months of home leave.

J. K. McCarthy describes Mack as "a tough, wiry man, who smoked black stick tobacco in his pipe" (1963:112). A photograph of Ian, given to me by his sister

Margaret, shows a short, slim, slightly balding young man with a pipe clamped between his teeth. On this leave, Margaret is a young woman of 15, proud of her glamorous older brother. Ian brought home a fellow patrol officer, whom she remembers as Penhalluriack but only recalls that the two men had a "terrible fight." Another day, Margaret remembers Ian taking her, their mother, and younger sister Josephine for a drive in a car, during which Ian

> had a heart attack of some kind. Drama—but he did stop the car and passersby came to our help. Mother tried so hard to prevent him going back to New Britain. But he recovered and was determined to return. . . . I think that . . . [the] trauma [of the tragic voyage from Witu] may have caused the heart attack. (M. Mack 1996)

Although Ian never married, he did have a long-standing friendship with a woman named Nancy. Margaret remembers that Ian and Nancy "were very fond of each other and I'm afraid I intruded on their last farewell on the Spencer St. Railway Station [Melbourne]" when they wanted to have a private farewell. Margaret never saw her brother again.

From New Britain to the Upper Ramu: The Final Patrols

When Mack returned to Rabaul in April, he set out on an eight-week patrol into the East Nakanai mountains to find and bring under administrative control the elusive Mokolkols, who again had attacked a patrol. They struggled up steep slopes on their hands and knees, slid down ravines, picked their way across treacherous limestone karst formations, and hacked their way through bamboo thickets, and though they caught glimpses of the nomadic Mokolkol, they failed to make any meaningful contact with the people.[21] With only two weeks' rest after two months on patrol in East Nakanai, Mack departed from Talasea Station on a sixteen-week patrol that took in fifty-seven villages in the Kaliai, Bariai, and Kilenge-Lolo subdistricts on the northwest coast, around the western tip of the island to the southern coast to Gilnit on the Itni River. Following ancient trade routes from the south coast, Mack traveled back through unexplored territory over the mountains and to Gurissi in the Bariai subdistrict on the northwest coast. Mack had built up enormous familiarity of the peoples and cultures he had encountered, but he was always aware of his dependence on others in his daily life—personal servants, cooks—and in executing his duties—constables, carriers, and especially interpreters. In what turned out to be his last patrol report, Mack related

> a striking example of how dependant one is on the good faith of interpreters. . . . An old man approached me, and speaking in Maliu, told me that, his wife having died, he wished to leave the village . . . and spend the last few years of his life with his son in another village. His speech was very indistinct

through loss of teeth so to make certain that I had heard aright I called out to the Tultul (who was unaware that I had more than a very small smattering of the language). The Tultul's interpretation of his request showed that I had heard him correctly, but when I told the Tultul to tell the old man that it was a free country, and he was quite at liberty to go to his son's village I was amazed to hear the Tultul interpret my remarks into Maliu as: "The white man says that there are very few men in this village and if you leave it, and go to your son he will tie you and take you away, and you will never come back again." Enquiry revealed that the Tultul had been an objector to his leaving the village, and one wonders how many times one has ones [sic] remarks distorted, or, as in this case, wilfully altered by interpreters who are interested in the case being dealt with.

Mack seemed aware that at least some local people did not simply acquiesce to colonial rule, but actively manipulated the colonizer's presence to their own ends. Perhaps he did not learn this lesson well enough before he had to deal with people and local politics in the Upper Ramu area of his next posting.

Because of severe shortages of senior officers in Morobe and the Upper Ramu District, Mack and District Officer E. [Ted] Taylor were transferred from New Britain to Salamaua. Mrs. Sarah Chinnery, wife of the government anthropologist E. W. P. Chinnery, was also sailing the *Montoro* for Salamaua to visit her brother who had a gold stake at Edie Creek. In her January 27, 1933, diary entry, Mrs. Chinnery writes:

> There are a number of administrative officials going round—Mr. Eric Feldt, who was at Salamaua five years and has just returned from south with his bride, a very nice girl who is intensely interested in the new life she is seeing for the first time.... Then Mr. and Mrs. Ted Taylor, who have been seven years at Kokopo, are going to Salamaua—Ted Taylor knows Morobe District well as he was there years ago.... Also for Salamaua is Mr. Ian Mack. (1998:65)

Mack, it seems, had been due for leave, but Taylor "had persuaded him to postpone his leave until staff shortage was rectified" (Radford 1987:102–103). And, "within a few weeks of arrival, Taylor sent Mack to the Upper Ramu to replace Jim Taylor.... Mack arrived as gold-prospecting activities were approaching their peak and the administrative load had reached a level and a complexity well beyond the resources available to him" (ibid.).

The situation in the Upper Ramu area was indeed complex. In 1932, James Taylor (Australian Archives:CRS A7034 Item 30) assessed the population to be "something like 200,000 people—none of whom are under control." Gold had been found in the area, and prospectors, unconstrained by administrative edict, were pushing into uncontrolled territory. Some villagers were extremely hostile to the

European intruders. Others clashed among themselves for access to the prospectors' material goods or engaged in their own long-standing rivalries and hostilities. One such conflict resulted in a woman's death and, when the patrol from Ramu Post attempted to restore peace and arrest the person(s) responsible for the killing, the villagers resisted and one man was killed by the patrol. Six men were eventually arrested by the officer-in-charge and detained in a grass-and-wire hut that served as the jail at Kainantu. A month later, the prisoners escaped: three reached their home area safely, one turned himself in, and two were killed as they made their way through enemy Aiamontina territory (Watson 1960; 1992:178; Radford 1977; 1987:118). Mack took the returned prisoner, a local interpreter, and a line of police to capture and bring to trial the remaining escaped prisoners.

Watson (1992:177) points out that, "in principle a last resort, armed attack by constabulary was viewed by a number of *kiaps* as the most effective measure they had" to impose control over intervillage conflict. He thus suggests that Mack's patrol into Aiamontina to capture the murderers of the men who escaped from Kainantu jail was such a punitive patrol. Watson relates villagers' memory of the event. Under cover of darkness, "the police surrounded the men's house. Shooting through the walls at whoever might be within, they fired point blank at survivors attempting to escape. Nine or ten men were remembered to have been killed" (ibid.:178). In Radford's account (1977:65–66), villagers recall that the first two men killed by the patrol were shot as they exited the men's house; others were shot or injured as they escaped the men's house into the bush. When things settled down, one constable "with rifle in hand crept into the house to check the casualties"; he was shot with an arrow, "forcing him to drop his rifle" as he retreated out of the men's house. Radford describes Mack as "a man of short temper," who was "angry at the loss of the rifle and the policeman's reluctance to retrieve it," so he entered the men's house "with pistol in one hand and torch in the other . . . to retrieve the rifle, firing as he went." Mack, shot with an arrow and mortally wounded, escaped the men's house, whereupon he "ordered the police to surround the men's houses once again and fire into them." The random shooting and attack on *one* men's house reported by Watson's informants seems, in Radford's account, to take place after most of the men had escaped from the *three* men's houses into the bush.

Radford (1977, 1987) argues that local events, intrigues, and tribal fighting, complicated by government intentions, by Mack's ignorance of the area and its people, and by his stubborn determination to bring the episode to closure in favor of the administration, all confounded this fateful patrol, which eventuated in Mack being mortally wounded and in the death of six to thirteen Aiamontina men.[22] In particular, Mack was unfamiliar with Anarai'i, a local leader. When he encountered Mack in pursuit of escaped murderers, Anarai'i

> saw a chance to assert his own power through collaboration with the government, and in so doing he not only improved his personal standing

with the Europeans but also diverted their recognised superiority of weaponry onto a rival village [Aiamontina]. The results showed him that while the government undoubtedly possessed superior arms it was also vulnerable to deception and guerilla-like tactics—its weakness lay in its ignorance, innocence and impetuosity. (Radford 1987:70)

It is the case that Mack was new to the area; however, he was not an unseasoned, naive young officer inexperienced in dealing with unfamiliar people or terrain. His patrols to bring in escaped prisoners and capture murderers in New Britain were not undertaken as a punitive expedition, nor with any anger, stubbornness, or "impetuosity" on Mack's part. Mack had achieved the rank of assistant district officer, reporting to Ted Taylor, who had, according to Sarah Chinnery (1998:65), five years' experience in the area and, if Taylor's instructions to Mack in New Britain are anything to go by, he probably informed and cautioned Mack as to the circumstances he would likely encounter and the need for due caution. We can never know all that happened or why.

The Death of Ian Mack

Sarah Chinnery's diary reads:

> *15 June 1933.* News came in that Ian Mack, the Assistant District Officer in Morobe District who was on the *Motoro* trip to Salamaua in January, was shot by bow and arrows on 13 June. This morning I heard that he was to be brought to Rabaul. They are going to put floats on a Junker and fly him in with Dr. B. A. Sinclair to be X-rayed as there is an arrow splinter they can't locate. . . . He is dangerously ill.

> *20 June 1933.* They were not able to get floats to the plane, and Ian Mack died of his wounds on Sunday morning, June 18. Chin[nery] arrived back from Port Moresby on the same Sunday, with ten new patrol officer cadets. Hearing of Mack's death on board the *Macdhui*, Chin has decided to go out to Morobe District and the upper Ramu area and supervise patrols to bring in his attackers. . . . The ten cadets came to afternoon tea on Monday. They are generally fine-looking young fellows—and so they should be as they are chosen out of 2000 applicants. (1998:117)

Also on June 15, Daisy Mack received a telegram from the prime minister's department in Canberra (Australian Archives:Series A518/1 Item 852/1/334) informing her that her son had been admitted to Salamaua Hospital suffering from arrow wounds in his upper back and shoulder, "inflicted by natives in attack on patrol party Upper Ramu last Sunday [June 12, 1933]." Daisy immediately replied asking the secretary to telegram Salamaua Hospital with her message, "All send love including Nancy hope speedy recovery" (ibid.). J. K. McCarthy had also arrived in Salamaua severely wounded in the leg and abdomen from an altercation with the "Wild Men of Menyamya" (McCarthy 1963:106–113).

Three days later, Daisy received the news that Ian had died of his injuries. On the same day, the Sydney *Sun* ran an announcement of Mack's death under the bold-type headline "Hero's Death; N. Guinea Clash Ends in Tragedy" (*Sun*, June 18, 1933). The newspaper reported that Mack and his police were attacked when they "came upon the natives who had murdered the [escaped prisoners]," but the natives had "retreated to a blockhouse to make a stand with their bows." The paper went on to say, "Braving their arrows, Mack led his men in an advance on the blockhouse, and forced his way in, although hit by four arrows." The newspaper quotes Mr. C. W. C. Marr's description of Mack as

> typical of the men of the service in the Mandated Territories—young, keen, resourceful and efficient, and of a remarkably pleasing personality. . . . He showed gallantry and disregard of personal safety which in the Great War would have gained him the highest honour. . . . I extend to his mother, on behalf of the Commonwealth Government, very deepest sympathy on the loss of her gallant son.

Days later, on June 30, 1933, D. S. Wanliss, acting administrator, Territory of New Guinea, mailed a lengthy official account of Mack's death to his mother, an account that was also released to the press and published, almost verbatim, in the *Rabaul Times* (June 30, 1933). Mack's death is attributed to loss of blood from a punctured artery, despite three transfusions from fellow officers. DO Taylor noted that Mack's recovery was compromised by his "weakened constitution . . . occasioned by his keen and arduous bush work" (*Rabaul Times*, June 30, 1933).[23] Taylor flew back to Salamaua from his investigations of the scene in the Upper Ramu on the day that Mack was buried. According to the *Times*,

> [Taylor's] plane passed over the grave where the mourners were paying their last homage to a brave man. It was an impressive moment as the District Officer's plane soared overhead, with the rays of the afternoon sun striking the fuselage, and the drone of the engine mingling with the solemn words of the missionary who conducted the service.

So began the legend of the death of Ian McCallum Mack, Patrol Officer.

Conclusion

In this chapter, I have presented several perspectives on the early years of the colonial mandate in New Guinea. First, there is the letter from Mack's mother that opens this chapter, a poignant attempt on the part of a bereft woman to find a greater purpose in the life and death of her sons. Her sentiments are very much at odds with attitudes of today, in much the same way as present-day sentiment rejects the concept and practice of colonialism. Other inquiries and notes from both of Ian's parents speak to the distance, geographically and generationally, that had developed between them and their son in New Guinea.

Second, I have considered, however briefly, some of the sociohistorical and biographical details that constituted the life of Patrol Officer Ian Mack, which I believe make it much easier to gain some understanding of Mack and his peers in New Guinea. These are the men who symbolized and represented the colonial mandate to the people of New Guinea and who, in turn, represented the people to the colonial government. Mack and others of his generation were molded by a culture caught up in national and international events such as the depression of 1890 and the First World War and its aftermath. Against the backdrop of the vast country of his birth, Mack's personal background, like that of so many Australians of his time (and later), developed within the history of a former penal colony, fraught with personal and national issues of identity, maturity, and self-respect, and an ambiguously experienced connection to Mother England. Mack was brought up to honor a particular ethic of work and service to King and Country that, thwarted by his youth, he was unable to fulfill by sacrificing himself in the Great War as had his brother before him, but that found expression in service to the Commonwealth's mandate in New Guinea. Mack went to New Guinea for myriad reasons we can never know; but the glimpses of his biography presented here suggest that his reasons were more profound than simply to experience a *Boys Own Annual* fantasy of adventure in the savage tropics or to shoulder a Kiplingesque "white man's burden."

Third, I have included a very few examples of how newspapers in Australia represented the country and the people of New Guinea to a public sublimely indifferent to the whole enterprise (see Foster, Chap. 5). The quote in the title of this chapter is taken from a newspaper advertisement soliciting applicants to the colonial service in New Guinea. The words "must like adventure" were added by the newspaper, as they were not part of the press-release copy of the job description provided by the ministry, which saw the job of *kiap* as a routine undertaking of bringing a foreign people and land under paternalistic government control. Dr. Cilento's account of the Nakanai incident in the Sydney papers completely ignores the intrusion of prospectors into "uncontrolled areas" and the ineffective leadership and presence of Thurston and others, in favor of demonizing the local inhabitants to render the punitive expedition a heroic undertaking. The *kiap* as hero is also found in the *Rabaul Times* description of Ian Mack's death and funeral, an account very different from the pragmatic voice of *kiap* J. K. McCarthy (1933), who wrote to his mother that

> Mack had a few arrow wounds but one had cut an artery in his arm. He collapsed under the aneasthetic [*sic*] and the operation had to stop—

Mack had three blood transfusions but he never rallied and on Sunday last he died—poor chap. . . . So he passed out—perhaps it was just as well as he would have lost his arm if he would have lived . . . in fact the death of Mack was caused by his trying to stop tribal fighting—an effort that was a bit premature, I think—he raided a village and was filled with arrows when he went into a house. None of his police were hurt—Poor chap . . .

McCarthy's comments suggest that Mack's efforts to stop tribal fighting were "premature" and thus embroiled him in *local* events and histories of which he had no experience or knowledge. McCarthy's comments also speak to the complexity of the colonial situation. Mack was a seasoned *kiap*, but his experiences with the peoples and cultures of New Britain, while administratively similar, could not prepare him for the local situation, based as it was in local history and local experiences with colonialism in that particular area of the highlands.

McCarthy's version of the Nakanai incidents and the role of Constable Bai, Radford's informants' accounts of intervillage rivalries and Anarai'i's struggle for power, the traumatic experience shared by the survivors of the sinking of the schooner *Langu*, and Mack's awareness that what he said was not necessarily what his interpreter translated are just a few examples of the complex and conflicted relationships that entangled colonizers and colonized alike. Ian Mack, whose death lingers "firmly but imprecisely in the European oral tradition" (Radford 1987:4), is not an exemplar of an era; however, his life and death are part of the mosaic of experiences encapsulated by the sociopolitical mandate that was colonialism in New Guinea.

Seven

Paternalism, Progress, Paranoia
Patrol Reports and Colonial History in South Bougainville

Jill Nash

This chapter is an attempt to write a colonial history for a specific region of Papua New Guinea: the southern part of the island of Bougainville, also known as North Solomons Province. The colonial history of this area, from the post–World War II period to home rule in Bougainville, is documented by records of patrols of the Australian colonial administration that governed New Guinea from the end of World War I to the independence, in 1975, of the nation of Papua New Guinea. Regrettably, earlier records dating from the time of pacification in the 1920s were destroyed in World War II.[1] This study raises questions about the intentions of the colonial government and the factors involved in the creation of an official record through the writing of patrol reports (Kaplan 1995), focusing especially on understanding events in the Nagovisi region of south central Bougainville. As the patrol reports represent an official view, the value of retrieving the local point of view assumes importance (see Scaglion, Chap. 9). My fieldwork experiences provide a basis for amplification and alternative interpretations of the official record: I spent about two and one-half years in south Bougainville during the late colonial period.[2] I also briefly utilize the concept of "negative consciousness" associated with subaltern studies of colonial India (e.g., Guha 1983).

Here, I discuss three pervasive themes that, in my opinion, characterize this corpus of patrol reports: paternalism, progress, and paranoia. The first two are shaped by notions of hierarchy: in regard to native affairs, *paternalism* denotes the need for native leaders to do the "right" thing, but not to challenge the administration in any way; *progress* denotes the idea that the native people, though assumedly backward, with administration guidance might advance.

Hierarchy not only strongly colored field observations and reportage, but was evident in the structural organization of the administration itself, with junior officers reporting to senior ones, men in the field to those in offices, the provincial centers to the capital. Patterns of review and response seemed to reveal the existence of a sort of received wisdom that field observations ought not to contradict. To do so would invite correction or even rebuke.

The last theme, *paranoia*, seemed to subsume the various concerns that administration plans might fail or were failing, and that local people were somehow traveling a dangerous path of their own devising or, perhaps worse, being led by others less qualified or less entitled to do so than the administration—including possibly the Catholic Church, long a rival in providing services and brokering influence, but perhaps shadowy others as well. This theme became increasingly evident as plans for construction of the large open-pit copper mine at Panguna, just outside the study area, and movement toward home rule and independence proceeded. Periods of greater or lesser fear are probably inherent to colonial situations (Inglis 1975; Reay 1993:151). In the circumstances described here, the breakdown of hierarchy, concerns about managing the conclusion of Australian control, worry about breakaway political movements, and other matters were at issue.

Paternalism

One of the tasks of the colonial administrators was to identify and encourage liaisons between themselves and the villagers. Even though this aim was more a prewar pattern than a postwar one, in Nagovisi, it seemed to be important when the civilian leadership reassumed authority after 1945. In Bougainville, powerful chiefs were lacking. The indigenous leader was a "big man" (Sahlins 1963, but see Keesing 1985; Godelier 1986). Yet, in neighboring Siwai, Oliver (1955) asserts that the traditional feast-giving *mumis* (big men) deliberately separated themselves from the appointed officials, as they were no doubt aware of the limitations that acting as "middle management" would create on their influence and actions. The exemplary case of paternalistic attitudes emanating from the administration in Nagovisi involves Mesiamo, a big man of Biroi village.

I knew Mesiamo as a slightly stooped, pot-bellied old man with very black skin, a gray Afro, and thick glasses. He regularly smoked foot-long newspaper cigarettes, which were stained crimson at the mouth by the juice of betel mixture. During his youth and prime middle years, this man had been respected and feared all over South Bougainville. He is mentioned by name and referred to as the "Black Brigadier" in the official histories of the war (Long 1963). He had been a force to be reckoned with by the white population, be they mission or government. In the years from 1969 to 1973, I found him to be wryly humorous and extremely intelligent, still active in local affairs.

Mesiamo had been born around 1905, the youngest child in a family of some prominence. His father was described as having been a *momiako* (big man); what is more unusual, his mother and sister were said to have been *momiako* as well. All his siblings had died by the end of the 1930s, however. Relatives described him as having been hot-tempered in his youth. He had the usual growing-up experiences of a Nagovisi man of those days, including work on an east coast plantation and in Kieta's Chinatown.

During the fighting of World War II, he began to show his leadership abilities. Turning against the Japanese early in their occupation of the island, he aided the Allied cause and was awarded the Loyal Service Medallion on March 12, 1945, with the following commendation:

> MISIAMO [sic] has continually fought against the Japanese since their land-ing in the Bougainville District and remained loyal throughout to the Aus-tralian Administration and the Allied Cause. He took his people to the NAGOVISSI [sic] hills and defied all enemy attempts to enlist his assistance. He organized native resistance in the NAGOVISSI tribal lands and over a pe-riod of many months he and his people accounted for many Japanese. He has captured large quantities of rifles and other Japanese arms, including machine guns and mortars and has brought in many valuable enemy documents.
>
> MISIAMO learned to use hand grenades taken from the enemy and in using these, many casualties were inflicted on the enemy. From the bod-ies of the enemy he took identification tags, plans and maps which were of great value to American Intelligence Officers. One of the last docu-ments he brought in proved to be a warning from the Japanese Com-mander to beware of natives of MISIAMO's locality and to shoot them on sight.
>
> Since the time of the enemy occupation, MISIAMO has displayed out-standing loyalty, initiative and courage and a determination to resist all forms of enemy aggression. (Morris 1945)

At the end of the war, Mesiamo's reputation with the administration was high. The first patrol report after the war by C. W. Slattery (1945) includes the following statement:. "The native MUSIAMO of BIROI village is recommended when the time comes for consideration of the appointment of a Paramount Luluai." In 1949, again, there is general praise for his efforts, but also suspicion in Brian Connolly's lengthy report. Connolly (1949) admits to seeing Mesiamo as a "puzzle: . . . out-wardly . . . very deferential, yet he gives one the feeling that in many ways he re-sents anyone except himself having authority in 'his' area." Without the tacit as-sumption that natives must defer to the administration, it makes sense that Mesiamo would not want to share authority with others; there is no puzzle. Mesiamo was a leader and he knew he was good at it. Why should he acknowledge a young patrol officer as his superior? Connolly's attitude is the "puzzle," until the element of paternalism is added.

Several years later, while referring to earlier reports on Mesiamo, Patrol Officer Norton says it is embarrassing to let Mesiamo continue with road work, village improvement, and settling disputes, since he is acting unofficially. Norton makes a comparison to Yali, later the subject of Peter Lawrence's *Road Belong Cargo* (1964a), and speaks (presciently for Mesiamo, as it turned out) of Yali's ending in prison. Norton wanted to appoint him as *luluai* (village headman), but this did not happen (Norton 1952).

In 1951–1952, B. B. Butcher says Mesiamo is "of phenomenal intelligence . . . strongly pro-administration . . . having the personal magnetism of the fanatic." Because Boku Patrol Post was unmanned at this time, close supervision was not possible, and the patrol officers chose to "leave him like that" (Butcher 1951–1952).

Mesiamo's troubles start in 1955. He was called to give testimony to the court in the matter of £500 missing from his cousin Veniai's tradestore. He refused to appear and attempted to hide with relatives in Siwai. He was captured, however, by D. J. Hook, who wrote a lengthy account of Mesiamo that makes him out to be a rogue and a murderer who played both sides in World War II and, generally, as a petty tyrant in the postwar era (Hook 1955). In ten years, Mesiamo went from war hero to scoundrel. Hook states, however, that it was not possible to show that Mesiamo had taken any of the money from Veniai's store, so this theft or embezzlement cannot be the reason he went to jail. Neither the charge nor a conviction appears in the records of the patrol reports.

In mid-1956, noting that Mesiamo has recently returned from jail, the district commissioner attaches the following to K. Graham's report: "The activities of Misiamo should be observed vigilantly and constantly, as he has great influence throughout the area, and his activities in the past have been most harmful to the settling effect and administrative control in this region. . . . An effort should be made to counter MISIAMO's influence in the selection of new officials" (Gow 1956–1957).

I know from talking to Mesiamo that he did go to jail in Lae for a number of months. I also know that many people outside his village distrusted and feared him. However, when he returned from jail, people in his village and environs still followed his advice, which, as far as I could tell, was very sensible. His power had been broken, however; newer styles of leadership were soon to emerge.

The story of Mesiamo tells something about the kind of person the administration wanted to encourage. The *kiaps* appreciated someone who was effective in hearing disputes, who made sure that the villages were neat and that road work was done. Such a person, however, should definitely be subordinate to the administration. Such a person should resemble a middle-level public servant, rather than a Melanesian leader of his people. The Melanesian big man was apt to be highhanded or ruthless if it suited him. Mesiamo had enemies—and he knew it.[3] The postmortem on Mesiamo's downfall implied that he had not been properly "supervised." The message is that native leaders are only acceptable when supervised. On their own, what they do may be "harmful."

In a lesser way, there was concern about other unauthorized activities—however beneficial they might seem. The administration saw problems with the planting of cocoa by a man named Widokoma, who lived outside my research area and whom I never met. He was widely credited by local people with increasing interest in cocoa planting through his early example. However, patrol reports refer to these sorts of efforts as "unsponsored ventures" (Robson 1958–1959). A considerable portion of patrol reports devoted space to discussion of the cocoa problem (Hook 1954–1955; Graham 1956–1957; Wearne 1956–1957; Robson 1958–1959; Robson 1961–1962). Growing cocoa was often linked to the problem of "unofficial cooperatives," with their possibilities for embezzlement and mismanagement, or with increased agitation for road building. Native peoples must be led into ventures; they must not show initiative.

In connection with concerns about local initiatives to grow and market cash crops, officials viewed as troubling the plans involving the formation of a "black committee" to deal with produce-marketing ventures through a Rural Progress Society (Robson 1961). Mr. Robson's concerns about the influence of Paul Lapun (later Sir Paul) drew a response from his superior to counter "black leadership with white leadership."

Paternalism seems to be a marked theme in the organization of the administration, as well. The "office" appeared to be valued over the "field," for one thing, implying policy was highly rated, even when challenged by empirically based observations. The patrol reports repeat in various places the sentiment that junior officers' reports—when they disagree with what their superiors have written—are wrong. This takes the form of a rebuke and a pulling of rank: the junior officer is said to be inexperienced and thus mistaken, and a kindly higher-up may mention that, with time, he will come to see the situation as it truly is, to wit, as the senior officers have described it in their reports.

In 1968, a young patrol officer's report so diverged from prevailing administration beliefs that it occasioned a two-page letter from his superior officer detailing the misapprehensions it was said to contain. The young officer, Mr. J. R. Gyngell, had reported no evidence of anti-CRA,[4] anti-administration, or anti-European feeling and had described certain Nagovisi men as friendly and helpful. Among other points of clarification and disagreement, the letter sought to counter the apparently positive picture the junior officer had painted of the Nagovisi people. The senior officer, Mr. Hoad, asserts that "most people in this administrative area are paranoid in their behaviour . . . and express a feeling of deep resentment and hostility towards foreigners, especially Australians." He also gives this prediction: "I am sure that as Mr. Gyngell spends more time in the NAGOVISI area he will detect misconceptions, distrust, and even fear of CRA activities. The signs of this state may be indiscernible as the activity of CRA is mainly outside the NAGOVISI area. Furthermore they probably feel it difficult to discuss their feelings with

Administrative officers who appear to support CRA activity" (Hoad 1968). If the signs are "indiscernible," how the author of this letter has been able to discern them is not clear. This assertion suggests the existence of a culture or belief system at the official level shaping perceptions of the people and their problems, with higher-level officers' opinions taken as the truth. Without perusal of patrol reports from other parts of Papua New Guinea, it is not possible to tell how widespread this pattern was.[5]

Progress

From the beginning, patrol reports freely used language implying stages of development: the Nagovisi were "backward," real "bush kanakas" (Ormsby 1945), and, sometimes, "the most backward" in the district. Brian Connolly in 1949 described Nagovisi as people who were "shrewd and leaned toward being cunning." In 1951, they are said to be "by far the most backward" in the Buin Subdistrict, according to B. B. Butcher. In 1957, they are still "backward, but ready for economic development" (Graham 1957). A patrol to Banoni in 1958 finds people now at the "stage" at which they can get rid of their ground-level cookhouses (Robson 1958). Mr. Pitt notes in 1960 that they are "dirty, lazy, and backward." They would have to be dependent on the administration for "a great many decades" to come, as they represent "one of the more backward and primitive areas of Bougainville" (Robson 1961).

Frequently, they were compared unfavorably to their neighbors, the Baitsi (Butcher 1951–1952), the Siwai, or the Banoni, with the Nagovisi always occupying the low rung of the ladder. In 1948, their villages were said to be "not equal to the SIWAI village" (Cole 1948). In 1957, D. J. Hook notes that, "unlike their SIWAI neighbors in the east and their BANONI neighbors on the west coast, the Nagavisi [sic] natives are rather unintelligent and are inclined to be rather lethargic" (Hook 1956–1957).

Siwai is described in largely positive terms, not only by comparison with Nagovisi, but by any standard. For example, an early report noted that "all the villages seen on this short patrol were well-situated and clean." Carriers were "willing and cheery workers." Criticism is tempered with a modicum of praise: the use of streams for defecation is "not perfect [but] . . . does the job quite well." The village officials were described as "a mediocre lot who with encouragement can be made quite competent" (Connolly 1949). The next patrol notes that in one village, people wanted to begin to grow rice as a cash crop. On health matters, "Siwai was found to be surprisingly free of sickness" (Robinson and Cole 1947–1948). By 1951, Siwai in general are said to want to grow rice and hope to finance the project with their war damages money (Jackson 1951). The officer cautioned them about potential difficulties but noted that "many aspects [of their plans] are good." Similar comments continue throughout the next two decades.

Negative comments about the Siwai area tend to be specific—a particular village may be cited as dirty or ramshackle—rather than the Siwai area or people generally. In addition, the label "backward" is not applied to the Siwai, in contrast to the Nagovisi. One exception is in the report of 1951 cited above in which the patrol officer states that Siwai is "*economically* backward" (Jackson 1951; emphasis added) due to a poor road system.

Whether village leaders were more effective or "civic pride" (as the patrol reports use the phrase) more widespread or whether the lack of rugged terrain in Siwai kept patrol officers in a good mood (as a Nagovisi informant suggested to me) cannot be determined with certainty. It is clear that Siwai also had a reputation among Europeans for superior housing and village maintenance; G. R. Wearne notes in 1957 that although conditions are satisfactory, "the standard of housing was lower than I had been led to believe from conversations with others who had preceded me to the area" (Wearne 1956–1957).

What is striking is that these assertions were not questioned, nor was evidence usually brought to bear on such conclusions. Was part of the reason simply the distance from Buin—the geographical remoteness—that caused people to be "backward?" Evidently this was taken for granted, as I never saw a query from a higher-up as to the reason for this sort of assertion.

Thurnwald (1938) and Oliver (1943) characterized Nagovisi as representing the endpoint of a South Bougainville continuum, with kinship rather than political leadership structuring social relationships, an undeveloped rank system, greater equality of women, relative scarcity of shell valuables, and fewer material items and pigs for feasting. Thus, among "primitive" people, there were differences and those dwelling closer to the coastlines could be considered more advanced than others. It is perhaps not surprising, then, that patrol officers used comparisons of different cultural groups in their work.

I would further suggest that the ranking of groups over a region such as South Bougainville may have been an implicit management principle of the administration. To see some areas as progressive and others as backward provides direction—work is always needed in one area that may be lagging. Since innovations of "development" can only be introduced in the most "progressive" group, the one "ready" for them or at the right "stage" for them, the less advanced will never really catch up. Thus, the system is dynamic, but the work is always incomplete.

It is notable that in the two instances I came across in which a reportedly uncontacted group is encountered, it is not described as "backward." Instead, for a remote Buin Subdistrict group, the people are said to be nomadic, shy, and unable to speak Pidgin (Robinson and Cole 1947–1948). The Aita people of the central mountain ranges are described as the "most primitive" (presumably in the area served by the Wakunai Patrol Post), but not "backward" (Elder 1956–1957). The term "backward" seems reserved for those balky or contrary populations who were exposed to new ideas, but failed to accept or implement them (Errington and Gewertz 1995:23). The connotation is of resistance. Although "backward" groups fall within the orbit of the administration's control, they fail somehow to come up to its expectations.

Paranoia

More general-purpose epithets were occasionally used in place of the progressive/ backward tropes (cf. Nash and Ogan 1990), but a new way of describing the Nagovisi as "anti-white" or "anti-European" began to appear in the mid-1960s. By and large, this seemed to be connected to the context of increasing political aspirations and mineral prospecting on the part of the natives.

Acting District Commissioner D. J. Clancy attaches a letter to a patrol report stating that the only people who raise objections to the presence of the mining company are the Nagovisi. He claimed that their objections come from beliefs that the Buin people were cheated by the administration in the Tonolei Harbor project, a logging venture on the southern coast of Bougainville that failed to materialize. "Such talk cannot be understood by the unsophisticated NAGOVISI and they have become so bemused and upset that they start at shadows" (Clancy 1965). In 1966, hostility to a patrol is seen in the Nagovisi's refusal to carry drums of DDT (presumably without pay; Staples 1966–1967a). In the same year, school teachers are said to have negative feelings about land resumption and the mine (Staples 1966– 1967b). By 1967, they were said to be "volatile and suspicious" (Redmond 1966– 1967).

In the last part of the 1960s, Malcolm Lang worked at Buin as Assistant District Commissioner and Robert Hoad was the patrol officer at Boku. Reports by both show concerns about the perceived hostility of Nagovisi. Lang provided a patrol-officer-in-training with a series of questions to ask on his patrol to Torakina (Lang 1970). The questions on mining activity and political activity are reproduced here:

Mining Activity

1. What do you know about C.R.A.?
2. Do you think it is a good thing or a bad thing?
3. Do you think that companies should be allowed on your land for prospecting or mining?
4. Do you know that more than half of C.R.A.'s profits will be paid to the Administration in taxes and that this money can be used to develop the Territory?
5. Do you think all the money should be kept in Bougainville?
6. Do you know that in a few years time Kieta will be a town almost as big as Rabaul?
7. Do you know that this will make a lot of jobs available?

8. Do you think other companies should be allowed to look for minerals in Bougainville?
9. Would you be afraid if a mining company came to the Torakina area?

Political Development

1. What do you think about the work of local government councils?
2. Do you think that your council is doing enough to help you?
3. What would you like your council to do to help you?
4. What do you know about the work of the House of Assembly?
5. What work do the Members of the House of Assembly do?
6. Do any of the Bougainville Members ever visit you?
7. Have you heard of the Napidakoe Navitu at Kieta?[6]
8. Have you heard of Barry Middlemiss?
9. What do you think of self-government?
10. Do you think that the Territory or Bougainville is ready for self-government yet?
11. Have you heard about the Bougainville secession movement?
12. Do you think that the island of Bougainville should secede or stay with the rest of the Territory?
13. Have you heard about the referendum which Napidakoe Navitu is holding in Bougainville about secession?
14. Has Napidakoe Navitu distributed any ballot papers in your area?
15. Have Napidakoe officials visited your area?
16. Have you heard of Hahalis Welfare Society?[7]
17. Have you heard of John Teosin, the Secretary of Hahalis?
18. Have any Hahalis men visited Torokina to tell you about the Society or to collect money?

It is notable that there are twice as many questions on political matters as there are on economic or mining activity.

Two meetings about further prospecting on Bougainville were held at Konga in Siwai and in the Bana (i.e., Banoni-Nagovisi) council chambers. At both meetings, people were unequivocally opposed to further mineral exploration. Lang explains the attitude in Siwai in his letter to the Sohano District Office:

> The attitude expressed in the Siwai area is typical of the response gener-
> ated in those other parts of Bougainville already affected by mining activ-
> ity. The principal concern is that land on which mining operations are
> carried out may be permanently ruined for agricultural user (*sic*), and a
> rather sceptical attitude toward compensation. In addition, there is a
> fairly prevalent attitude that minerals should not be developed by an ex-

patriate company, but should be left in the ground for the development by the next generation of Bougainvilleans, who will be more sophisticated and better educated than the present one. The principal task of the Community Education patrols is to expose the flaws in this type of reasoning to the people themselves, but unfortunately, success to date has been limited. (Lang 1968)

As assistant district commissioner at Buin, Malcolm Lang was not well known to me, but Robert Hoad was the patrol officer in charge at Boku, the local patrol post, during my first stay in Nagovisi. Hoad seemed convinced that the Nagovisi were anti-European. For example, Nagovisi good manners include asking a passerby his destination; Hoad told me he regarded these queries as a kind of verbal harassment directed uniquely toward himself. Nagovisi complaints (to me) about Hoad involved his invitation of Nagovisi women to visit him. It was suspected that he was seeking sexual liaisons with some of them. His nickname was "Kokomo" (Hornbill) due to his prominent nose, but Nagovisi give nicknames freely, often with reference to physical distinctions; the practice does not imply hostility.

Certainly the unrest about prospecting had created stress among administration personnel, who perhaps feared an outbreak of violence. The questions in Lang's letter about the Hahalis Welfare Society, widely regarded as a cargo cult, seem to indicate additional fears, perhaps related to impending political independence from Australia. An enduring problem of "enlightened" colonialism was that though the intent was to foster political sophistication among local people, manifestation of social and political movements not initiated by the administration caused worry.

Discussion

In this chapter, I have presented patrol reports and my fieldwork interviews and observations for the events following World War II to self-government in central south Bougainville. The patrol reports speak without irony of the concerns of the colonial establishment and its local representatives. The reports reveal policy concerns plus impressions and interpretations of native behavior.

What was the historical context of the policy concerns? The postwar period brought political change globally, including the independence of former colonies in Asia and later Africa. In Papua New Guinea, the postwar era was affected by Labor Party policies in Australia, which put the emphasis on the provision of native welfare rather than on the extractive aims of colonialism (Oliver 1991:78). Paul (later Sir Paul) Hasluck's policy of "uniform development" meant in part that focus would shift to the areas under least administrative influence in order to raise them to the territorial standard. Many new efforts took place in the highlands of New Guinea, where there were no "classic" plantations typical of the lowlands. Bougainville became a backwater, the patrol post closest to Nagovisi was closed in 1947, and the lack of records seems to indicate gaps of years between patrols to the region, even from Buin.

Attempts to introduce better village hygiene, effective local leadership that would result in local government councils, and cash cropping thus proceeded by fits and starts (Rowley 1966:82). When it came to cash cropping, in which local people showed the greatest interest, concerns that such projects always be under administrative authority led to erratic implementation.

But the writings by administration personnel contain attributions of motive and interpretations that do not always correspond to my impressions from the time I was resident in Nagovisi—approximately two and one-half years toward the end of the period covered by official records. During this time, I interviewed informants about earlier times and discovered an alternative point of view from that of the reports. So discordant in some ways is my understanding of events compared to theirs that I sought to treat the patrol reports (as noted above) as a literary convention—a discourse of colonial writing.

Is it possible to get these colonial writings to reveal other points of view? I have been impressed by the potential usefulness of the subaltern studies approach of developing formulae that may be applied to the colonial record in order to recover the voice of the colonized. It may prove a useful exercise to appropriate and adapt some of this approach to Bougainville.[8] With certain historical caveats in mind, then, one of Guha's ideas in particular suggests new ways of decoding patrol reports. The notion of "negative consciousness," in which "for each sign we have an antonym, a counter-message, in another code" (Guha 1988:58) gives clues to local thinking. Guha shows that it is possible to produce a chart with phrases that correspond to each other, one being words of the colonizer, the other, the evaluation of the colonized (ibid.:59). The phrases of one imply the phrases of the other, but they are opposites (e.g., terrible/fine).

In Nagovisi, some of the simplest opposed pairs involve the "unofficial cooperatives," that is, the joint efforts made by villagers to sponsor tradestores or cash-cropping efforts independent of administration input. Patrol reports condemned them, but from the point of view of local people, they were highly desirable. These reversals or "negative consciousness" seem especially to characterize the "paranoia" period during which the mine was being established. Now, the impact of colonialism becomes much stronger. Hoad reports that the Nagovisi are paranoid; inverted, this would mean that the Nagovisi are justified in their concerns about the mine. Perhaps "native" and "administration" can be reversed: the administration is paranoid. Lang (and others) claim that the Nagovisi objections to the mine are foolish; the inversion is that the Nagovisi (and other Bougainvilleans) are wise.

The patrol officers report that the Nagovisi are lethargic and "backward"—are these labels denoting failure to cooperate with administration schemes a form of unrecognized assertion, resistance, or protorebellion? The misconstrual of the style of local greetings as hostile interrogation noted above seems to confirm that we do have two lists of corresponding signifiers.

Other interpretations may be more tentative. The expanded understanding of Mesiamo's life and its evaluation by patrol reports is a question that necessitates further study. It is tempting to regard Mesiamo as a sort of "bandit-hero" (Guha 1983) revered by natives and unjustly branded as a criminal by the colonial authorities. One problem with this interpretation is that Mesiamo was first esteemed during the war years by the Allies, and evidently not simply for having killed many Japanese. Mesiamo told me that army officers told him to kill off a number of troublesome Bougainvilleans who were thought to have given comfort to the enemy. Unfortunately, he states, the officials made no record of these instructions, and so he was blamed after the war for "murdering" people. The other half of the coin has to do with his reputation among local people: he was always viewed as controversial, and his own nephew and sole surviving lineage-mate reminisced with ambivalent affection and bitterness about having had his lips rubbed with chili peppers as a child by his irate uncle over some trivial frustration. The extent to which his actions can be seen as a form of anticolonial insurgency is uncertain. By the same token, Mesiamo was hardly a simple swindler or criminal, as Hook's patrol report may imply.

Guha's approach, with its fine-grained analysis of local politics, reminds us that colonial policies can never be uniformly applied or perceived. Certainly, this is the case in Papua New Guinea, Bougainville, and Nagovisi. In more remote inland Nagovisi, colonial dislocation and reaction to it was infrequent. What were the local agents of colonialism? There were no plantations or "plantocracy," with its characteristic consumption patterns, social exclusiveness, and random physical brutality toward native people. Missionaries came later than in the east (Sovele Roman Catholic Mission was established in the 1930s), and Catholic hegemony was shortly challenged by Methodist (United Church) encroachment, with ensuing skirmishes between the two denominations (Laracy 1976). Last came the Seventh Day Adventists. Men from the southwest part of Bougainville went early to plantations, and doing so became fairly universal in the years before World War II. As a result of that practice, an awareness of ethnic difference (Chowning 1986; Dureau 1998) and the unity of Bougainvilleans (i.e.,"Buka boys") was formed.

Although the first government patrols into the area date from the mid-1920s, administrative attention was limited. World War II created a brief but highly disruptive interlude. The Japanese occupied a camp at Mosigeta (a large village in southeast Nagovisi) and, in November 1943, the successful Allied beachhead at Torokina was made, with the subsequent building of a base and airfield from which to attack Rabaul. Thereafter Nagovisi (and other) stragglers came to Torokina and were evidently fed and housed there.

Administrative patrols resumed after the war, but the patrol post at Boku, near the junction of Baitsi, Banoni, and Nagovisi, was left unmanned for long periods of time. Errington and Gewertz (1995) have described the inscriptions in the village books and the writing of the patrol reports themselves as instances of control;

in Nagovisi, "neglect" seems to be the correct characterization of administrative posture, with few visits, spotty records, and frequent personnel changes. In the meantime, as I have outlined above, a large part of the Nagovisi region was under the control of Mesiamo and his lieutenants, who organized the postwar resettlement of the area into what I have called "big villages" (Nash 1974). According to informants, a military lifestyle prevailed there, with all awakening to a bell in the morning, lining up for inspection in matters of hygiene, and other such exercises. Punishment in the form of public spankings ("stickings") was dispensed for a variety of small infractions. Marriage rules, other than those prohibiting unions between primary kin, as well as marriage prestations, were abolished. Patrol reports also speak of some "barracks"-style houses in Mendai, the home village of one of Mesiamo's closest subordinates, Lankas (Cole 1948).

Mesiamo told me that he had insisted on the large village pattern because people were not sure that the war was truly over, and he did not want people living scattered in bush hamlets where they might be caught unaware if renewed hostilities broke out. Inspiration from military sources is obvious, and rituals of daily life are evident here. But the "big village" era appears to have lacked any Christian elements, and this is consistent with what I saw as Mesiamo's outlook. Although he had occasionally attended church and was acquainted with all of the priests to some extent, I believe he had never been converted to Christianity. He seemed to have no inclination to utilize religious imagery in any form as part of his leadership. He was widely considered to be a sorcerer, and no doubt was able to perform spells. His attitude always struck me as essentially skeptical; he was, after all, an adult before significant mission influence appeared locally. This thus contrasts with the situation in other heavily missionized areas on Bougainville, a region where religion has surely been a significant, if not the major, colonial force.

The Catholic Church on Bougainville, a sort of de facto government in its provision of health and education services (Griffin 1990:6), took leadership in village projects and turned out a small number of relatively well educated men for positions of authority, who may have felt comfortable taking adversarial positions in regard to the administration. The monopoly held by the Catholic Church over the education of all young men meant that those who would become island leaders and act in politics were overwhelmingly ex-seminarians. Even those trained as primary school teachers received a heavy dose of religion to qualify for training: the mission selected the devout and smart, not just the smart. These religiously motivated men—not businessmen, who would later dominate politics in the highlands of New Guinea—were primarily concerned with issues of political morality—the good society, justice in regard to mining, and similar subjects.

The eastern coast of Bougainville has a somewhat different history. Colonized by the turn of the twentieth century, this area was the scene of the greatest number of social movements. It was here where, in the early twentieth century, plantations were cut from the forest, the colonial capitals of Kieta and alternatively Sohano were situated, and many mission stations were established. Furthermore, the eastern coast is where villager interests were most vigorously asserted. Here, movements using religious imagery or reacting to the mission presence ("cargo cults"), including the Hahalis Welfare Society of Buka (Rimoldi and Rimoldi 1992), were developed. This is the place about which the representatives of the United Nations were told in 1962 that the Australians had treated Bougainvilleans like "dogs" (Ogan 1972). This is the area where the women's protest against the appropriation of Roravana land for mine infrastructure took place during the resumption of Arawa Plantation, now the site of Arawa town. Napidakoe Navitu was formed here. No doubt, the length, intensity, and nature of European contact are correlated with the frequency, intensity, and nature of Bougainvillean social movements. Anthropologists will see these movements as forging novel reactions to European presence, not as the local people's persistent failure to fully esteem and emulate what colonials were offering.

Insurgency in the form of protracted physical combat—the civil war—came to Bougainville, but not during the colonial period. Animated by dissatisfactions with the mine, which continued to operate after independence, the conflict was a legacy of the colonial period. During the civil war, we see an insurgency distinct from criminality—it is public, collective, destructive, and total (Guha 1983). However, to understand that insurgency, we need to refer to an earlier time. Patrol reports provide a chronicle, but they dismiss local concerns as anti-European or paranoid. The upheaval of killings, dislocation, and disease that characterized the decade-long struggle starting in 1989 represents a tragic culmination of earlier events.

Eight

The Queen of Sudest
White Women and Colonial
Cultures in British New Guinea and Papua

Maria Lepowsky

When I was first living on Sudest Island, my neighbors took me five miles by canoe across the bay to Madawa, a narrow peninsula jutting from the south coast. As we sat on the edge of a fine white sand beach, shaded by a neat row of enormous orange trees, messily eating their lemonish, pulpy fruit, an old woman walked up and greeted me in respectful tones as Missis Kwin. I quickly learned from younger islanders that she did not mean the Queen of England, she was not categorizing me with white women in general, and this was not a figure of speech. She and some of the elders at Madawa—and in other island villages—had been discussing me since my arrival. They had decided I was the returned spirit of Mrs. Elizabeth Mahony, an Irish-born Australian who came to Sudest Island in the gold rush of 1888 and who, if she were alive, would have been about 120. Mrs. Mahony herself, around 1920, had planted (ordered planted, really) the orange trees under which we sat, down the beach from one of her old coconut plantations, Tetena, whose abandoned planked house and copra sheds we explored that afternoon. In the following weeks, other elders came up and addressed me directly, in friendly tones, in a pidgin I did not understand, as Miz Mahony. (Islanders pronounce her name like the local rendering of "money"; expatriate Europeans of Southeast Papua pronounce it similarly, with the accent on the first syllable.) The islanders eventually decided that I was not, in fact, the spirit of Miz Mahony. Instead, everyone I met who was a child before World War II came to the conclusion that I was the spirit of Taineghubwa, a recently deceased big woman whose land I was living on at Jelewaga. Everyone born during and after the war recognized me as quite mortal.[1]

This case of mistaken identity is the origin of my very personal interest in Mrs. Mahony, known in her time and ours as the Queen of Sudest. It was a frontier-era fancy of Europeans in the Pacific to bestow parodic but admiring royal titles on solitary white traders living on remote islands—such as King Cam of Kitava (see note 3) or Queen Emma of the South Seas (who was actually half-Samoan)—titles that reflected the trader's often autocratic though partial control of islanders, their bodies, and their wealth. Mrs. Mahony and her daughters were the only other white women to live on the island before I did. Being mistaken for the Queen of Sudest also began my intense curiosity about the few European women who lived scattered among the islands of New Guinea's East End during the long years of colonial rule, and about the mostly forgotten white traders and miners, male and female, who lived and died in the islands.

The anthropologist Camilla Wedgwood, in an unpublished paper from 1945 on Australian New Guinea, described "three broad interest groups; the colonial triad of Government, mission and commercial and settler interests" (Ogan, Chap. 11; Smith 1989:293). In 1914, at the start of the Great War, and the year Bronislaw Malinowski began his field research, some three-quarters of the 1,200 or so white residents belonged to this third colonial category (Territory of Papua 1914). But compared to the quantity of written material, official and unofficial, from former colonial government men and missionaries, few documents or published accounts of their experiences in British New Guinea or Papua have been left behind by representatives of "commercial and settler interests"—the "unofficial whites" (Roe 1962). White traders and miners in Papua came mainly from the laboring classes and were generally not highly educated or well connected back in England, Australia, or Europe. Quite a few came to this obscure territory because they could not, or would not, conform to metropolitan conventions, and they seemingly had no interest or ability to write for an audience of the kinds of people they had left behind. Many died of malaria or accident, and others of the results of drink. Few collections of traders' letters home have ever been published. Undoubtedly many journals and diaries have rotted in moldy corners of collapsing plantation houses and trading stations, or sunk to the bottom of the Solomon Sea from capsizing canoes and cutters. Few were repatriated to the attics of the writers' metropolitan heirs or found their way to national archives.

White traders and miners as a group were hostile to colonial government in general, and to Papua's Lieutenant Governor Hubert (later Sir Hubert) Murray and the upper-class toffs who were his closest aides in particular. Most were convinced that Murray and his administration had spoiled the Papuans for honest labor (working for whites) through coddling natives, forbidding land sales to Europeans, and passing laws prohibiting flogging of indentured laborers and servants. Their antipathy was a basic fact of life in colonial Papua, as the entire run of the Territory of Papua Annual Reports shows. Depictions of white traders, most highly uncomplimentary, tend to come from official government or missionary reports or correspondence, or else from the impressionistic accounts of book-writing travelers to the islands.

This has given disproportionate historical weight, in scholarly writings about colonial cultures, to the reports and memoirs left behind by government officers and missionaries who lived in New Guinea.[2] These were higher-status sojourners

sent by established institutions: metropolitan governments and missionary societies. Their influence, in their own day and in historiographic practice, inevitably
colors scholarly accounts of colonial Papua and New Guinea, other parts of the island Pacific, and likely many other colonial situations. The lives and actions of
small, independent traders, pearlers, and miners, the unofficial whites, are largely
submerged in most histories of Melanesia. So are the actions and responses of the
Papuans, who found these persistent strangers on their beaches and moving onto
their clan lands, and who often went on to establish exchange relations with the
whites who survived disease, accident, and attack.

White Women and Papua's Expatriate Enclaves

Frontier societies, like the Coral and Solomon Sea frontiers of what eventually
became British New Guinea and Papua, are heavily masculinist in their dominant
cultural ideologies and in the sex ratios of their white sojourners (e.g., Riley 1984;
Jameson and Armitage 1997; and Moynihan, Armitage, and Dichamp 1998 for the
North American West, and Lake 1998 for Australia). So, too, were the colonial societies that ensued in Southeast New Guinea's tropical periphery of empire. This
was especially pronounced among two of their three main constituent colonial
cultures: government and unofficial whites. Protestant missionaries, both Europeans and Polynesians, often came as married couples to Papua, the Catholics later
sent missionary nuns, and both Catholics and Anglicans contributed nursing sisters to their missions. Although mission colonial cultures were also decidedly
male-dominant, it is no coincidence that missionaries were often charged, by
white traders, some government officers, and irate members of the Australian
public, with being "soft on natives," a telling metaphor. Missionary wives and
nuns, and wives of the highest officials, had designated places in the global
British colonial pantheon as feminine agents of civilization and morality. As a result, their lives and experiences are somewhat better documented (e.g., Langmore
1989; Bulbeck 1992; Roberts 1996). But in the islands and coasts of the East End
of British New Guinea and Papua, the most visible European women were from the
"commercial class" of unofficial whites: they were traders, storekeepers,
hotelkeepers, planters, and goldrushers. Women such as Elizabeth Mahony, hotel
owner Flora Gofton of the island port town of Samarai, and writer and plantation
owner Beatrice Grimshaw were among the most influential white settlers in shaping expatriate colonial cultures, relations with Papuan neighbors and employees,
and Papuan images of Europeans that have persisted until the end of the twentieth
century. I focus on them in this chapter, and on women's agency, as a way, paradoxically, to gain insight into these highly masculinized frontier and colonial cultures and their legacies.

East of Port Moresby, there were no resident wives of government men for almost the entire near-century of colonial rule. European missionary wives of men
such as Charles Abel at Kwato, near Samarai, or the various Methodist missionaries

in the Trobriands and Dobu had very limited and localized influence either on Papuans or on the mores and actions of the white population of the district until after World War II. The Sacred Heart nuns only began their island missions in 1947. In the colonial government, even Lieutenant Governor Hubert Murray was a "grass widower" whose wife lived in Australia, refusing to join him in Port Moresby. (After she died, his second wife too remained "South.") Lower-ranking government officers were not permitted to bring wives to more remote posts in the Territory of Papua. They were considered too dangerous for a woman, and a wife too likely, in her lonely neediness—and purported vulnerability to sexual attack by Papuan men—to distract a colonial officer from patrolling his district. The prevailing ethos among the government officers was a contradictory amalgam of the British public school, military, and Australian white settler values of self-reliance, stamina, stoicism, physical courage, group loyalty, camaraderie—mateship, in the Australian idiom—and obedience to authority (see Foster, Chap. 5, and McPherson, Chap. 6).

These highly marked aspects of an idealized colonial masculinity extended, for the most part, to the heterogeneous category of the unofficial whites—the "pioneers," in Hubert Murray's public representations (see below)—even if these individuals varied greatly in social class, education, and ethnicity (though most were Australian, British, or Irish). But white male traders, miners, and small planters tended to express and act out a more anarchistic ideal of Australian frontier masculinity: self-reliant and anti-authoritarian, rather than deferential to authority; individualistic, highly mobile, and, except for a presumed loyalty to (male) mates, generally free of family or community ties or responsibilities (cf. Lake 1998).

This floating population of men—and much smaller number of women—who were the great majority of the white residents of Papua and New Guinea generally worked for themselves. They tended to try their hand at different enterprises over the years: buying an old cutter and setting up as a trader, pearl buyer, or labor recruiter; staking out a mining claim in the latest goldfield; or working as a store clerk, small vessel captain, or planter of coconuts on contract for an outfit like Burns Philp. Men with secondary schooling and reasonably untarnished reputations did stints as patrol officers or government clerks: the administration was chronically short of young, single, white men for lower-level positions (see McPherson, Chap. 6).

European women were always a distinct minority in British New Guinea and Papua, their presence generally unmentioned in the official and unofficial documents of the era (see Nash, Chap. 7, for more on colonial documents and colonial discourse). Still, there were significant numbers of women among the white planters, traders, and miners. Some women came to Papua on their own, mostly from Australia, and others came with their husbands and parents. A few, like Elizabeth Mahony, remained in the Territory after a husband's or father's death. There were also a fair number of divorcées. Divorced women bear far less stigma in frontier societies or colonies with small white populations, as the case of nineteenth-century California shows (e.g., Griswold 1983). In California and Papua alike, divorcées and widows operated businesses, chose new lovers and husbands from among a wide array of suitors, or remained unmarried and independent as respected community members.

The Territory of Papua census for 1921 showed 670 white women, 133 of whom were listed as breadwinners. In the same year, there were 1,408 white men, of whom 1,123 were breadwinners (Bulbeck 1992:91). Most of the white women who were not breadwinners were missionary wives, nuns, or the wives of higher-ranking government officers, and the majority lived in Port Moresby. The wage earners included nurses, stewardesses on Burns Philp and other ships, traders, planters, miners, barmaids, and store, boardinghouse, and hotel keepers. The lives, activities, and memories of the nongovernment, nonmissionary white women we know were present in colonial Papua and New Guinea are not easily visible from this end of the century, and they can only be investigated with difficulty. White settlers, traders, and miners as a whole left few records (cf. Lewis 1996:256), but the lives of the white women affiliated with neither church nor government are even more obscure.

The Golden Dream

Late in 1887, an Englishman named David White, who had been trading for pearl shell and *bêche-de-mer* in the Louisiade Archipelago, southeast of New Guinea, thought he saw gold in a stream on Joannet Island. He reported his discovery in Cooktown, a port in Far North Queensland named after the great discoverer, home to a polyglot group of *bêche-de-mer* fishers, pearlers, and miners who worked claims on the Palmer goldfield. In April of 1888, financed by local businessmen, White and nine local miners sailed north in the *Juanita*. The others were furious when they discovered no gold at Joannet, but the party crossed the lagoon to Sudest, where, along the river the white men called the Runcie and islanders know as Veora, they found quartz outcroppings with gold intrusions and gold dust in the fine dark muck of the riverbanks.

The rush was on. By the end of the year there were hundreds of white miners on Sudest Island, living in tents and purchasing goods at five tradestores, also housed in canvas tents. Some struck pay dirt; many others died of malarial fever and dysentery (British New Guinea Colonial Annual Reports 1888, 1889). Also by the end of the year, and because of the Sudest gold rush, British New Guinea, a protectorate since 1884, became a full-fledged colony of the British Empire. No longer just a money-losing, fever-ridden buffer between the newly proclaimed colony of German New Guinea and the uneasy white settlers of the British colonies of Queensland and New South Wales, British New Guinea became a land of promise, luring hundreds of men, and a few women, to journey there in search of wealth.

One woman arrived from Cooktown, Queensland, in 1888 among the hundreds of miners. Mrs. Elizabeth Mahony, then 33 years old, came in search of gold with her husband, John. Elizabeth Mahony's origins are uncertain, but she was clearly not from the propertied classes and had little formal education. In these ways she and her husband were representative of the majority of the great and then ongoing Irish-Australian migration (see Fitzpatrick 1994). She remained on Sudest Island until 1930, and she was by far the most successful white entrepreneur on the island until about the time of the First World War. For much of her adult life, she was one of the most prominent white traders in all of British New Guinea and Papua. Elizabeth Mahony was only the second white woman to live anywhere in New Guinea. The first, Mrs. Fanny Lawes, was the missionary wife of the Reverend William Lawes, sent by the London Missionary Society in 1874, and she lived near the harbor at Port Moresby (cf. Langmore 1989:1, 3). Mrs. Mahony lived for over forty years in what is still one of the most remote regions on earth.

The Sudest gold strike proved disappointing. Alluvial gold was soon panned out by too many hands, and no one to this day has ever located the mother lode, although many have tried. By 1889, most white miners had already moved on to new strikes on Misima Island, ninety miles north, located by disgruntled prospectors from Sudest, and then farther north again to Woodlark Island (Nelson 1976; Lepowsky 1993). The Mahonys were among the small number of white traders who stuck it out on Sudest. From hiding places along the ridges, Vanatinai men and women carried out a few months of cautious surveillance of the white miners panning for gold along streams where islanders had always bathed, drawn water, and fished for shrimp and eel. By the early 1890s, overcoming initial strong objections from white miners, they too learned to work gold, sluicing the soils of the creekbeds with heavy iron gold pans imported from Australia and purchased on credit, or book, from tradestores newly opened by whites. They paid for mining supplies, bush knives, steel axes, molasses-cured trade tobacco, pipes, calico, and other goods with pokes of gold dust, measured in pennyweights and ounces. Gold dust remained a primary medium of exchange for European goods with the few white traders on the islands into the 1960s, along with blacklip or goldlip pearl and trochus shell, copal gum, and copra. Harnessing the labor of island miners to pan for the gold meant that whites could branch out into other endeavors: importing European goods; selling pearl shell at Samarai, the tiny island capital of British New Guinea; keeping stores; owning plantations and hotels; and managing the "native labor" used to process copra, dive for shell and pearls, and crew small trading schooners.

Lieutenant Governor Murray leaves a benign public account of Mrs. Mahony and her enterprises in his book *Papua, or British New Guinea*, published a few years later:

> Though the Sud Est goldfield has been deserted by Europeans, many of the natives still fossick round in the neighbourhood of the old workings and weigh out their findings in exchange for goods, the price of which is

reckoned in grains and "weights" at the local store, kept by the widow of
an old pioneer, Mrs. Mahony, known to Europeans as "The Queen of Sud
Est," and, more affectionately, as "Mamma" to the native customers.
(Murray 1912:141)

None of my elderly island neighbors could recall anyone calling her "Mama," or
anything but "Miz Mahony" or "Missis Kwin." No one seemed to recall her with
affection; more characteristic reactions were some combination of amusement,
respect, and fear. I suspect Hubert Murray of an unrealistically sentimental public portrayal of his old adversary. Characteristically for his day, Hubert Murray
demotes Mrs. Mahony, who had lived and worked in a remote corner of the Territory since 1888, to "the widow of an old pioneer," rather than a pioneer herself.

On a Monday in April of 1918, Bronislaw Malinowski went to visit his friends
Raphael and Simone Brudo, who ran a pearl trading station at Sinaketa, on the
shore of Trobriand Lagoon. Malinowski writes in his diary:

In the morning wrote letter to E. R. M. [his future wife] and worked with
Raffael. Mrs. Mahoney [sic] came by. Wasted the whole day with her . . .
Conversations: Headon killed Dr. Harse's dog; the doctor sued him.
Samarai sympathizes with Headon. Dr. H. is a shark. Mrs. Mahoney wants
no trade; she has debts, wants to wind up affairs, but can't. He is in love
with Miss L.—problem: what is she to do about her future?—She tells us
about her interventions in struggles among the natives. This 63-year-old
woman, tall, strong, with an ultra-energetic Anglo-Saxon face, constantly
using profane language (damn, blooming), is quite likable. Went back. R.
dejected. (Malinowski 1967:263–264)

Besides being an eyewitness account of the minutiae of the social and economic
concerns of Papua's white expatriates of the era, this is a rare first-hand description of Elizabeth Mahony, her conversation, and her problems. Six feet in height,
with a commanding voice and personality, she was already a legendary figure
throughout the Territory.

Malinowski already knew Mrs. Mahony from prior meetings at the hotel, pub,
and trading depot she owned at Samarai (Lepowsky n.d.a, n.d.b.). Samarai, the tiny
and strategically located island off the East End, former capital of British New
Guinea, was still a district capital of the Australian Territory of Papua. Mrs.
Mahony's very presence in the Trobriand Islands is evidence of her far-flung and
varied business interests, characteristic of East End expatriate traders of the colonial period. It is likely she had come, in her own launch, to buy pearls. The
Trobriand diving season was November to March, and in March, buyers from all
over the world began making the trip from Samarai to the trading depots along the
shore of Trobriand Lagoon (Silas 1926:129). Mrs. Mahony also owned, and peri-

odically visited, coconut plantations on Woodlark Island, east of the Trobriands, and in the Calvados Chain near Sudest (cf. Lewis 1996).

Gold Dust and *Kula* Shells

Beginning with the 1888 gold rush, British officials, including Lieutenant Governor Sir William MacGregor, visited Sudest Island once a year to enforce the Pax Britannica. His private secretary, Basil Thomson, son of the archbishop of York, was appointed the first warden of the Sudest goldfield, empowered to adjudicate disputes and "deal with the disorderly contingent who are the curse of all gold fields and to issue miners' rights" (Thomson 1937:79).

When the governor's party first arrived on the yacht *Hygeia*, they found "a gunboat sent from the Australian station as soon as the 'rush' was reported.... Already about fifteen hundred men were on the field, and more were coming from Cooktown. They dispersed in pairs along all the stream beds, washing the gravel in pans, and many of them had a few natives to help them. Stories were current of deals with the natives which seemed to be lacking in strict honesty; of diggers who had bought large nuggets for a stick of trade tobacco" (Thomson 1937:78–79).

Governor MacGregor gave passage to "twenty of the most respectable miners" to allow them to prospect the archipelago as the government yacht proceeded. Basil Thomson, an old Etonian and Oxford graduate reared in a bishop's palace, writes, "Some of them were rough diamonds; there was a strong infusion of Queensland Irishmen, whose opinion of the mother country [Britain], as wafted to me through the cabin skylight, was disturbing to listen to, but they were sober and orderly" (Thomson 1937:80). John and Elizabeth Mahony were among the Queensland Irish gold prospectors, though Thomson records no notice of a white woman among the Sudest miners. By the mid-1890s, with few whites still on Sudest, the island rarely received official attention, a lack of oversight that continued during Australia's colonial control, which began in 1906. Absence of government supervision meant that white traders and islanders largely worked out their own relationships.

Elderly islanders remembered stories about "Mista Mahony" that date from the early years of the twentieth century. John Mahony, who was lame and who, they said, drank heavily, used to ride the steep mountain slopes of Vanatinai on his horse. He would appear suddenly in remote sago groves and gardens, tracking down debtors who had bought goods at his tradestore on credit. Mr. Mahony, my neighbors said, would rein in his horse and lash the debtor with his long whip, ordering him to go pan for gold in order to pay his "book," or debt.

The practice of advancing tradestore goods to islanders in order to place them in debt and force them to labor or produce commodities for sale was a common one in the islands of the Southwest Pacific. The goods were generally pegged at inflated prices relative to the prices offered for the tropical commodities or gold dust produced by islanders. Alexander Campbell (1898a, 1898b), Resident Magistrate for the South-Eastern District, documented "certain abuses" by Sudest

Island's white traders during an 1898 visit. They were "the result of the objectionable system of giving goods on credit to the natives which was introduced by some traders a few years ago." Gold being now scarce, the traders "at times adopt measures of an illegal character in the endeavor to urge the native to greater efforts in his search for gold" (Campbell 1898a).

A letter to the Government Secretary appends "several statements made to me by natives of Sudest regarding the ill treatment they have received at the hands of Messrs Mahoney [sic], Carvey, and their employe [sic], Henry Burfitt." John Mahony, Campbell writes, had two island men who were in debt to him "placed in irons" by a village constable called Jimmy. At one of the gold mines, "Mr. Mahoney handcuffed a boy to a truck in the tunnel and left him there for some time because he owed him money." The white traders, who Campbell (1898b) notes, "carry either guns or revolvers in a very conspicuous manner," received no official sanction (cf. Lepowsky 1991). D. C. Lewis (1996:150) notes an official complaint from 1924, a generation later, that Mrs. Mahony and her sons and daughters were not paying a fair price for copra obtained in the Calvados Chain islands, just northwest of Sudest Island.

Mrs. Mahony is remembered by several of my neighbors for having ordered her Papuan employees to tow debtors by a rope behind her launch through the lagoon waters until they were half-drowned in order to impress on them the need to work off their debts. "She was a real Tartar," Mother Antoninus, who had heard many such stories over the years, said to me once. (By then Mother Superior of the Sacred Heart Convents that stretch from the Trobriands to Rossel Island, she had come as a nun in 1953 to Nimowa Mission, on a small island just north of Sudest.) John Mahony died about 1906, leaving his wife with a large family of half-grown children. Mrs. Mahony declared in 1908 to the visiting lieutenant governor, Hubert Murray, that there was "no truth whatever in any of the allegations" printed in 1898 in the Annual Reports, and "that neither she nor her husband had had the opportunity of refuting these statements in open Court, as no legal proceedings had been instituted in connexion with them . . . and asked that, as the statements had been published, her contradiction should be published also" (Murray 1908).

What my elderly island neighbors most particularly remembered about Mrs. Mahony—and more of them had known her than her husband—was her refusal to let anyone speak the island language on her trading station on pain of banishment. These are Vanatinai people who, with their parents or as young adults around the 1910s and 1920s, visited "Miz Mahony" at her store and trading station at the place on the north coast islanders of all ages still call "Greep"—Griffen Point—or "Towni"—town. The islanders had to learn Papuan pidgin, which they call Vanga Lumo, "the language of Europeans," in order to sell gold dust and black-lip pearl shell for trade goods. The author Beatrice Grimshaw, who visited Mrs. Mahony's trading station at Griffen Point in 1908, also writes about the ban on island languages, attributing the islanders' fluency in "broken English" to this rule (1911:300).[3]

When I first heard these stories of islanders forbidden to use their own language, even to speak among each other, it seemed a capricious example of white arrogance and colonial power. It was, but other reasons beyond an unwillingness to learn a local language encouraged white arrogance to take this particular form. The Mahonys were not the only white traders to establish such a rule. Forcing islanders to trade in the "language of Europeans" put them at a disadvantage in negotiations with the storekeeper and creditor. It may also have partially protected white traders, at least in their own minds, against conspiracy and attack.

John Mahony and other European traders were accused of physically attacking and threatening their island debtors to force them to pan for gold. Mrs. Mahony, within a year or so of her husband's death and for the next two decades, was documented, by visiting Europeans and by islanders' eyewitness accounts given to me in the 1970s and 1980s, as using quite a different approach. Like other South Sea traders in the years before and after the turn of the century, she found that the best incentive for securing gold and labor was to provide a desired "native" valuable, shell-disc necklaces, in exchange.

The handful of Europeans who came to live in the islands off the East End of New Guinea provided a new market—one with a global reach—for the artifacts that traveled in the indigenous inter-island exchange systems called *kula* in the Trobriand Islands. Some Europeans themselves became sources of new *kula* valuables, hiring island laborers to dive for bivalve shells, manufacture the coral-colored shell discs, and string them into necklaces, belts, and earrings. White traders stocked what they called "native money" or "Papuan trade" in their stores, and Papuan patrons put it into circulation in inter- and intra-island ceremonial exchange networks (Lepowsky n.d.a, b, c).

The white traders of Papua had years' worth of observations of inter-island exchange and ceremonial valuables, and they were highly motivated to notice how shell necklaces, shell belts, and decorated armshells were used in the inter-island journeys and village rituals that consumed so much of the islanders' attention and labor. European traders learned, under pressure from islanders, to contract for raw shell and direct the manufacture of strings of shell discs, known as *sapisapi* throughout the islands of southeastern New Guinea. White traders also had their Papuan laborers make up necklaces and belts and even greenstone axe blades to sell to island pearl divers and goldminers. For Trobrianders and the other islanders of the Solomon and Coral Seas, pearls or gold dust were European commodities, gleaned by island labor from ancestral seas or streams, but useful only for their exchange value to white traders for steel tools, tobacco, trade goods, and— once those new needs had been largely sated—shell valuables.

Among the white traders, superior knowledge of islanders' desires for particular valuables, their sources, and inter-island trade routes was a competitive advantage. This explains why Bronislaw Malinowski's diaries and private letters show that he was relentlessly asking all the white traders of his acquaintance about "native trade." It also explains why those who barely knew him sometimes refused to share this information, much to Malinowski's annoyance. They probably saw him as a potential competitor for the labor and goods of the islanders—which he became in the Trobriands, to a limited extent—and perhaps even as a trader himself; he would not have been the first scientist or naturalist in Papua to turn to trade to finance his travels and amass his collections (e.g., Meek 1913; Lepowsky n.d.b).

While at Samarai for a month in 1917, waiting for a boat back to the Trobriands, Malinowski learned how to make tortoiseshell combs for his fiancée, flirted with hotel barmaid Mrs. Flora Gofton (of whom more below), and asked every white trader he ran into about *kula* and inter-island exchange. On November 17, he writes in his diary, "I talked with Mrs. Mahoney [sic] and a certain Osborne from Rossel Island. Their unwillingness to give any information whatever was amusing. I suppose it's just laziness and a kind of void? —I had a drink with Everett; he spoke about *kula* and maintained the Misima was not in the *kula*, but only Panayati and Panapompom; Tubetube and Wari; also Roge'a . . ." (the ellipse apparently represents place-names indecipherable to the editor of the diary; Malinowski 1967:118).

Mrs. Mahony was among the white traders who was especially prominent in the shell trade. Others were Charles Arbouin (once an employee of the Mahonys on Sudest and at Samarai, later Burns Philp's first agent at Samarai, and by 1920 a trader on Rossel) and the Osborne brothers of Rossel (cf. Allen 1920:119; Nelson 1976:42; Lewis 1996:37). D. H., or Harry, Osborne, whom Malinowski met in 1917, was on the Sudest goldfield in 1901 and the Gira field in 1904 (Nelson 1976:21, 157; cf. Osborne 1942). He and his brother, Frank, who arrived in Papua in 1903, lived, planted, and traded at Rossel Island through the 1930s. They routinely exchanged Rossel *sapisapi* for trade goods and shipped quantities of it to Samarai for sale to other whites to resell as what was locally known as "Papuan trade." By 1908, the Osborne brothers, their motor vessels, and their European customers at Samarai had largely supplanted Rossel Island big men, sailing canoes, and traditional exchange partners from Sudest Island in the *sapisapi* and shell necklace trade (Liep 1983:123). In the later 1920s, 100 raw *sapisapi* shells brought £1 from Rossel's white traders; Rossel Island men used the cash to buy trade goods and to pay their head tax (ibid.:127).

European pearl traders based at Trobriand Lagoon sometimes paid cash at Samarai for raw shells, *sapisapi*, and shell necklaces from Rossel and Sudest Islands, where the shells are plentiful on certain fringing reefs at a depth of fifteen or twenty feet. The shells were collected and the valuable manufactured by islanders under the direction of white traders, particularly Mrs. Mahony and the Osborne brothers, who sold them to islanders on their own trading stations as well as to other white traders at Samarai. Mrs. Mahony also sold the necklaces as curios and souvenirs to adventurous white tourists at her Samarai hotel.

One Sudest trader, an Australian (possibly Frank Mahony), imported a machine from London in the 1920s to manufacture shell discs, which he not only traded but also used to pay his island laborers, until a patrol officer shut down his "factory" (Mytinger 1946). The shell trade was extensive enough that there were established cash prices at Samarai stores. In 1913, the red-rimmed *sapisapi* shells retailed for £25 per (copra) sack, and the "pyramid shell," the brown-and-white speckled Conus used to make *kula* armshells, sold for £12 per sack (Roe 1962:474–475).

The visiting artist Ellis Silas observed that *kula* valuables were prominent among the wares of white traders on Trobriand Lagoon. They were made by island men to be traded for pearls and put into indigenous ceremonial exchanges.

> Necklaces of pink shell money, strings of beads, arm-shells and other trinkets much valued by the Trobrianders hang from the edges of the shelves. But of all these things, the one most important in bartering with the natives is the pink shell money, or sapi sapi, as it is called. . . . The white traders encourage the industry; they have made themselves the centre of it. For to get the sapi sapi which is so highly valued by them the natives will barter something which they do not value but which is most highly prized by the white men—pearls. The insignificant-looking stores are daily the scene of traffic in pearls of enormous value. (1926:122)

Beatrice Grimshaw, an Irish-Australian travel writer and novelist—and later, owner of a coconut plantation near Samarai—then on her first visit to Papua, documents the manufacture and barter of ceremonial valuables, this time on Sudest and Rossel Islands (Lepowsky n.d.a). She describes a visit to the East End islands and the Louisiade Archipelago in 1908, excerpts from which were quickly serialized in the *Sydney Morning Herald*. The full account is contained in her book *The New New Guinea* (1911:294–295). Grimshaw helpfully explains to her readers that "Papuan money" consists of long strings of shell discs, that the bivalve from which it is made is plentiful on Rossel Island, and that "many of the white traders use it in preference to European money for purchasing copra or pearlshells, or even pearls. Each disc is worth about threepence. . . . The trader resident on Rossel has instituted a mint on a small scale, where he employs the natives making money for him."

Grimshaw (1911:301) was told, apparently by Mrs. Mahony's children or managers, that Mrs. Mahony was "one of the largest purchasers of the Rossel shells from which the money is made," and shown numerous examples in Mrs. Mahony's house at Griffen Point, Sudest. In 1978, Vanatinai people told me that Mrs. Mahony actually imported Rossel Island men themselves to make shell-disc necklaces under her supervision. Her intention, elderly islanders said, was to induce Vanatinai people to pan alluvial gold and exchange their gold dust for necklaces.

On her 1908 visit to the Louisiade Archipelago, accompanying Hubert Murray on an official tour of inspection, Grimshaw stayed at Mrs. Mahony's trading station on the north coast of Sudest Island and wrote the following:

Grassy, rolling downs slope above the sea as one approaches; a coral jetty runs out into the bay; there are houses and sheds on the hill above. . . . The island is nominally, no doubt, owned and governed by the Commonwealth, but morally it is the property of the Queen of Sud-East, and of no one else. Mrs. Mahony, the adventurous Australian who bears this title, has been on the island, with an occasional holiday, for twenty years. . . . Mrs. Mahony was absent at the time of our call, much to the regret of the party; but we were hospitably entertained in her house, and shown many local curios. Shell money is among the most interesting of these. Mrs. Mahony is one of the largest purchasers of the Rossel shells from which the money is made, as already described. Native armlets also, carved out of a single large white shell, thick and firm as a slab of marble, bring an amazing price among the natives and are profitable to trade in. (1911:297, 301)[4]

Mrs. Mahony was away, and on an errand of mercy, visiting an ailing and elderly Australian lady—annoyingly unnamed by Grimshaw—somewhere on a lonely island plantation. Beatrice Grimshaw thus has a free hand in elevating Mrs. Mahony to a symbol of the pluckiness and self-sacrifice of the British Australian pioneer woman. While Mrs. Mahony clearly merits the greatest admiration for raising her children as a widow in the farthest reaches of a distant colony, and for running a string of difficult and risky enterprises to support them all, the portrait of the noble pioneer recorded by Grimshaw is quite untarnished by the profanity and the allegations of shady business practices and abuse of islanders that show up in Malinowski's diary, colonial government records, and oral accounts. What is more, Mrs. Mahony, quite likely as a result of these official accusations, was well known in her day for her strong hostility toward the Territorial government, even more than most of the small planters and traders among the expatriates. That very year, 1908, Mrs. Mahony was demanding of Hubert Murray that the government print a retraction of its published charges against her husband of abusing islanders.

Most of Beatrice Grimshaw's writings focus primarily on male heroic figures: Sir Hubert Murray in her nonfiction, and courageous white plantation owners and prospectors of high moral character in remote parts of the Territory in her novels. But her books are also noteworthy for the attention they pay to strong white female characters in the Papuan bush, both real (in *The New New Guinea*) and imagined. For example, after visiting Mrs. Mahony's trading station, Lieutenant Governor Murray's party steamed north to Misima Island, or St. Aignan. Grimshaw (1911:304–305) offers her readers a lengthy anecdote about a white woman who came to Misima with her husband in the gold rush. After being widowed, living alone on the island for many years, and by then elderly and ill, she returned to Misima from a trip to Queensland with a companion, another elderly woman who had been left financially destitute, to continue working her gold claim. Both women died shortly before Grimshaw's arrival.

Suspiciously sentimental as this story is, Mrs. Mahony was far from the only widow in Papua or New Guinea who continued to work a gold claim or plantation, or to run a tradestore, after her husband's death (e.g., Bulbeck 1992:91–92). Elizabeth Mahony was not at home when Hubert Murray and Beatrice Grimshaw called because she was tending an ill and elderly white woman on another island, perhaps one of the pair that Grimshaw describes.

Hotels, Pubs, and Colonial Cultures

Port-town hotels and pubs were the crucibles of the most geographically and numerically pervasive of the colonial cultures of British and Australian New Guinea, cultures with a strong inheritance from the masculinist, cosmopolitan, British-inflected maritime frontier culture of a precolonial era only recently ended.

The social and economic elite among the commercial sector, the white settlers of Papua, consisted largely of the highest-level managers of corporate-owned plantation, trading, and shipping enterprises: those of Burns Philp, Carpenter's, British New Guinea Development Company, Steamships Trading Company, and Lever Brothers. These planters and managers founded the Planters' Association and the Papua Club at Port Moresby, and socialized primarily with one another, occasionally including a congenial Resident Magistrate. Samarai's colonial geography mirrored the social pyramid and the division between government and planter interests: the two highest houses, regarding each other from the tops of the island's two hills, were those of the Burns Philp manager and the Resident Magistrate, the most senior government officer east of Port Moresby (Lewis 1996:88, 265, 278).

The smallholder planters, tradestore owners and managers, pearlers, and miners kept less rarefied company: each other. Almost all the white settlers, whatever their wealth and station, used the hotels and attached pubs of Port Moresby and Samarai in Papua (and Lae, Rabaul, and Madang in New Guinea) as entry points, rendezvous and gathering places. Their numbers were occasionally augmented by adventurous travelers, and, after World War I, by a few package tourists arriving every six weeks or so on Burns Philp or Steamships mail boats, early forerunners of adventure tourism (cf. Douglas 1996).

Independent travelers, mostly young Englishmen and Australians descended from the British landed gentry, had been making their way to New Guinea since the Protectorate days (e.g., Bevan 1890; Baden-Powell 1892). By the early twentieth century, American travelers, too, had found their way to Southeast New Guinea, some by steamer, others by yacht. Quite a few of these early independent and package tourists were women, traveling singly or in pairs, some of whom wrote of their colorful or alarming encounters with resident expatriate men and women on coastal steamers and cutters and in port-town hotels (e.g., Forbes 1919; Mordaunt 1930; Mytinger 1946; see Lepowsky n.d.a for more on travelers and travel writing in British New Guinea and Papua). The accounts of women field scientists, like entomologist Evelyn Cheeseman (1957, 1965) and anthropologists Margaret Mead

(1972) and Hortense Powdermaker (1966), also illuminate the social life of colonial port towns and hotels.

A surprisingly high number of Papuan hotels and pubs were owned or managed by white women who were longtime residents and central figures in port towns and mining communities. Of the three hotels at Samarai in the early 1900s, one, the Cosmopolitan, was owned by Mrs. Mahony, who made frequent supervisory visits on her own launch from her home on Sudest Island, 150 miles to the southeast.[5] Another hotel was owned by Mrs. Anna Clunn (and her husband, but she held the liquor license), and the third, by "W. Widdells" (that would have been the hotel popularly known as Billy the Cook's; cf. Roe 1962:141).

European women in frontier societies—particularly on mining frontiers, where there tended to be very few white women, few services, and plenty of floating wealth—often parlayed the domestic skills they were expected to command as part of the European sexual division of labor—cooking, baking, housekeeping, sewing, and laundering—into successful businesses such as hotel, restaurant, and boardinghouse keeping; tailoring; and commercial laundries. This pattern is quite visible in gold rush California (e.g., Levy 1992; Rohrbough 1997; Zanjani 1997; prostitution, the commercialization of women's sexual services, was far less commonly reported among white women in British New Guinea or Papua than in the gold and silver rushes of nineteenth-century California and Nevada). The most entrepreneurial and successful women, such as Elizabeth Mahony, delegated the physical labor and direct contact with customers to "native" men or indentured servants (Papuans in Samarai and Chinese in California), or to lower-status, poorer, or more newly arrived women. Flora Gofton, whose story we take up below, was a generation younger than Mrs. Mahony and first worked for Mrs. Mahony at the Hotel Cosmopolitan before setting up her own rival hotel. Less well capitalized than the Queen of Sudest, Mrs. Gofton had to act as her own barmaid and waitress.

Samarai, a mile off the east end of mainland New Guinea, was a key port for the East End goldfields and a stop en route to German New Guinea from Sydney, Brisbane, Cairns, and Cooktown. Rising from the deepwater trench of China Strait, it was named in 1873 by Captain John Moresby, who saw it as a potential route from Australia to China, avoiding the treacherous shallows of Torres Strait or having to beat to windward around the Louisiade Archipelago. Samarai was the center of economic and social life for the expatriates and visitors of the East End. George Munt, an English planter, trader, and storekeeper at Misima, Panapompom, and Nivani Islands since at least 1909, told a reporter from the *Papuan Courier* in 1937 that he had "never been to Port" (the prewar term for Port Moresby; Lewis 1996:94).

The Hotel Samarai, as of 1934 licensed to a Mrs. L. M. Skully, advertised itself in *Pacific Islands Monthly*, under a picture of the verandahed, two-story establishment (just below a similar advertisement for its competition, the Hotel Cosmopolitan), as "Samarai Hotel. The Rendezvous of the Miners of Eastern Papua. Comfortable

Accommodations for Tourists, Travellers and Residents. Best Brands of Spirits and Wines—Victorian Lager Beers. Fishing Excursions Arranged" (*Pacific Islands Monthly*, November 22, 1934:67; cf. Roberts 1996:219).

The tiny island community, which, as several generations of visitors have pointed out, you can walk around in half an hour, was crowded with warehouses, trading and transshipping depots, wharves, stores, two or three hotels and pubs, a movie theater, a hospital, private residences, government buildings, and a jail. In a Papuan version of apartheid, "natives," except for the indentured laborers and personal servants of whites, were forbidden to spend more than twenty-four hours on Samarai. There was a separate landing for "native" canoes. Samarai's Papuan laborers and servants had a 9:00 P.M. curfew. The one exception was if their masters were out carousing at pubs and parties: personal "boys" were supposed to squat outside in the dark and wait to escort them safely home (e.g., Mytinger 1946; Lewis 1996).

Ringed by forested, mountainous islands, with the tip of mainland New Guinea rising across the intense blue of the China Strait, Samarai, one of the most lovely spots in the South Pacific, brings out strong emotions in expatriate visitors. Malinowski writes, in November 1917, of "the contradiction between the picturesque landscape, the poetic quality of the island set on the ocean, and the wretchedness of life here" (1967:112).

> It is the contrast between this wonderful little island bathed in light and sea, with its palm-fringed walks and wide perspectives on smooth blue bays—and the miserable existence of the white men absolutely out of harmony with all this. (Wayne 1995, 1:51)

The English artist Ellis Silas (1926:42) praised the (unnamed) Samarai hotel where he stayed in 1924 as "light and airy," with two "very handsome" verandahs with "stained flooring, rattan cane chairs, chaises longues, occasional tables of wickerwork, and one large deal table" painted black, a vase of flowers on it. As in Port Moresby hotels, there were two dining rooms, the "best people" dining in the front, enjoying the "privilege of punkahs," and the rest dining in the back in their shirtsleeves. But his neighbor "appeared to have found life in the town somewhat exhilarating: with the result that he experienced difficulty in getting into bed and still greater difficulty in remaining there. The partition between us was thin, and although, to my relief, it resisted his apparent efforts to break into my room, sleep for me proved out of the question." Still, Silas praises the men who were "down and out" as

> usually the fine old characters who were the pioneers of the country many years before. The beachcomber is now a mythical figure, but there are still old men living in the loneliness of the jungle who come to the townships

occasionally to purchase stores. And there are others, whom adverse circumstances have forced from their quest—the stores can no longer finance them: they hang about the verandahs of the hotels or pace listlessly up and down the jetties. They are now old and broken, but they are veterans of better days, never admitting defeat, and still ready, given but the chance, to renew their old endeavours and adventures in the search for gold. Many and varied were the tales they narrated. (Ibid.:43)

Other visitors left a grimmer portrait. The English author Elinor Mordaunt (1930:25–31), who visited in the mid-1920s, commented on its residents' unhappiness and mutual dislike. One young man told her that all there was to do was "walk to one hotel and get a drink, then back to the other and get another so long as your money or your pals last out." In the six weeks Mordaunt spent in Samarai, three men attempted suicide, and two were successful (cf. Roe 1962:498–499). Two young yachtsmen who sailed out of New York on a world cruise in 1935 saw in Samarai

> more excitement than we had seen since distant Suva [the capital of Fiji].... Two steamers came during our first day there.... At ten o'clock we were walking quietly along the only street of the town. At ten-two Sheridan lay outstretched in a pool of blood. A man, coming up from behind, had snarled: "You murderer!" and cracked a bottle over Sher's head. At ten-ten there was a free-for-all in the streets of Samarai.... Everyone bloody, everyone cursing, everyone letting fly everything he could reach.... A man rushed us into a bar, where it developed Sher had been attacked by an Australian recruiter who accused all Americans of having killed the famous Australian racehorse, Phar Lap. (Fahnestock and Fahnestock 1938:227–228)

Survivors of the brawl gathered in the same bar the next day to drink mint juleps and toast President Roosevelt. The yachtsmen conclude: "Lord knows where he had found bourbon or mint.... When we sailed away for Port Moresby a few days later, half the town was on the pier singing their idea of our National Anthem: 'Dixie' and 'California, Here I Come!'" (ibid.:228).

In the first four decades of the twentieth century, women, though well in the minority, were among the most prominent white residents of this less-than-genteel port. They, and their husbands, if any, often had plantations on nearby small islands and the Milne Bay region of the mainland, traveling back and forth to the tiny island capital by boat for provisions and mail, especially on "steamer day," when a Burns Philp liner came in from Sydney, Port Moresby, or Rabaul. Mrs. Mahony bought the appropriately named Cosmopolitan Hotel, the biggest establishment east of Port Moresby, along with its attached pub and tradestore, from

Burns Philp early in the 1900s. She often passed through the island port on her way to and from her scattered plantation holdings. Three of Elizabeth Mahony's adult daughters lived at or near Samarai. Hanorah Kathleen married William John Leetch, and they ran a coconut plantation, Hihila, on Milne Bay. Interestingly, Hanorah is listed in *Stewart's Handbook of the Pacific Islands* for 1920, taken from the Papuan census, as "planter," but no occupation is given for her husband. Another daughter, Tagula Mahony, is listed in 1920 as a nurse at Samarai, apparently still single. (Tagula is the Misima language name of Sudest Island.) A third Mahony daughter had much earlier married Charles Owen-Turner, who in 1902 became Assistant Resident Magistrate for the Eastern District, based at Samarai. They took out a lease on a plantation called Eabuli, on the mainland along China Strait opposite Samarai, which Mrs. L. M. (Ellen) Owen-Turner managed. Owen-Turner later left government service and turned to planting. Roe (1962:239, 244–245) notes that "family connections" seem to have affected Owen-Turner's lax enforcement, as magistrate, of labor and liquor laws as they applied to his in-laws.

Mrs. Mahony's primary business partner later in life was her son, Frank. He was often accused—wrongly, he and his mother claimed—of unfair treatment of "native" labor or of violating trading regulations. Frank Mahony enlisted in the Great War. He is enumerated in the Territorial Census as a Sudest Island resident in 1920, as is his mother; the occupation of both is given as "planter." (Mrs. Mahony is listed twice, also at Samarai, occupation: storekeeper.) In the early 1920s, Frank was pointed out, extremely drunk in a Rabaul pub, to a visitor as the son of the Queen of Sudest. He had gone to the Mandated Territory of New Guinea as part of a colonial settlement scheme designed to offer returned servicemen plantation land that had been expropriated from former German owners. This venture must not have worked out, because Frank Mahony later became a planter near Daru, on the Gulf of Papua, where he tried to grow cotton (Allen 1918, 1920; cf. Lewis 1996:92, 96–98, 194, 283, 306). Elizabeth Mahony finally retired to Sydney in 1930 to live with one of her daughters, twelve years after complaining to Malinowski that she wanted out.

Mrs. Arthur Bunting, wife of Mrs. Mahony's business partner, was another dominant female figure at Samarai. She probably helped him manage the Hotel Cosmopolitan. Her husband, storekeeper at Samarai since 1903, later brought his brothers, Robert and Fred Bunting, out from England. Bunting Brothers soon owned numerous plantations on various East End islands, becoming the most important white planters in that part of Papua (Lewis 1996:90, 305–306; cf. Roberts 1996:219). Calling on Mrs. Bunting for eleven o'clock tea was, for respectable visiting white women at Samarai, "the done thing," according to Malinowski's Australian sister-in-law, who paid her respects in 1921 (Bassett 1969:12–13).

Another white woman of note in the town was Mrs. Elizabeth Whitten, wife of William, an early pearl trader, originally from London, and one of the first miners in the Sudest gold rush of 1888. William, with his brother, Robert, in 1892 founded Whitten Brothers, a trading empire that included coconut plantations on China Strait, Milne Bay, and Cloudy Bay; ships; stores at Samarai, Port Moresby, and several goldfields; and numerous mining claims. Whitten Brothers had previously owned the Cosmopolitan Hotel, in 1905 (Stuart 1970:176–177; Nelson 1976:11, 85; Lewis 1996:fig. 1, 249–250, 305–306).

Mrs. Anna Clunn was the wife of John Clunn, a Cooktown publican who in 1889 shipped an entire two-story hotel, complete with wrought-iron balconies, to Samarai, where it was reassembled to outfit the Sudest and Misima goldfields. Clunn's Hotel, which she managed, was at the main anchorage, across the parade from the Cosmopolitan (Nelson 1976:25, 156; Lewis 1996:37, 296). Anna (Granny) Clunn died at Ramaga, her Milne Bay coconut plantation, in 1938.

In 1917, Malinowski stayed at a hotel in Samarai run, he says, by a mother and her four daughters. The oldest daughter, Mrs. Gofton, starred in Malinowski's erotic fantasies, although he never writes down her first name (e.g., Malinowski 1967:112, 122, 123). "Mrs. . . . ," whose name is censored in the published diary on page 109, seems to be Mrs. Gofton as well: "I made up to Mrs. . . . , who is not stupid, though quite uncultured. I fondled her and undressed her in my mind, and I calculated how long it would take me to get her to bed" (cf. Wayne 1995, 1:66–67). Mrs. Gofton's given name was Flora, but she was often called Flo. This same woman, at 31 the object of Malinowski's desires in Samarai, much later became the "Territorial identity" known as Ma Stewart. (Middle-aged and elderly female hotelkeepers and boardinghouse keepers in colonial Papua were generally known to white male residents as Ma or Mother, as with Mother McGrath or Ma Wright of Port Moresby—an acceptable fictive kin role for these women of ambiguous status, many divorced or widowed, in the colonial pantheon [Lepowsky n.d.a; cf. Stuart 1970]). Mrs. Stewart lived in retirement at Lae, along the northeast coast of the mainland, into the 1970s. Flo Gofton was not only the barmaid, and the "waitress" whose "liver" Malinowski patted—a lewd Polish expression that loses something in translation—but the founder, owner, and manager of the Hotel Samarai. Flora Shaw Young was born in Scotland in 1886, and left Edinburgh with her parents and a sister for Cooktown, North Queensland, three years later. Gifted at languages, Flora worked as a court interpreter for Aborigines at Cooktown, and as an adult learned Motu and several other Papuan languages (unlike, for example, Elizabeth Mahony and her children, who learned no island languages in all their years in Papua).

Flora first went to Papua at age 20 to take a hotel job at Samarai. She quit almost immediately and left for Port Moresby, then came back to Queensland, where she married Englishman Hardy ("Harry") Gofton, whose family owned a bakery in Port Moresby. Hardy worked as the Port butcher in 1914 and as a plantation assistant at Kanosia, down the coast. He enlisted in the RAF—the marriage seems to have been troubled—and was sent to France. Flora went to work at Steamships' store at Sapphire Creek, a copper-mining area in the mountains behind Port Moresby, while her mother, Mrs. Kate Young, took care of Flora's two young children, a son named Moresby, and a daughter, Ela (after Ela Beach, near Port Moresby). Flora, her mother, her children, and later, her younger sisters, soon moved to Samarai, where Flora worked at the Hotel Cosmopolitan, before quitting in 1917 to found her own establishment, the Hotel Samarai (Roberts 1996:50–56).

Hardy Gofton was killed late in the war. Word of this tragedy obviously came after Malinowski had left Samarai for the Trobriands on November 29, 1917. He writes to his fiancée, Elsie Masson, that day, seemingly feeling a need to confess: the imminent departure of his boat for Kiriwina meant, he says, that he had successfully avoided sexual entanglements: "I also had some temptations out here: not brown skins of course. . . . Only there is a woman here, who is undoubtedly an extremely clever and capable individual, coarsened and banalized in these conditions and married to a somewhat loathsome man. Physically she is very fine, though she is just beginning to be on the descending line. . . . I did not make any advances," he hastily assures Elsie, contra his diary, "but I could not help admiring her and thinking what a pity it is she was wasted." He continues, a bit later: "I am on very friendly relations with the family (mother and 4 daughters) who own this pub. They ask me to have morning and afternoon teas with them and I also play cards with some of them. The eldest daughter is the one I mentioned to you above. She has the same type of face as Marnie [Elsie's sister] and is tall and well built" (Wayne 1995, 1:66–67).

Flora Gofton also owned a house in the Ela Beach area of Port Moresby, but it burned down around 1923, luckily with no injury to her tenants, a Mrs. Mustard and her children.[6] Popularly regarded as a beautiful woman, fashionably dressed when she visited Port Moresby or Sydney, and known as "Samarai's own Merry Widow," Mrs. Gofton was still running the Hotel Samarai in 1928. The following year she headed to another frontier, the new goldfields of Bulolo and Wau in the Mandated Territory of New Guinea. Unmarried, divorced, and widowed women were banned altogether in 1926, the year of the gold discoveries, from the Australian-controlled Mandated Territory because of the perceived dangers of white prostitution and female immorality to colonial prestige and order. This meant that entrepreneurial white women in Papua, such as the widowed Flora Gofton and the divorced gold miner Doris Booth (1929), had to arrange what seem to be marriages of convenience before heading off to the gold camps. As Flora's daughter, Ela Gofton, remembers, even the woman known as "Tiger Lil" had to marry "poor old Toby" Millar before she could set up her service business in New Guinea.

So in 1929, at 43, Flora Gofton remarried; her new husband, a Mr. James (Jim) Stewart, was a carpenter she knew from Samarai. They walked inland for several days from Salamaua, and together built the first hotel in the New Guinea goldfield of Wau, the Hotel Bulolo, overlooking the aerodrome, as their advertisements in *Pacific Islands Monthly* say. There is little further mention of Mr. Stewart following his marriage to Flora, even in Ela Gofton's oral account of her mother (Roberts 1996).

Flo Stewart liked to boast that she was the first person in the world to import a pianola, a billiard table, and a racehorse (a mare) by airplane. A noted horse-woman, she also raised and butchered her own stock for the hotel, attended the births of white women in far-flung mining camps, and kept order in her establishment by throwing well-aimed tins of baked beans or sweet corn at miscreants (Lewis 1996:250; Roberts 1996:54–56, 195–200). She "retired" and accompanied her daughter to Lae, on the coast, where they managed the Hotel Cecil. Her son, Moresby, who, like his father, joined the RAF, died over Germany in 1940, a second family casualty of world war. Evacuated in 1942 under protest ahead of the Japanese advance, Flo and Ela retreated to Sydney, where on Sundays they hosted a polyglot crew of displaced Papua and New Guinea expatriates, including Charlie Ong from Madang, five Eastern European Catholic brothers who had been in the Sepik so long they only spoke Pidgin, and "Madam Brudeau of the Trobriand Islands."

Flora Stewart was the first white female civilian to return to the Territory of Papua and New Guinea after World War II. She at first operated the Hotel Lae in abandoned military barracks. Marjorie Murphy, who went to Rabaul in 1940 to work as a secretary and married Patrol Officer John Murphy, recalled the Hotel Lae of 1949, and "Ma Stewart":

> It was quite comfortable, but it was raining all the time and you had to put your raincoat on to go to the toilet or the showers. Ma was wonderful. She only had this funny old stove to cook for the whole hotel. She put native spears up so I could put the nappies there to dry . . . [She] dressed in man's sandals and was burned black by the sun. (Bulbeck 1992:92–93, 254–255)

Flora Stewart later reopened the Hotel Cecil. She remained "one of [Lae's] most respected residents" as late as 1970 (Stuart 1970:252; Bulbeck 1992:10, 92–93; Roberts 1996:240–241, 282–283, 293). Remarkably, this was three years after Malinowski's private diaries were published.

European Women on Maritime Frontiers and Colonial Borderlands

There has been a burgeoning of scholarly attention to global and local manifestations of European colonialism and empire. Since the challenges of Talal Asad (1973), we have been pressed to examine as well the "colonial situations" in which anthropological knowledge has long been gained (Stocking 1991; cf. Ogan, Chap. 11). Recent scholarship emphasizes the interconnections between colonizers and colonized, and the uniqueness and fluidity of imperial frontiers, colonial contact zones, and borderlands as sites of cultural metamorphoses and reinvention. Some writers have emphasized the singularity of these phenomena, and their lack of fit with established social categories of culture, nation, tribe, and homeland, by devising or adopting neologisms such as "transculturation" (Pratt 1992) and "interculturality" (Shaw 1995). Their depictions of times and places of colonial synergy and cultural metamorphosis resemble historical precursors of "ethnoscapes": the neologism for the transcultural global flows and recombinations that Arjun Appadurai (1990) sees as unique to the late twentieth century. They fit as well into the more encompassing framework of "traveling cultures," cultural displacements such as seasonal migration, trade, pilgrimage, conquest, diaspora, and tourism (Clifford 1997).

Recent writings on colonialism stress the blurriness and lack of coherence within the two overarching social categories, colonizer and colonized. They document the diverse, often competing interests of persons within the larger category of colonial subject, or expatriate, who are perceived differently by diverse others, see themselves differently, act differently, and pursue differing and sometimes antagonistic "colonial projects." Patterns of difference in identity, belief, and action can in part be accounted for by studying colonial or metropolitan classification systems and hierarchies based on ethnicity, race, gender, class, education, residence, and occupation. Such hierarchical classification systems—and the changing and contradictory forms they take in particular eras and places, in metropole and colony—are themselves cultural responses to colonial and imperial situations (cf. Stoler and Cooper 1997). Indeed, one could argue further that so, too, are the social and political categories of culture, nation, tribe, and homeland, which are basic to social science and—in European nation-states and former colonies alike—ubiquitous in the global political rhetoric of the last century and a half of colonial domination, anti-imperialist resistance, and postcolonial reality.

These are fruitful lines of investigation and analysis for the study of frontier and colonial New Guinea and Papua. Stoler and Cooper (1997) encourage us to go beyond the Manichean colonizer-colonized rhetoric—central, they point out, to all colonial regimes—and investigate social differences and blurred boundaries, focusing on multiplicities of colonial cultures and on the political economies that shape them and respond to them. They also urge us to be aware of how colonial states organize knowledge, and how their aims and projects constrain us as scholars working in the archives of the present day. These perspectives help illuminate the great imbalances of the archival record for British New Guinea and Papua, and of the histories that tend to be written based on this material. The majority of New Guinea's and Papua's traders, miners, and planters were of working-class origin. They had little formal education, and their economic situations were usually precarious. Most were from England, Scotland, Ireland, Australia, and New Zealand—but others were Greek, Turkish, Chinese, Filipino, Malay, Polynesian, or "mixed race." Some traders and miners adhered to metropolitan European standards of decorum, but many consorted openly with Papuan women, lived in palm-thatched houses, dressed in pajamas, worked only when necessary to pay off a creditor or buy supplies, and consumed prodigious amounts of alcohol. A few whites, as well as other expatriates, were spectacularly eccentric, delusional, or violent. None of this was how official Papua and New Guinea wished to represent the colonies to superiors or the general public back in Britain or Australia (see also Foster, Chap. 5). Even missionaries, whose private letters and journals are full of complaints about evil examples set by nearby debauched and gin-soaked white traders, preferred, in public lectures and reports back home, to represent themselves as fighting Satan in the forms of native cannibalism, sorcery, and idolatry, not in struggles with tropical versions of the drunken wastrels found in London or Sydney.

As a result of this official selective amnesia, traces of the white traders and miners in government documents are faint, appearing as depersonalized entries in colonial annual reports of ounces of gold won or tons of copra shipped, or in reports of generic complaints about colonial government policies. They appear only briefly by name in census enumerations, lists of trading licenses or plantation leases issued, reports of charges brought before resident magistrates, or investigations of solitary deaths in lonely outstations. Since few unofficial whites wrote their own memoirs, and few of their descendants preserved their personal papers, their lives, opinions, values, and emotions and their contributions to the formation of maritime frontier cultures and colonial cultures of New Guinea and Papua remain obscure. So, therefore, do their influences on the thoughts and actions of the Papuans who lived with or near them, except, importantly, as reflected in the reminiscences and oral traditions of the Papuans and their grandchildren.

Except for Papuans who lived near Port Moresby or Samarai, government stations, or mission stations, for most indigenous residents of the coastal and small island districts of the Territory, the white trader, planter, or miner was the European with whom they were most familiar and in most frequent contact over many years. The government officer only appeared for days or hours on infrequent patrols, and most missionaries stuck close to their stations. White traders, planters, and miners—including the women among them such as Elizabeth Mahony—are the people who were most influential in shaping Papuan images of Europeans and their ways. In turn, the Papuans and their ideologies, desires, and customs had the greatest impact on the outlook and practices of the unofficial whites, who lived the most closely, and sometimes intimately, among them—though always unequally, with the most disreputable trader who had "gone bush" still claiming racial superiority and colonial privilege. In regional variants of what Sahlins (1989) calls "cosmologies of capitalism" and Thomas (1991) epitomizes as "entangled objects," Papuan and European quests for wealth, and the ideologies that underlay them, intersected and transformed one another on the Coral and Solomon Sea frontiers. White traders, like Mrs. Mahony, the Osborne brothers of Rossel Island, or the

Greek Mick George of Trobriand Lagoon, were socialized over the years by their Papuan neighbors, who strategically withheld their labor unless compensated with objects they held to be valuable. The traders gradually became more Melanesianized. Seeking gold dust or pearls, they not only extracted Papuan labor by coercion and persuasion, but developed complicated exchange relations with their neighbors, accumulating and bartering shell-disc necklaces and hosting the occasional feast (cf. Wayne 1995, 1:77; see Lepowsky n.d.a,b,c). Even Mrs. Mahony's "interventions in struggles among the natives" that she recounted to Malinowski (1967:263–264) took on—from what I heard on the island—a Melanesian big-woman-like cast in the eyes of her neighbors.

Papuan colonial society was a masculine one. Physical prowess and notions of racial superiority were prized, even respectable men in private drank heavily and dressed oddly, and quite a few men had clandestine or public sexual liaisons with Papuan women or pubescent girls. European women were deeply threatening to this white male colonial pastorale, representing to European men (whether the women wanted to or not) ambivalently regarded values of civilized morality. They also symbolized the danger, to white male hegemony, of crossing the color line in the other direction: the illicit desire of Papuan men for white women or, worse yet, the other way around (cf. Inglis 1974). White women, as one strain of British colonial thought long maintained, were "the ruin of empire"; their arrival in any numbers disrupted the formerly close, though properly hierarchical, interracial relations between white colonial men and the "native" population in its roles as laborers, servants, and concubines.[7]

Among the unofficial whites, European women, though far outnumbered by men, were often central figures to their contemporaries, prominent as they were among the traders, hotelkeepers, boardinghouse and bar managers of Papua. Time has eroded their presence and visibility; their traces appear today mainly in the letters, diaries, and reminiscences of B4s—"Befores," the expatriate term for whites who resided in the Territory before World War II—the jottings of the occasional travelers, and the stories of their Melanesian former neighbors.

Unattached European women—single, divorced, and widowed—were among the most threatening figures of all to the colonial hierarchy. Due to a high death rate among European males from tropical disease, accident, and suicide, the percentage of white widows was fairly high. Other European, and Papuan, women found their marriages to expatriates insupportable and filed for divorce, which was less stigmatized for women on the frontier than it was back "home" in Sydney, London, or New York. Most newly single women either left the Territory or quickly remarried, but of those who stayed and remained single, quite a few, like Elizabeth Mahony, Flora Gofton, Doris Booth, and the unmarried Beatrice Grimshaw, were among the most visible white settlers to their contemporaries, European and Papuan.

Single women, who also included adult, Papua-born daughters and visitors, like Grimshaw, who decided to settle, had an ambiguous status. Their virtue unprotected by spousal supervision, many ran public houses or took in paying lodgers, while others lived "alone" with Papuan servants on remote plantations and trading stations. The model white settler in tropical colonies was not, in imperial ideologies, supposed to be a lone female or an entrepreneurial female head of household. These women challenged ideals of female domesticity, physical delicacy, dependence, respectability, and sexual vulnerability that were prevalent in both metropole and colony.[8]

White women on the colonial frontiers of British New Guinea and Papua were disturbing to the highly masculinized prevailing ideologies of the self-reliant, independent, brave, and stoical frontiersman, pioneer, and white settler that were characteristic of British colonies such as Australia and British New Guinea, and of the Australian colonial frontier in Papua. The "pioneer woman" archetype—familiar in white-settler colonies and former colonies such as Australia, the United States, Canada, and South Africa as the brave and exalted being who brought civilization and morality to the new country—was not part of official ideologies of British New Guinea and Papua because white-settler families were actively discouraged by the colonial administration.

Colonial policies mitigated against the alienation of large blocs of land for use by white entrepreneurs. When Beatrice Grimshaw sought to recruit a "better class" of settler for Papua in her semi-official book The New New Guinea (1911), she aimed it toward the unmarried, younger sons of the British gentry. White women and children were perceived by colonial officials as potential victims of killing fevers, headhunting raids, and sexual assault by "natives." Their widespread presence would be disruptive to the colonial projects of extending government influence to "uncontrolled areas" and the efficient harnessing of indigenous male labor in the service of European-led, government-supervised commodity production and the extraction of gold, timber, and shell.

The white women who did come to British New Guinea and Papua without the sanction of government or mission, alone or with husbands or fathers, were generally trying to escape from poverty and lack of prospects back in Ireland or Queensland. Like their male counterparts, they sometimes created problems for the official whites: the government officers and missionaries. The goals and attitudes that accompanied their entrepreneurial colonial projects of extracting wealth and finding personal security were often at odds with the aims of government or mission. White men, too, not just Beatrice Grimshaw, admired Elizabeth Mahony and other white women in the Papuan islands for their "pluck" and resourcefulness in the face of physical and economic hardships. Still, Elizabeth Mahony was, to Lieutenant Governor Hubert Murray, merely "the widow of an old pioneer." It was more convenient for the colonial regimes to ignore white women entrepreneurs in the great majority of their official representations.

The colonial cultures of British New Guinea and the Territory of Papua were highly marked by British and Australian ideologies of frontier masculinity.

Paradoxically, they were at the same time shaped and maintained in no small part through the agencies of the small minority of European women who ran stores and plantations on distant islands, and whose hotels, boardinghouses, and pubs were the gathering places for the dispersed, mobile, and mostly male population of white entrepreneurs and fortune seekers. It was this population of unofficial whites, like Mrs. Mahony, the Queen of Sudest, whose actions and values had the greatest impact on the lives of Papuans living along the shores of the more remote islands and coastal reaches. Papuan memories of these women and men are a cultural legacy of colonialism that persists into the present day.

Nine

Juxtaposed Narratives
A New Guinea Big Man
Encounters the Colonial Process

Richard Scaglion

In all too many studies of colonial encounters, the perspectives and agency of the colonized are underrepresented or completely absent. Yet colonial cultures actually arise from intercultural interactions and, moreover, interactions that are created by historically situated actors. Essentializing colonizers as victimizers in a hegemonic global ideology trivializes the field of action of the colonized. While recognizing that very real power differentials exist in colonial cultures, we can still acknowledge that "individuals and local groups resist, subvert, accommodate, embrace, transform, or transcend the discourse, policies and practices from the center" (Shaw 1995:15). Thus, in order to fully appreciate the dialectics of the colonial process, we need to attend to the perspectives of local people.

In this chapter, I examine the perspectives and opinions of one of the colonized, Moll Apulala, an Abelam big man, juxtaposing his viewpoints with those of other historically situated actors who shared in particular events. Born in the 1920s, Moll was among the first of his people to engage in plantation labor. He worked as a cargo carrier and guide for the first European gold miners in the Sepik foothills, was an eyewitness to the construction of the first government patrol post in the region, and worked as a domestic for one of the early Australian government officers. During the Second World War, he was employed as a cook for Japanese troops in the Sepik area, and then later became a guide for Allied troops during the reoccupation of the Sepik. During the postwar years, Moll played an active role in a variety of local development projects and government services. After independence, he became the first Chairman of the Balupwine Village Court in his area. During all these activities, he continued to remain in touch with local life in his village. He passed through all of the male initiation ceremonies and became a village leader of considerable renown. After a rich life, Moll passed away toward the end of 1998, while I was writing this paper.

Many of the activities in which Moll was involved, including plantation labor, gold mining, colonial government expansion, World War II, and postcolonial development, are critical historical issues throughout the Pacific. However, the well-rehearsed "public" histories created by the colonial participants to these events, with their stress on themes of social and economic development, structural change, and colonial government agency, perforce minimize the contributions of and effects on individual local people. Consequently, the biographies of these persons can act as a corrective to the more structural and monocultural versions of the historical process. During fieldwork in 1983, 1988, and 1990, I recorded Moll's biography in his own words. In this essay, I juxtapose some of his own observations and descriptions not only with accounts from the public histories of his colonizers, but also with narratives of other historically situated actors. I concentrate on the early colonial period through World War II, when divergent views of colonial encounters were most marked. My goal is to interweave narratives from varied perspectives in an attempt to shed light on the complex entanglements of colonial encounters in the Sepik foothills in the early colonial era.

Overview of Sepik Foothills History: The Colonizers[1]

When the German Imperial Government assumed administrative control of the Sepik coast following the turn of the twentieth century, the foothills hinterland of the Sepik began to be explored and organized for labor recruitment, primarily for coastal plantation work. The first European to travel through the Abelam area was Richard Thurnwald in 1913. Earlier in the year, he had explored the grassland country between the Sepik River and the sea in a relatively sparsely populated region to the east of Abelam territory. On his second trip, he encountered the densely populated foothills and the Abelam people. He remarked,

> I have nowhere in the South Sea come on a country with as dense a population as this, even when I consider the thickly populated south end of Bougainville.... From a practical viewpoint, recruiting would be a primary consideration in this region. To introduce recruiting with skill and without violence would be well worth the trouble for those interested in it. The powerful inhabitants of the inland are also usually more resistant than the coastal people especially against fever. (Thurnwald 1914:81–84)[2]

Unfortunately, it would seem that recruiters did not follow Thurnwald's advice because, as events unfolded, early labor recruitment in the foothills became particularly violent and coercive. As the events of the First World War eroded government influence throughout the Sepik, recruiters took advantage of the ensuing power vacuum and kidnapped laborers in a heavy-handed manner (see, for example, Scaglion 1983:471–475; 1985:77–78; 1990). It was not until several years after the Australian civil administration began in 1921 that Australians were able to reorganize the Sepik coastal area. Interestingly, the first Australian administrative patrol (of which we have record) that ventured into the area near Moll Apulala's village was undertaken by G. W. L. Townsend (then acting deputy district officer of the Sepik) in July of 1924, in response to reports of recruiting excesses. With six policemen, Townsend (1968:111–112) followed a "trail of broken clay pots, smashed plants, and tales of abduction." In Kulingai, an Abelam settlement roughly seven kilometers northwest of Moll's village of Neligum, he found a man dying of "an array of pellet holes" apparently fired from a recruiter's shotgun.

During this time, Australian administrative control was gradually being established in the Sepik hinterland through a series of patrols for the purpose of "asserting government influence, preventing fighting, arresting murderers, and gradually enforcing the Native Regulations, which imposed standards of hygiene, sanitation, cleanliness, and so on upon the villagers" (West 1968a:13). One or more government officers with an escort of armed native police would enter a new area and establish a base camp.

In the mid-1920s, large goldfields were discovered in the Wau-Bulolo Valleys of the Morobe District, encouraging enterprising Australian prospectors to move "up from the south" (O'Neill 1979). In the early 1930s, some of these prospectors, many of them completely unfamiliar with New Guinea and its people, began exploring the streams and rivers of the Sepik foothills, then relatively uncontrolled territory, searching for gold. O'Neill (1979:1–2) describes the circumstances of his recruitment to the ranks of New Guinea prospectors:

> Christmas 1930. I was twenty-three years old, and camped at Burleigh Heads on the South Queensland coast with a few mates. We were enjoying ourselves in traditional holiday style—sun, surf and more of the same. At the beach I ran into Alan Corrigan, who had plans to go to New Guinea where good gold had been discovered a couple of years earlier. . . . I knew that gold was yellow in colour and heavy, and more pertinently that it was hard to come by, but I was at a loose end, having just completed an abortive attempt to matriculate. Then again, things were grim in those days: no jobs to be had even in the West, where I had put in five years before going back to school. Also I was lucky, having a stake which a thoughtful, but misguided, ancient relative had willed to me. Finally, I had an adventurous streak.
>
> One month later, we—Bill McNamee, an old New Guinea hand; George Henderson, a successful wolfram gouger [tungsten miner] from North Queensland; Alan and myself—were on our way.

The Sepik foothills goldfields were initially located far in the hills, in streams draining northward to the coast. It soon became clear that the claims were often more easily reached from the Sepik Plains than from the coast. Before long, gold was discovered in the Amogu (Screw) River near Moll's village, and miner interest in Moll's home area increased. Recruiting activity also increased, since laborers were needed to work the new goldfields as well as the coastal plantations, and conflicts with local people ensued. Tuzin (1976:25–27) reports on recruiter Charlie Gough, "speared to death by the men of Lehinga" while "employing recruiting methods of dubious legality." Another recruiter during this period was Hunter Kirke, who later become a gold miner and employed Moll Apulala, as we shall see. In a report to the director of District Services in Rabaul, dated March 18, 1937 (Sepik District 31/1; Pacific Manuscripts Bureau #602), G. W. L. Townsend, now district officer, wrote the following under the heading "Native Disturbances— Sepik District—Maprik Area":

> Last Month it was reported to Mr. Bilston that Messers. Kirke and Holland had been menaced by natives of GATNIGUM and forced to leave the village. GATNIGUM is south of Leihinga and had once been visited by Mr. Bilston.
>
> After enquiry, Messers. Kirke and Holland were charged with sending a native unaccompanied by a person holding a recruiter's license to recruit in Gatnigum Village.
>
> The story is exactly as Gough's. A Native brought in a recruit who ran away during the night. The recruiters followed next day to recover the recruit.
>
> With the example of Gough before them, one wonders at their madness.
>
> The upshot was that it was impossible to get witnesses without raiding Gatnigum Village, which probably [would] have led to loss of life. The case therefore was dismissed. After this lapse of time, I suppose we cannot very well close the area and I have instructed Mr. Bilston to disregard everything else in favour of getting into villages ahead of recruiters and prospectors.
>
> I have instructed Mr. Woodman—a cadet is with him—Mr. Reading—to work north up the Screw towards Maprik. However the population as you will see is immense and we can only trust that nothing will happen.

Accordingly, Maprik station, the administrative center nearest Moll's village today, was established in late 1937. Townsend writes (1968:234):

> By 1937 Maprik had become established as the main sub-station of the grass country. Two huge, two-story, sago-leaf bungalows had been built there through the energy of Patrol Officer Johnny Miller and Medical Assistant Tom Ellis.
>
> They were made completely of native materials, shook and reverberated with every footstep and, although entry to the second story was effected by ladder, the two architect-builders were exceedingly proud of them and of the hospital of native materials nearby.

The events of the Second World War brought a fairly abrupt halt to these developments, however. Japanese aircraft began an assault of the north coast of New

JUXTAPOSED NARRATIVES

Guinea in early 1942, and by December of that year had landed at Wewak, the coastal center nearest Moll's village. The miners had by then left the area and the Australian civil administration, suspended in February of 1942, had abandoned Maprik station. In 1943, Japanese troops established themselves along the north coast. However, following defeats in the Madang and Morobe areas, the Japanese 18th Army, their supply lines cut, began to establish "self-support" units in the foothills area in mid-1944. Initially, troops curried favor with locals, stressing themes of brotherhood against the Australian "Other." By late 1944, the situation for the roughly 15,000 Japanese troops remaining in the foothills had become desperate. With supplies already exhausted, local game killed, and local gardens depleted, Japanese relations with local people had deteriorated badly. Lt. Gen. Tsutomu Yoshihara's account of the New Guinea campaign reflects this breakdown of local support:

> There are many people who believe the natives are savage, like fighting, and are fond of human flesh but this is completely opposed to the truth. . . . On the contrary they are obedient, gentle and friendly and their cooperation during the New Guinea campaign was no small matter. They help with offering food and carrying the wounded. (1955:80)

But later, Yoshihara writes:

> The natives west of MAPRIK were comparatively numerous and because they liked fighting it was convenient to use them for action against the enemy; but in our area the natives were meek and because for a long time they had been in contact with our self-support units there was this difference. . . . Now that the enemy were close, there were attempts to escape by natives who did not like their task of carrying supplies, and crimes such as the killing of small garrisons of troops who had been despatched to various points. Really after April, 1944, the state of public order on the western front was very disturbed. (1955:164)

Late in 1944, the Australian 6th Division began to advance east through the foothills, and Japanese troops often dug in at village sites. Numerous Australian air strikes strafed Japanese positions, villages were often leveled, and Japanese troops withdrew only after considerable resistance. The 2/5 Battalion, 17th Brigade Australian Forces, secured the Maprik area in April and May of 1945, and by the general surrender in August, troops were well east of Moll's village.

On the first postwar patrol through the area in April and May of 1946, Patrol Officer J. E. Wakeford (1945–1946:5) recorded his impressions of the conditions of the villages visited:

Speaking generally, the condition of the native villages seen on this patrol was bad, but this was expected as it must be understood that for some years now the villages have been occupied, firstly by the Japanese, then Australian soldiers and NGIB [New Guinea Infantry Battalion]. In some cases villages have been the centres of severe fighting and targets for bombing.

One of the worst cases is the village of Ulupu. This village was devastated, every coconut tree and house was destroyed. The village site is a mass of shell craters. A 500 lb bomb which was unexploded was removed from the village and disposed of over a cliff.

After the war followed a period of rebuilding villages and replanting gardens in Moll's home area. By the 1950s, the themes of "paternalism" and "progress" described by Nash (Chap. 7) and concern with the "degree of advancement" of particular groups described by Westermark (Chap. 4) were much in evidence in patrol reports and other colonial narratives of the period. Patrol Officer K. A. Brown (1954–1955:3) writes:

My previous patrols in the Maprik sub-district were besieged from beginning to end with numerous petty complaints over bride price, pigs, sacsac, land boundaries and so on. I had painted much the same picture in my mind when setting out on this patrol. It was not, however, until the last day of the patrol that I heard such a complaint. This was very trivial and was settled to the apparent satisfaction of all parties.

The proximity of the Sub-district Office has considerable bearing on this state of affairs but it is also indicative that the people are on the "move."

Throughout the late 1950s and 1960s, "development" moved along much as it did in other parts of the Territory of Papua and New Guinea (TPNG): local development projects were encouraged, agricultural development officers were assigned, Local Government Councils were established, and so on. The themes that Foster describes in his chapter—land, labor, and individual character; mateship; a new start; and no heroes/all heroes—which were very evident in pre–World War II narratives, also appear in some texts from this era. However, by the late 1960s, increasing concern with showing success in "civilizing" local peoples (but at the same time questioning whether natives were sufficiently "advanced" for independence) became more evident in colonial government texts (see Foster, Chap. 5), and the area was no longer being portrayed largely as an untamed wilderness in which courageous (but modest) colonial officers and rugged fortune hunters were operating.

Overview of Sepik History: The Colonized

In other publications (Scaglion 1999, 2000; see also Scaglion 1983), I have contrasted prevailing Western notions of time, which I call "linear," with Abelam notions of time, which I call "episodic." I believe that the fundamentally different orientations toward time, of Westerners on the one hand and Abelam on the other, result in quite different historical orientations. The episodic perspective of the Abelam sees social and cultural structures as generally unchanging, and the flow of events as merely process. What Westerners would call "change" is usually perceived merely as repetition or "replacement" of events or persons and objects in the same unchanging structure of reality. People die, and others are born to replace them. Yams die, but others grow from the harvested tubers to take their place. In this perspective, "real" change can only occur cataclysmically or millennially in a total restructuring of reality. In contrast, the linear (or "evolutionary") historical orientations of Westerners see structure as coming into being and changing cumulatively.

Abelam views of historical time are not unique in Melanesia. Peter Lawrence, in his classic *Road Belong Cargo* (1964a), suggests that episodic thinking may have conditioned the "cargo" beliefs of Yali and his followers. In similar fashion, Errington (1974:257) links beliefs concerning a Duke of York Island cargo cult movement with episodic time logic. Counts and Counts (1976:304) report on how the Kaliai of West New Britain feared the approach of independence in Papua New Guinea because they "foresee change, not as a process occurring by degree, but rather as a sudden qualitative transformation that alters fundamental relations." Similarly, McDowell (1985, 1988) for the people of Bun, Burman (1981) for the Simbo, and Kempf (1992) in Sibog describe the importance of episodic time in the interpretation of ethnohistory and for an understanding of social constructions of historical change in Melanesia.

Western linear orientations toward time and history accord very well with notions of "progress," "advancement," "development," and, as Patrol Officer Brown put it, "being on the 'move.'" But Abelam people, like the other Melanesians referenced above, tend to see the flow of time as a kind of "punctuated equilibrium," that is, a steady state ruptured by catastrophic events that restructure the world and result in a new steady state. As a result, the Abelam see the past as divided into eras or epochs: the "time of the ancestors," the "time of the Germans," the "time of fighting," and so forth (Scaglion 1985). From an Abelam perspective, nothing really changes within each era. Events clearly linked with change tend to be "telescoped" or "foreshortened" in time, in comparison with a Western calendrical orientation, to better fit a model of rapid change associated with the cataclysm that accompanies transition periods.

Moll's narrative uses these "epochs" as points of reference. The precolonial era, or time of the ancestors, he describes much as a structural-functionalist anthropologist would. It is a period of unchanging time in which a "traditional" culture existed. This era was shattered by the arrival of the *tuang*, or light-skinned people, thought at first to be spirit beings, but now recognized as Europeans. In the first encounter of Moll's people with the *tuang*, which ushered in the "Time of the

Germans," labor recruiters surprised the people of his village, who were preparing for a male initiation ceremony. Thunderclaps emanated from the midst of the *tuang*; people were terrified and ran away. The *tuang* captured one young man, trussed him up like a pig, and carried him off to work on a plantation (as it was later discovered when he finally returned). The time of the Germans is remembered firsthand by very few living Abelam, and, apart from labor recruitments, it actually had relatively little impact on their lives, beyond making them aware of the colonial culture developing on the distant coast.

Moll's next era is the "Time of the English," an epoch roughly corresponding to the 1930s, in which gold mining and the establishment of Maprik station play prominent roles. Moll tends to see the arrival of the miners, the establishment of the station, and other dramatic events (such as the arrival of the first airplane) as all occurring at about the same time, telescoping change in keeping with his episodic view of history. Following this period is the "Time of Fighting" (World War II), which was, once again, ushered in with apocalyptic events from his perspective. The "Time of the Australians" ensued, a period accompanied by the suppression of many traditional customs such as house burials, tribal fighting, and other practices. For Moll, this was yet another "colonial" era. Western linear calendrical history and Moll's episodic framework come together neatly with the arrival of the "Time of Independence," ushered in on September 16, 1975.

Moll's Narrative

I recorded the bulk of Moll's narrative in June and July of 1983. By that time, he and I had developed a very close relationship. He had adopted me as his son in 1974, during my Ph.D. field research of 1974–1976, throughout which he had been my local sponsor and main informant. At that time I maintained a separate household in Neligum Village on lineage land adjacent to his own. During this period, he was very much the teacher and I the student. From 1976 through 1983, I revisited Neligum often, especially during 1979–1981 when I was based in Port Moresby working for the Law Reform Commission of Papua New Guinea. By 1983 I had developed some agency of my own, as I had been visiting Maprik in a governmental capacity, acting as a principal legal officer, investigating and supervising legal development in the area. Whenever I could, I based myself in Neligum Village. Because Moll was chairman of the Balupwine Village Court at the time, we had a professional as well as a personal relationship.

I had often talked of recording Moll's "story," because the many incidents he had described to me over the years fascinated me. We began the task in earnest in June of 1983. On seven separate occasions over the next two months, Moll came to my field house in Neligum, in the evening, to tell his story. We sat on the floor of an enclosed verandah in front of my house, often with an audience of onlookers, mostly children. Each evening, I would generally fill a 90-minute audiotape. The sessions actually took much longer than this, because periodically Moll would ask me to turn off the tape recorder so that he could compose his thoughts, eat, chew betel nut, smoke, etc. Moll does not speak English, and his narrative unfolded mostly in Tok Pisin (in which we are both fluent) and sometimes in Ambulas, the Abelam language (in which I am less fluent). By 1983, Neligum had become a bilingual village (Ambulas and Tok Pisin). Discussions involving *gavman* and *bisnis* (i.e., government and business matters mostly related to the colonial and postcolonial legacy) were typically discussed in Tok Pisin, whereas "traditional" matters such as yam growing, ceremonial life, and so on were most often conducted in Ambulas. Consequently, the portions of the narrative that appear in this chapter were recorded almost exclusively in Tok Pisin.

In the beginning, I tried to let Moll tell his own story just as he wished, with little interruption or structuring by me. At times he would allude to something I already knew, and I would have to remind him to retell it "for the tape." His narrative did not unfold chronologically, but because I have a Western historical orientation, I mentally organized his episodes this way. Toward the end of our sessions I asked him to fill in temporal gaps by asking him to tell about what he did in the years between certain temporal markers. During subsequent field trips in 1988 and 1990, I asked him to fill in other gaps, received clarification of certain matters about which I was confused, and so on. Translations given here are my own. Editorial clarifications have been made in square brackets (in both Moll's and other narratives). I have tried to keep to Moll's own words as closely as possible, leaving digressions, redundancies, and inconsistencies in place. However, I have not translated his Tok Pisin "literally"; instead, I use a more subtly nuanced English that I think better reflects his actual ideas. Although he was uneducated, he was exceedingly bright, and oratory was his special skill. If he had used English, he would most certainly have used it well. In the next section, I juxtapose sections of Moll's narrative with observations of European witnesses to the same historical events.

Juxtaposed Narratives

One of the events that particularly impressed a young Moll Apulala was the building of the Maprik airstrip and the arrival of the first airplane. Following his description of the death of his father, it was the second issue he chose to explore on tape. Although the event was little more than an afterthought in the broader Australian narrative of "opening up the Sepik," Australian texts of the event nicely illustrate the colonial themes highlighted in this volume. Juxtaposing Australian descriptions of this event with Moll's recollections draws these differing perspectives into sharp relief. Lloyd Rhys, in his account of the development of the New Guinea goldfields, writes of pilot Ray Parer's inaugural run into the new airstrip at Maprik:

> Back at Wau, however, [Parer] heard accounts of good gold finding on the Screw River, one of the tributaries of the Sepik, and once more he and Glasson set out. This was the beginning of the opening up of a new field.

The Screw River tests proved to be up to expectations, and five miles of it were pegged in their joint names. Glasson cleared an aerodrome at Maprik for his partner to bring in his plane.

Parer has told me how he flew into Maprik in the "old bus" —the Fairy 3F which had brought him fame in the England to Australia air race in 1920. As a result of a forced landing on the Sepik during one of his trips he was without food for three days. Then with the plane in order once more he began regular trips, carrying in rice, meat and mining materials. On each trip the little machine was loaded to its utmost capacity. "Every possible thing was stowed inside the bus," said Parer, "but the overflow was a bit of a problem, so we put the bags of rice in bomb-racks on the wings and lashed them with rope; sometimes they were left swinging in the wind." (1942:198–199)

District Officer G. W. L. Townsend records a similar story in his memoirs: "By the end of 1936 Ray Parer, Guinea Airways, and Stephens' air service were flying between the beach [at Wewak] and Maprik. These were haphazard flights—Parer simply using his plane as a farmer in Australia would use a utility truck" (1968:228).

The not-very-subtle subtext of the Australian version of the story is one of Australian personal agency. Local people rarely if ever appear in these texts. Rather, they are seen as part of the "wildness" that must be tamed. Australians are "can-do" sorts of individuals, accomplishing what they can under difficult circumstances. Parer appears as one of Foster's "all heroes/no heroes" as he goes for days without food, outfits the goldfield by flying rather literally "by the seat of his pants," and establishes formal air services in the region in the process.

Moll's recollections provide a different perspective, with somewhat different agents. First of all, in the Australians' versions of the story, gold simply "is discovered" in the Sepik foothills. Moll suggests it was actually an Abelam man who discovered it, at least in his area:

> Gold was really discovered in our area by Kenny Masalein. He found some gold in the Amogu [Screw River]. He was digging in a salt pit, clearing it out, digging out the ground and throwing it up on the sides. As he threw the dirt up on the banks, he saw the gold sparkle and he found three pieces. He had previously worked for a gold miner [in the highlands], so he knew what gold was and what it looked like.... He looked at it and said, "Oh gee, I think that that's gold." He gave the gold nuggets to some of the white men who were supervising the work on Maprik airstrip and they sent it to Australia. Australians looked at the gold, and then came and asked, "Where did you find this?"... and he showed them where he had found it.

In Rhys's version of the events, "Glasson cleared an aerodrome at Maprik for his partner to bring in his plane." Typically, there was no mention of the local people who actually did the work! Moll remembers it as follows:

> When they built Maprik airstrip, I was still a young boy. Nevertheless, I tagged along with everyone who went down there. The place where they built the airstrip was originally a swamp overrun with cane and the type of sago that has spines on the leaves. There were many areas where the ground was rough, and there were holes. Prisoners[3] were digging out the bases of the thorny sago trees and leveling the ground. There was a small stream, and all of these guys had to fill that in too. It was really a lot of work.

As for the heroic Ray Parer and his flight into Maprik, Moll says the following:

> After the airstrip was ready, a plane came. This was the first time any of us had seen an airplane. We thought, "What the heck is going on? What *is* this thing?" When the plane first approached, I was at Iresikwu. At the time I was holding Musuayel, who was still young. We heard the engine of the plane begin to drone. Someone said, "What is that, a huge cassowary bird?" Everyone was running around grabbing their spears so that they would be ready in case the strange thing landed. One of my uncles had worked at a mission station before and had seen airplanes. He went up to Mangaambu, stood on the ceremonial ground, and called out to all the people. By this time, we had all run away and hidden in the jungle. But when I heard him cry out, I took Musuayel and went up to Mangaambu. We sat there and watched as the plane circled around, and around, and around, and around, and finally touched down at Maprik.
>
> Then everyone for miles around gathered at Maprik. Everybody was climbing all over the plane—looking at the wheels, looking at the wings, touching it. When the second plane came, my father went down to Maprik to look at it, and it was just after that he became sick. But all those who went down to Maprik on that very first day looked at that plane and said, "Ah, so this is an airplane!" The pilot of that first plane was Masta[4] Parer. He was a short, bald guy. I saw him.

Careful readers, well versed in Western linear historical constructs, will recognize an apparent inconsistency in Moll's narrative. If gold had not yet been discovered in the area, why were the white men, to whom Kenny Masalein gave the gold, building an airstrip? But from an Abelam episodic temporal perspective, this is not really inconsistent at all, because events happened "all at once." The careful sequencing of discrete events that characterizes Western telling of history are not at all important for the Abelam. Places and objects are much more likely to be the touchstones of history.

In a subsequent chapter of his life, Moll worked for one of the gold prospectors who worked the claims, the aforementioned Hunter Kirke, who played a small part in a sad chapter in Australian colonial history. Australian narratives from the gold-mining era often have the same theme of "taming" the Sepik as described above: lone prospector overcomes odds, works hard, survives hardships, and accomplishes much through the strength of his personal character and strong will. Again, the agency of local people is underplayed. What is much less heralded, and barely chronicled at all in surviving documents, however, is the rather ignominious retreat of the Australians from the Maprik area in 1942. Initially, Kirke displayed a philosophical bravado about the war. In a letter dated "Think it's about 10th-10-39," Kirke (Pacific Manuscripts Bureau #610) wrote to fellow gold miner Ted Fulton (1936–1948):

> I shall put a "kanda" [length of cane] on to Mr. Hitler's pants when I see him, for upsetting things & folks so. Since I "listened-in" at Mick's to Chamberlain's announcement that "we are at war with Germany" I have been in a "dither": all else seems to fade into insignificance—It looks to me that ere many moons have vanished, the "teams" shall be choosing to take part in a conflict the likes of which the world has never witnessed & maybe shall never again witness—Shall be the greatest show on earth, knocking Barnum's Circus into a cocked hat! I believe that eventually most of us shall be fully occupied in scattered parts of the universe curbing the wily Hun & his hard case allies and as far as I can see it matters little, as we are all heading for the mat-mat [grave] in any case & just dying of sickness is a lousy way to die.

By the time the Japanese invasion of the north coast began in early 1942, all of the Europeans in the Sepik District were essentially cut off, and no effective plans had been made for their evacuation. In the end, it was left to individual enterprise as to how to escape. Moll remembers Hunter Kirke's departure as follows:

> When Masta Hunter left right before the war, I was a young man, and strong enough to help carry his cargo. We started at the mission near Maprik, and went all the way up to the headwaters of the Amogu. All of the other miners had already run off, but Masta Hunter was the last to leave, since he had been staying up there at the headwaters. However, the *kiaps* [government patrol officers] were still in Maprik, looking after the area.
>
> At the time, I was staying in the village, and Masta Hunter came to ask

us to go up to the headwaters to help him: me, Sakikun, Taminja, all of us. One group, escorted by police, took a lot of his cargo down to the Sepik River near Pagwi. Then the police returned and got another group to take away still more cargo. We were in the very last group to go: me, some men from Kuminibis, and some men from Neligum. We went at night, got as far as Burui, and left the cargo in a house there.

A lot of goods were left behind at the headwaters of the Amogu and Biam. People from Neligum and Kuminibis went up there and either ate or used up all the remaining cargo. Some of his stuff—they broke into his storehouse at the Amogu and brought things like canned goods and rice to the hill above Ndingé and ate it.

Assistant District Officer George Ellis was then in charge of the Sepik River region, and "appears to have resented all plans for evacuating these men, to a point where it had become a neurosis" (Townsend 1968:227). Len Odgers, a clerk at Wewak before the war, takes up the story in his diary:

> Saturday 14 Feb 1942
> Went for a run on the "Osprey" with George Ellis and Roy up the [Sepik] river to where the "Thetis" is hidden. At about half past five when Roy and I went over to MacGregor's Station to see Len Bridger. Had a yarn and then later the "Duai" arrived from Yimas bringing Roy MacGregor and "Blue" Cook, Hunter Kirke, Garry Keagh, Geoff Shaw, Simncocks. [An argument ensued] . . . this led to a fight between Kirke and Ellis, the former winning after a rough and tumble.

> Sunday 15 Feb 1942
> Up at a quarter of seven as usual this morning to find that George Ellis had a beautiful black eye.

> Thursday 19 Feb 1942
> Later we learnt Shaw, Cook, Keagh and Kirke had gone down the river presumably with an idea of getting into Australia. (1942–1943)

Hunter Kirke eventually did make his way safely to Australia. His adversary, George Ellis, was not so fortunate. As Townsend (1968:227–228) tells it:

> When Assistant District Officer Jim Taylor and Patrol Officer Charles Bates arrived to assist the men on their way [Ellis] barricaded himself and about 40 native police in the Station and gave the newcomers half an hour to get clear. Taylor, Bates and some of the civilians who were camped in the neighbourhood then armed themselves and advanced on the station.

In the shooting that followed Taylor was shot in the groin. The party withdrew down-stream to Marienberg where they were joined by the District Officer from Wewak who swore the civilians in as Special Constables and with 10 of his own police returned to Angoram.

They found Ellis dead in his house, shot through the head,[5] and leaving only a note for his people. The police had gone, most of them eventually finding their way back to their own villages. One group, however, went completely berserk and set out to kill every European still living on the River. Their first victim was Patrol Officer R. B. Strudwick who was stationed at Timbunke, which is a little above Angoram, and who was unaware of what was going on. They shot him in cold blood while he was eating a meal.

Further up-river they came upon a party of miners. They killed George Eichorn, Jack Mitchell, Reg Beckett and a Chinese carpenter while two other miners, J. Wilton and Freddy Eichorn, escaped.

The war years brought with them considerable turmoil, destruction, and death throughout the foothills. The broad outlines of events, told from a Western structural perspective, have been given earlier, but there are many unwritten individual stories. Perhaps among the most poignant are those involving cultural differences, miscommunications, and, in some cases, actual understandings. After the Japanese occupied the north coast, Moll worked as a cook for the Japanese troops. In the passage below, he describes his decision to desert. (He successfully made his escape at night, carefully avoiding trip wires and mines.)

I think that we had been working for the Japanese for about a month and a half before we had a problem. Ndunjamba stole a little bit of fish from their cookhouse. It was salt fish. The Japanese would catch all these really small fish, dry them well, put them in bags, and send them over to us. We would take them out of the bags and make a kind of soup out of them. Ndunjamba just wanted to see what the fish tasted like, so we all watched for the Japanese to make sure they were not looking, and then he took a little piece and tried it. It must have tasted pretty good to him, and besides, he was hungry. He began to reach into the bag, hold more fish in his hand, and then slip them into his mouth when no one was looking.

At the time, I myself was over by the soup, stirring it with this very large paddle used for the purpose. The supervisor of the cooking facilities came up unexpectedly and saw Ndunjamba put a fish in his mouth. He was really angry and screamed, "Ah, you fuckhead! Stealing is no good!" He then picked up a piece of plank and began to beat Ndunjamba over the head with it. I think he gave him about five shots to the head. The blows knocked Ndunjamba down and he was badly hurt. I think he must have

JUXTAPOSED NARRATIVES

had a concussion because his eyes were rolling around in his head. He just sat down and began to cry.

This really upset me. I thought to myself, "What kind of people are these, who would beat a big-man like that, to the point where he would cry?" It was then that I determined to run away. Some big-men from our village who had been carrying cargo to Aitape for the Japanese had already run away because of the treatment that they had received. They would be beaten around the face and heads, and the Japanese would swear at them and yell at them constantly. So they had already returned to the village. But you know, Japanese would even strike each other in this way. If a Japanese soldier did something wrong, an officer would strike him.

Yet even as Moll is repelled by certain cultural behaviors of the Japanese, at the same time he credits individual Japanese with acts of kindness and bravery as we see below:

Later, when the Australians came, they cut the supply lines of these Japanese soldiers, who had no way to escape. Their ships and planes could not come to their rescue. They were trapped. So they began to raid our gardens, and steal our food, and, eventually, they began to kill and eat local people. They killed a number of men from Kalabu and ate them.[6] There were even some Papua New Guineans who participated with the Japanese in this cannibalism, and were later put in jail for it. And I have already told you the story of how the Japanese very nearly killed everyone in our village.

[Scaglion: Yes, but since I don't have it on tape, could you please tell it again?]

Well, they lined up everyone in the village at Mangaambu. The line was so long that it stretched right to the top of the village. They were going to start firing at one end of the line and just go right down the line and kill everyone. I think we all would have died right there had it not been for this one Japanese named Unda. He tried to talk the other soldiers out of killing us by reminding them that we had not done them any wrong, that we had never refused them food, that we had looked after them, and that we should not be treated in this way. Finally he said, "I will stand up with these people, and you shoot me first, and then you kill the rest of them." After this, the Japanese dispersed us.

In 1977 in Tokyo, Bryant Allen conducted a remarkable interview with Kikuo Kajizuki, a former captain of the 41st Division, 238th Regiment, of the Japanese forces who held the foothills during this period. Kajizuki's perspectives on inter-cultural understanding, and the agency of local peoples, provide yet another per-spective. I quote from notes kindly provided by Dr. Allen:

> In the Maprik area our only aim was to stay alive and the lack of coopera-tion by the native people did not worry us because we had no equipment to carry. We took food from the gardens. Only if they tried to kill us did we defend ourselves. Depending on the fighting situation a number of men were assigned to collect food. Sago, pawpaw, cooking bananas and coco-nuts were the most common foods. Sometimes we ate dogs, less often pigs and poultry. We were never attacked by village people while collecting food. Everywhere the villages were deserted. It is only now, I realise they were hiding close by. The only natives to attack my unit were native sol-diers. . . .
>
> Just before the end of the war I had closer contacts with native people. At a village we called Mikau No. 2, we occupied the village before the Aus-tralian forces had moved into this area. The villagers had run away when we arrived but the next day they came back. We lived there with them for several days. Although we could not speak pidgin we managed to commu-nicate using a few words of English. Gradually we also learned some pid-gin. On the fourth day there was heavy rain. The villagers brought Austra-lian troops to the village and we were attacked.
>
> In this attack I was wounded. I still have the two bullets which I carried in my body for many weeks. My headquarters believed I had been killed and prepared documents for my funeral. Even though these people caused us to be attacked, I do not want them to think that we maintained animosity towards them for this. But when I tried to return to see them in 1972 they took one look at us and fled into the bush. Only last year after the old *luluai* had died could we make contact with them. I think the people thought we were going to kill them in revenge. The village is still much the same as it was then, except the location of the houses has changed, the people who were adults then, many have died.

Kajizuki's narrative clearly shows the agency of local people, who brought the Aus-tralian forces to rout the Japanese.

In the Australian structural versions of the retaking of the Maprik area, the emphasis is very much on facts, tactics, and the contributions of various Australian officers. Local people are much less visible, their roles minimized, the impacts on their lives virtually ignored. In a series of books on Australia in the war of 1939–1945 published by the Australian War Memorial, Gavin Long (1963:334–336) wrote simply of the taking of Moll's village:

Next day there were two patrol clashes. A native reported that bombing had driven a party of 20 or 30 Japanese out of the Neligum villages but on 25th April a patrol under Lieutenant A. H. Seekamp found three there, drove these away, and burned the villages, which were occupied the next day. Also on the 25th a patrol under the ubiquitous Sergeant Hedderman found Mangumbu [Mangaambu, the hamlet of Neligum referred to above] strongly held. . . . During May the 2/6th on the northern flank continued to patrol eastward, and the enemy, harassed by patrols and air attack, slowly moved back. Mangumbu was found to be empty of Japanese on 1st May and occupied the next day.

Moll's recollections are, of course, more detailed and provide complementary information by concentrating on the impact of these bombings on local populations:

There was another time, I remember, that people actually did get killed, this time by the Australians. I was planning to carry my [infirm] father down to a place called Wallapiai, where Borsimbi's clan's water spirit is. It is right near where Rakambwe's father's garden house was in those days. We had just passed Mangaambu and were standing at the head of the path when we saw a line of planes come and bomb Mamembel. First the planes came down, made a run, and dropped the first set of bombs. Then they circled around and made a second bombing run. We could see huge explosions all over the place. We just hid out there at the top of the path until they began to make yet another run. This time they flew low over the village and began strafing it with machine gun fire. I grabbed my father, threw him on my shoulders, ran down the path to where the base of Borsimbi's sago is, and hid there until the firing ceased. When the planes had gone, I carried my father back up to our hamlet. Afterward I went to see the people who had been killed by the explosions and the fire. There was my father's cousin, Bokwa, and Bawtaakwi, who was Kapmukisik's big brother. I think that altogether four people were killed. . . .

After this we were bombed nearly every day. It was miserable. We would have to wake up very early in the morning before daybreak and go and scatter in the bush and hide near little streams in valleys. After a long time, the bombing ceased, and the Australian ground troops began to close in on Maprik.

In other parts of his narrative, Moll gives his eyewitness accounts of still more events of the Second World War. Particularly moving are his recollections of sometimes innocent people who were shot for reportedly collaborating with the enemy:

Men from Kuminibis, Mamblep, and Imbia, who had previously run off to Aitape, were the ones who led the Australians back in. We ourselves had stayed in our village in Japanese-occupied territory. This turned out to be a real problem for us, because there followed a series of very harsh reprisals by native police working with the Australians who thought that we had been with the Japanese when war atrocities took place in their villages. Since some New Guinea people had helped the Japanese to destroy gardens and had raped women in other villages, some of these native police from Kuminibis and Mamblep decided to seek payback revenge on our people. They beat many of our men and raped some of the women. One of these native police shot Yuambil, the father of Paul Angou, and then defaced his body by taking a pocketknife and slicing his nose. But this man later faced trial in Aitape.

Well, actually, the authorities did not tell this man that he was going to court and he never had a real trial. He was just sitting down near Marap. They had written his name down on a piece of paper, and they called it out. He got up and said, "Yes, I am this man." They just shot him on the spot, and dug a hole and buried him. If you and I go up to Marap sometime, I can show you the grave.

Needless to say, such accounts of summary executions are rarely reported in the public documents of the period.

Discussion

I hope that the episodes in Moll's narrative that I have recounted here illustrate that we have much to learn from what Susan Rodgers (1995:3) calls, "the interpenetration of autobiographical memory and public history." While researching the colonial history of the Tolai people of New Britain, Klaus Neumann was frequently urged by Tolais to (as they put it) "set the record straight." Neumann (1992:259) observes:

> *Vatakodo* 'setting the record straight' could and should mean encircling hegemonical History with a colorful diversity of counterhegemonical histories. It should mean contradicting colonial History through anticolonial histories, male History through women's histories, big man History through histories centered around the lives and experiences of the nobodies, *ol rabis man,* as they are called in Tok Pisin. It should mean contradicting the singular, "capital 'H'" History through a plurality of histories.

Clearly, there are no single Histories, no objective truths. Instead, histories are inevitably constructed, manufactured, or fabricated by using multiple voices and multiple truths. Anthropologists should contribute to the historical enterprise not so much by seeking to tell "how it really was" as by "setting the record straight" by collecting, writing, and referencing the autobiographical narratives and voices that are typically missing in public histories, that is, by writing against hegemonical History.

Neumann describes his own project as follows (1992:36–37):

> I do not intend to write a history that places a particular sequel to events of the past firmly between a before and after. Nor do I try to reconcile the account based on written sources with that based on Tolai histories to establish what *really* happened in Toma. There are many realities in those accounts. There is, for example, the reality of a colonial project that could only succeed if the colonized were subdued by military conquest and by making them into images that could be conquered. There is also the reality of two old men in Tamanairik in 1987 who recreate their past by telling it. By structuring the accounts, by incorporating particular histories, by selecting different styles and a particular form, by juxtaposing different realities I propose a truth, but the truth is open-ended. It then becomes your turn to tell a history.

In like manner, I have not attempted to tell "the truth" here about colonial events in the Sepik foothills, but only to help "set the record straight." By giving voice to one of the colonized, I have tried to provide a corrective to the public history of the colonists by presenting an alternative historical reality for consideration. Long ignored or downplayed, indigenous perspectives such as Moll's are only recently beginning to achieve the recognition they deserve (see, for example, Lindstrom and White 1990 on the Pacific war), and these accounts are helping to flesh out a clearer understanding of the complex dynamics of colonial events in the Pacific.

Anthropologists would seem to be in a unique position to help counter the reification of public colonial History by engaging in such projects. But surprisingly, anthropological writings on colonial enterprises have been relatively few. In a review of such writings, Nicholas Thomas (1991:3) has criticized contemporary scholars for downplaying the importance of the colonial encounter. He writes, "Anthropologists . . . have resisted the implications of colonial history and transcultural exchange for the sorts of people typically studied. . . . Such a perspective seems also to depend upon a radical denial of history." Because anthropologists wish to present their subject peoples as "pristine," Thomas argues, they have minimized the importance of historical events that have brought various types of outsiders into contact with colonized peoples. These events "are part of a shared history which has continuing ramifications in the process of 'development.'"

Unfortunately, Thomas's criticisms ring all too true. Although anthropologists can broaden studies of the colonial history by integrating the perspectives of the local people with whom we work, we rarely have done so. Narratives such as Moll's, when combined with Western views of history and with biographical and autobiographical accounts of other actors, particularly those typically underrepresented in public histories (see Lepowsky's account of Elizabeth Mahony, Chap. 8), can shed considerable light on the complex entanglements of the colonial encounter. We hope that, in some small way, the alternative voices presented in this volume have helped to "set the record straight" on colonial New Guinea.

Ten

Three-Day Visitors
The Samo Response to Colonialism
in Western Province, Papua New Guinea

R. Daniel Shaw

Not long after established contact and the designation of village sites on
the Strickland Plain of Papua New Guinea, a young, energetic, Australian
government patrol officer entered the village of Kwobi. Anxious to do his
job, he inspected the community, noting with satisfaction the presence
of two recently constructed longhouses. However, his inspection did not
turn up any latrines, and since the officer's handbook said there were to
be latrines for every family, he ordered the government interpreters to
instruct the people in the art of building outhouses. The people of
Kwobi, anxious to please, did as they were instructed and not only built,
but dutifully used the little houses for their intended purpose. A year
passed, and another officer entered the community to take a census and
keep in touch with the native population. Upon arrival, he nearly became
sick from the odor hanging over the community. Recognizing the source
of the stench, he ordered that the maggot infested outhouses be burned.
That done, the Samo happily returned to using the forest as was their
custom. About a year later another officer arrived and seeing no latrines,
demanded that the code book be honored and a new round of houses
built. By this time, the Samo had learned both how to please administrative officers and how to maintain their traditions. They built new "small
houses" and then used the forest. Thereafter, they passed inspection and
maintained their own hygienic traditions. (Field notes)[1]

This incident reflects a typical Samo response to colonialism. It demonstrates an active agency in the process of adapting in the postcontact period.
Their response was not just passive acquiescence but surviving in a manner that
enabled them to express through sociopolitical relationships a means of coping
with internal constraints as well as a new set of restraints introduced by outside

agents of change. Although colonialists brought their ideas to bear upon the Samo, they rarely remained long enough to carry them out or see the impact they made— local residence was rarely more than three days. The Samo, for their part, desired to comply with outside requests at least to the extent necessary to maintain harmonious relationships within the rubric of their social structures. Visitors came and went, but the Samo remained. This was their *sa*,[2] their "place," their "land." Their response to colonialism reflects a propensity for developing coping strategies that enabled them to live their lives in accordance with cultural intentions while adapting to the strategies of the outsiders.

Introduction

The Nomad River region in the center of the island of New Guinea was the last to be contacted and officially de-restricted (meaning outsiders could enter without police protection) in November of 1969. This recent contact, even by New Guinea standards, largely factors out the need to establish an ethnographic present and provides a unique opportunity to explore the nature of a contact situation at the end of the colonial period in New Guinea.

This chapter seeks to demonstrate how the interaction between colonizers and indigenous populations combines to establish what Thomas (1994) calls the "colonial project," which allows each side to develop an "interculturality" that is both unique and meaningful (C. M. Shaw 1995). Wagner (1995) demonstrates the need to account for the intent of both the colonialists and those they contacted. The colonialists had an "intent" for the colonized that produced changes, including new "technologies" such as outhouses, that were beyond the purview of the "contacted" peoples. For the Samo, contacted in a near "virgin" context (Ogan 1996b), this was doubly so. They dug the holes and built outhouses, knowing that would please the outsiders, while maintaining their own, more appropriate hygienic practice. Such agency ensured their survival, a reality on which the colonial project depended—were the people not to survive, colonialism by definition would have failed.

My analysis involves appreciating the "socially transformative endeavor," which I take to mean the unfolding of the situation over the life of the outside influence, extending from the early 1960s to the present. As I see it, this requires (1) isolating what "new" thing comes out of the interaction, (2) understanding the intent of both colonial and local agents, and (3) appreciating the interrelationships that impacted colonizers and colonized alike—all of which is integral to the "anthropology of colonialism" as discussed in this volume. As the Samo expanded their understanding of the fringes of their world they were forever changed: human enemies of the precontact era were largely eliminated, and foreigners, who served as a window to the world beyond the rain forest, were added. In short, their understanding of themselves and those around them underwent dramatic transformation.

Colonialism Begins

Soon after my family's arrival in the Samo village of Kwobi, I discerned a growing uneasiness. Despite the local people's apparent delight at showing off their "white family," they began to question how long we would stay. Through our meager knowledge of the language and a helpful interpreter, we tried to communicate our intent to live with them, to learn to speak their language, to document their culture, and eventually to translate the Bible. From conversations with local residents years later, it is obvious all this was completely lost on the people of Kwobi at the time. The only visitors they knew were government officers and missionaries, who always arrived for a particular purpose (to take census, communicate government messages, preach a sermon) and promptly left. Initially we caused them great concern because we had no apparent message to communicate and we quickly outstayed the typical visitor. Rather, we hung out with them, ate their food, learned their language, and, to the extent possible, tried to enter into Samo life—activities never before attempted by visitors. After three years, they included me in an initiation ceremony, providing me with an established identity—we were no longer "visitors"; we belonged there.[3]

Visitors arrived in the Upper Strickland Census Division under three general rubrics—government administrators reflecting political issues, service providers reflecting socioeconomic issues, and missionaries reflecting spiritual issues—all of which included expatriates (primarily from Australia) and nationals from various parts of what is now Papua New Guinea. Below I outline the contact situation on the Strickland Plain that established the intent of colonialism on the one hand, and the Samo response to it on the other.

Government Administration

The Samo were first contacted by a reconnaissance patrol from Kiunga on the Fly River in 1953. Patrol Officer D. G. Calder noted in his journal that "the people were very wary and distrustful of their first sight of white men and did everything possible to side track the patrol . . . and get it out of their tribal boundaries without delay" (1953).

The Samo had to wait until 1959 for a more extended view of the Australian-administered government. In that year, Brian McBride made an extensive patrol throughout the region and, again, the wary Samo were suspicious of visitors.[4] Noting these concerns, McBride (1959) wrote: "The population has had little or no contact and . . . there is no semblance of our ideas of law and order in the area. Tribal fighting, killings, and cannibalism frequently occur and are openly talked about."

Late in 1961 Assistant District Officer Malcolm Lang crossed from Kiunga to establish a patrol post and build an airstrip at the confluence of the Nomad and Homami Rivers. During the eighteen months of station construction, carriers passed by several

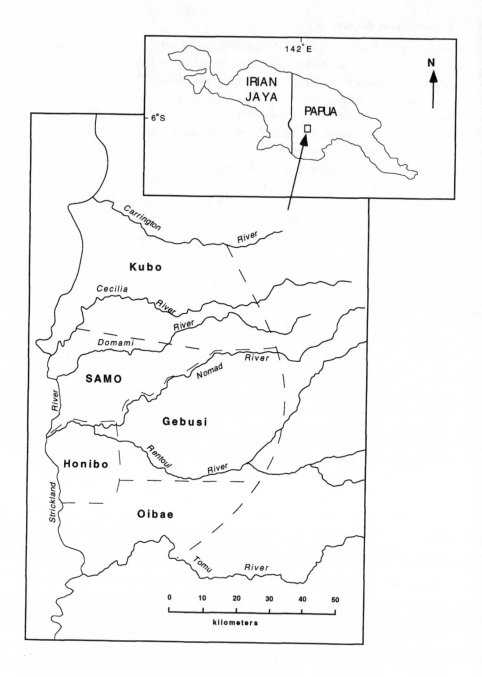

From a map in Rensel and Rodman, Home in the Islands, *University of Hawaii Press, 1997.*
Reprinted by permission of the publisher.

Samo longhouses and eventually the Samo shed their fears and contributed to the work force largely out of curiosity. Those who worked for a month received a steel ax head for their effort. In this way about one hundred steel axes were introduced to the area. By mid-1963, Patrol Officer Ian Douglas noted that steel axes had largely "replaced the traditional stone ax, but in all other respects the Supei[5] are as primitive as their forebears one hundred years ago" (Douglas 1963).

The first census was conducted in 1966. At the same time, headmen and deputies were chosen to serve as government representatives in each designated "rest house" community. As a form of taxation, government work days were established in order to cut and maintain bush tracks for easy access between communities throughout the region. Of particular concern to administrators were the endemic raiding and counter raiding (particularly perpetrated by the Bedamini on the nearby Great Papuan Plateau), subsequent cannibalism, and issues of control (see Brown, Chap. 2). The burgeoning community of Nomad River, situated in the vast rain forest, provided a base of operations from which to administer the entire region.

Support Staff

In support of administrators, a police force,[6] clerks, agricultural and medical assistants, trade store operators, and schoolteachers all began to arrive at Nomad. Initially these individuals were commissioned to assist the overworked patrol officers, but gradually control turned to administrative maintenance, and these colonizers were able to turn their attention to local development and incorporating the Samo into the life of the nation.

In 1973, a team of scientists from Australian National University (ANU) was invited to do a baseline study of the area surrounding Nomad. The team included a biologist, a botanist, a geologist, and a medical doctor.[7] Working together, this group trudged from village to village collecting specimens of flora and fauna, soil and water samples, and examining the geological structure of the region. They also examined the people, taking blood samples and performing physical examinations.

After two weeks, the preliminary conclusions confirmed what was already evident: the well-leached soil was poor, barely supporting forest life. A rich proliferation of hardwoods was found in the forest, but except for local use, this resource was of little economic value because of the difficulty of exporting timber from such a remote region. The geological make up of the district suggested the presence of oil and natural gas, but, again, removal was not feasible. Finally, medical examinations determined that the people were generally malnourished (especially the children) and infested with a proliferation of parasites that made them susceptible to illness and disease, a fact made painfully evident two years earlier when a flu epidemic had decimated nearly 10 percent of the entire population. The study enabled the administration to bring in specialists as time went on. Along with government personnel came other trappings of civilization: schools, medical facilities, stores, and mission activity.

Mission

Following close on the heels of the administrative presence at Nomad, missionaries of the Asia Pacific Christian Mission arrived and set out to build a small airstrip at Hanonabi, about seven miles northwest of Nomad. Then they encouraged indigenous pastors from the Gogodala region far to the south to evangelize the Samo. Pastors, however, found themselves in strange territory and rarely stayed for more than two years.

The Seventh-Day Adventists established small church-schools at Nomad and two Samo villages in 1971. However, they were unsuccessful in their attempt to open an airstrip among the Kubo at Tiyamobi in 1977, and their use of Tok Pisin and interpreters rather than the vernacular resulted in their having minimal impact upon the Samo.

The missionary intent of this group of outsiders focused on encouraging the Samo to convert to Christianity and join congregations all across the nation who based their faith and values on the Bible. What the Samo understood, however, was a negative message based on what they could not do (raid, eat human meat, eat pork, chew betel nut, drink kava, and perform their rituals and ceremonies). This negative approach produced misunderstandings that were only corrected when translated portions of the Bible allowed the Samo to go beyond their understanding of both government and mission and begin to appropriate God's intent to interact with human beings. God's Word, they discovered, was in contrast to the behavior of government officers and missionary pastors. Neither, it seemed, were in line with Samo expectations about human relationships or the spiritual world surrounding them, as attested by the Bible.

Anthropologist

To this list of foreigners I must add my family and myself. Spurred by a list of "urgent research" areas around the world (Reining 1967), I conducted an initial linguistic survey in December of 1969 under the auspices of the Summer Institute of Linguistics (SIL). In February 1970, we went to live in the village of Kwobi, five miles north of Nomad River. In the course of the next twelve years, we lived among the Samo about 50 percent of the time. The Samo subsequently incorporated us into their community life.[8] But as they were with other visitors, the Samo were initially unsure of our intentions and viewed us with suspicion. The demise of our first house provided an example of the Samo response to us and our respective development of relationships over time.

> After eight years of habitation, our house is beginning to totter on its posts. I discovered this today when Rick came running into my office

to give me a demonstration of his growing strength. I followed him under the house, where he put his arms around a post and began to move it about—it had completely rotted through just below ground level. He was proud of his strength, but I feared for our safety. I subsequently called my brothers from the village and encouraged Rick to demonstrate his strength to them. When they saw the post move, they fell into gales of laughter. I failed to see the humor and sought an explanation. Recovering their composure, they asked, "How long have you lived in this house?" My response was common knowledge—eight years. More raucous laughter. "It's amazing," they said, "that the junk wood we brought for you to build this house has lasted so long. We have all had to rebuild our houses several times, but yours has lasted eight years—amazing." They went on to explain that when we came, the longest an outsider had stayed among them was three days. They did not understand what outside interest could possibly keep a foreigner there for a prolonged period. So they brought the most accessible and easily collected wood to build our house. Now that they knew our objectives, and they had incorporated us into their cultural system, they would build us a real house. (Personal journal)

They were true to their word, and today the "new" house (built in 1978) still stands, a monument to Samo building expertise and architectural design. When visitors arrive today and ask about longhouses, they are taken to see that house.

With this background, I now discuss issues outsiders brought to their interaction with the Samo, namely, eliminating raiding and its subsequent cannibalism, initiating village nucleation, and encouraging regional development. The Samo, in turn, responded to these issues in their typical survival mode. For them, this was manifested by an intentional adjustment to the colonial project while maintaining their own identity through harmonious relationships.

Colonial Issues and Samo Responses

The culture of colonialism on the Strickland Plain began as outsiders brought themselves and their values to a new context. Over time, two governments (colonial and national) established and maintained an administrative presence, and two missions vied for the hearts and souls of the people. Government support staff were intent upon encouraging development and assisting the people in their national integration, while missionary pastors focused on conversion in order to bring Samo beliefs and practices into line with Christians in other parts of the nation. Into this context, I weave my own intent to understand the Samo in terms that reflected their values while attempting to integrate that understanding with the values of a translated Bible.[9]

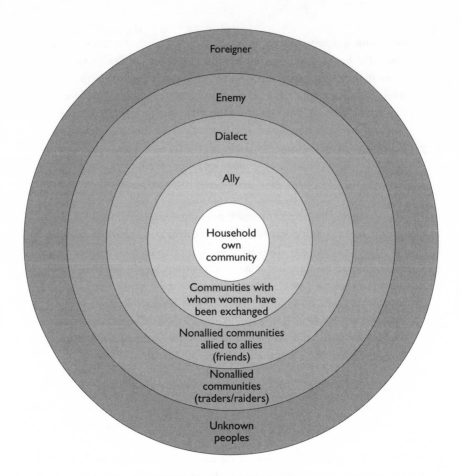

A Network of Social Relationships

Raiding and Cannibalism

Prior to contact, Samo social structure revolved around members of a single household isolated in the forest and utilizing the land to maximize their survival. Each longhouse was occupied by 25 to 75 people who, in turn, protected themselves from enemies through a carefully orchestrated network of alliances with other households established when men arranged sister exchanges (Shaw 1974). The reciprocity resulting from this exchange of females required allied males to cooperate in a supportive network that placed each community at the heart of a self-created, protective circle, making a surprise raid by enemies less likely and providing the human resources to mount a counter raid in the event of a breach of security (see figure above). Allies, then, provided the protection necessary to enable a community to survive in what they perceived to be a hostile environment in which enemies, though at the fringe of their network, had a strategic affect on their lifestyle.

Trading was often a prelude to raiding. The geography of the region made trading for goods essential. Limestone for mixing with betel nut, granite for stone axes, soft stones for making ochre paint, and fibers for string bags all had specific allocations. Because trading was organized to procure goods not otherwise available within the region, it required going beyond the protection of the alliance structure. At the same time, trading afforded an opportunity to view the houses and the layout of surroundings, providing valuable information for a future raiding party. Thus, women and children were carefully secluded, and men on both sides of the displayed goods were wary of each other.

Administrative Officers

Into this aboriginal environment came foreigners (both *bou*, "light-skinned," and *kooohage*, "dark-skinned") from beyond the known extremities of the Samo world (cf. Nash, Chap. 7).[10] From the Samo view, these outsiders necessitated incorporation into their social structure in order to be understood. Though at the fringe of Samo social structure, these newcomers were not enemies to be raided; rather, they brought a cessation of raiding. In due course, foreigners replaced allies in the protective role so crucial to the precontact social structure. Thus magistrates, judges, and courts became part of an extended alliance structure that enabled the Samo to interface with an ever expanding world. Conversely, foreigners viewed themselves as operating under a mandate extending back to Paul (later Sir Paul) Hasluck. This, they reasoned, gave them the right to "bring the Samo out of the stone age and into the twentieth century." Administrators and Samo alike had an agency respective to the other that communicated intent and demanded response.

Australian administrators, assisted by an extensive national police force, quickly established "control" with demonstrations of power. One of their first administrative objectives was to put an end to raiding and cannibalism. All reports of such activity were quickly followed up.

> On an early census patrol, the interpreters heard about a raid on a Kubo longhouse to the north. Upon hearing the story the officer returned to Nomad for police reinforcements and then proceeded to launch his own "raid" upon the Komifia raiders. Surrounding the house in the predawn darkness, several police entered the house and apprehended the men, bringing them to Nomad for trial. (Personal journal)

One early book about the region (Anderson 1970) detailed the administration's response to a raid among the Bedamini. These dwellers of the Papuan Plateau were particularly recalcitrant and kept the *kiaps* busy searching out and bringing raiders to justice.[11] The perpetrators of raids were tried and sent off for extensive jail terms (typically five to seven years) in the provincial capital at Daru.[12] Samo stories about Bedamini raids were frequent and portrayed both brutality and a focus on food as a primary rationale. When collecting texts for linguistic analysis, my wife came upon a group of children acting out a raid and a cannibalistic feast in front of their house. Accompanied by appropriate animation, the children said:

> The Biami [Samo name for Bedamini] come for the purpose of killing. Having hit, they cut you up and stuff you into a string bag. Having stuffed you, they carry you home. Arriving home they cut you up. Having cut you up, they put you with sago and greens for the purpose of cooking. Having cooked you, they eat you. That is all. (Elicited language text)

Cannibalism continued as an expected outcome of a raid—activity supported by a common aphorism that "a certain pitch in a baby's cry indicated that only human meat would satisfy." The administrative efforts to eliminate raiding subsequently reduced opportunities for cannibalism, and by pacification in 1969, cannibalism was little more than a memory (albeit vivid) for most people in the region. However, despite the available bounty of protein-rich foods such as sago grubs, forest animals of all kinds, including cassowary, wild boar, many different marsupials, crocodile, and a rich bird life, the administration-perceived need for protein in the Samo diet became the rationale for introducing certain crops, as I will discuss shortly.

Although the law required a government response to raiding, cannibalism was largely treated as a "custom," a local manifestation of behavior that, though contrary to "civilized" activity, was not criminal. In a test case documented in the Australian press, seven Gebusi men (a related dialect south of the Homami River; see Knauft 1985) were brought to trial at the district headquarters in Daru. Judge J. Prentice subsequently dismissed the case. Basing his ruling on extant Queensland laws, he responded that

> on a full consideration of the evidence I have come to the conclusion that the conduct of the Yulabi villagers and of the man from Dadalibi in eating the body of the deceased Sabasigi villager, in all the circumstances of the case, was neither improper nor indecent behaviour on their part, being normal and reasonable behaviour for them as most primitive villagers living in the Gabusi area of the Nomad Sub District in early 1971, in the limited condition of pacification and administration to which that area had then been reduced. (Report 1973)

Given the absence of legal precedent on cannibalism and the value of local custom regarding the proper disposal of a body, Judge Prentice had no choice but to acquit the accused who had no part in the preceding murder. These seven men, therefore, had only engaged in what reporters labeled "a bizarre funeral" (*Pacific Islands Monthly*, September, 1971:47). The court contended that under the Queensland Criminal Code, which served as the jurisdiction for Papua prior to its independence in 1975, cannibalism was little more than "improper and indecent interference" with a corpse, and thus the accused were sent home.

Though this may have been the "point of law," the broader public, represented by agriculturalists, teachers, and pastors, were not amused. For them, not only was murder inappropriate, but consuming the remains of the deceased in a feasting atmosphere was beyond their sensibility. This ever expanding "public" assisted government administrators in their effort to bring civilization to this remote region. They built and maintained the airstrip, housing, and administrative buildings at Nomad, but also introduced material culture and sought to ameliorate the Samo propensity for cannibalism by altering their diet. Accordingly, the Samo began to interact with this group of well-intentioned but often culturally naive individuals.[13]

Agriculturalists

Prominent among those providing support services were agricultural officers who sought to improve the people's diet by adding protein, the lack of which was perceived by the administration as being in some way linked to cannibalism. In their travels around the area, agricultural specialists introduced crops that took little care, could be grown in the forest environment, and could add significant nutrition. Accordingly, squash, corn, and peanuts were introduced to supplement a painfully bland, uninteresting diet (the outsiders' view) of sago, greens, and plantains. Seeds for the introduced crops could easily be carried on patrols, along with instructions for the care and harvest of the plants. In addition, legumes (such as peanuts) would add protein and at the same time enrich the leached-out soil. Agriculturalists, hoping to create a more nutritious diet, also instructed people to combine fruits and vegetables (including coconut) with sago. Outsiders who traveled in the area always brought their food with them and thereby introduced a variety of new foods. In this way *saporas*, a type of lime, were tossed out and in some cases took root and grew to produce reasonably good fruit. Today lime trees are part of every village. Similarly, papaya, pineapple, tomatoes, and other nutritious fruits and vegetables were introduced. At first, the new produce did not match the Samo palate, but gradually the Samo increased the amount of introduced fruits and vegetables they planted in small, fenced-in gardens near their villages. Eventually this supplemented the forest produce and reduced the amount of time people needed to spend foraging for food.

The intent of agricultural specialists was to provide additional foods and new sources of protein for the Samo, thereby reinforcing the strenuous efforts by the *kiaps* to reduce raiding. It was another group of outsiders, the teachers and mission pastors, who reflected the reaction of the general population to cannibalism.

Teachers

Government teachers arrived at Nomad in 1967 and established a school primarily for the children of the growing number of staff, particularly policemen, necessary for government control. However, some of the children of Samo interpreters and others living near Nomad began to attend the school. Though many were older than their grade level indicated, they were eager to learn and proved to be reasonably good students.[14] Through their teaching, it became clear that teachers abhorred cannibalism. Though rarely part of a lesson, their attitudes toward Samo life often came through in their discussions with youngsters, who, in turn, took these ideas home and discussed them with their parents. Consequently, a perception that cannibalism was bad gradually permeated Samo consciousness.

Pastors

While *kiaps* were busy dealing with raiding from an administrative perspective, mission-sponsored pastors were busy preaching sermons that reflected a religious morality they hoped would convert the "savage mind." The mission station and accompanying airstrip at Hanonabi initially represented Christianity to inquisitive Samo. Airstrip construction was punctuated with sermons telling what God expected of human beings. Gradually the Samo came to understand the Christian message as a list of taboos, which, they quickly realized, closely matched what they were being told by government officers and teachers alike. Principal among these prohibitions were raiding and cannibalism.

Identified with neither government nor mission, I sought to independently understand the context within which Samo presuppositions clashed with external prohibitions. Using their own norms and cultural expectations, I sought to provide a biblical perspective. On the subject of cannibalism, the Bible was unclear. Though I intuitively knew God would not have condoned it, I could not point to chapter and verse. However, in the process of translating the Book of Genesis, we arrived at the place where God talks to Noah after the flood and lays down some principles for living. In the narrative, God expresses regret for having wiped out so many people and tells Noah that he does not want humans or animals taking the life of other human beings. An extract from my journal continues the story:

> When we got to Genesis chapter nine, where God tells Noah that human beings should not take the life of another, Hogooanobiayo became indignant: "You mean God doesn't want us going on cannibal raids?" He went on to explain that the government had come and said raiding was bad and put the men they caught into prison. Similarly missionaries had come condemning cannibalism. Frustrated, he blurted out, "No one ever told us why." He concluded that finally, through the Bible story, they had a rationale for the cessation of what they considered to be normative behavior.

With this new understanding, he reasoned, "God, who made human beings, did not want other human beings to take matters into their own
hands—he alone was the giver and taker of life." This perspective was in
keeping with their understanding of interaction within the social context
of a community but offered new insight into their interaction with enemies and outsiders. (Personal journal)

Indeed, both government and mission had reduced behavior to a list of prohibitions against much of what the Samo had traditionally considered normative. The
style of life they substituted made little sense to the Samo. Hearing a story from the
Bible, however, resonated with their understanding of relationships. The focus was
not on murder or even what to do with the body of an enemy, but rather on their
relationship with God, and subsequently with each other. It was the discourse
genre that enabled the Samo to respond—the story, rather than a list of rules,
made sense. For the Samo the focus shifted to cosmic and social harmony and away
from simply doing what they were told. Bible translation served as a medium of
effective communication to which the Samo responded. Anthropologically, this
necessitated a probe into the religious and social expectations of the Samo (c.f.
Shaw 1990, 1996). Again, my dual role as anthropologist and translator impacted
my own understanding of the context and reflected on the Samo response to the
ministrations of government and mission personnel alike.

Village Nucleation

In reducing raiding and cannibalism, outsiders largely assumed for the Samo the
role of protector. If they were protected from the raiding activity of enemies, then
the rationale for living in isolated longhouses scattered throughout the forest no
longer obtained. This presented the Samo with a whole new set of relationships
based on their understanding of both the natural and the spiritual world. The
former was seen to be under the jurisdiction of government personnel and con-
comitant support staff, while the latter fell under the missionary purview.

Without doubt, government protection was not Patrol Officer Ian Douglas's
objective when, weary of searching out what he considered to be nomadic peoples,
he declared it was time to establish sites in the forest where people could gather for
administrative purposes. His objective was ease of administration and establishing viable villages, as is clear from his patrol report (1963): "In due course these
rest houses may well act as magnets, drawing in the various outlying houses as their
current dwellings become uninhabitable. In this way the area would be eventually
reduced to eight or nine villages worthy of that name, thus greatly easing the job of
administering the area."

Indeed, this was almost prophetic, because over the next ten years the Samo did
move to these sites as their houses fell into disrepair and they were forced to rebuild. Not wanting to spend undue amounts of time traveling from a forest-house

site to the nearest government rest house, and never knowing when someone might show up demanding a hearing, they began the process of establishing new communities at the government-designated localities. As already noted, a longhouse community was a caring, extended family that served as the primary socioeconomic and political unit, engineering its future survival through the effective distribution of its women in order to establish a protective network of alliances. Those communities that were most closely allied to each other congregated in order to form new social units that came to be known as *gaboo monsoon*, or "white man said place." The openness that resulted from building multiple-house communities in a cleared space in the rain forest also created a greater opportunity for observation and attack by human enemies. Hence, the protective value of the administration, realized through inhibiting raiding, was central to the success of household aggregation.

Census Requires a Name

Keeping track of people as they moved into villages was a further responsibility of administrative patrols. The initial census was taken in mid-1966. When taking a census, the officials questioned the native people and carefully recorded their responses. The first question was always: "What is your name?" Out of fear of upsetting the spiritual relationship with the ancestors no Samo ever directly answers this question.[15] Therefore, in order to respond, many Samo came up with fictitious names, which they thereafter called their "census name"—often a nonsensical string of syllables or references to the circumstances around them, such as "thorn in my foot," "under a palm tree," or "standing in front of a table."[16] Without meaning or frequent use, however, these names were often forgotten by the next census, which resulted in an amusing tangle of names that caused *kiaps* no end of frustration. Fitzpatrick reports on his 1971 patrol that the census was "very trying, with many people forgetting the names they had used at other census takings." He frequently mentions spending the evening compiling statistics and rewriting the village books.

Early census takers made a point of telling people to remain in the place where their names were written in a "village book." As a result, some people actually changed their place of residence in order to accommodate what the book said. Those who did not move either incurred the wrath of the next census officer or learned of a census in time to rush to "their village" before the census patrol arrived. This example from the village of Mogwibi was typical.

> Wohonlen, a man from Fogoisu longhouse to the north of the Cecilia River, was visiting his allies at a longhouse near the present site of Mogwibi when the first census patrol arrived there in late 1967. Since his name was recorded in that location, he felt compelled to remain there. Some weeks later he returned with his wife and small baby boy and joined the Mogwibi community.

Also visiting Mogwibi was Bugooin, a man who had recently married a Mogwibi woman. There had been a raid in which two women and a man had been killed while processing sago. While the men were discussing the possibility of launching a counter-raid, the census patrol arrived and Bugooin's name went into the Mogwibi village book. Bugooin was persuaded to remain there, and soon after, he brought his wife back to her natal community to settle. (Field notes)

Such historical accidents are reflective of adjustments that people living throughout the Nomad region had to make. Villages had their basis in the cultural rubric of alliance. Longhouse communities had previously engineered their alliance structure to maximize protection. Under the rubric of protection, the collective group now occupying a village began to apply the same rationale to relationships with other villages and to extend alliances to provide for the spiritual protection the government could not guarantee.

Villages Protect from Spiritual Enemies

As longhouses were built in close proximity to government rest houses, people began to exploit the forest in the immediate vicinity. Gardens were planted, sago was processed, and the forest was gradually pushed away from the habitation site. As the distance between forest and houses grew, protection from *hogai* (evil forest beings) increased. The increasing space between a village and the surrounding forest created a spiritual buffer zone that Patrol Officer Douglas could not have anticipated.

The protective value of this space around a village contributed to the growth of the Christian community at Hanonabi. With its airstrip, a growing number of buildings, and a retreating forest, this community attracted more and more people, whom the pastors assumed were all interested in Christianity. However, the administration recognized Hanonabi only as a mission station and not as an administrative site. Therefore, administrators encouraged people living there to return to their villages for census, work-day projects, and other government-recognized activity, resulting in a considerable flow of traffic and well-worn trails to nearby villages. This development of an infrastructure for contact with each other and with the administration served as yet another Samo response to colonialism that, in turn, helped the Samo prepare for self-determination.

Regional Development

As the 1960s gave way to the 1970s, the region was derestricted and villages were established, allowing colonialists to turn their attention to introducing services and assisting the people in becoming more "civilized" and fostering development commensurate with the rest of the nation, whose people were rapidly approaching self-determination and independence. Central to this development was the need for easy access between communities.

Administrative Taxation

Nomad River was a growing town that served as the hub for the entire region. Connecting villages dispersed throughout the expanse of jungle and swamp that characterizes this portion of Western Province were essential for effective administration. To provide the labor force for such an enterprise, the administration implemented a tax. Because the forest was the source of the people's only livelihood and they therefore had no money for taxes, the administration set up a labor tax, requiring people to devote one day per week for "government work." In the beginning, this took the form of clearing the necessary bush tracks for easy access between newly established villages and the administrative center. Later, road construction for four-wheel-drive vehicles, village and school maintenance, and any other form of community service came under the taxation rubric.[17]

Taxation was not a concept that made any sense to the Samo. To begin with, they liked their forest the way it was. Initially they viewed the bush tracks as ways to assist enemies who might use them to implement an attack—remaining isolated was one rationale for moving a household about communal territory in order to avoid detection. Furthermore, this work to pay taxes was viewed as an onerous interruption of the important work necessary for daily survival. Cutting bush tracks only one day per week extended some projects beyond belief and often wore supervising police, interpreters, and village headmen to a frazzle. Moreover, the Samo had no sense of marking days of the week and often showed up on the wrong day. Clearly, government expectations of work for taxes were not understood and were consequently abused by people who did not like to be so occupied. People frequently disappeared or had "urgent" responsibilities that took them away on government workdays.

Despite these interruptions, villages were eventually connected and support personnel were able to have relatively easy access to the communities surrounding Nomad River. Patrol reports always included a notation on the condition of tracks/roads. Besides administrative patrols, those who provided support services began to gather at Nomad River in order to implement the suggestions from the ANU report.

Driven by both government and mission agendas, support personnel—including agricultural and medical officers, teachers, entrepreneurs, and pastors—came to give assistance to the people and improve the quality of their lives and livelihood. It was their values and intent of goodwill that precipitated a Samo response that was often misunderstood.

Agricultural Projects

An early, well-meaning attempt to assist the Samo in their need for cash demonstrated the clash of values between administration and local people. The increasing need for money to pay school fees and buy goods led an observant young agricultural officer to introduce chilies as a cash crop. When government-chartered aircraft brought supplies, the planes frequently departed Nomad empty. Back-loading local produce for sale to an external market could be an answer to the people's need for cash. Noting this pattern, the *didiman* (Tok Pisin: agricultural officer) reasoned that chilies were easy to grow, required minimal care, were lightweight for easy transport, and were a valuable crop on the world market. Acting on this knowledge, he ordered some seed and instructed interpreters to educate the Samo about this new source of economic vitality for the region.

Skeptical at first, but desirous of cash, the Samo obediently began to plant chili bushes in small gardens as well as along paths and around houses.[18] In keeping with the Samo division of labor, women dutifully cared for the plants through the bearing stage, and then picked and dried the fruit. The agricultural officer was excited about the first intake. The crop was abundant and the market such that he could offer top dollar. The Samo were equally pleased and headed for the closest tradestore to spend their money or turned school fees over to teachers. However, chilies require constant harvesting to maintain the quality of a bush—a fact not accounted for by the *didiman*. Eventually, the Samo need for cash slackened, and they responded by picking chilies only when they needed money. This, in turn, resulted in a decreasing crop, and most bushes eventually dried up. Though disappointed that a cash source had deteriorated, the Samo could never understand the value of a food that hurt the mouth and had no flavor. For most, it was simply another manifestation of foreign irrationality. Within two years there were virtually no chili bushes left (except around my house), and people had forgotten the allure of cash cropping.

In fairness, the *didiman* had done his job: researching the need, determining an effective and cheap means of transport, selecting a product that was lightweight and had high market value. His well-meaning attempt went astray not for lack of involvement, but because he did not understand the Samo context. They already spent one day per week away from their own subsistence activity to pay taxes. Producing chilies was a side issue that provided luxuries they could live without. For centuries they had effectively utilized the forest without having children go to school, without tradestores, and without money. At this stage in their development they saw little benefit in these accouterments of civilization. The tradestores sold clothes (ill-fitting and of poor quality), food (tasty and sometimes exotic), and some utensils (lamps, cookware, bush knives, and axes), but all at an exorbitant price for items that were rarely necessary. Time spent to earn money carrying goods for patrols, doing contract labor, or even selling local produce to outsiders at Nomad or Hanonabi took them away from their daily labors and placed an added burden on people engaged in traditional activities necessary for personal survival.

In response to the ANU report of poor, leached-out soil, another agricultural officer decided to focus on the survival aspect of Samo livelihood by trying to improve the quantity and quality of produce. Accordingly, he set out to demonstrate the slash-and-burn technique of forest utilization. He chose the month of March to cut a small patch of forest near Nomad and invited village headmen from throughout the region to come and view his handiwork. When they arrived, however, the heavy rainfall, typical in March, made burning the underbrush and logs impossible. It was July before the plot dried to the extent that the *didiman* was able to burn the brush and plant a garden. By then the soil was so leached from torrential rains that the garden would not grow without massive amounts of fertilizer delivered by government-chartered aircraft. The Samo shook their heads knowingly and returned to their time-honored seasonal cycle that called for planting during July and August when there was a minimum of rain. Furthermore, they allowed the new shoots to be protected by the forest canopy, which they cut only when certain the crop would take hold and bear to fruition. Not only did they know the forest and its habits, but they also had no money for fertilizer, much less for chartered aircraft. Clearly, under the circumstances, the Samo way was best for them. An embarrassed *didiman* learned a valuable lesson in paying attention to the local agricultural cycle and styles of utilization. Schieffelin (1975) reports a similar pattern among the Kaluli on the northern slopes of Mt. Bosavi.

Despite such setbacks, the need for cash in dealing with the encroaching world did not diminish, and many further attempts to introduce cash cropping were made. The crops tried included sweet potatoes (pig food from the Samo perspective) to sell to government policemen and their families, who often came from the highlands; coffee (bitter and too hot to drink), which was only of interest to expatriates and was expensive to transport, not to mention painstaking to produce; and even rubber (smelly, sticky, and useless, as the Samo saw it), which requires at least seven years to begin producing and then demands specific care as well as expensive transport. Though these endeavors were instigated by well-meaning individuals, the complexities of the environment and the temporary nature of staff assignments to Nomad (few government personnel could follow through on what they began) contributed to the failure of most projects. Replacement officers had their own new ideas and sought to implement these, often to the detriment of previous projects.

Medical Assistance

As the network of roads connected Samo communities to Nomad River, access to medical assistance improved. A large clinic was established at Nomad and a medical orderly assigned who made frequent patrols to instruct people in basic hygiene. The people's response to apparent medical miracles was enthusiastic. Injections seemed to cure the dreaded sores and eventual disfigurement of yaws. Pills could, overnight, put an end to malarial chills and fevers. Early success in treating pneumonia (the most frequent cause of death) with penicillin encouraged the Samo to seek medical assistance. However, many were brought in with advanced stages of illness and when they died despite the best efforts of medical personnel, the Samo lost confidence and would not allow people to remain in a "doctor's" care over-night. This eventually led to the government establishing aid posts with attendant orderlies in key villages and upgrading the Nomad clinic to a regional medical cen-ter with a resident doctor and nurses.

However, the Samo view of quality health care often diverged considerably from the concerns of outside orderlies. What the medical orderlies considered to be assistance to the people was often taken negatively by the Samo—viewed as an af-front to their sensibility. So, for example, the modesty of Samo women prevented male medical staff from assisting them in matters of pregnancy and childbirth. This resulted in a high incidence of death in childbirth and of infant mortality continuing long after contact. The use of increasing numbers of female nurses and medical doctors by government and mission alike has improved the situation, re-versing the high incidence of infant mortality and turning an earlier 8 percent population decline into a 10 percent population increase during the 1990s. A fe-male mission doctor makes regular visits to villages for maternal and infant care. Additionally, some aid-post orderlies were equipped with two-way radios that could be used to call in an aircraft for a medical emergency—a practice that saved many lives.

Education

Prominent in the development of the region was the education of Samo children. Government and mission alike developed schools—proximity and a place for chil-dren to stay served as the criteria for where children went to school. At Hanonabi, a school was built and a new grade added each year. Teachers were imported, and soon the noise of children learning reverberated across the playground and around the community.

Samo children have done well in national exams and many have gone on to trade schools and, upon completion, returned home to assist their people. Ap-proximately 50 percent of the present adult population have been educated through at least grade three. This means they are able to read at a basic level, do simple math computations, and understand the broader political context of pro-vincial and national government. Given this basic awareness, they can comprehend newscasts on the radio, listen to and respond to simple English, and communicate more effectively using the national trade languages. Many of the students now fit back into village life and can help their elders understand the changes taking place.

Village Tradestores

A more recent response to the need for cash has been investment in tradestores. Sev-eral villages have, under the direction of grade-six graduates, established cooperative stores to generate the capital necessary to purchase goods. Profits have been redistrib-uted to those who contributed, thereby enabling them to pay school fees and handle other matters requiring cash. Many, however, reinvested their funds to be used as the cooperative needed them, thereby accumulating interest while enabling the project to succeed. Such successes have produced a sense of well-being and financial control never possible in the "cash-crop" era. Nevertheless, those crops, together with contract labor and occasional work for the government or its ancillary staff, produced the capital necessary for investing in the first place.

Culturally Appropriate Response

In fairness to the foreigners who frequented the Nomad Patrol Post, many were genuinely interested in the people. Their objective, despite the inevitable misunderstandings, was the development of people throughout the region. Though not well trained anthropologically, many outsiders showed an interest in local customs and sometimes struggled with the clash of personal responses and administrative responsibility.

The transition from expatriate to national administration further illustrates outside influence and disjunction with local values. Independence in 1975 represented a transformation Mave O'Collins called "neo-colonial" (1979). Nationals, she maintained, continued the colonialist attitudes and practices of their predecessors. Those who trained at the Administrative College in Port Moresby soon found themselves in remote places like Nomad River. In the transitional years from 1973 to 1975, expatriate officers introduced national officers to the rigors of administrating native peoples. Former police and other Papua New Guineans themselves became colonial officers. This transition from colonial to neocolonial government meant little change for the Samo. What the retiring Australian officers began, Papua New Guineans continued. The *kooahage*, "national outsiders," came from regions of the country where there had been a hundred or more years of contact. These men had little appreciation for the circumstances under which the Samo lived. In fact, the Samo lifestyle was as remote to them as it was to the expatriate officers who preceded them. The reactions of national teachers, medical personnel, and others who frequented Nomad clearly indicated they did not understand such a "primitive context," and they sought to remove the Samo from it with haste. This same attitude was reflected in other parts of PNG, where people from outside the geocosms of the local populations simply did not comprehend the context of the native people nor were they able to deal with such differing sociopolitical values (Scheiffelin and Crittenden 1991).

I recall an incident when a magistrate from New Britain presided over a case of what a teacher considered "bridal abuse." Acting in accordance with the custom of taking an unsuspecting girl from her natal community and introducing her to the new husband, a group of men were literally dragging a kicking and screaming woman who, in so doing, demonstrated her character by attempting to escape. Responding to the ruckus, a teacher had interrupted the proceedings and taken the entire group to Nomad in order to inflict justice upon these "ignorant savages." My journal continues the story:

Early Friday morning, Hogalibo and I went to Nomad to discuss the matter with the magistrate. I tried to impart some cross-cultural understanding and compassion for customs beyond his experience. I explained the importance of women demonstrating their value through the display of uncooperativeness. . . . I also explained the need for the exchange to be completed in order to establish an alliance between the two communities. The rationale for the rather harsh treatment of the woman was to ensure that she arrive at the destination and the marriage alliance be completed with all haste.

During my exposé, the magistrate nodded his understanding and reiterated stories he had heard from old men about their own marriage customs. Though the customs were not the same and had not been practiced in his region for many years, the magistrate acknowledged the right of the Samo to express their customs so long as they did not interfere with the laws of the country. We then went out to the flimsy jailhouse, where he verified my analysis of Samo marriage with the incarcerated wedding party. Hoga was still, appropriately, sulking, and the men were no longer brash and strong. Using Hiri Motu, he questioned them about their activities in light of what he had learned from me. The men supported my analysis and hung their heads while the magistrate cautioned them about being so rough on women and about their need to fit into the larger national society. He thereupon released them. Their animated discussion all the way home and the subsequent conclusion to the exchange demonstrated that all was well with marriage alliances in Samoland. However, they were understandably cautious about displaying their culture before the teachers for some time after that. (Personal journal)

For me, the amazing thing about this incident was the power one outside teacher had to halt the procession and hand the entire exchange party over to the "authorities." Clearly, Papua New Guineans have replaced the Australian officers of yesteryear as authority figures. Although my Samo brothers had more physical power than the teacher, the latter represented outside authority and so they acquiesced and went to Nomad with him. Foreigners with dark skins exhibit paternalism and carry on the outside dialogue just as their light-skinned instructors did. For their part, the Samo maintained their basic approach to economic and social viability within the structure of the contact situation. For them, the culture of contact was an extension of aboriginal beliefs and values within the framework of villages, connecting roads, and the encroachment of the outside world.[19] Foreigners were "other" regardless of skin tone, which made little difference to the way the Samo perceived the ministrations of those who saw themselves as benefactors.

Conclusion

Truly, the Samo know how to survive in their world, and they received visitors based on their understanding of that world. Outside views, even when they didn't make much sense, were greeted with respect based on perceived outside power and a desire for harmonious relationship. In short, the Samo initially responded to outsiders with suspicion in much the same way they treated traders and enemies prior to contact. When the outside community grew at Nomad, regardless of personnel turnover, it became clear to them that the authority of outside influence was not going away. Thus, their response was to build relationship in some way. In my family's case, that relationship was cemented through trust and close interaction consummated by my initiation. For government and mission personnel, the relationship was somewhat tenuous yet permanent, and outsiders were accordingly incorporated into the social structures. In fact, the reality of Samo life today is a product of their adaptive response to outside influence within a structure that makes sense to them. In the process of adapting, they have (1) established "new" structures, (2) interpreted the colonial intent vis-à-vis their own understanding, and (3) responded to the circumstances by establishing new interrelationships—all of which corroborates Nicholas Thomas's (1994) "colonial project" and redefines visitors for the Samo.

It is important to recognize that there is no notion of pan–New Guinea-ness when discussing the nature of colonialism in its various manifestations throughout this book. As several other contributors to this volume note, the colonial effort was largely designed to encourage native peoples to interface with the world at large, not to bring the world to the people. Thus, in the Samo context, much activity today revolves around precedents set during colonialism. Many "new" aspects of life exist that were not extant at the point of contact: living in villages, work-day activities, church attendance, schools, tradestores, clinics, and other manifestations of what the colonizers consider an improved quality of life, including outhouses. Yet, despite this heavy colonial agency, the Samo have adapted all these changes to their particular interests and needs, which include harmonious relationships within an adjusted alliance structure, greater protection as well as contact with each other through a network of roads, and corporate worship designed to consolidate spiritual power, including use of the Bible, to handle problems of daily living. An increasingly educated and literate population is able to respond by adjusting these outside issues to its own transforming structures. The agents of change are both outsiders bringing their issues and insiders responding to those issues in ways that allow them to maintain their cultural identity while incorporating change that enables them to join other colonized New Guineans in the "nation of a thousand tribes," as Albert Maori Kiki (1968) liked to call it.

For the colonialists, the culture of contact is now largely sustained by memories, dusty patrol reports, dog-eared photo albums, and yellowing letters. Their legacy, however, remains imprinted upon the people long after their visitations are over. The Samo have accomplished the goals set for them by these outsiders: raiding and cannibalism are but a memory of the aged, as is the wandering nomadic existence or aboriginal paganism. These former elements of Samo life have been replaced by peaceful coexistence with old enemies; nuclear families and individuated housing in aggregated villages; cultivation rather than foraging; Western education that teaches outside values, health care, cash cropping and tradestore capitalism; and, finally, Christianity represented by a book.

Colonialism came in with young patrol officers demonstrating their power by killing a pig and ended with an elaborate system of roads connecting permanent, but often deserted, villages. These structures represent a "new" interculturality that is neither colonial nor Samo but is a new autonomy with broad national connections—a testimony to the resilience of a people who remain aware of their surroundings, relationships, and structures. There is a whole new field of intentionality represented by both sides of the "colonial discourse." This has been a study of the nature of sociocultural cohesion and the versatility of the human struggle for identity and survival. As Foucault (1965) demonstrated how the residents of an insane asylum survive the madness of the "civilization" created for them, so I have attempted to show how the Samo have adjusted to, and will persevere beyond, the impact of colonial hegemony. Without a doubt, they will continue to develop new tropes, which neither they nor their colonial benefactors could have imagined.

Eleven

Afterword:
An Anthropology of Colonialism
Out of the "Last Unknown"

Eugene Ogan

A Long Gestation

Despite decades of promises and portents, a genuine Anglophone anthropology of colonialism has been slow to develop. By an *anthropology* of colonialism, I mean bringing the concepts and techniques of anthropology to bear on colonial situations.[1] This includes recognizing such situations as sociocultural systems worthy of study; focusing on social relations *between* colonizer and colonized, with the understanding that these two categories themselves may comprise multiple agents and projects that can be variably in cooperation or conflict; recognizing that, like all social relations, colonial situations can be a matter of negotiation rather than simple oppression; attending to emergent cultural forms; and placing all studies in a comparative and historical context.

I specify *Anglophone* to indicate that Francophone scholars much earlier produced distinctive analyses of colonialism. Octave Mannoni ([1950] 1964), Georges Balandier ([1953] 1970), and Albert Memmi ([1957] 1967) provided studies that might have pointed American anthropologists in particular toward this area of research, but their contributions have often been ignored even to the present time. When Americans finally took up colonialism as a topic for serious disciplinary consideration, their discussion took a rather different direction.

Anglophone anthropologists appeared to have discovered (with the amazement of Moliere's character upon finding he spoke prose) the discipline's historical connections to colonialism in the 1960s (see Stocking 1991). In the United States, this was connected with more general unrest in universities particularly associated with opposition to American policy in Southeast Asia. However, this new awareness did not result in the study of colonialism from an anthropological perspective, but rather in a series of studies in the history of anthropology, trying to determine the extent to which the discipline served colonizer interest (see, for example, Asad 1973; also see Francophone anthropologists like Maquet 1964 and Panoff and

Panoff 1968, especially Chapter 2, which also examined this issue). Here I confess that I see a touch of anthropological hubris at work in overestimating the possibility of such an effect. This overestimation is perhaps not surprising, given the efforts by British anthropologists between the World Wars to sell their work as valuable to colonial administrations (cf. the unedifying picture drawn by Kuklick 1991, chap. 5). In fact, any serious student of this relationship can only conclude by echoing Asad (1991:315): "The role of anthropologists in maintaining structures of imperial domination has, despite slogans to the contrary, usually been trivial."[2]

To borrow a subtitle from Stocking (1991), this new concern with anthropology's possible service to colonialism did indeed help to "contextualize the production of ethnographic knowledge." But despite the main title of Stocking's book, the individual contributions in that volume were less about "colonial situations" *per se* than about the activities of the anthropologist in those situations. Most books in this genre did not bring anthropological insight to bear on the phenomenon of colonialism itself. Such research did not really begin to develop, at least in the United States, until the 1980s. Then, thanks to collaboration between anthropologists and historians, especially those associated with the Universities of Chicago (e.g., Comaroff 1985; Cohn 1987) and Michigan (e.g., Dirks 1987), American anthropology began to take colonialism as a matter worth serious study. However, what resulted is more fairly labeled "colonial studies" rather than an anthropology of colonialism in the sense described above.

The Birth of Colonial Studies

Much of this work dealt with colonial situations in Africa and India; in the latter case, there was cross-fertilization with "subaltern studies" (e.g., Guha 1985). The journal *Comparative Studies in Society and History* published many articles in this vein, while the November 1989 issue of *American Ethnologist* (Cooper and Stoler 1989, later revised as Cooper and Stoler 1997) may be regarded as a landmark publication locating such studies within anthropological boundaries.

It is not my purpose to provide a complete survey of work developed in the 1980s, but two general points may be made about what I will caricature as the Chicago/Michigan axis. First, like many such circles in anthropology (I cannot speak for history), the major contributors formed a relatively tight group intellectually and seldom drew on relevant studies by others. Thus, even after anthropologists working in the Pacific began, as noted below, to write more about colonialism, less than 5 percent of the works in Stoler and Cooper's (1997) extensive bibliography deal exclusively with that region.[3] Second, and more important, the colonial studies described here seemed to draw more from literary theory than from anthropology. Indeed, so much was written under the rubric of "colonial discourse studies" that even one of its "founders" felt compelled to warn that "it is all too often the case that the *historical* experience of colonialism—along with the contemporary *politics* of post-colonialism—gets lost in the elegant new textualism of colonial discourse studies" (Dirks 1992a:175; emphasis added). I will argue below that this has already happened in some recently published work on Papua New Guinea.

What many would regard as the major contribution to colonial studies centered on Pacific Island material is, of course, Nicholas Thomas's *Colonialism's Culture* (1994). It is the one Pacific book that has attracted the attention of writers whose research is carried out in other parts of the world. This attention is thoroughly merited, though the book is not above criticism (e.g., Mason 1995). An emphasis on cultural factors as an antidote to defining colonialism solely in terms of politics or economics is certainly laudable. I would only underline here that Thomas's explicit focus on theories of colonial discourse in the work of writers like Homi Bhabha creates its own constraints, such as those noted by Dirks.

The View from Papua New Guinea

I have elsewhere (Ogan 1996a) commented critically on the long-standing tendency on the part of ethnographers of Papua New Guinea (hereafter PNG) to write their monographs in an artificial ethnographic present, ignoring the important influences that changed the lives of the indigenous population. Many of these influences can, of course, be grouped under the rubric "colonialism." One consequence of this way of writing ethnography is that much of our understanding of PNG colonialism until very recently has been provided by historians, political scientists, and others, rather than by anthropologists.[4] It is not necessarily surprising that a symposium volume for the centenary of colonial contact in PNG (Latukefu 1989) lists no anthropologists among its twenty-four contributors, but surely it is worth noting that, of 310 items in the bibliography, a mere 27 were authored by anthropologists in the usual sense of that term.

Even a preliminary glance at PNG's history reveals how varied were the colonial situations that developed after 1884. Newbury (1989:39) says that, at various times, government in PNG was

> an externally-directed executive carrying out a poor man's paternalism in Papua; a nonexistent executive for a German chartered company; a military administration supervising enemy aliens who were the mainstay of the cash economy; a set of Australian public servants safeguarding Commonwealth assets and paying lip-service to principles laid down by League visionaries; and finally it has become the political executive of a national government which has its own assets to safeguard and principles laid down in the Eight Aims of 1972 cooked up by local planners and University of East Anglia development visionaries.

The diversity within the colonized population is one point on which anthropologists have frequently commented. Less often have they been explicitly concerned to write about what Wedgwood (1945, quoted in Smith 1989:293) called the "colonial triad of Government, mission, and commercial and settler interests." The relative strength of each of these colonizer elements in specific cases is vital in assessing, comparing, and contrasting colonial situations in PNG.

Berating anthropologists in PNG for neglecting the study of colonialism serves no good purpose now. Rather, it seems more important to put on record what I believe to be significant contributions by those scholars whose works are insufficiently cited in anthropological accounts of PNG. Although the government anthropologists E. W. P. Chinnery (the Mandated Territory) and, especially, F. E. Williams (Papua) did excellent work, they could no more examine colonialism as an institution than a fish could analyze the water in which it swims. However, in his "Creed of a Government Anthropologist," Williams ([1939] 1977) provides insightful commentary on the differences between then prevailing anthropological theory and the practical requirements of an administration charged with the welfare of a colonized population. He reminds modern readers that villagers themselves might embrace the changes colonialism brought.

The work at least a few anthropologists regard as the premier contribution to an anthropology of PNG colonialism written before World War II began as a dissertation in sociology. Stephen Reed's *The Making of Modern New Guinea* (1943) was based on research in the Mandated Territory 1936–1937, but it can still be read with profit. Reed had a sharp eye for all the contradictions of colonialism, whether in the overarching "caste system" or in the conflicts prevalent among the "triad" of planter, missionary, and administrator.

The Second World War brought major changes to PNG, not least the beginning of a single administrative structure for what had been separate territories. It also involved a number of anthropologists in considering more carefully how that administration might be carried out to the greater benefit of the indigenous population. H. Ian Hogbin was one who, under administrative direction, made what could be considered a rare early contribution to the anthropology of colonialism in his 1951 *Transformation Scene* about Busama.[5] He explicitly considered the respective impacts of administration, mission, and wage labor. If the final chapter, "Race Relations," seems naive today, one should consider that, in its historical context, his argument was probably very radical. It is therefore surprising that in a subsequent monograph about Busama (Hogbin 1963:170), he downplayed the changes that had earlier been his main focus. On the other hand, his Josiah Mason lectures (Hogbin 1958) drew on both his PNG and Solomon Island experiences to provide a more generalized picture of colonial influence on Melanesians.

Two other books that might have presaged an anthropology of PNG colonialism appeared in the early 1960s. Kenelm Burridge's *Mambu* (1960) gave a somewhat different view of the "triangle," which he saw to be formed by administration, mission, and villager, but added further evidence for the agency of villagers who sought to deal with change.[6] Peter Lawrence's *Road Belong Cargo* (1964a) provided the kind of historical perspective too often neglected in PNG ethnography, and it clearly showed the interplay of different kinds of colonizers with Madang people. Yet most anthropologists who wrote about "cargo cults" in the next few years failed to give adequate attention to all aspects of the colonial situations in which these movements emerged.

Another 1960s book that should have advanced our understanding of PNG colonialism was written not by an anthropologist but by a kind of social science polymath, Charles Rowley (1966). This is not to downplay his earlier contribution analyzing the Australian takeover of what had been German New Guinea (Rowley 1958). However, the later book showed how much he had been able to absorb from his principalship of the Australian School of Pacific Administration and his consequent interaction with both junior and senior administration personnel and anthropologists (e.g., Peter Lawrence; see Westermark, Chap. 4). What is particularly useful about Rowley's book—especially as an introduction to any younger anthropologist essaying to study PNG today—is the detailed attention paid to all the agents who had been involved in PNG's colonial history, showing how the separate projects of administrator, planter, and missionary sometimes conflicted, sometimes reinforced each other in their effects on the colonized.[7]

A 1970s volume, Edward Wolfers's (1975) *Race Relations and Colonial Rule in Papua New Guinea,* can enlighten anthropologists who began their research after PNG independence and may have therefore missed some of the brutality of colonizer racism that existed particularly in coastal and island regions. As he says elsewhere (1989:417), "it is only through an awareness of the nature and impact of colonial rule that certain aspects of contemporary Papua New Guinean society can be understood," and that impact certainly includes, for many living Papua New Guineans, experiences of "racial prejudice, personal slights and/or systematic adverse discrimination" (ibid.:419).[8]

The Reed, Rowley, and Wolfers books in particular provide a basis from which to draw comparisons and contrasts with the studies of colonialism from other parts of the world described earlier.

In 1992, a spirited critique of the neglect of history and change in ethnographies of Melanesia was mounted by James Carrier and his contributors (Carrier 1992). Three of the chapters (by Carrier, John Barker, and Margaret Jolly) deal specifically with PNG material. I have elsewhere (1994; 1996a) discussed some aspects of this book and will not go further into the matter here except to say that, indeed, more and more anthropologists are today providing fascinating analyses of modern PNG society, abandoning the fiction of an "ethnographic present." Yet I would voice a mild criticism: postcolonial PNG, with all its efforts to build a nation (see, for example, Foster 1995; Otto and Thomas 1997), must be examined for the effects of almost a century of colonial rule. As Allen (1990:185; emphasis added) argues, "inadequate recognition has been given to the manner in which the colonial experience transformed and *continues to influence* the way in which the present generation confronts the world in which, from almost every viewpoint, the terms of exchange are unequal." For example, colonial PNG was very reluctant to provide a secular education to indigenous populations (Smith 1989), leaving education in the hands of Christian missions for decades. To what extent do mission-educated personnel still dominate the ruling elite, and what role do both the older mission, and the newer government, higher education centers play in modern politics? How does mission-influenced ideology affect nation-building efforts?

Another general question to be raised about the laudable increase in anthropological studies of colonial and postcolonial PNG concerns the choice of appropriate comparative and theoretical models. This problem was highlighted in a special issue of *Oceania* entitled "Alienating Mirrors: Christianity, Cargo Cults, and Colonialism in Melanesia" (Lattas 1992). All the journal articles deal with PNG. Looking at the bibliography, one finds Foucault,[9] Gramsci, and Ricoeur, but no mention of Balandier, Mannoni, or Memmi. Nor are there any citations of Reed, Rowley, or Wolfers. The result is to privilege colonial discourse studies at the expense of other possible analytic frameworks.

I do not intend to be dogmatic about the way one approaches history, including colonial history, in improving anthropological studies of PNG. As one who admits to being cheerfully, if not uncritically, eclectic, I can only applaud the currently increasing attention to history and change. In this context, I feel I must single out Frederick Errington and Deborah Gewertz's (1995) *Articulating Change in the "Last Unknown"* as a landmark in the development of a genuine anthropology of colonialism in PNG. The book seems to me exemplary in its scholarly attention to both PNG history and theoretical approaches to colonialism. Errington, of course, had the dubious advantage of having been caught up in the kind of "plantation colonialism" (Ogan 1996b) that still existed in the last years before independence. However, a number of the papers in the present volume show that those who began their anthropological research after PNG's independence can make equally valuable contributions.

What Can PNG Add to the Anthropology of Colonialism?

If anthropology is always a comparative discipline, one might argue that the contributions to this volume are worthwhile simply for adding to a body of literature in which the Pacific has been so poorly represented in the past. However, as Robert Foster (pers. com. 1997) has suggested, perhaps this is not enough. I would underline further some points demonstrated by the preceding chapters.

Echoing Newbury's comments quoted earlier, Brown's and Jaarsma's contributions emphasize the changing historical context of colonialism in PNG, the latter adding a comparative dimension by contrasting the situation in the western half of the island of New Guinea itself. They also serve to remind us of the late date of this colonialism, which relates directly to the particular strength of the individual chapters.

That strength lies in the ethnographic component in the present volume, lacking in so much of "colonial studies" literature that rests solely on documentary materials. What the chapters by Lepowsky, McPherson, Nash, Scaglion, and Shaw in particular illustrate is what Sanjek (1998:397, following the ethnohistorian Fenton) calls "upstreaming": interpreting earlier written records on the basis of direct ethnographic knowledge of a particular community or people.[10] The opportunity to interview participants in colonial situations (or their survivors) has produced a biographical bias in most of the chapters. This ethnographic component also makes some progress toward recovering the voice of the colonized, a particularly worrisome problem faced by colonial studies based on the analysis of texts provided by the colonizer.

At the same time, contributors to this volume have paid attention to what the colonial studies literature can offer. This is seen especially in Foster's chapter, but it does not seem excessive to say that all the authors have been more far-reaching in their comparisons and theoretical searches (e.g., Nash's use of Guha's subaltern studies) than have some students of other geographical areas who have maintained a more parochial focus.

This is not to claim that what is presented in this volume is in any way definitive, even for PNG. All elements of the "triad" have not been adequately treated in most of the chapters. Partly this is a limitation of space, and partly it is because one cannot describe what did not exist in a particular situation. The recent availability of patrol reports has inevitably tipped the balance toward administration, but one regrets that the chapters on *kiaps* do not include the insights on the indigenous police force provided by Kituai (1998).

Although Shaw's chapter demonstrates the contrast between administration and mission projects, overall, the volume slights the varied ways missions and commerce fit into PNG colonialism. Lepowsky cogently notes that planters or traders are less likely to provide archives than are missionaries or *kiaps* (but see, for example, Stuart 1977), though her own thoroughgoing scholarship shows how much might still be found. Most contributors do not delve as deeply into conflicts among the different colonizer projects as did Dorothy Counts (1978) more than two decades ago, although she did not have the advantage of the now extant literature to guide her.[11]

However, to make these points is only to say that there is still much work to be done in proving how much material from Papua New Guinea can add to a burgeoning anthropology of colonialism. It also remains to be seen whether this volume, and those that one hopes will follow, can attract the attention of the established scholars of colonial studies who persist in regarding the area as the "Last Unknown."

Notes

Chapter 1. Introduction

1. By way of example, see Carrier 1992; Errington and Gewertz 1995; Gordon and Meggitt 1985; Jolly and Thomas 1992; Lewis 1996; Rosenberry and O'Brien 1991; Schieffelin and Crittenden 1991; Thomas 1994.

2. A mandated territory is one judged not to be capable of self-government (in a European sense, of course).

3. The Microfiche of Patrol Reports by province is available at the Papua New Guinea National Archives or from the Melanesian Archives at the University of California, San Diego.

4. Dwyer, and the administration generally, was very concerned about malaria, and he comments: "At Marika [Bariai] a native child died in the nearby hospital. Native Medical Assistant in charge of the area was treating his patient for dysentery. In light of experience gained at the malaria control school at Minj recently, it is reasonable to conclude that the deceased had been suffering from malaria and that the dysentery symptoms were merely complications" (Dwyer 1954–1955).

5. Elsewhere, Lepowsky (n.d.b) presents an intriguing assortment of personalities and stories about white women during the early years in colonial New Guinea. Among many others, there is the famous author Beatrice Grimshaw, whose fiction captures much of the tone of colonial culture at the time and whose travelogues of the Pacific, published in Britain, extol the virtues of the country in order to promote white settlement in Papua. Speculations about her long friendship with the Papuan Administrator Hubert Murray continue to this day. There is also Evelyn Cheesman, an entomologist who spent twenty years collecting specimens in New Guinea, accompanied by native "carriers, assistants and servants" in complete disregard of "official and unofficial disapproval" of a white woman traveling "alone." And there is the beautiful Mrs. Flora Gofton, who founded the Samarai Hotel and, as "Samarai's Merry Widow," arranged a marriage of convenience in 1929 in order to join the rush to the gold fields. As Mrs. Flora Stewart, she and her husband built the Hotel Bulolo in Wau, where she "kept order in her establishment by throwing well-aimed tins of baked beans" at miscreant miners.

Chapter 2. Colonial New Guinea

1. See the biographical studies of recently contacted persons by James Watson (1960) and by Virginia Watson (1997).

2. A general review of colonial Papua New Guinea is found in Latukefu 1989.

3. I took this as acceptance of my place in the local community.

Chapter 3. Conceiving New Guinea

This article is based on research done since 1986, financed by grants from the Foundation for Social and Cultural Sciences (SSCW, ref. nr. 500-276-001) and the

Foundation for Economical, Sociocultural and Geographical Sciences (ESR, ref. nr. 510-76-504), subsidized by the Netherlands Organization for Scientific Research (NWO). I thank Naomi McPherson, Gene Ogan, Paula Brown, Ann Chowning, and George Westermark for their constructive comments on previous versions.

1. Contact is, of course, like any relation, always about the exchange of goods and services. However, at the early stages, the parties involved did not deal on an equal footing (either in terms of power or of available information on each other's nature) and were uncertain of what was being exchanged (Jaarsma 1998).

2. Though certainly no rule, this practice lasted well into the 1960s. The fact that very few, if any, researchers have been killed while in the field by any cause other than accident or disease may of course be interpreted as a result of circumspection on the part of anthropologists and other ethnographers. In that regard, the administrative officers and missionaries preceding the researchers were more at risk. Nowadays, however, anthropologists definitely have to be more careful in this respect in certain areas of Papua New Guinea or even have to avoid specific areas. This implies that in the past the safety of researchers in the field may have relied to a large extent on the (implicit) threat of retaliation.

3. By the 1960s, however, most anthropologists tried to avoid being identified with the administration, either by the people they studied or their audience, and the fact is usually only mentioned in passing.

4. *Translation at Sight* (1968) is Jan Pouwer's inaugural lecture as Foundation Professor of the Department of Anthropology and Maori Studies at Wellington University (1966–1976). Jan Pouwer did his research (1952–1954) among the Kamoro as a government anthropologist working for the Dutch Kantoor voor Bevolkingszaken (Native Affairs Bureau).

5. New Guinea ethnography has in the past developed in two distinct and to some extent alien directions. On the one hand, we have the ethnography of West New Guinea, or Irian Jaya, that looks west to the Indonesian Archipelago for, among other things, contact influences. On the other hand, for the eastern part of the island, Papua New Guinea, we look east—outward across Melanesia as a whole—for evaluative models. These days we know, based largely on archaeological and linguistic evidence, that this division cannot be maintained, yet it still pervades much of our academic anthropological discourse.

6. On the reverse side, opinions of the indigenous population toward the administration developed differentially, at least in terms of racial issues. In Papua New Guinea, racial tensions largely developed between the indigenous population and the Europeans. In West New Guinea, similar tensions existed between the indigenous population and the Indonesians and Indo-Europeans who filled the lower echelons of both the administration and missions.

7. Westermark (Chap. 4) refers in several places to the distrust such "old hands" expressed concerning anthropologists and their influence on the training of new personnel. Elsewhere (Jaarsma 1994), I have pointed to similar sentiments existing in the Dutch administration.

8. The decreasing importance of this position may very well relate to the person of Charles Julius himself, who was the government anthropologist in the postwar period, but too little is known of him to be sure.

9. Both Williams and Chinnery were active researchers in their own right. Williams, however, published more extensively, and his work is fairly well known in anthropological discourse (Kohn 1988). Chinnery's contribution to anthropology was more that of gatekeeper (Stocking 1982a), introducing several academic researchers to the field.

10. An important difference, however, stems not from a difference between the missions in either area, but from the involvement of the churches in Dutch politics of the time. The missions' evaluation of change and development of the indigenous population carried considerable weight, oftentimes influencing administrative policies. In the 1920s, the Roman Catholic mission successfully applied political and popular pressure to force the Dutch government and the East Indies administration to start a large-scale health campaign on the south coast against an epidemic venereal disease (granuloma inguinale). In a similar vein, several authors in a recently published collection of memoirs of Dutch administrative personnel (Schoorl 1996) carry the conviction that throughout the 1940s and 1950s the local missions could influence policies, if not directly then indirectly, through their links to parliamentary politics (see Jaarsma 1993).

11. Examples are the work done by Schoorl (1953) on the workforce of the Netherlands New Guinea Petrol Company in the Bird's Head area. Similarly, Bougainville Copper financed some anthropological and economic research on Bougainville Island to assess the impact of the new mine in the 1960s (Ogan 1996b).

12. For an overview of urban research in Papua New Guinea, see Levine and Levine (1979); for West New Guinea, see Jaarsma (n.d.b).

13. Ann Chowning (pers. com. January 1988) pointed out to me that the attention given to African ethnographic "models" in Papua New Guinea was largely an Australian National University influence by the early 1950s. Terence E. Hays quotes Marie Reay as having trouble with the narrow focus on social structure advocated by S. F. Nadel and W. E. H. Stanner at the ANU. Reay's training at Sydney University, as well as her previous fieldwork experience, had given her a wider interest in "social change and the dynamic nature of social relations" (Hays 1992:33). Chowning adds that American anthropologists, too, were less affected by these priorities. Nevertheless, Australian anthropology—and Sydney University is certainly no exception—developed against a background of British social anthropology (Campbell 1998) and implicitly echoed its focus on African ethnography. Two main factors gradually caused a shift away from this predominantly theoretically dictated focus: (1) a growing body of New Guinea ethnography, and (2) a growing influx of American anthropologists. Both factors already influenced Sydney University by the early 1950s, whereas the ANU was still developing its research program.

14. Although the number of researchers active in Papua New Guinea is less than one hundred for the 1950s and first half of the 1960s taken together, this number was

surpassed for the second half of the 1960s and more than doubled for the first half of the 1970s. Throughout these years there are about two male researchers for every female one active (Current and Projected Research 1968–1974; Bulmer 1970). It is impossible to give reliable figures for the number of researchers active in West New Guinea during these same decades.

15. In the late 1950s and early 1960s, Dutch academic research in West New Guinea gained dedicated financial sponsoring (from the Foundation for Scientific Research in New Guinea), but this development was cut short by political reality, with only a handful of research projects realized.

16. In 1968, the Roman Catholic and the main Protestant churches (Anglican, Evangelical Lutheran, and United Church) in Papua New Guinea founded the Melanesian Institute for Pastoral and Socio-Economic Service in order to be able to systematically study Melanesian cultures. Apart from occasional papers, the Institute publishes the journals *Catalyst* and *Point,* as well as a Tok Pisin publication, *Umben* (MacDonald 2000:161).

17. There are distinct similarities between the first three stages I identify and the stages distinguished by both Ian Downs (1980:179) and George Westermark (Chap. 4) for postwar Australian administrative activity in the highlands (for an extensive description, see Westermark). Downs and Westermark, however, distinguish their phases based on the administrative activities in a specific locale. My more extensive division follows the increasingly complex nature of contact itself as it occurs across New Guinea.

18. Ethnographic research itself will, of course, cause further sophistication in contact, through long-term research, repeated short-term research, or concurrent research in neighboring areas. Even the large-scale ethnographic surveys done by the Dutch administration that usually lasted only a few months—J.Th. van Logchem, for instance, visited twenty-three villages in four months for his survey of the Argoeni Bay region (1963)—occasionally caused considerable reaction both inside and outside the area visited (cf. Jaarsma 1990:114–118).

19. Schieffelin (1991:288) points to the fact that, for the Onabasulu, the Strickland-Purari Patrol of 1935 was not the watershed event for first contact; rather it was the second patrol, in 1953. The gap of some eighteen years was simply too large to keep the initial event sufficiently alive in memory.

20. In Irian Jaya, on both the northern and southern coasts, and especially in the Bird's Head area, trade systems existed a considerable time prior to European contact. Even though these links carried little contact information into the interior of New Guinea, they were doubtless formative for the later (European) contact situation. This can and should be contrasted to the contact situations in the highlands and on the eastern half of the island.

21. After the Pacific War, however, in both West New Guinea and Papua and New Guinea, the role of the missions as independent pacifying agencies decreases as the scale of the administrative effort grows.

22. The Australian administration was probably the first to enforce such a ban explicitly. Paula Brown (1995:89) indicates that these restrictions prevented new missionaries from entering the highlands and limited the existing missionary pres-

ence to their main stations. In 1936 these restrictions were relaxed slightly, but until 1947 missionaries remained restricted to a radius of five miles around their stations. She adds that this minimally affected commercial interests, as "there were hardly any commercial people or miners in the highlands at that time, only a few around Kainantu" (pers. com. December 1988). In the 1950s, the Dutch administration enforced similar policies both to safeguard the safety of European personnel (missionary and administrative) and to prevent the spread of communicable diseases to the interior of West New Guinea. Here, too, given the lackluster economic development of West New Guinea, its perceived lack of readily exploitable resources, and the ambiguous international political situation, there was little need to implement such restrictions to curb commercial interests.

23. Representations of *kiaps* can be found in several contributions to this volume (see, for instance, McPherson [Chap. 6] and Westermark [Chap. 4]), but also in *Kiap*, by Sinclair (1984). A good representation of the first missionaries can be found in *The Bishop's Progress*, by Mary Huber Taylor (1988).

24. The discussion on cargo cults developed in the wake of a debate in *Pacific Islands Monthly*, where the term seems to have entered public discourse. From there it entered academic discourse, where it—to quote Lamont Lindstrom (1993:34)— "broke through and prospered . . . became a proper scientific and analytical category." Even though attempts had been made, and were made at later stages, to place the discussion in wider comparative frames, none of these efforts ever took hold of the discourse on cargo phenomena in any definitive fashion (see Lindstrom 1993; Jaarsma 1996, 1997).

25. Increasingly, too, the struggle also applies to the ways in which the indigenous population being described represents this change. In some cases, like Andrew Lattas's recent study of cult activity among the Kaliai of West New Britain (1998), this lets ethnography make a curious double take: "us" representing "them" representing "us."

26. Appreciably, there is no necessary relation between the nature of the colonial setting and this increase or onset of self-reflexivity. Watson's research itself may have contributed to it, as may other factors. The interesting aspect, though, is not the exact nature of its causality, but the fact that it occurs and the effects it has on the process of gathering ethnographic data.

27. The other prerequisites Schoorl formulates may give some depth to this statement. He indicates a need for three further things: (1) a certain familiarity of the administrator with either the process of gathering ethnographic data or the specific area he is studying; (2) the availability of archives or documents relevant to the research questions; and (3) the existence of a *lingua franca* or knowledge of the local language. Although Schoorl refers in his statements specifically to the short-term research of specified problems, he still touches upon a number of characteristics of research done where contact experience is on the increase. In fact, we might say that the one prerequisite mentioned earlier presupposes the three mentioned just now, and vice versa. Contrary to the situation in the first- and early-contact settings, the researcher has the possibility to familiarize her/himself with a *lingua franca* or a locally spoken language, may have long-term access to her/his infor-

mants, and can provide her/himself with information based on administrative reports and ethnographic descriptions on neighboring cultures. The result is that s/he can maximize her/his time in the field.

28. If we express what happens in terms of an exchange or trade, then overall information is exchanged for goods and services. Additionally, only one party involved— the researcher—has a clear and full view of the purpose s/he is trading for. The people studied are in most cases neither informed enough to appreciate the potential of the exchange, nor are they empowered enough to realize its potential. Also, to stretch the exchange analogy, it is a "buyer's market." If the people in the field tend to drive too hard a bargain, the researcher can usually opt out and look for another field location. Still, what is said here is not all negative. The position of the people studied is vastly improved if we compare it to first- and early-contact situations. If we compare this situation to trade or exchange, the first- and early-contact situations are best compared to robbery and swindling (Jaarsma 1998).

29. The extent of literacy, of course, varies in each research situation. With the increase in local literacy, ethnographers will be more likely to send their reports back to the field, although this will vary with the institutional context of the research done. As Chowning points out in her comments on a previous version of this chapter (pers. com. January 1988), it is not even literacy that is at stake here. Even if the people we study can read what we write, it is not necessarily true that they are able to comprehend the message that we try to convey to our audience. The ability to reflect on one's culture and to appreciate this reflection as done in European concepts by an outsider demands quite a lot of contact experience.

Chapter 4. Anthropology and Administration

I would like to thank Santa Clara University for the Presidential Research Grant that covered expenses for the research on which this chapter is based.

1. For analyses of early colonial ethnography from Africa, see Kuklick (1978, 1991), and from India, see Morrison (1984). For studies of the work of anthropologists within post–World War II Pacific Islands colonial systems, see Falgout (1995) for Micronesia, and Jaarsma (1994) for Dutch New Guinea.

2. For the development of other national traditions, see Bender (1965), Gerholm and Hannerz (1982), and Stocking (1982b).

3. Rick Giddings served as a *kiap* from 1956 until Papua New Guinea's independence in 1975. Thereafter, he held several administrative and legal positions with the government of Papua New Guinea. He was interviewed by the author in 1989.

4. This point was brought to my attention by Paula Brown (pers. com., July 21, 1997).

5. This differentiation of information on economic, social, and political change from the "traditions" encompassed within anthropology reflects the earlier ethnographic traditions that Ogan (Chap. 11) critiques.

6. See also Patrol Reports Nos. 1 and 5 of 1956–1957, Kainantu, and Patrol Report No. 11 of 1957–1958, Goroka; Watson (1992:185) comments on the place of patrol reports in the *kiap*'s knowledge of local peoples: "It [i.e., knowledge] thus was limited to his own immediate contacts with local people and to the written records his office might afford him, such as patrol reports, supplemented by whatever infor-

mal comments might have been passed to him by seniors and other predecessors on the station."

7. Letter from Donald Tuzin to the author, February 1, 1995.
8. See also Patrol Report No. 4 of 1948–1949, Goroka.
9. See also Patrol Report No. 2 of 1956–1957, Goroka.
10. See also Patrol Report No. 5 of 1949–1950, Goroka.
11. See also Patrol Report No. 3 of 1948–1949, Goroka; Patrol Report Nos. 2 and 6 of 1957–1958, Goroka; and Patrol Report No. 3 of 1956–1957, Goroka.
12. For a comparison of settlement patterns south of Henganofi, see Patrol Report No. 1 of 1949–1950, Goroka.
13. See also Patrol Report No. 2 of 1949–1950, Goroka, for the cultural variation west of Gimi.
14. For Gadsup, see Patrol Report No. 5 of 1947–1948, Kainantu; for Awa, see Patrol Report No. 6 of 1956–1957, Kainantu; for Fore and Chimbu, see Patrol Report No. 2 of 1949–1950, Goroka; for Kamano, see Patrol Report No. 1 of 1950–1951, Goroka, and Patrol Report No. 1 of 1957–1958, Goroka; for Ungai, see Patrol Report No. 13 of 1956–1957, Goroka.
15. Patrol Report No. 10 of 1955–1956, Kainantu; Patrol Report No. 7 of 1957–1958, Kainantu; Patrol Report No. 6 of 1957–1958, Goroka. Local government councils were the democratically elected bodies that the Australian administration introduced to the highlands starting in the late 1950s. They replaced the village headmen, referred to as *luluais*, who had served as the earliest form of colonial government at the community level. Unlike the *luluais*, councilors met across the lines of village and language to reach decisions pertaining to entire districts.
16. See also Patrol Report No. 4 of 1956–1957, Kainantu, and Patrol Report No. 5 of 1947–1948, Kainantu; see also Watson (1992:186) on the reputation of the "Terrible Tairora." See Nash (Chap. 7) for a similar situation in South Bougainville.
17. See also Patrol Report No. 2 of 1948–1949, Goroka.
18. For the Aiyura related case, see Patrol Report No. 8 of 1955–1956, Kainantu; for the Henganofi cases, see Patrol Report No. 1 of 1957–1958, Goroka; and for the diffusion from Papua, see Patrol Report No. 2 of 1957–1958, Goroka. A later report on the Bena Census Division mentions a cargo cult that was linked to leaders who had supposedly been trained by Yali (see Patrol Report No. 8 of 1965–1966, Goroka).
19. See also Patrol Report No. 12 of 1956–1957, Goroka, and Patrol Report Nos. 1, 2, 3, and 7 of 1957–1958, Goroka, and Patrol Report No. 5 of 1959–1960.

Chapter 5. Unvarnished Truths

I thank the late Maslyn Williams for his generous help with my research for this chapter. (Williams died August 11, 1999, at the age of 88.) Staff members at the National Library of Australia and the National Film and Sound Archive offered important assistance. I also thank Chris Ballard for passing on a copy of Sinclair's patrol report, and participants in the ASAO sessions from which this volume derives for their constructive criticisms. I have benefited from conversations with numerous colleagues in Australia, including Margaret Jolly, Nicholas Thomas, Gary Kildea, and Andrew Lattas. I gratefully acknowledge the financial support of The Spencer Foundation and the

University of Rochester. The data presented, the statements made, and the views expressed are the sole responsibility of the author.

1. I follow MacKenzie (1984:3) in defining the word *propaganda* as "the transmission of ideas and values from one person, or groups of persons, to another, with the specific intention of influencing the recipients' attitudes in such a way that the interests of its authors will be enhanced."

2. See, for example, Bertrand and Collins 1981; Lansell and Beilby 1982; Bertrand 1989; Moran 1991; Shirley 1994. I refer readers to this literature (especially Moran 1991) for more detailed descriptions of the institutional contexts and political circumstances of Australian government film during the postwar period.

3. In 1995, the National Library of Australia screened *Mike and Stefani*, along with films directed by Roberto Rossellini and John Huston, in a series of important cinematic works about the problems of postwar (1945–1949) adjustment.

4. For more information on Williams's family history and biographical background, including his Catholicism, consult the taped 1967 interview with Williams held in the oral history collection (Hazel de Berg Recordings) of the National Library of Australia.

5. In 1947, Williams himself had traveled to Canada to study the operations of the Canadian Film Board, which Grierson had founded and from which came Stanley Hawes—British filmmaker and Grierson protégé—who headed Australian government film production from 1946 to 1970.

6. MacKenzie (1984:84) observes an apparent irony in the work of Grierson and his followers, who, although they cultivated their reputations as radicals, dedicated themselves to imperial propaganda funded by an imperial body, the Empire Marketing Board. For Grierson, "Empire was a fact of life, . . . a source of moral and economic improvement for both home and colonial populations" (ibid.:85). Yet despite their advocacy for this sort of ethical imperialism, Grierson and his followers were sometimes characterized as Bolsheviks, a symptom of "the paranoia of the right rather than the revolutionary intent of the film makers" (ibid.:86). Similar tensions and paradoxes characterized the work of the Australian CFU in the 1950s, when "the unit was under a cloud, both because of the imagined close association of the parent Department of Information with the deposed Labor Government and the apparent leftism of many of the filmmakers" (Moran 1991:53–54). In 1976, the unit—by then called Film Australia—did become part of an independent statutory body, the Australian Film Commission.

7. Among the emendations made by McCarthy to Williams's proposal was the elimination of Williams's suggestion to produce a film focusing mainly on the work of the missions in the Territory. McCarthy also recommended that Williams pay more attention to matters of health, education, and agriculture and that he produce a general "development" film covering as wide an area as possible of social, political, and economic activity.

8. The group of students included a young Dame Josephine Abaijah.

9. Likewise, the image of Duna men "scampering after packages" disguises indigenous motivations. Biersack (1995:30) notes that Duna people interpreted the appearance of Europeans and planes in terms of local cosmological assumptions that

connected these celestial events with the return of *mbingi*, a time of darkness in which volcanic ash falls and renews the world's fertility.

10. Much of the material in this section draws on this interview, conducted at Williams's home in Bowral, NSW, in April 1996.

11. In retrospect, some of these opinions seem tragically misguided. Upon his return in late 1964 from a few months' tour of Indonesia, Williams reported that "while Indonesia had not yet done very much for West Irian materially, it had made the people 'first class citizens' by giving them a 'nationality'" (*Sydney Morning Herald*, date unknown; "Maslyn Williams" Clippings File, National Library of Australia).

Chapter 6. "Wanted: Young Man, Must Like Adventure"

This chapter is based on two years of anthropological research conducted in West New Britain and six months in Australia—all generously supported by funding from the Social Sciences and Humanities Research Council of Canada. I am also grateful for financial support from the Professional Development Fund and the Grants-in-Aid of Scholarly Activity at Okanagan University College. Thanks to Adeja Chrisara and Tyee Bridge for their research assistance and to Kathy Creely of the Melanesian Archives, UCSD. My appreciation extends also to Ann Chowning, David Counts, Dorothy Counts, Rik Goulden, Bil Thurston, Lawrence McPherson, Bob Pulsford, an anonymous reviewer, and contributors to this volume, all of whom commented on earlier drafts of this chapter. Very special thanks go to Miss Margaret Mack and Mr. Richard Mack for their generous assistance, letters, e-mails, and comments on earlier drafts of this chapter. Any errors of fact or analysis are, of course, my own.

1. Mr. C. W. C. Marr was, at the time, the minister for Health and Repatriation.

2. I have spent a total of twenty-four months during the years 1981, 1982–1983, and 1985 living and working with the Kabana of the Bariai District in northwest New Britain.

3. I am privileged to be in contact with members of Ian Mack's family in Australia, particularly his sole surviving sibling, Miss Margaret Mack, and his nephew, Mr. Richard Mack, both of whom have shared with me information about Ian and the Mack family history. Many of Ian Mack's reports on microfiche are illegible, and I am particularly indebted to Richard Mack, who, with the help of Katy Mack, transcribed and edited copies of Ian Mack's patrol reports that had been kept safe by Margaret Mack. Without a copy of these clearly typed records generously given to me by Richard Mack, the particular project of this chapter would have been impossible.

4. Miss Margaret Mack, now retired, is a recipient of the Medal of the Order of Australia for her years of service to the Australian Physiotherapy Association and her work with the disabled.

5. Although I have been unable to learn what, if any, connection existed between Mack and Hunt, Atlee Hunt was an excellent choice for a personal reference. Born in 1864 (d.1935) in Baroondah, Fitzroy River, Queensland, "A.A. Hunt, Esq. C.M.G. [was] Secretary, Department of External Affairs, 1901/17; Department of Home and Territories, 1917/21" (Mackenzie 1987:356). He had also been "private secretary to the first Prime Minister, Edmund Barton. . . . [Hunt] was to remain the

Commonwealth officer responsible for relations with the administration in Papua through many changes of federal ministry and years of hope, conflict and disappointment" (Lewis 1996:60).

6. The Burns Philp invoice to the ministry (Australian Archives: Series A518/1 Item 852/1/334) for Mack's "1st saloon passage . . . Sydney to Rabaul," at a cost of £14/8, has an interesting sketch in the left corner showing a map of Australia and New Guinea flanked by the exotic flora and fauna of the area: a loin-clothed aborigine, two kangaroos, and tropical palms. Burns Philp's branch offices also show the extensive reach of this company, nicknamed the "octopus of the Pacific" (Lewis 1996:34).

7. I am grateful to Dr. Ian Campbell, University of Canterbury, for helping me to clarify Mack's rank at hiring.

8. Keeping track of government issue and expenditures was often the bane of a patrol officer's existence. Handwritten on the bottom of a letter from his district officer, in which he is reminded to "keep a careful record of expenditure incurred" on an upcoming patrol, J. K. McCarthy wrote: "All these bastards think of is money. The Administration even charged me £30 for medical expenses when I was wounded in the first Menyamya patrol" (McCarthy 1933; see McCarthy 1963:109–113).

9. I take Mack's point here to mean that because of the small, scattered population, there were few choices of sexual partners and not that the Bainings had any intrinsic propensity to inbreed.

10. Names of rivers and important geographic sites, villages, and names of New Guineans who had come to the attention of the patrol officer/administration were highlighted in capital letters to make visual scanning of the report easier.

11. See Pels (1997:174), who comments that "to further study the culture of colonialism, it seems especially important to continue interrogating how the boundaries and relationships between public and private were constructed." Among other things, this includes "the ubiquitous infantilizing of the colonized."

12. The Other is not always white and of European extraction.

13. In "Weaver of the Border," Margaret Mead (1960:183) wrote of Phoebe Parkinson that "when the war came, the Germans did not include Mrs. Parkinson among the Germans who were protected, and for the first time she was left deserted, citizen only of an in-between world where there were no principalities and powers to whom to turn for help. The Australians brought in even greater racial self-consciousness, and after the war she withdrew almost entirely into plantation life, helping now one child and then another to set up plantations, recruit labor, trade in the bush."

14. *Luluais* were government appointed village headman; their seconds in command were called *tultuls*.

15. According to Amendment of Regulation 45(4) of the Native Labour Regulations, posted in the July 1915 *New Guinea Gazette*, flogging could occur for such things as rape, attempted rape, theft, robbery, and gross insubordination, but this punishment could only be inflicted if "the surrounding circumstances present features of cruelty or deliberation or violence or torture or immorality or defiance of authority," and only if the individual had been convicted of those offenses by the "judge

of the Central Court, the Officer in Charge of Native Affairs, or a District Officer, after duly hearing the case." A further amendment posted in the August 1915 *New Guinea Gazette* stated that anyone in contravention of this ordinance would face a penalty of "two thousand marks or six months' imprisonment." In 1919, an amendment to labor regulations absolutely abolished any form of corporal punishment of native laborers. The Nakanai events took place in 1926.

16. If Nicholls hadn't resigned, he may very well have faced those penalties noted above for illegal flogging of a native; however, his mishandling of the affair seems to have been overlooked in the furor of murders and punitive expeditions, as I can find no indication that he was ever called to account on this incident.

17. The final paragraph in the newspaper report reads: "It is a curious condition that the two Victorians who lost their lives [Collins and Fischer] were only sons, were both former members of the Australian Imperial Forces, and had both been employed on the expropriated plantations. Mr. Noel Tracy Collins, who was 48 years of age, had served the Crown in South Africa, Australia, and in the Mandated Territories. He was sent to New Guinea in 1920 and on his retirement early this year was deputy district officer at Kieta. Mr. Collins was an only son and was nephew of Captain Richardson, late, of the Royal Australian Navy."

18. In Mack's reports, this village is referred to as Kuma-Kuma or Guma-Guma; no such village now exists.

19. My account of this event is based on Ian Mack's patrol report contained in R. Mack (1994). Known full names of the passengers were: Reginald Percy Brake Mills of Ningau Plantation, Witu; Lionel Cyril Saunders, Plantation Overseer, Witu; Mr. Paku and Mr. Garu of Kuravu Village, Ningau (labor line recruits); Mr. Kavulio of Bali Island; Mr. Tanguri of Ilia Plantation; Police Constable Geiti; and Mack's personal servants, Mr. Nali with his unnamed wife and infant, and the brothers Mr. Mataiu and Mr. Launa.

20. Mr. Saunders described the M.S. *Langu* as "a boat of five and a half tons (gross) . . . and had a good 15 h-p Kelvin engine in her. . . . The schooner was 32 feet long and 10 feet in beam" (quoted in R. Mack 1994:196).

21. On the elusive Mokolkols, see Fenbury 1968.

22. Watson (1960, 1992), Radford (1977, 1987), and Acting Territory Administrator Wanliss, in a letter to Daisy Mack (Australian Archives: Series A518/1 Item 852/1/334), all differ as to the number of Aiamontina men killed.

23. Watson (1992:178) points out that "according to a fellow *kiap*, however, Mack had a well-known medical problem from which he later succumbed, in the hospital at Salamaua, his weakness aggravated by the stress of the Aiamontina experience."

Chapter 7. Paternalism, Progress, Paranoia

1. I would like to thank Kathy Creely, of the Melanesian Archives at the library of the University of California, San Diego, and Don Tuzin, of the Department of Anthropology, University of California, San Diego, for their help in facilitating my access to the patrol reports used in this chapter. I further thank Eugene Ogan for his many helpful suggestions, my co-authors and editor, and an anonymous reviewer for the University of Pittsburgh Press.

2. My thanks to the National Institutes of Health for predoctoral support and to the Australian National University for postdoctoral funding.

3. He once told me that the reason he didn't believe that sorcery worked was because "if it did, I'd be dead now."

4. ConZinc Riotinto Australia (CRA), the copper-mining company in question operating in Bougainville, later reorganized as Bougainville Copper Proprietary Limited (BCPL).

5. I ran across a similar case from the Tiop area of North Bougainville, a correction of Mr. Young-Whitford's wrong impression in a letter by Acting District Officer R. M. Farlow, File 30/1/1-1002 from November 9, 1948, roughly twenty years before Mr. Hoad's remarks were written.

6. Napidakoe Navitu was an organization of ethnic groups on the east coast of Bougainville, headed by Barry Middlemiss, former overseer at Arawa Plantation. The organization was supported by Paul Lapun, as well. Its goals were not always clear to an outsider, but a consideration of secession and independence for Bougainville was one of its concerns. It was seen as a general *bête noire* by the white establishment, and Middlemiss was considered a race traitor in a sense.

7. The Hahalis Welfare Society was a political organization centered in Buka, reputedly involving supernaturalistic practices (see Rimoldi and Rimoldi 1992).

8. It may be asked whether the methods of subaltern studies, developed in the context of Indian colonial history, are applicable more generally. Some appear to think so; for example, Nelson has recently elucidated insurgency in nineteenth-century Chiapas (Mexico) by reference to such formulations (1997). But Mexico and India resemble one another in having borne a heavier weight of colonial distortions than Bougainville ever did. In the former two, the colonial periods were lengthy and for most of the time utterly uninformed by any notion of "democracy." The tenure of colonials was sweeping, brutal, and exploitative. In Bougainville, the colonial experience was much shorter in duration and, especially inland, surely not so intense. Furthermore, after World War II, preparation for independence, not extraction of resources, was the official mission.

Chapter 8. The Queen of Sudest

Portions of earlier drafts of this chapter were presented at "The Culture of Contact in Papua New Guinea," Sessions of the Association for Social Anthropology in Oceania Annual Meeting, San Diego, California, in February 1997, and in Pensacola, Florida, in February 1998. I thank Naomi McPherson, Gene Ogan, Paula Brown, and session participants for their comments. Sections of earlier drafts of this chapter were presented at the Borders Symposium of the Institute for Research in the Humanities of the University of Wisconsin, Madison, March 1998. Thanks to Susan Friedman and members of the University of Wisconsin's Borders Research Group for their comments. I am grateful for Kirin Narayan's critical reading and valuable suggestions. The ethnographic and archival research on which this chapter is based, dating from 1977 to 2000, has been supported by the National Science Foundation; the University of California, Berkeley, Chancellor's Patent Fund, Department of Anthropology, and Lowie (now Hearst) Museum; the National Institute of Child Health and Human Development, National

Institutes of Health; the Wenner-Gren Foundation for Anthropological Research; the National Endowment for the Humanities; the American Philosophical Society; the American Council of Learned Societies; the Graduate School of the University of Wisconsin, Madison; and the William F. Vilas Trust of the University of Wisconsin, Madison.

1. The island shown as Sudest or Tagula on maps and charts, at fifty miles by ten the largest in the Louisiade Archipelago, is known to its 2,300 inhabitants as Vanatinai, literally, Motherland. The islanders speak their own language. The pidgin spoken by Vanatinai elders is a variant of Papuan coast pidgins, which derive from contacts in the 1880s with European *bêche-de-mer* and pearl fishermen, gold miners and traders, and from indentured servitude on Queensland sugar plantations. This pidgin, which linguists had thought extinct since before World War II, is not the same as Tok Pisin, the Neo-Melanesian Pidgin that is an official language of Papua New Guinea. I have always denied all spirit identities, with only mixed results (Lepowsky 1993).

2. Admirable exceptions by historians and anthropologists include Stocking (1977), Nelson (1976, [1982] 1990), Young (1992, 1998), Bashkow (1996), and Lewis (1996). Malinowski's diary (1989) and letters to his future wife (Wayne 1995) contain brief but valuable references to traders and other expatriates he met in Papua.

3. The generation born in the first two decades of this century, almost all dead by now, are the last speakers of this Vanatinai variant of Papuan Pidgin. I have cassette tapes from the 1980s of elders pretending they were visiting Miz Mahony's store and speaking Vanga Lumo. While the Pidgin itself, as a naturally spoken language, is, finally, virtually if not actually extinct in the 1990s, many of its lexical items have diffused into Vanga Vanatinai, the island's language, and they are used in daily speech by people of all ages (Lepowsky 1993). The eccentric Scottish trader Cyril Cameron, known to Papuan whites as King Kam of Kitava, who lived in the eastern island of the Trobriand Group for thirty years early in the twentieth century, similarly forbade all island men on his trading station and banned the speaking of the Trobriand language, making islanders speak Papuan Pidgin. King Kam was also notorious locally for keeping an ever-changing harem of young Kitava girls, and for making his rare appearances in Samarai clothed only in a burlap copra sack. I heard these stories in the 1970s from longtime Papua residents. Gordon Saville (Saville and Austin 1974) heard them while resident in the Trobriands during World War II (cf. Lewis 1996:94). The English remittance man who operated a plantation and tradestore near Rehua, on the south coast of Sudest, until his death in the early 1970s would only let women and girls onto his trading station.

4. White traders and planters in the East End islands used Papuan forms of wealth to buy land as well, often without colonial government approval. One example is the purchase in 1910 of a piece of land near Rambuso, on the north coast of Sudest Island, by a European for one steel axe, an eighteen-inch shell-disc necklace, one large empty bottle, one parcel of trade tobacco, and a bag of rice wrapped in a woven mat. The land was planted in coconut palms (Territory of Papua 1972). The use of shell necklaces as a medium of exchange between islanders and Europeans during the colonial era was not limited to New Guinea's East End islands. For example, the Englishman Eric Muspratt,

who lived on San Cristoval in the Solomon Islands in 1920, writes, "In certain parts of the Solomons [the string of shell discs] is the only currency recognized so that white traders, before they can deal with these people, must have shell money. This is difficult as few natives will sell it for white man's money. The trade price for it was about thirty shillings a fathom" (Muspratt 1931:166).

5. The Cosmopolitan Hotel appears on the front cover of D. C. Lewis's *The Plantation Dream*, in a photograph taken in 1927, and in Figure 1, in a 1905 photograph showing its name spelled out below the second-story verandahs.

6. Flora Gofton's tenant, Mrs. Mustard, was apparently the head of another fatherless white family in Papua. A list of white residents of Papua in 1918 shows Archibald Mustard, miner, and Charlotte Mustard, no occupation and no children (probably an error, unless the children were in Australia), at Woodlark Island, a gold-mining area east of the Trobriands. By 1920, the Mustard family is at the Laloki mine, in the mountains behind Port Moresby, with four children: Charlotte, Jr., Clara, Ivy, and Robert. Archibald Mustard disappears from view before the fire (Allen 1918:31; 1920:111; Stuart 1970:252; Roberts 1996:21, 50–57).

7. Some male historians have subscribed to these views as well (e.g., Hyam 1990). For feminist historical perspectives, see Inglis (1974) on sexual anxiety and politics in colonial Papua; Bulbeck (1992) and Roberts (1996) on Australian women in New Guinea; Woollacott (1997) on Australian women and colonial whiteness; Bulbeck (1992:236–249) on white women as the ruin of empire in the eyes of prominent male colonials and historians; Knapman (1986) on "white women and the ruin of empire" in Fiji; Shaw (1995) on race, sex, and class in colonial Kenya; Chaudhuri and Strobel (1992) and Midgely (1998) on white women and empire in global perspective; Grewal (1996) on gender and empire in India; and Stoler (1989, 1991, 1992b, 1995, 1997) on race and sex in the Dutch East Indies and other colonial possessions.

8. Similarly ambiguous and threatening to colonial racial and sexual hierarchies were the individuals known in Papua as "the coloured population," "mixed race," and "half castes." The "coloureds" were mostly non-European men who came to New Guinea in the frontier days from all over the world—China, the Philippines, Japan, the Malay Peninsula, Polynesia—to dive for pearl shell, fish *bêche-de-mer*, and pan for gold. Many of them took island wives, and their children—along with the offspring of Europeans, such as Greek pearl trader Mick George and English goldminer Henry Morley—were the "half castes" so troubling to those who upheld the dual systems, defined by race, of laws and mores that governed colonial Papua. Stoler has documented how attention to the position of "mixed race" individuals brings into sharper focus Dutch and French imperial projects and colonial cultural ambiguities in Southeast Asia (1989, 1991, 1995, 1997). Papua's white colonials, especially those of higher social standing and authority, were similarly preoccupied with the "problem" of mixed race (e.g., Inglis 1974).

Chapter 9. Juxtaposed Narratives

First and foremost, I acknowledge my deep intellectual and personal debt to my Abelam father, Moll Apulala. *Némaandu ndémbu kiyaadék nde mi pukao.* I thank the East

Sepik Provincial Government and the government of Papua New Guinea for opportunities to pursue my work. This research has been supported at various times by the Fac-
ulty Research Grants Committee and Central Research Development Fund of the University of Pittsburgh. Some of the archival work was done while I was a Visiting Fellow
at the Research School of Pacific and Asian Studies of the Australian National University. Special thanks go to Bryant Allen for many discussions of foothills history, and also
for permission to quote extensively from transcripts of his interview with Kikuo
Kajizuki. I am grateful to Naomi McPherson and the other authors in this volume for
helpful suggestions, and especially to Dan Shaw, who encouraged me to join the ASAO
session on which this book is based.

1. This essay is one of a series in which I examine the history of colonial encounters
   in the Sepik foothills. I have described the broad outlines of salient historical
   events in three previous papers (Scaglion 1983, 1985, and 1990), and borrow generously from those publications in providing historical background. Parts of Moll's
   narrative have also been used in another paper (Scaglion and Norman 2000), and
   again there is some overlap. That piece explored the limits of using the term "resistance" to describe Moll's agency as he manipulates colonial encounters to facili-
   tate his own ends.
2. Translation courtesy of David Lea.
3. This labor gang did not consist of "prisoners" in the ordinary sense of the word.
   Older informants report being dragooned into the work and being physically mis-
   treated (Scaglion 1983:476–477; 1985:87–88).
4. Moll calls European actors during the colonial era "Masta," as in "Masta Hunter,"
   "Masta Tom," and so on. But for him, the connotations are quite different than
   their usage in English might suggest. In his mind, it would seem, "Masta" is more
   a part of a name than a title or term of respect. The linguistic tag is generally absent when he names European actors in the postcolonial era.
5. It was fairly clear that this was a suicide.
6. See Tuzin (1983) for a discussion of similar events.

Chapter 10. Three-Day Visitors

1. All references to "field notes" and "personal journal" refer to my own anthropological records made in the field. Fieldwork on which this chapter is based was
   funded, in part, by the New Guinea Research Fund of the Summer Institute of Linguistics and is gratefully acknowledged.
2. The sounds of the Samo language are pronounced much as corresponding
   sounds in English, with a few notable exceptions. The sound symbolized by the
   letter /l/ can be either an [n] sound at the beginning of a word or when surrounded by nasalized vowels, or the usual sound for [l] when found in the
   middle of a word. Thus the word to eat, *nala*, is orthographically symbolized as
   lanla. This brings up discussion of Samo vowels. There are six phonemic vowels, *a, e, i, o, u,* and *ə*. For orthographic ease, *ə* is represented by "o" and *o* by
   "oo." All vowels can be either oral or nasal (sound is forced through the nose).
   The nasalized vowels are symbolized using an "n" after the vowel. A sound
   comparison chart with English follows:

English: a b d e f g h i k l m ŋ o   s t u
Samo: a b d e f g h i k l m o oo s t u
Nasalized vowels: an en in on oon un

When spoken rapidly, the transition from high to low vowels in diphthongs, such as ia, creates a [y] sound, and that from low to high vowels in diphthongs, such as ua, creates a [w] sound. These sounds are a normal part of speech flow and are, therefore, not symbolized in the orthography. For a detailed phonological description and orthographic decisions based on psycholinguistic testing, see Shaw and Shaw (1977). The glossed meanings that accompany Samo words and phrases are translations based on meaning rather than a word-for-word translation.

3. I had two roles in this field context that are sometimes perceived as self-contradictory: anthropologist and Bible translator. Anthropology enabled me to focus on data collection and analysis that helped me appreciate the rationale behind Samo behavior patterns and make them known to other anthropologists (Shaw 1990 and 1996). The role of Bible translator demanded a long-term relationship that both facilitated the collection of cultural data and necessitated the application of cultural data to the translation process, that is, each role favorably impacted the other. Twelve years of spending half our time with the Samo produced valuable linguistic and anthropological data (Shaw and Shaw 1977; Shaw 1986). This dual role, with its resulting approaches, is reflected in the way this presentation takes colonial issues and emphasizes the Samo response to them. As in any colonial context, the Samo did not have the freedom of choice, but responded to the issues colonialists confronted them with as their culture conditioned them to do.

4. The Samo viewed the intrusion of the government much as they did encounters with their traditional enemies. When preparing for a raid, a group of warriors would mount a trading expedition designed to return with both desired trade goods and information that would assist a raiding party eager to attack a particular community. Hence, trading parties were always viewed with suspicion and encouraged to move on without delay.

5. In early reports, the name Supei appears instead of Samo. Inasmuch as patrols came from Kiunga in the west and crossed the Strickland River, officers applied the name as known to the Pare people on the west side of the river. The people, themselves, as do all groups on the east side of the river, use the name Samo, which is currently used by the administration. This reflects the colonial approach to accept external sources rather than inside information from the people themselves.

6. At one point in 1968 over one hundred policemen and their families were billeted at Nomad River.

7. No reason was given for this grouping. Perhaps the team reflects colonial interests in the viability of the land and its resources—documenting the fauna, flora, and mineral value along with an interest in the medical condition of the people was important at the time. The absence of a social scientist seems significant.

8. Our more-or-less constant contact with the Samo over a lengthy time period allowed me to take a long-term, unpressured approach to anthropological research. This arose from a confidence that, given enough time, I would be able to observe

most cultural activity. Thus we learned the language (Samo was my second son's first language) and entered into the community life in a way that eventually led me to data unavailable to short-term visitors. Indeed, my initiation in March 1973 opened a level of trust and interaction that created many opportunities for relationship that would otherwise have been impossible.

9. The SIL is not a mission or a church, and members are strictly forbidden to engage in "ecclesiastical activities." Therefore, there should be no competition with missions. The sole reason for being involved with the people is to do linguistic and cultural research that can be applied to doing Bible translation. One would think this would please missionaries, but the truth is, my relationship with expatriate missionaries was often confrontational. As for the pastors from other parts of Papua New Guinea (primarily the southern part of Western Province and the Southern Highlands), they simply followed the example of the missionaries and attempted to make the Samo like them: bathe daily, wash before coming to church, come to church when the bell rings, and obey all the "station" rules. None of these practices bore any resemblance to biblical concerns or Samo life, hence the Samo considered them largely irrelevant. With the Bible available to them, the Samo could compare what they were taught about the Bible with the translation of the Bible itself. When the Samo found differences, they would go to the pastors and say, "you say 'x,' but we don't see that in the Bible." Needless to say, this frustrated the pastors and missionaries. However, we were also very colonial in our approach, which was based largely on a print model. This forced the Samo to learn to read. In retrospect, I would prefer to have used nonprint communication styles unique to them, as the United Bible Society is doing in many parts of the world today (Sundersingh 1999).

10. Both types of foreigners had the power and authority to impose their will upon the Samo, and they could support that authority through a show of force epitomized by a gun. A favorite object lesson of young *kiaps* and policemen involved bringing a large pig into the cleared space in front of a longhouse. With one shot, the pig collapsed on the spot. Such demonstrations were not lost on the Samo. Whatever officers, police, and interpreters said became law. Following the independence of PNG in 1975, the Samo experienced the national officers to be equally as foreign and ethnocentric as the white Australians before them.

11. Bruce Knauft (who has chronicled the high incidence of homicide through sorcery among the Gebusi [1985]) has noted (pers. com. November 1997) that the focus of official attention on the Bedamini allowed the Gebusi to come across as peaceful, thereby leading the administration to be tough on their feared neighbors to the east. This "ruse" enabled the Gebusi (and to a lesser extent others on the Strickland Plain) to carry on much as they always had, with little government intervention—patrols to the south of the Homami River were infrequent and primarily administrative rather than punitive.

12. Ironically, for many of these former cannibals (everyone ate the meat raiders brought home), raiding became the doorway to opportunity. While in jail they learned to speak the trade language (either Hiri Motu, spoken throughout Papua, or Tok Pisin, used more broadly throughout the nation). Some also learned to read

and write, use basic math, and in some cases learned carpentry, mechanics, and other skills. During their long prison stay some would write letters home. Inevitably a letter began "I am, name. I write this letter in order that you not forget me." I had the privilege of reading many of these letters, usually written in a mixture of Samo, Motu, and Tok Pisin. Upon their release from prison, these men returned home only to discover that life had gone on without them. In many cases, wives had been given to younger brothers, and relationships in the village were maintained to support the women and children whose lives had been disrupted by the absence of the accused. With their new knowledge of the world, many returnees found it difficult to settle back into village life. Consequently, some of these displaced men gravitated to Nomad, where they offered their services to the administration. With one foot in each world, they could at once assist their people and outsiders. This resulted in some of them becoming government interpreters, while others became clerk's assistants and medical orderlies. Some even became policemen or joined the army.

13. Despite the role of ASOPA and later of the Administrative College in Port Moresby (see Westermark, Chap. 4) in training officers, support staff were selected primarily because of their expertise (medical, educational, agricultural, etc.) and were sent to work with little, if any, cultural training.

14. This age factor, combined with cultural responsibility, sometimes got in the way of education: "One of the teachers came to me today enraged because a second grader said she could no longer attend school because she was getting married. Upon investigation, I discovered that the student in question was Homebeuyo, a women well past puberty whom her brothers were now ready to exchange. When I pointed out that this girl was at least twenty years old, the teacher sputtered something about her needing to complete her education before getting married. The Samo, however, had other priorities" (personal journal).

15. In the daily context of life, names are replaced by kin terms, which identify everyone in a community of residence with respect to relative age and position within an initiation cycle (cf.: Shaw 1990: 59–61). The dead are never referred to by name, and name taboos among kinsmen are common.

16. These "circumstantial" names resemble names given by mothers when a child is born. Not certain how long a baby will live, and not knowing which ancestral spirit is energizing the child, mothers give babies a name that often serves as a nickname throughout childhood, such as "mother of a tree," "frightened by thunder," or "bright stars." Some of these names also found their way into the census books.

17. More recently, the plan to extend the highland highway requires road builders to survey and engineer a road that bisects the entire region, with Nomad River serving as a crucial staging point for the section between Komomanunda in the Southern Highlands and Kiunga on the Fly River. When completed, this road will reconnect the Samo to the origin of early patrols and their colonial roots.

18. I recall the first time someone asked me what chilies were and I simply responded that they were food. Since the Samo seem to always be in search of food, it was only natural that the inquirer should reach out to the nearest chili bush and, before I could warn him, pop a chili into his mouth. The response to the first bite was pre-

dictable: a wild and vocal attempt to rid himself of the burning sensation. However, when someone came to investigate the noise, he quickly calmed down and told those who had gathered that chilies were "good food" and encouraged them to try it. They did so and were surprised that something so "strong" could be considered valuable as a food. Soon everyone in the village had been encouraged to try this strange "white man's food." Despite my attempts to tell them the chile was to be ground up and used sparingly for flavoring, they wanted no part of spicing up their own food with this new discovery.

19. The Samo have responded by increasingly entering into the life of Papua New Guinea as a nation, seeking higher education (the first Samo entered the University of Papua New Guinea in 1996), running for political office (the most recent speaker of the Western Province Assembly was an enterprising Samo), and paying attention to what is going on around them (most villages have at least one radio and people often gather to listen to the news). With this broader awareness from education comes a changing perspective of themselves. Communities like Nomad and Hanonabi resemble many other small towns throughout PNG—houses, businesses, and service facilities clustered along an airstrip. These communities now act as magnets for population growth.

Chapter 11. Afterword

1. Although Georges Balandier's ([1953] 1970:52) definition of "colonial situation," quoted below, was written almost a half-century ago, I still find it a useful starting point for this discussion, particularly since it so well described the conditions under which I did my first fieldwork in Papua New Guinea:

> (1) the domination imposed by a foreign minority, racially (or ethnically) and culturally different, acting in the name of a racial (or ethnic) and cultural superiority dogmatically affirmed, and imposing itself on an indigenous population constituting a numerical majority but inferior to the dominant group from a material point of view;
> (2) this domination linking radically different civilizations into some form of relationship;
> (3) a mechanized, industrialized society with a powerful economy, a fast tempo of life, and a Christian background, imposing itself on a non-industrialized "backward" society in which the pace of living is much slower and religious institutions are most definitely "non-Christian";
> (4) the fundamentally antagonistic character of the relationship between these two societies resulting from the subservient role which the colonial people are subjected to as "instruments" of the colonial power;
> (5) the need, in maintaining the domination, not only to resort to "force," but also to a system of pseudo-justifications and stereotyped behaviors, etc.

2. This applies to academic anthropologists, not to those gazetted as anthropologists in colonial administrations. In Africa, the latter had typically served earlier as political officers (cf. Kuklick 1991:203–205).

3. Pacific items represent less than 10 percent of Pels's (1997) bibliography, while works by Comaroff, Cohn, et al. make up almost 17 percent. Of course, in both bibliographies, composite volumes listed may contain Pacific material.

4. Even those anthropologists who focused on change (e.g., those who wrote monographs published in the New Guinea Research Bulletin series) were more concerned with "development" than colonialism as it is usually defined.

5. Lucy Mair's ([1948] 1970) *Australia in New Guinea* is a straightforward history of administration and does not really have the analytic impact one might have expected from an anthropologist.

6. As noted below, he is not alone among anthropologists for neglecting the significance of commercial interests. On the other hand, yet another French anthropologist, beginning as early as 1969, has consistently emphasized the significance of plantations in PNG colonial situations (Panoff 1969; see also the special issue Panoff edited of *Journal de la Société des Océanistes* 42, 1986.)

7. Peter Hempenstall (1992), a self-identified "colonial historian," singles out the Reed and Rowley volumes for particular commendation and notes Lawrence's contribution as well. He is one of a number of currently active historians whose work can be recommended to anthropologists concerned with colonialism.

8. On this point, one should also consult the autobiographical writings of the older generation of PNG leaders (e.g., Albert Maori Kiki 1968).

9. Anthropologists who persist in trying to apply Foucault's work to situations where its relevance is questionable should certainly read Stoler's (1995) challenging book.

10. Another outstanding example from a PNG historian is Kituai (1998).

11. Most recently, Bronwen Douglas (1998) has compared historical texts provided by different participants to demonstrate in a striking fashion the complexities of a single colonial situation.

References

Achebe, Chinua. 1988. The Truth of Fiction. In *Hopes and Impediments: Selected Essays*, 138–153. New York: Doubleday.

Aitken, R. B. 1957–1958a. Territory of Papua and New Guinea, Patrol Report No. 7, Goroka. National Archives of Papua New Guinea.

———. 1957–1958b. Territory of Papua and New Guinea, Patrol Report No. 8, Goroka. National Archives of Papua New Guinea.

———. 1959–1960. Territory of Papua and New Guinea, Patrol Report No. 2, Goroka. National Archives of Papua New Guinea.

Allen, Bryant. 1990. The Importance of Being Equal: The Colonial and Postcolonial Experience in the Torricelli Foothills. In *Sepik Heritage: Tradition and Change in Papua New Guinea*, ed. N. Lutkehaus et al., 185–196. Durham, N.C.: Carolina Academic Press.

Allen, Percy. 1918. *Stewart's Handbook of the Pacific Islands: A Reliable Guide to All the Inhabited Islands of the Pacific Ocean for Traders, Tourists, and Settlers.* Sydney: McCarron, Stewart.

———. 1920. *Stewart's Handbook of the Pacific Islands: A Reliable Guide to All the Inhabited Islands of the Pacific Ocean for Traders, Tourists, and Settlers.* With a Bibliography of Island Works. Sydney: McCarron, Stewart.

Anderson, James L. 1970. *Cannibal.* Sydney: A. H. and A. W. Reed.

Appadurai, Arjun. 1990. Disjuncture and Difference in the Global Cultural Economy. *Public Culture* 2 (2): 1–24.

Asad, Talal. 1991. Afterword: From the History of Colonial Anthropology to the Anthropology of Western Hegemony. In *Colonial Situations: Essays on the Contextualization of Ethnographic Knowledge*, ed. George Stocking, 314–324. Madison: University of Wisconsin Press.

———, ed. 1973. *Anthropology and the Colonial Encounter.* London: Athlone Press.

Australian Archives, Canberra. ACT, Series A518/1 Item 852/1/334, Ian McC. Mack, Patrol Officer.

———. CRS A7034 Item 30: Report on Ramu, Purari Areas, March 1933, Morobe District. J. L. Taylor.

———. Series A452/1 Item 1959/3484.

———. Series A518/1 Item U141/3/1.

Baden-Powell, Baden F. S. 1892. *In Savage Isles and Settled Lands: Malaysia, Australasia, and Polynesia 1888–1891.* London: Richard Bentley and Son.

Balandier, Georges. [1953] 1970. *The Sociology of Black Africa: Social Dynamics in Central Africa.* Translated by D. Garman. London: Andre Deutsch.

Barwick, Diane, Jeremy Beckett, and Marie Reay. 1985. W. E. H. Stanner: An Australian Anthropologist. In *Metaphors of Interpretation: Essays in Honour of W. E. H. Stanner*, ed. D. Barwick, J. Beckett, and M. Reay, 1–52. Canberra: Australian National University Press.

Bashkow, Ira. 1995. "The Stakes for Which We Play Are Too High to Allow of Experiment": Colonial Administrators of Papua on Their Anthropological Training by Radcliffe-Brown. *History of Anthropology Newsletter* 22 (2): 3–14.

———. 1996. "To be his witness if that was ever necessary": Raphael Brudo on Malinowski's Fieldwork and Trobriand Ideas of Conception. *History of Anthropology Newsletter* 23 (1): 3–11.

Bassett, Marnie. 1969. *Letters from New Guinea 1921*. Melbourne: The Hawthorn Press.

Beckett, Jeremy. 1989. *Conversations with Ian Hogbin*. Oceania Monograph 35. Sydney: University of Sydney Press.

Bender, Donald. 1965. The Development of French Anthropology. *Journal of the History of the Behavioral Sciences* 1 (2): 139–151.

Bergmann, Wilhelm. n.d. Vierzig Jahre in Neuguinea. 11 vols. Mimeograph.

Berndt, Ronald. 1958. Anthropology and Administration. *South Pacific* 9 (13): 611–619.

Bertrand, Ina, ed. 1989. *Cinema in Australia: A Documentary History*. Kensington: New South Wales University Press.

Bertrand, Ina, and Diane Collins. 1981. *Government and Film in Australia*. Sydney: Currency Press.

Bevan, Theodore. 1890. *Toil, Travel, and Discovery in British New Guinea*. London: Kegan Paul, Trench, Trubner.

Biersack, Aletta. 1995. Introduction: The Huli, Duna, and Ipili Peoples Yesterday and Today. In *Papuan Borderlands: Huli, Duna, and Ipili Perspectives on the Papua New Guinea Highlands*, ed. A. Biersack, 1–54. Ann Arbor: University of Michigan Press.

Biskup, Peter, Brian Jinks, and Hank Nelson. 1968. *A Short History of New Guinea*. Sydney: Angus and Robertson.

Booth, Doris. 1929. *Mountains, Gold, and Cannibals*. Sydney: Cornstalk Press.

Boutilier, James. 1985. Papua New Guinea's Colonial Century: Reflections on Imperialism, Accommodation, and Historical Consciousness. In *History and Ethnohistory in Papua New Guinea*, ed. D. Gewertz and E. Schieffelin, 1–25. Oceania Monograph 28. Sydney: University of Sydney Press.

British New Guinea. 1888. Colonial Reports-Annual.

———. 1889. Colonial Reports-Annual.

Bromilow, William E. 1929. *Twenty Years among Primitive Papuans*. New York: AMS Press.

Brookfield, Harold C. 1972. *Colonialism, Development, and Independence: The Case of the Melanesian Islands in the South Pacific*. Cambridge: Cambridge University Press.

Brown, K. A. 1954–1955. Territory of Papua and New Guinea, Patrol Report No. 5, Maprik. National Archives of Papua New Guinea.

Brown, Paula. 1990. No Dialogue: Premises and Confrontations in Intercultural Encounter. *American Anthropologist* 92: 468–474.

———. 1995. *Beyond a Mountain Valley: The Simbu of Papua New Guinea*. Honolulu: University of Hawai'i Press.

Buck, Pem D. 1988. Cargo-Cult Discourse: Myth and the Rationalization of Labor Relations in Papua New Guinea. *Dialectical Anthropology* 13 (2): 157–172.

Bulbeck, Chilla. 1992. *Australian Women in Papua New Guinea: Colonial Passages, 1920–1960*. Cambridge: Cambridge University Press.

Bulmer, Ralph N. H. 1970. Intense Ethnographic Studies. In *An Atlas of Papua and New*

Guinea, ed. R. G. Ward and D. A. M. Lea, 93–96. Port Moresby: University of Papua and New Guinea.

Burman, Rickie. 1981. Time and Socioeconomic Change on Simbo, Solomon Islands. *Man* 16: 251–267.

Burridge, Kenelm. 1960. *Mambu: A Melanesian Millennium*. London: Methuen.

Butcher, B. B. 1951–1952. Territory of Papua New Guinea, Patrol Report 2, Buin. National Archives of Papua New Guinea.

Cahill, Peter. 1997. A Prodigy of Wastefulness, Corruption, Ignorance, and Indolence: The Expropriation Board in New Guinea 1920–1928. *Journal of Pacific History* 32: 2–23.

Calder, D. G. 1953. Report of Patrol between the Cecilia, Nomad, and Rentoul Rivers. July–August. National Archives of Papua New Guinea.

Campbell, Alexander M. 1898a. Report of the Resident Magistrate for the South-Eastern Division. Colonial Reports-Annual. British New Guinea. Appendix o.

———. 1898b. Letter from A. M. Campbell, Resident Magistrate, with appended typed copies of statements, dated 7th July 1898, Samarai, British New Guinea, to The Government Secretary, Port Moresby. National Archives of Papua New Guinea.

Campbell, Ian C. 1998. Anthropology and the Professionalisation of Colonial Administration in Papua and New Guinea. *The Journal of Pacific History* 33 (1): 69–90.

Carrier, James G., ed. 1992. *History and Tradition in Melanesian Anthropology*. Berkeley: University of California Press.

Chaudhuri, Nupur, and Margaret Strobel, eds. 1992. *Western Women and Empire: Complicity and Resistance*. Bloomington: Indiana University Press.

Cheeseman, Evelyn. 1957. *Things Worth While*. London: Hutchinson.

———. 1965. *Who Stand Alone*. London: Geoffrey Bles.

Chinnery, E. W. Pearson. 1932–1933. Applied Anthropology in New Guinea. In *Annual Report to the Council of the League of Nations on the Administration of the Territory of New Guinea, 1932–1933*, 153–162. Canberra: Commonwealth Government Printer.

Chinnery, Sarah. 1998. *Malaguna Road: The Papua and New Guinea Diaries of Sarah Chinnery*. Edited and introduced by Kate Fortune. Canberra: National Library of Australia.

Chowning, Ann. 1986. The Development of Ethnic Identity and Ethnic Stereotypes on Papua New Guinea Plantations. *Journal de la Société des Oceanistes* 4 (82–83): 153–162.

Clancy, D. J. 1965. Territory of Papua New Guinea, Letter attached to Patrol Report 7, Kieta. National Archives of Papua New Guinea.

Clark, Manning. [1963] 1987. 3rd rev. ed. *A Short History of Australia*. New York: NAL Penguin.

Cleland, Donald. 1969. An Administrator Reflects. *Journal of the Papua and New Guinea Society* 2 (2): 35–45.

Cleleand, R. D. M. 1956–1957. Territory of Papua and New Guinea, Patrol Report No. 4, Kainantu. National Archives of Papua New Guinea.

Clifford, James. 1997. *Routes: Travel and Translation in the Late Twentieth Century*. Cambridge: Harvard University Press.

Cohn, Bernard. 1987. *"An Anthropologist among the Historians" and Other Essays*. Delhi: Oxford University Press.

Cole, R. R. 1948. Territory of Papua New Guinea, Comment attached to Patrol Report 9, Kangu, by B. R. Connolly. National Archives of Papua New Guinea.

Colman, J. 1956–1957a. Territory of Papua and New Guinea, Patrol Report No. 3, Kainantu. National Archives of Papua New Guinea.

———. 1956–1957b. Territory of Papua and New Guinea, Patrol Report No. 5, Kainantu. National Archive of Papua New Guinea.

———. 1956–1957c. Territory of Papua and New Guinea, Patrol Report No. 6, Kainantu. National Archive of Papua New Guinea.

Comaroff, Jean. 1985. *Body of Power, Spirit of Resistance*. Chicago: University of Chicago Press.

Commonwealth of Australia Gazette No. 59, 1927. [Government publication]

Connolly, Bob, and Robin Anderson. 1987. *First Contact: New Guinea Highlanders Encounter the Outside World*. London: Viking Penguin.

Connolly, Brian R. 1949. Territory of Papua New Guinea, Patrol Report, Nagovissi [sic] Area. National Archives of Papua New Guinea.

Cooper, Frederick, and Ann L. Stoler, eds. 1989. Tensions of Empire: Colonial Control and Visions of Rule. *American Ethnologist* 16 (4): 609–619.

———. 1997. *Tensions of Empire: Colonial Cultures in a Bourgeois World*. Berkeley: University of California Press.

Counts, David, and Dorothy Counts. 1976. Apprehension in the Backwaters. *Oceania* 46: 283–305.

Counts, Dorothy. 1978. Christianity in Kaliai: Response to Missionization in Northwest New Britain. In *Mission, Church, and Sect in Oceania*, ed. James Boutilier et al., 355–394. Ann Arbor: University of Michigan Press.

Covenant of the League of Nations. 1974. In Appendices to *Australia and Papua New Guinea*, ed. W. J. Hudson, 179–180. Sydney: Sydney University Press.

D'Albertis, Luigi Maria. 1881. *New Guinea: What I Did and What I Saw*. Boston: Houghton.

Denoon, Donald, ed. 1997. *The Cambridge History of the Pacific Islanders*. Cambridge: Cambridge University Press.

Dirks, Nicholas B. 1987. *The Hollow Crown: Ethnohistory of an Indian Kingdom*. Cambridge: Cambridge University Press.

———. 1992a. From Little King to Landlord: Colonial Discourse and Colonial Rule. In *Colonialism and Culture*, ed. N. Dirks, 175–208. Ann Arbor: University of Michigan Press.

———. 1992b. Introduction to *Colonialism and Culture*, ed. N. Dirks, 1–25. Ann Arbor: University of Michigan Press.

———, ed. 1992. *Colonialism and Culture*. Ann Arbor: University of Michigan Press.

Douglas, Bronwen. 1998. Reading Indigenous Pasts: The "Wagap Affair" of 1862. In *Across the Great Divide: Journeys in History and Anthropology*, ed. Bronwen Douglas, 159–191. Amsterdam: Harwood Academic Publishers.

Douglas, Ian M. 1963. Report of Survey and Building of Rest Houses in the Supei Area. July–August.

Douglas, Ngaire. 1996. *They Came for Savages: One Hundred Years of Tourism in Melanesia*. Alstonville, NSW: Southern Cross Press.

Downs, Ian. 1980. *The Australian Trusteeship 1945–1975*. Canberra: Dept. of Home Affairs, Australian Government Publishing Service.

———. 1986. *The Last Mountain: A Life in Papua New Guinea*. St. Lucia, Queensland: University of Queensland Press.

Dureau, Christine. 1998. Decreed Affinities: Nationhood and the Western Solomon Islands. *Journal of Pacific History* 33 (2): 197–220.

Dwyer, T. 1954–1955. Patrol Report TAL. No. 6 of 54/55. Wariai-Kaliai [*sic*] Subdivision.

Eisenhauer, D. W. 1947–1948. Territory of Papua and New Guinea, Patrol Report No. 1, Goroka. National Archives of Papua New Guinea.

Elder, David. 1956–1957. Territory of Papua New Guinea, Patrol Report, Aita. National Archives of Papua New Guinea.

Errington, Frederick. 1974. Indigenous Ideas of Order, Time, and Transition in a New Guinea Cargo Movement. *American Ethnologist* 1: 255–267.

Errington, Frederick K., and Deborah B. Gewertz. 1995. *Articulating Change in the "Last Unknown."* Boulder, Colo.: Westview Press.

Fahnestock, Bruce, and Sheridan Fahnestock. 1938. *Stars to Windward.* New York: Harcourt, Brace.

Fajans, Jane. 1997. *They Make Themselves: Work and Play among the Bainings of Papua New Guinea.* Chicago: University of Chicago Press.

Falgout, Suzanne. 1995. Americans in Paradise: Anthropologists, Custom, and Democracy in Postwar Micronesia. *Ethnology* 34 (2): 99–111.

Fenbury, David M. 1968. Those Mokolkols! New Britain's Bloody Axemen. *New Guinea and Australia, the Pacific and Southeast Asia* 3 (2): 33–50.

———. 1978. *Practice without Policy: Genesis of Local Government in Papua New Guinea.* Development Studies Centre Monograph No. 13. Canberra: Australian National University.

Finney, Ben. 1973. *Big Men and Business: Entrepreneurship and Economic Growth in the New Guinea Highlands.* Canberra: Australian National University Press.

Firth, Stewart. 1982. *New Guinea under the Germans.* Melbourne: Melbourne University Press.

Fitzpatrick, David. 1994. *Oceans of Consolation: Personal Accounts of Irish Migration to Australia.* Ithaca: Cornell University Press.

Fitzpatrick, P. 1971. Report of Census Revision and Routine Administration in Upper Strickland Census Division #27, February 2–March 25.

Forbes, Rosita. 1919. *Unconducted Wanderers.* London: John Lane.

Foster, Robert J. 1995. *Nation Making: Emergent Identities in Postcolonial Melanesia.* Ann Arbor: University of Michigan Press.

Fulton, Edward T. W. Papers 1936–1948. Canberra: Pacific Manuscripts Bureau #610. Microfilm, 1 reel.

Gammage, Bill. 1996a. Police and Power during Contact in the Papua New Guinea Highlands. In *Work in Progress: Essays in New Guinea Highlands Ethnography in Honour of Paula Brown Glick,* ed. Hal Levine and Anton Ploeg, 123–142. Frankfurt am Main: Peter Lang.

———. 1996b. Police and Power in the Prewar Papua New Guinea Highlands. *Journal of Pacific History* 31: 162–177.

———. 1998. *The Sky Travellers.* Melbourne: Melbourne University Press.

Gerholm, Tomas, and Ulf Hannerz. 1982. Introduction: The Shaping of National Anthropologies. *Ethnos* 47 (1–2): 5–35.

Gewertz, Deborah B., and Frederick K. Errington. 1991. *Twisted Histories, Altered Contexts:*

Representing the Chambri in a World System. Cambridge: Cambridge University Press.

Gewertz, Deborah B., and Edward Schieffelin, eds. 1985. *History and Ethnohistory in Papua New Guinea*. Oceania Monograph 28. Sydney: University of Sydney Press.

Giddings, Richard J. 1969–1970. Territory of Papua and New Guinea, Patrol Report No. 12, Kainantu. National Archives of Papua New Guinea.

———. 1989. Personal interview with the author, Kundiawa, Simbu Province, July 30.

Goddard, David. 1972. Anthropology: The Limits of Functionalism. In *Ideology in Social Science: Readings in Critical Social Theory*, Robin Blackburn, 62–75. London: Panther Books.

Godelier, Maurice. 1986. *The Making of Great Men*. Cambridge: Cambridge University Press.

Goldman, Marion. 1981. *Gold Diggers and Silver Miners: Prostitution and Social Life on the Comstock Lode*. Ann Arbor: University of Michigan Press.

Gordon, Robert J. 1983. The Decline of Kiapdom and the Resurgence of "Tribal Fighting." *Oceania* 53 (3): 205–223.

Gordon, Robert J., and Mervyn J. Meggitt. 1985. *Law and Order in the New Guinea Highlands: Encounters with Enga*. Hanover: University Press of New England.

Gow, A. F. 1956–1957. Territory of Papua New Guinea, Letter attached to Patrol Report No. 8, Buin, of K. Graham. National Archives of Papua New Guinea.

Graham, K. 1956–1957. Territory of Papua New Guinea, Patrol Report No. 8, Buin. National Archives of Papua New Guinea.

———. 1957. Territory of Papua New Guinea, Patrol Report No. 9, Boku. National Archives of Papua New Guinea.

Greenwood, Emma. 1995. No Migrants Here: Migrant Absence within Australian Migration Publicity Films. *Antithesis* 7 (2): 108–122.

Grewal, Inderpal. 1996. *Home and Harem: Nation, Gender, Empire, and the Cultures of Travel*. Durham, N.C.: Duke University Press.

Griffin, James. 1990. Bougainville Is a Special Case. In *The Bougainville Crisis*, ed. R. J. May and M. Spriggs, 1–15. Bathurst: Crawford House Press.

Griffin, James, Hank Nelson, and Stewart Firth. 1979. *Papua New Guinea: A Political History*. Richmond, Victoria: Heinemann Educational Australia.

Grimshaw, Beatrice. 1908. The Truth about Papua. Series. *Sydney Morning Herald*.

———. 1911. *The New New Guinea*. London: Hutchinson.

Griswold, Robert. 1983. *Family and Divorce in California, 1850–1890: Victorian Illusions and Everyday Reality*. Albany: State University of New York Press.

Grosart, Ian. 1980. Australian School of Pacific Administration (ASOPA). In *Encyclopedia of Papua New Guinea*, Peter Ryan (general editor), 50–52. Melbourne: University of Melbourne Press.

Grove, D. S. 1947–1948. Territory of Papua and New Guinea, Patrol Report No. 5, Kainantu. National Archives of Papua New Guinea.

Guha, Ranajit. 1983. *Elementary Aspects of Peasant Insurgency in Colonial India*. Delhi: Oxford University Press.

———. 1988. The Prose of Counter-Insurgency. In *Selected Subaltern Studies*, ed. Ranajit Guha and Gayatri Chakravorty Spivak. New York: Oxford University Press.

———, ed. 1985. *Subaltern Studies IV: Writings on South Asian History and Society*. Delhi: Oxford University Press.

Handler, Richard, and Daniel Segal. 1993. Introduction to *Nations, Colonies and Metropoles*. *Social Analysis* 33: 3–8. Special Issue, *Nations, Colonies and Metropoles*, edited by D. Segal and R. Handler.

Harding, Thomas. 1997. Across the "Great Divide": Tarosi, Yali, and Darwinian Evolution. Paper presented at the Annual Meeting of the Association for Social Anthropology in Oceania, San Diego, Calif.

Hasluck, Paul. 1976. *A Time for Building: Australian Administration in Papua and New Guinea 1951–1963*. Melbourne: Melbourne University Press.

Hays, Terence E. 1992. A Historical Background to Anthropology in the Papua New Guinea Highlands. In *Ethnographic Presents: Pioneering Anthropologists in the Papua New Guinea Highlands*, ed. T. Hays, 1–36. Berkeley: University of California Press.

———. 1996. What Does One Do with White People Who Stay? In *Work in Progress: Essays in New Guinea Highlands Ethnography in Honour of Paula Brown Glick*, ed. Hal Levine and Anton Ploeg, 173–184. Frankfurt am Main: Peter Lang.

———, ed. 1992. *Ethnographic Presents: Pioneering Anthropologists in the Papua New Guinea Highlands*. Berkeley: University of California.

Hempenstall, Peter. 1992. "My Place": Finding a Voice within Pacific Colonial Studies. In *Pacific Islands History: Journeys and Transformations*, ed. Brij V. Lal, 60–78. Canberra: The Journal of Pacific History.

Hides, Jack G. 1935. *Through Wildest Papua*. London: Blackie and Sons.

Hoad, Robert. 1968–1969. Territory of Papua New Guinea, Letter attached to Patrol Report No. 1, Boku, of J. R. Gyngell. National Archives of Papua New Guinea.

Hogbin, H. Ian. 1951. *Transformation Scene: The Changing Culture of a New Guinea Village*. London: Routledge and Kegan Paul.

———. 1958. *Social Change*. London: Watts.

———. 1963. *Kinship and Marriage in a New Guinea Village*. London: The Athlone Press.

Hook, D. J. 1954–1955. Territory of Papua New Guinea, Patrol Report No. 2, Buin. National Archives of Papua New Guinea.

———. 1955. Territory of Papua New Guinea, Appendix B, Special Report on Misiamo [sic] of Nagavisi [sic], Patrol Report No. 1, Boku. National Archives of Papua New Guinea.

———. 1956–1957. Territory of Papua New Guinea, Patrol Report No. 1, Boku. National Archives of Papua New Guinea.

Huber, Mary Taylor. 1988. *The Bishops' Progress: A Historical Ethnography of Catholic Missionary Experience on the Sepik Frontier*. Washington, D.C.: Smithsonian Institution Press.

Hudson, W. J. 1974. Introduction to *Australia and Papua New Guinea*, ed. W. J. Hudson, 1–7. Sydney: Sydney University Press.

Hudson, W. J., and Jill Daven. 1974. Papua and New Guinea since 1945. In *Australia and Papua New Guinea*, ed. W. J. Hudson, 151–177. Sydney: Sydney University Press.

Humphries, W. R. 1923. *Patrolling in Papua*. New York: Henry Holt.

Hyam, Ronald. 1990. *Empire and Sexuality: The British Experience*. Manchester: Manchester University Press.

Inglis, Amirah. 1974. *"Not a White Woman Safe": Sexual Anxiety and Politics in Port Moresby 1920–1934*. Canberra: Australian National University Press.

——. 1975. *The White Women's Protection Ordinance: Sexual Anxiety and Politics in Papua.* London: Sussex University Press.

Jaarsma, Sjoerd R. 1990. *Waarneming en interpretatie: Vergaring en gebruik van etnografische informatie in Nederlands Nieuw Guinea (1950–1962).* Utrecht, Neth.: ISOR.

——. 1993. "More Pastoral Than Academic . . .": Practice and Purpose of Missionary Ethnographic Research (West New Guinea, 1950–1962). *Anthropos* 88: 109–133.

——. 1994. "Your Work Is of No Use to Us . . .": Administrative Interests in Ethnographic Research (West New Guinea, 1950–1962). *The Journal of Pacific History* 29 (2): 153–171.

——. 1996. Cults as Ethnography: On Acknowledging Reflexivity in the People We Study. Paper presented at the Third Biannual Conference of the European Society for Oceanists (ESfO), Copenhagen, December.

——. 1997. Ethnographic Perceptions of Cargo: The Invention of a Concept. In *Cultural Dynamics of Religious Change in Oceania,* ed. Ad Borsboom and Ton Otto, 67–86. Leiden, Neth.: KITLV Press.

——. 1998. Ethnography: Authority and "Voice": Some Thoughts on the Changing Nature of Ethnography. In *Anthropology of Difference: Essays in Honour of Professor Arie De Ruijter,* ed. Selma van Londen and Els van Dongen, 27–45. Utrecht, Neth.: ISOR.

——. n.d.a. Some Remarkable Work Indeed: A Colonial History of West New Guinea. Manuscript.

——. n.d.b. An Unacknowledged Tribe: Colonial Imagination of "Urban Papuans" and Indigenous Elites in Netherlands New Guinea. *The Journal of Pacific History.* Forthcoming.

Jackson, A. K. 1951. Territory of Papua New Guinea, Patrol Report, Bougainville. National Archives of Papua New Guinea.

Jackson, H. H. 1947–1948. Territory of Papua and New Guinea, Patrol Report No. 4, Kainantu. National Archives of Papua New Guinea.

Jackson, Keith. 1983. Postcolonial Mood at Australia's Development Institute. *Pacific Islands Monthly* 54: 25–28.

Jameson, Elizabeth, and Susan Armitage, eds. 1997. *Writing the Range: Race, Class, and Culture in the Women's West.* Norman: University of Oklahoma Press.

Jinks, Brian. 1982. Australia's Postwar Policy for New Guinea and Papua. *Journal of Pacific History* 17 (1): 86–100.

Johnson, E. R. 1956–1957. Territory of Papua and New Guinea, Patrol Report No. 10, Goroka. National Archives of Papua New Guinea.

——. 1957–1958a. Territory of Papua and New Guinea, Patrol Report No. 1, Goroka. National Archives of Papua New Guinea.

——. 1957–1958b. Territory of Papua and New Guinea, Patrol Report No. 3, Goroka. National Archives of Papua New Guinea.

Jolly, Margaret, and Nicholas Thomas, guest editors. 1992. Introduction: The Politics of Tradition. *Oceania* 62 (4): 241–354.

Joyce, Roger B. 1971. *Sir William MacGregor 1876–1919.* Melbourne: Oxford University Press.

Kapferer, Bruce. 1988. *Legends of People, Myths of State: Violence, Intolerance, and Political Culture in Sri Lanka and Australia.* Washington, D.C.: Smithsonian Institution Press.

Kaplan, Martha. 1995. *Neither Cargo nor Cult: Ritual Politics and the Colonial Imagination in Fiji*. Durham, N.C.: Duke University Press.

Keesing, Roger. 1985. Killers, Big Men and Priests on Malaita: Reflections on a Melanesian Troika. *Ethnology* 24: 237–252.

Keesing, Roger, and Margaret Jolly. 1992. Epilogue to *History and Tradition in Melanesian Anthropology*, ed. James G. Carrier. Berkeley: University of California Press.

Kempf, Wolfgang. 1992. The Second Coming of the Lord: Early Christianization, Episodic Time, and the Cultural Construction of Continuity in Sibog. *Oceania* 63: 72–87.

Kent, J. 1956–1957. Territory of Papua and New Guinea, Patrol Report No. 8, Goroka. National Archives of Papua New Guinea.

Kettle, Ellen. 1979. *That They Might Live*. Sydney: F. P. Leonard.

Kiki, Albert M. 1968. *Kiki: Ten Thousand Years in a Lifetime: A New Guinea Biography*. Melbourne: F. W. Cheshire.

Kituai, August Ibrum K. 1998. *My Gun, My Brother: The World of the Papua New Guinea Colonial Police, 1920–1960*. Honolulu: University of Hawai'i Press.

Knapman, Claudia. 1986. *White Women in Fiji 1835–1930: The Ruin of Empire?* Sydney: Allen and Unwin.

Knauft, Bruce M. 1985. *Good Company and Violence: Sorcery and Social Action in a Lowland New Guinea Society*. Berkeley: University of California Press.

———. 1999. *From Primitive to Postcolonial in Melanesia and Anthropology*. Ann Arbor: University of Michigan Press.

Kohn, T. 1988. A Text in Its Context: F. E. Williams and the Valaila Madness. *Journal of the Anthropological Society of Oxford* 19 (1): 25–42.

Kuklick, Henrika. 1978. The Sins of the Fathers: British Anthropology and African Colonial Administration. *Research in Sociology of Knowledge* 1: 93–119.

———. 1991. *The Savage Within: The Social History of British Anthropology, 1885–1945*. Cambridge: Cambridge University Press.

Kuper, Adam. 1983. *Anthropologists and Anthropology: The British School 1922–1972*. 2d ed. London: Allen Lang.

———. 1991. Anthropologists and the History of Anthropology. *Critique of Anthropology* 11 (2): 125–142.

Lagerberg, Cees S. I. J. 1962. Jaren van reconstructie: Nieuw-Guinea van 1949 tot 1961. Den Bosch, Neth.: Zuid-Nederlandsche Drukkerij.

Lagerberg, Kees. 1979. *West Irian and Jakarta Imperialism*. New York: St Martin's Press.

Lake, Marilyn. 1998. Australian Frontier Feminism and the Marauding White Man. In *Gender and Imperialism*, ed. Clare Midgly, 123–136. Manchester: Manchester University Press.

Lambden, W. J. G. 1956–1957. Territory of Papua and New Guinea, Patrol Report No. 1, Kainantu. National Archives of Papua New Guinea.

Lang, Malcolm. 1968. Territory of Papua New Guinea, Letter to Sohano, Buin. National Archives of Papua New Guinea.

———. 1970. Territory of Papua New Guinea, Letter to L. U-Yassi, Buin. National Archives of Papua New Guinea.

Langmore, Diane. 1989. *Missionary Lives: Papua, 1874–1914*. Honolulu: University of Hawai'i Press.

Lansell, Ross, and Peter Beilby, eds. 1982. *The Documentary Film in Australia*. Melbourne: Cinema Papers.

Laracy, Hugh. 1976. *Marists and Melanesians*. Honolulu: University of Hawai'i Press.

Lattas, Andrew. 1996. Humanitarianism and Australian Nationalism in Colonial Papua: Hubert Murray and the Project of Caring for the Self of the Coloniser and the Colonised. *The Australian Journal of Anthropology* 7: 141–165.

———. 1998. *Cultures of Secrecy: Reinventing Race in Bush Kaliai Cargo Cults*. Madison: The University of Wisconsin Press.

———, ed. 1992. Alienating Mirrors: Christianity, Cargo Cults, and Colonialism in Melanesia. *Oceania* 63 (1).

Latukefu, Sione, ed. 1989. *Papua New Guinea: A Century of Colonial Impact 1884–1984*. Boroko, PNG: The National Research Institute and the University of Papua New Guinea.

Lawrence, Peter. 1964a. *Road Belong Cargo: A Study of the Cargo Movement in the Southern Madang District, New Guinea*. Manchester: Manchester University Press.

———. 1964b. Social Anthropology and the Training of Administration Officers at the Australian School of Pacific Administration. *Anthropological Forum* 1 (2): 195–208.

Leabeater, T. J. 1948–1949. Territory of Papua and New Guinea, Patrol Report No. 3, Goroka. National Archives of Papua New Guinea.

———. 1949–1950. Territory of Papua and New Guinea, Patrol Report No. 1, Goroka. National Archives of Papua New Guinea.

League of Nations. 1926–1927. Report to the Council of the League of Nations on the Administration of the Territory of New Guinea, 1 July 1926–30 June 1927.

Leahy, Michael. 1991. *Exploration in Highland New Guinea, 1930–1935*. Tuscaloosa: University of Alabama Press.

Lepowsky, Maria. 1991. The Way of the Ancestors: Custom, Innovation, and Resistance. *Ethnology* 30 (3): 217–225.

———. 1993. *Fruit of the Motherland: Gender in an Egalitarian Society*. New York: Columbia University Press.

———. n.d.a. Gold Dust and Kula Shells. Manuscript.

———. n.d.b. Malinowski, White Traders, and the History of Anthropology. Manuscript.

———. n.d.c. Historicizing Kula. Manuscript.

Lett, Lewis. 1935. *Knights Errant of Papua*. Edinburgh: William Blackwell and Sons.

Levine, Hal B., and M. Wolfzahn Levine. 1979. *Urbanization in Papua New Guinea: A Study of Ambivalent Townsmen*. Cambridge: Cambridge University Press.

Levy, Jo Ann. 1992. *They Saw the Elephant: Women in the California Gold Rush*. Norman: University of Oklahoma Press.

Lewis, D. C. 1996. *The Plantation Dream: Developing British New Guinea and Papua 1884–1942*. Canberra: Journal of Pacific History.

Liep, John. 1983. "This Civilizing Influence": The Colonial Transformation of Rossel Island. *Journal of Pacific History* 18 (2): 113–131.

Lindstrom, Lamont. 1993. *Cargo Cult: Strange Stories of Desire from Melanesia and Beyond*. Honolulu: University of Hawai'i Press.

Lindstrom, Lamont, and Geoffrey M. White. 1990. *Island Encounters: Black and White Memories of the Pacific War*. New York: Smithsonian Institution.

Linsley, G. 1948–1949. Territory of Papua and New Guinea, Patrol Report No. 7, Kainantu. National Archives of Papua New Guinea.

Loizos, Peter. 1977. Personal Evidence: Comments on an Acrimonious Argument. *Anthropological Forum* 4 (2): 137–144.

Long, Gavin. 1963. *The Final Campaigns: Australia in the War of 1939–1945.* Series 1, Army Vol. 7. Canberra: Australian War Memorial.

Lovett, Richard. 1903. *James Chalmers: His Autobiography and Letters.* London: The Religious Tract Society.

Lutkehaus, Nancy. 1986. "She was Very Cambridge": Camilla Wedgwood and the History of Women in British Social Anthropology. *American Ethnologist* 13 (4): 776–798.

Lyons, Peter. 1968–1969. Territory of Papua and New Guinea, Patrol Report No. 12, Kainantu. National Archives of Papua New Guinea.

MacDonald, Mary N. 2000. Writing about Culture and Talking about God: Christian Ethnography in Melanesia. In *Ethnographic Artifacts: Challenges to a Reflexive Anthropology,* ed. Sjoerd R. Jaarsma and Marta A. Rohatynskyj, 150–173. Honolulu: University of Hawai'i Press.

Macintyre, Stuart. 1986. 1901–1942: The succeeding age. In *The Oxford History of Australia,* Vol. 4., G. Bolton (general editor).

Mack, Ian McCallum. 1926–1931. Patrol Reports, New Britain. PMB1036. 35mm Microfilm. Canberra: Pacific Manuscripts Bureau.

Mack, Margaret. 1996–1999. Personal correspondence with the author.

Mack, Richard. 1996–1999. Personal correspondence with the author.

———, ed. 1994. On Patrol: The New Britain Patrol Reports (1926–1931), Territory of New Guinea of Patrol Officer Ian McCallum Mack (1900–1933). Victoria, Australia: Richard Mack.

MacKenzie, John. 1984. *Propaganda and Empire: The Manipulation of British Public Opinion, 1880–1960.* Manchester: University of Manchester Press.

Mackenzie, S. S. 1987. *The Australians at Rabaul: The Official History of Australia in the War of 1914–1918.* Vol. 10. Brisbane: University of Queensland Press. [Originally published by the Australian War Memorial, 1927]

Mair, Lucy. [1948] 1970. *Australia in New Guinea.* 2d ed. Melbourne: Melbourne University Press.

Malinowski, Bronislaw. 1989. *A Diary in the Strict Sense of the Term.* Stanford: Stanford University Press. [Originally published 1967]

Mannoni, Octave [1950] 1964. *Prospero and Caliban: The Psychology of Colonization.* Translated by Pamela Powesland. New York: Frederick A. Praeger.

Maquet, Jacques. 1964. Objectivity in Anthropology. *Current Anthropology* 5: 47–55.

Marcus, George. 1990. Imagining the Whole: Ethnography's Contemporary Efforts to Situate Itself. *Critique of Anthropology* 9 (3): 7–30.

Marcus, George, and Michael Fischer. 1986. *Anthropology as Cultural Critique: An Experimental Moment in the Human Sciences.* Chicago: University of Chicago Press.

Mason, Peter. 1995. Colonialism's Culture and Its Limits. *Anthropos* 90: 576–581.

Mayo, John. 1973. A Punitive Expedition in British New Guinea 1886. *Journal of Pacific History* 8: 89–99.

McAuley, James. 1953a. Anthropologists and Administrators. *South Pacific* 6 (10): 518–522.

———. 1953b. Australia's Future in New Guinea. *South Pacific* 6 (11): 544–549, 556.

————. 1974. *The Grammar of the Real: Selected Prose, 1959–1974*. Melbourne: Oxford University Press.

McBride, Brian. 1959. Report of Contact with Tribes to the East of the Strickland River October–November. National Archives of Papua New Guinea.

McCall, Grant. 1982. Anthropology in Australia: Introductory Remarks. In *Anthropology in Australia: Essays to Honour Fifty Years of "Mankind,"* ed. G. McCall, 1–21. Sydney: The Anthropological Society of New South Wales.

McCalman, Janet. 1984. *Struggletown: Public and Private Life in Richmond, 1900–1965*. Carlton, Victoria: Melbourne University Press.

————. 1993. *Journeyings: The Biography of a Middle-Class Generation 1920–1990*. Melbourne: Melbourne University Press.

McCarthy, J. Keith. 1933. Patrol Reports and Other Papers, 1926–1952. PMB616. Canberra: Pacific Manuscripts Bureau. Microfiche.

————. 1963. *Patrol into Yesterday: My New Guinea Years*. Melbourne: F. W. Cheshire.

McDowell, Nancy. 1985. Past and Future: The Nature of Episodic Time in Bun. In *History and Ethnohistory in Papua New Guinea*, ed. D. Gewertz and E. L. Schieffelin, 26–39. Sydney: Oceania Monograph 28.

————. 1988. A Note on Cargo Cults and Cultural Constructions of Change. *Pacific Studies* 11: 121–134.

McMurchy, Megan. 1994. The Documentary. In *Australian Cinema*, ed. S. Murray, 179–200. St. Leonards, NSW: Allen and Unwin.

McRae, Keith. 1974. *Kiaps, Missionaries, and Highlanders. New Guinea and Australia, the Pacific, and Southeast Asia* 9 (2): 16–28.

Mead, Margaret. 1960. Weaver of the Border. In *In the Company of Man: Twelve Portraits of Anthropological Informants*, ed. Joseph P. Casagrande, 175–210. New York: Harper and Row.

————. 1972. *Blackberry Winter: My Earlier Years*. New York: William Morrow.

Meek, A. S. 1913. *A Naturalist in Cannibal Land*. London: T. Fisher Unwin.

Memmi, Albert. [1957] 1967. *The Colonizer and the Colonized*. Translated by Howard Greenfeld. Boston: Beacon Press.

Midgely, Clare, ed. 1998. *Gender and Imperialism*. Manchester: Manchester University Press.

Miedema, Jelle. 1984. *De Kebar 1855–1980: Sociale structuur en religie in de Vogelkop van West-Nieuw-Guinea*. Dordrecht, Neth.: Foris.

Mikloucho-Maclay, Nikolai N. 1975. *Mikloucho-Maclay: New Guinea Diaries 1871–1883*. Translated by C. L. Sentinella. Madang: Kristen Press.

Milar, I. R. 1966–1967. Territory of Papua and New Guinea, Patrol Report No. 10, Goroka. National Archives of Papua New Guinea.

Monkton, Charles A. W. 1921. *Some Experiences of a New Guinea Resident Magistrate*. London: John Lane.

Moran, Albert. 1991. *Projecting Australia: Government Film since 1945*. Sydney: Currency Press.

————. n.d. Interview with Ron Maslyn Williams, undated. Cover title No. 271790. Canberra: National Sound and Film Archives.

Mordaunt, Elinor. 1930. *The Further Venture Book*. London: John Lane.

Morris, B. M. 1945. Territory of Papua New Guinea, GOCAGAU, Document 252. National Archives of Papua New Guinea.

Morrison, Charles. 1984. Three Styles of Imperial Ethnography: British Officials as Anthropologists in India. *Knowledge and Society* 5: 141–169.

Moynihan, Ruth, Susan Armitage, and Christiane Dichamp, eds. 1998. *So Much to Be Done: Women Settlers on the Mining and Ranching Frontier*. 2d ed. Lincoln: University of Nebraska Press.

Murray, J. Hubert P. 1908. Report on Visits to Sudest, Rossel, and Misima Islands. Papua Annual Reports 1907–1908.

———. 1912. *Papua, or British New Guinea*. New York: Charles Scribner's Sons; and London: T. Fisher Unwin.

Muspratt, Eric. 1931. *My South Sea Island*. New York: William Morrow.

Mytinger, Caroline. 1946. *New Guinea Headhunt*. New York: Macmillan.

Nash, Jill. 1974. *Matriliny and Modernisation: The Nagovisi of South Bougainville*. New Guinea Research Bulletin 55. Canberra: Australian National University Press.

Nash, Jill, and Eugene Ogan. 1990. The Red and the Black: Bougainvillean Perceptions of Other Papua New Guineans. *Pacific Studies* 13 (2): 1–18.

Nelson, Diane M. 1997. Crucifixion Stories, the 1869 Caste War of Chiapas, and Negative Consciousness: A Disruptive Subaltern Study. *American Ethnologist* 21 (2): 331–354.

Nelson, Hank. 1976. *Black, White, and Gold: Goldmining in Papua New Guinea 1878–1930*. Canberra: Australian National University Press.

———. [1982] 1990. *Taim Belong Masta: The Australian Involvement with Papua New Guinea*. Crows Nest, NSW: Australian Broadcasting Corporation.

Neumann, Klaus. 1992. *Not the Way It Really Was: Constructing the Tolai Past*. Center for Pacific Islands Studies Monograph Series No. 10. Honolulu: University of Hawai'i Press.

Newbury, Colin. 1989. Land, Labour, Capital, and Colonial Government in Papua New Guinea. In *Papua New Guinea: A Century of Colonial Impact, 1884–1984*, ed. S. Latukefu, 37–48. Boroko, PNG: The National Research Institute and the University of Papua New Guinea.

New Guinea Gazette. 1915. July.

New Guinea Patrol. 1958. 35mm Eastmancolor, 43 min. Producer: R. Maslyn Williams. Director: Peter Dimond. Script: R. Maslyn Williams. Cameraman: John Leake. Australian Commonwealth Film Unit and Supreme Sound Studios.

Nilles, J. 1987. *They Went Out to Sow*. Rome: Analectica SVD 62.

Norton, John R. 1952. Territory of Papua and New Guinea, Report on Musiamo [*sic*] of Nagovisi, following Territory of Papua New Guinea, Patrol Report No. B. N. 1, Buin, 1951–1952. National Archives of Papua New Guinea.

O'Collins, Mave. 1979. Social Justice and Neocolonialism. Inaugural Lecture. Port. Moresby: University of Papua New Guinea.

Odgers, Len. 1942–1943. Diary and Transcript. Canberra: Pacific Manuscripts Bureau #610. Microfiche.

Ogan, Eugene. 1972. *Business and Cargo: Socioeconomic Change among the Nasioi of South Bougainville*. New Guinea Research Bulletin 44. Canberra: Australian National University Press.

———. 1994. Review of History and Tradition in Melanesian Anthropology. *The Contemporary Pacific* 6: 224–229.

————. 1996a. The (Re)making of Modern New Guinea. *Reviews in Anthropology* 25: 95–106.

————. 1996b. Copra Came before Copper: The Nasioi of Bougainville and Plantation Colonialism, 1902–1964. *Pacific Studies* 19 (1): 31–51.

Ohnuki-Tierney, Emiko, ed. 1990. *Culture through Time: Anthropological Approaches*. Stanford: Stanford University Press.

Oliver, Douglas L. 1943. *The Horomorun Concepts of South Bougainville: A Study in Comparative Religion*. Papers of the Peabody Museum of American Archaeology and Ethnology 29 (1): 1–27.

————. 1955. *A Solomon Island Society*. Cambridge: Harvard University Press.

————. 1991. *Black Islanders: A Personal Perspective on Bougainville 1937–1991*. Melbourne: Hyland House Publishing.

O'Neill, Jack. 1979. *Up From the South: A Prospector in New Guinea 1931–1937*. Melbourne: Oxford University Press.

Ormsby, R. G. 1945. Territory of Papua New Guinea, Comment attached to Patrol Report, ANGAU, Toko, by C. W. Slattery. National Archives of Papua New Guinea.

Osborne, D. H. 1942. How Sudest Gold Was Found. *Pacific Islands Monthly* 13, no. 5 (December): 16–17.

Otto, Ton. 1991. *The Politics of Tradition in Baluan: Social Change and the Construction of the Past in a Manus Society*. Nijmegen, Neth.: Centre for Pacific Studies.

Otto, Ton, and Nicholas Thomas, eds. 1997. *Narratives of Nation in the South Pacific*. Amsterdam: Harwood Academic Publishers.

Pacific Islands Monthly. 1971. September, pp. 47–48.

Panoff, Michel. 1969. An Experiment in Intertribal Contacts: The Maenge Labourers in European Plantations 1915–1942. *The Journal of Pacific History* 4: 111–125.

————. 1979. Travailleurs, recruteurs et planteurs dans l'Archipel Bismarck de 1885 à 1914. *Journal de la Société des Oceanistes* 35 (64): 159–173.

————. 1990. Die Rekrutierung von Arbeitskräfter für die Plantagen in Neuguinea und ihre demographischen Folgen. *Sociologus* 40 (2): 121–132.

Panoff, Michel, and Francoise Panoff. 1968. *L'Ethnologue et Son Ombre*. Paris: Payot.

Parker, F. 1964–1965. Territory of Papua and New Guinea, Patrol Report No. 2, Kainantu. National Archives of Papua New Guinea.

Parker, R. S. 1995. Appraising the Colonial Record: Australia in Papua New Guinea. In *Lines across the Sea: Colonial Inheritance in the Post-Colonial Pacific*, ed. Brij V. Lal and Hank Nelson. Brisbane: Pacific History Association.

Pels, Peter. 1997. The Anthropology of Colonialism: Culture, History, and the Emergence of Western Governmentality. In *Annual Review of Anthropology*, Vol. 26, ed. William H. Durham et al., 163–183. Palo Alto, Calif.: Annual Reviews.

Petersen, Glen. 1996. Colonialism as a Fractured Project, Review of Thomas. *Current Anthropology* 35 (5): 885–886.

Pike, Andrew, and Merrilyn Fitzpatrick. 1977. *Interview with Ron Maslyn Williams*. Episode title No. 220557. Series 286882. Film Pioneers Oral History Project. Canberra: National Sound and Film Archives.

Pitt. A. D. 1960. Territory of Papua New Guinea, Patrol Report No. 3, Boku. National Archives of Papua New Guinea.

Ploeg, Anton. 1979. The Establishment of the Pax Neerlandica in the Bokondini Area. In *The Pacification of Melanesia*, ed. M. Rodman and M. Cooper, 161–177. Ann Arbor: University of Michigan Press.

Pouwer, Jan. 1968. *Translation at Sight: The Job of a Social Anthropologist*. Wellington, NZ: Victoria University.

Powdermaker, Hortense. 1966. *Stranger and Friend: The Way of an Anthropologist*. New York: W. W. Norton.

Pratt, Mary Louise. 1992. *Imperial Eyes: Travel Writing and Transculturation*. London: Routledge.

Rabaul Times. 1933. June 30.

Radford, Robin. 1977. The Death of Aiamontina and Ian Mack. *Oral History* 5 (7): 58–73.

———. 1987. *Highlanders and Foreigners in the Upper Ramu: The Kainantu Area 1919–1942*. Melbourne: Melbourne University Press.

Read, Kenneth E. 1986. *Return to the High Valley: Coming Full Circle*. Berkeley: University of California Press.

Reay, Marie. 1993. An Innocent in the Garden of Eden. In *Ethnographic Presents: Pioneering Anthropologists in the Papua New Guinea Highlands*, ed. Terence E. Hays, 137–166. Berkeley: University of California Press.

Redmond, H. J. 1966–1967. Territory of Papua New Guinea, Letter attached to Patrol Report No. 2, Boku. National Archives of Papua New Guinea.

Reed, Stephen Winsor. 1943. *The Making of Modern New Guinea*. Philadelphia: American Philosophical Society Memoirs, Vol. 18.

Reining, P. 1967. Urgent Research Projects. *Current Anthropology* 8: 362–416.

Report of Australian National University Findings in the Nomad River Region. 1973. Supreme Court Document #634, 1971.

Rhys, Lloyd. 1942. *High Lights and Flights in New Guinea*. London: Hodder and Stoughton.

Riley, Glenda. 1984. *Women and Indians on the Frontier, 1825–1915*. Albuquerque: University of New Mexico Press.

Rimoldi, Max, and Eleanor Rimoldi. 1992. *Hahalis and the Labour of Love: A Social Movement on Buka Island*. Oxford: Berg.

Roberts, Jan. 1996. *Voices from a Lost World: Australian Women and Children in Papua New Guinea before the Japanese Invasion*. Alexandria, NSW: Millenium Books.

Robinson, J. R., and R. R. Cole. 1947–1948. Territory of Papua and New Guinea, Patrol Report No. 10, Bougainville. National Archives of Papua New Guinea.

Robson, A. C. 1958–1959. Territory of Papua New Guinea, Patrol Report No. 2, Boku. National Archives of Papua New Guinea.

———. 1961. Territory of Papua New Guinea, Patrol Report No. 2, Boku. National Archives of Papua New Guinea.

———. 1961–1962. Territory of Papua New Guinea, Patrol Report No. 3, Boku. National Archives of Papua New Guinea.

Robson, Robert W. 1971. *Queen Emma: The Samoan-American Girl Who Founded a Commercial Empire in Nineteenth-Century New Guinea*. Sydney: Pacific Publications. [Originally published 1965]

Rodgers, Susan. 1995. *Telling Lives, Telling History: Autobiography and Historical Imagination in Modern Indonesia*. Berkeley: University of California Press.

Rodman, Margaret, and Matthew Cooper, eds. 1979. *The Pacification of Melanesia*. Ann Arbor: University of Michigan Press.

Roe, Margriet. 1962. A History of Southeast Papua to 1930. Ph.D. diss., Department of Pacific History, Australian National University. Canberra, Australia.

———. 1971. Papua-New Guinea and War, 1941–45. In *Australia and Papua New Guinea*, ed. W. J. Hudson, 138–150. Sydney: Sydney University Press.

Rohrbough, Malcolm. 1997. *Days of Gold: The California Gold Rush and the American Nation*. Berkeley: University of California Press.

Rosenberry, William, and Jay O'Brien, eds. 1991. *Golden Ages, Dark Ages: Imagining the Past in Anthropology and History*. Berkeley: University of California Press.

Rowley, Charles D. 1958. *The Australians in German New Guinea*. Melbourne: Melbourne University Press.

———. 1966. *The New Guinea Villager: A Retrospect from 1964*. New York: Praeger.

Sack, Peter, and Dumphna Clark. 1980. *Albert Hahl: Governor in New Guinea*, ed. and trans. Peter Sack and Dumphna Clark. Canberra: Australian National University.

Sahlins, Marshall D. 1963. Poor Man, Rich Man, Big-Man, Chief: Political Types in Melanesia and Polynesia. *Comparative Studies in Society and History* 5: 285–303.

———. 1985. *Islands of History*. Chicago: The University of Chicago Press.

———. 1989. Cosmologies of Capitalism: The Trans-Pacific Sector of "the World System." Radcliffe-Brown Lecture in Social Anthropology, read March 17, 1988. *Proceedings of the British Academy* 74: 1–51.

Sanjek, Roger. 1998. *The Future of Us All: Race and Neighborhood Politics in New York City*. Ithaca, N.Y.: Cornell University Press.

Saville, Gordon, and John Austin. 1974. *"King" of Kiriwina: The Adventures of Sergeant Saville in the South Seas*. London: Leo Cooper.

Scaglion, Richard. 1983. The "Coming" of Independence in Papua New Guinea: An Abelam View. *Journal of the Polynesian Society* 92: 463–486.

———. 1985. *Kiaps* as Kings: Abelam Legal Change in Historical Perspective. In *History and Ethnohistory in Papua New Guinea*, ed. D. Gewertz and E. L. Schieffelin, 77–99. Oceania Monograph No. 28. Sydney: University of Sydney.

———. 1990. Reconstructing First Contact: Some Local Effects of Labor Recruitment in the Sepik. In *Sepik Heritage: Tradition and Change in Papua New Guinea*, ed. N. Lutkehaus et al., 50–57. Durham, N.C.: Carolina Academic Press.

———. 1999. Yam Cycles and Timeless Time in Melanesia. *Ethnology* 38: 211–225.

———. 2000. Zero Hour: Reflecting Backward, Looking Forward. *Ethnohistory* 47 (1): 227–270. Afterword for Special Issue: *Millennial Countdown in New Guinea*, ed. P. J. Stewart and A. J. Strathern.

Scaglion, Richard, and Marie Norman. 2000. Where Resistance Falls Short: Rethinking Agency through Biography. In *Identity Work: Constructing Pacific Lives*, ed. P. J. Stewart and Andrew Strathern. ASAO Monograph Series No. 18. Pittsburgh: University of Pittsburgh Press.

Schieffelin, Edward. L. 1975. Felling the Trees on Top of the Crop. *Oceania* 46: 25–39.

———. 1995. Early Contact as Drama and Manipulation in the Southern Highlands of Papua New Guinea: Pacification as the Structure of the Conjecture. *Comparative Studies in Society and History* 37: 555–580.

Schieffelin, Edward L., and Robert Crittenden, eds. 1991. *Like People You See in a Dream: First Contact in Six Papuan Societies.* Stanford: Stanford University Press.

Schoorl, J. W. 1953. Toestanden en verhoudingen in de nederzettingen van autochtone werklieden, in dienst van de NNGPM te Sorong. Hollandia: University of Utrecht. Mimeograph.

———. 1967. The Anthropologist in Government Service. In *Anthropologists in the Field,* ed. D. G. Jongmans and P. C. W. Gutkind, 170–192. Assen, Neth.: Van Gorcum.

———. ed. 1996. Besturen in Nederlands-Nieuw-Guinea, 1945–1962: Ontwikkelings-werk in een periode van politieke onrust. Leiden, Neth.: KITLV.

Segal, Daniel, and Richard Handler. 1992. How European Is Nationalism? *Social Analysis* 32: 1–16.

Shaw, Carolyn M. 1995. *Colonial Inscriptions: Race, Sex, and Class in Kenya.* Minneapolis: University of Minnesota Press.

Shaw, R. Daniel. 1974. Samo Sibling Terminology. *Oceania* 44: 233–239.

———. 1986. The Bosavi Language Family. *Pacific Linguistics* A-70: 45–76.

———. 1990. *Kandila: Samo Ceremonialism and Interpersonal Relationships.* Ann Arbor: University of Michigan Press.

———. 1996. *From Longhouse to Village: Samo Social Change.* Case Studies in Anthropology Series, ed. George and Louise Spindler. Fort Worth: Harcourt Brace.

Shaw, R. Daniel, and Karen A. Shaw. 1977. Samo Phonemes: Distribution, Interpretation, and Resulting Orthography. *Workpapers in Papua New Guinea Languages* 19: 97–135.

Shirley, Graham. 1994. Australian Cinema: 1896 to the Renaissance. In *Australian Cinema,* ed. S. Murray, 5–44. St. Leonards, NSW: Allen and Unwin.

Silas, Ellis. 1926. *A Primitive Arcadia: Being the Impressions of an Artist in Papua.* Boston: Little, Brown.

Sinclair, James P. 1956–1957. Patrol Report No. 8, Duna. National Archives of Papua New Guinea.

———. 1969. *The Outside Man.* Melbourne: Angus and Robertson.

———. 1984. *Kiap: Australia's Patrol Officers in Papua New Guinea.* Bathurst, NSW: Robert Brown and Associates. [Originally published 1978]

———. 1988. *Last Frontiers: The Explorations of Ivan Champion of Papua.* Broadbeach Waters, Queensland: Pacific Press.

Skinner, R. Ian. 1946–1947. Territory of Papua and New Guinea, Patrol Report No. 2, Kainantu. National Archives of Papua New Guinea.

Slattery, C. W. 1945. Territory of Papua New Guinea, Patrol Report, ANGAU, Toko. National Archives of Papua New Guinea.

Smith, Peter. 1989. Education Policy in Australian New Guinea: A Classic Case. In *Papua New Guinea: A Century of Colonial Impact, 1884–1984,* ed. S. Latukefu, 291–315. Boroko, PNG: The National Research Institute and the University of Papua New Guinea.

Sørum, Arve. 1980. In Search of the Lost Soul: Bedamini Spirit Seances and Curing Rites. *Oceania* 50: 273–296.

Staples, R. J. 1966–1967a. Territory of Papua New Guinea, Patrol Report No. 1, Boku. National Archives of Papua New Guinea.

————. 1966–1967b. Territory of Papua New Guinea, Patrol Report No. 2, Boku. National Archives of Papua New Guinea.

Stocking, George. 1977. Contradicting the Doctor: Billy Hancock and the Problem of Baloma. *History of Anthropology Newsletter* 4 (1): 4–7.

————. 1982a. Gatekeeper to the Field: E. W. P. Chinnery and the Ethnography of the New Guinea Mandate. *History of Anthropology Newsletter* 9 (2): 3–12.

————. 1982b. Afterword: A View from the Center. *Ethnos* 47 (1–2): 173–186.

————, ed. 1991. *Colonial Situations: Essays on the Contextualization of Ethnographic Knowledge*. Vol. 7 of *History of Anthropology*. Madison: University of Wisconsin Press.

Stoler, Ann. 1989. Rethinking Colonial Categories: European Communities and the Boundaries of Rule. *Comparative Studies in Society and History* 13 (1): 134–161.

————. 1991. Carnal Knowledge and Imperial Power: Gender, Race, and Morality in Colonial Asia. In *Gender at the Crossroads of Knowledge*, ed. Micaela di Leonardo, 55–101. Berkeley: University of California Press.

————. 1992a. Rethinking Colonial Categories: European Communities and the Boundaries of Rule. In *Colonialism and Culture*, ed. N. Dirks. Ann Arbor: University of Michigan Press.

————. 1992b. "In Cold Blood": Hierarchies of Credibility and the Politics of Colonial Narratives. *Representations* 37: 151–189.

————. 1995. *Race and the Education of Desire: Foucault's History of Sexuality and the Colonial Order of Things*. Durham and London: Duke University Press.

————. 1997. Sexual Affronts and Racial Frontiers: European Identities and the Cultural Politics of Exclusion in Colonial Southeast Asia. In *Tensions of Empire: Colonial Cultures in a Bourgeois World*, ed. Frederick Cooper and Ann Stoler, 198–237. Berkeley: University of California Press.

Stoler, Ann Laura, and Frederick Cooper. 1997. Between Metropole and Colony: Rethinking a Research Agenda. In *Tensions of Empire: Colonial Cultures in a Bourgeois World*, ed. Frederick Cooper and Ann Stoler, 1–56. Berkeley: University of California Press.

Strathern, Andrew. 1992. Looking Backward and Forward. In *Ethnographic Presents: Pioneering Anthropologists in the Papua New Guinea Highlands*, ed. T. Hays, 250–270. Berkeley: University of California Press.

————. 1996. Structures of Disjuncture. In *Work in Progress: Essays in New Guinea Highlands Ethnography in Honour of Paula Brown Glick*, ed. Hal Levine and Anton Ploeg, 253–268. Frankfurt am Main: Peter Lang.

Strathern, Marilyn. 1992. The Decomposition of an Event. *Cultural Anthropology* 7: 244–254.

Stuart, Ian. 1970. *Port Moresby: Yesterday and Today*. Sydney: Pacific Publications.

Stuart, Robert. 1977. *Nuts to You!* Sydney: Wentworth Books.

Sun, The (Sydney). April 17, 1929; June 18, 1933.

Sundersingh, Julian. 1999. Toward a Media-Based Translation. Ph.D. diss., Fuller Seminary, Pasadena, Calif.

Swadling, Pamela. 1997. *Plumes from Paradise: Trade Cycles in Outer Southeast Asia and Their Impact on New Guinea and Nearby Islands until 1920*. Port Moresby: Papua New Guinea National Museum.

Swinton, A. R. 1957–1958. Territory of Papua and New Guinea, Patrol Report No. 3, Kainantu. National Archives of Papua New Guinea.

Sydney Morning Herald. November 4, 1926; December 30, 1928; March 26, 1960.

Taylor, James L. 1933. Mt. Hagen Patrol. AA CRS A7034 no. 218.

———. 1939. Report of the Hagen-Sepik Patrol.

Taylor, Mary Huber. 1988. *The Bishop's Progress: A Historical Ethnography of Catholic Missionary Experience on the Sepik Frontier*. Washington, D.C.: Smithsonian Institution Press.

Territory of Papua. 1914. Annual Reports.

———. 1918. Annual Reports.

———. 1920. Annual Reports.

———. 1972. Patrol Report, Sudest Island.

Thomas, Nicholas. 1991. *Entangled Objects: Exchange, Material Culture, and Colonialism in the Pacific*. Cambridge: Harvard University Press.

———. 1994. *Colonialism's Culture: Anthropology, Travel, and Government*. Princeton: Princeton University Press.

Thompson, Roger. 1986. Hubert Murray and the Historians. *Pacific Studies* 10 (1): 79–96.

Thomson, Basil. 1937. *The Scene Changes*. Garden City, N.Y.: Doubleday, Doran.

Thurnwald, Hilde. 1938. Ehe und Mutterschaft in Buin. *Archiv fur Anthropologie und Volkerforschung*, n.s., 24: 214–226.

Thurnwald, Richard. 1914. Vom mittleren Sepik zur Nordwestküste von Kaiser-Wilhelmsland. *Mitteilungen aus den Deutschen Schutzgebieten* 27: 81–84.

Thurston, William R. 1994. The Legend of Titikolo: An Anêm Genesis. In *The Children of Kilibob: Creation, Cosmos, and Culture in Northeast New Guinea*, ed. A. Pomponio, D. R. Counts, and T. G. Harding. *Pacific Studies* 17 (4): 183–204.

Townsend, George W. L. 1937. Sepik District Report 31/1. Canberra: Pacific Manuscripts Bureau #632. Microfiche.

———. 1968. *District Officer: From Untamed New Guinea to Lake Success, 1921–46*. Sydney: Pacific Publications.

Tuzin, Donald. 1976. *The Ilahita Arapesh: Dimensions of Unity*. Berkeley: University of California Press.

———. 1983. Cannibalism and Arapesh Cosmology: A Wartime Incident with the Japanese. In *The Ethnography of Cannibalism*, ed. P. Brown and D. Tuzin, 61–71. Washington, D.C.: Society for Psychological Anthropology.

Urry, James. 1997. Writing Yourself into History. *Anthropology Today* 13 (5): 1–2.

van Baal, Jan. 1953–1954. Algemene sociaal-culturele beschouwingen in Nieuw-Guinea: De ontwikkeling op economisch, sociaal en cultureel gebied. In *Nederlands en Australisch Nieuw-Guinea*, Vol. 1, ed. W. C. Klein, 230–258. Den Haag, Neth.: Staatsuitgeverij.

van der Veur, Paul. 1966. *Search for New Guinea's Boundaries: From Torres Strait to the Pacific*. Canberra: Australian National University Press.

van Logchem, Jan Th. 1963. *De Argoeniers: Een Papoea-volk in West Nieuw-Guinea*. Utrecht, Neth.: Schotanus and Jens.

Verschueren MSC, Jan C. 1953–1954. De katholieke missie. In *Nieuw-Guinea: De ontwikkeling op economisch, sociaal en cultureel gebied*, in *Nederlands en Australisch Nieuw-Guinea*, Vol. 1, ed. W. C. Klein, 160–229. Den Haag, Neth.: Staatsuitgeverij.

Wagner, Roy. 1995. Hazarding Intent: Why Sogo Left Hweabi. In *Other Intentions: Cultural Contexts and Attribution of Inner States*, ed. Lawrence Rosen, 163–175. Santa Fe: School of American Research Press.

Wakeford, J. E. 1945–1946. Territory of Papua and New Guinea, Patrol Report No. 1, Maprik. National Archives of Papua New Guinea.

Ward, Alan, et al. 1979. The Hasluck Years: Some Observations. Discussion Paper. Bundoora, Victoria, Australia: Research Centre for Southwest Pacific Studies.

Watson, James B. 1960. A New Guinea "Opening Man." In *In the Company of Man: Twenty Portraits of Anthropological Informants*, ed. Joseph B. Casagrande, 127–174. New York: Harper and Row.

———. 1972. Talking to Strangers. In *Crossing Cultural Boundaries: The Anthropological Experience*, ed. Solon T. Kimball and James B. Watson, 172–181. San Francisco: Chandler.

———. 1992. Kainantu: Recollections of a First Encounter. In *Ethnographic Presents: Pioneering Anthropologists in the Papua New Guinea Highlands*, ed. T. Hays, 167–198. Berkeley: University of California Press.

Watson, Virginia. 1997. *Anyan's Story: A New Guinea Woman in Two Worlds*. Seattle: University of Washington Press.

Wayne, Helena, ed. 1995. *The Story of a Marriage: The Letters of Bronislaw Malinowski and Elsie Masson*. Vol. 1,1916–1920; Vol. 2, 1920–1935. London: Routledge.

Wearne, G. R. 1956–1957. Territory of Papua New Guinea, Patrol Report 6, Buin. National Archives of Papua New Guinea.

Webster, E. M. 1984. *The Moon Man*. Melbourne: Melbourne University Press.

Wedgwood, Camilla. 1945. Education and the Native Environment. Typescript.

Weiner, Annette. 1987. Anthropology and the Colonial Legacy (guest editorial). In *Cultural Anthropology: A Perspective on the Human Condition*, ed. E. Schultz and R. Lavenda, 392–393. St. Paul: West Publishing.

Wesley-Smith, Terence. 1994. Australia and New Zealand. In *Tides of History: The Pacific Islands in the Twentieth Century*, ed. K. R. Howe et al., 195–226. Honolulu: University of Hawai'i Press.

West, Francis James. 1968a. The Historical Background. In *New Guinea on the Threshold: Aspects of Social, Political, and Economic Development*, ed. E. K. Fisk, 3–19. Pittsburgh: University of Pittsburgh Press.

———. 1968b. *Hubert Murray, the Australian Pro-consul*. Melbourne: Oxford University Press.

Wetherell, David. 1982. Charles Abel of Kwato. *Journal of Pacific History* 17: 195–200.

Wetherell, David, and Charlotte Carr-Gregg. 1990. *Camilla: C. H. Wedgwood, 1901–1955, A Life*. Kensington, NSW: University of New South Wales Press.

White, Richard. 1981. *Inventing Australia*. North Sydney, NSW: Allen and Unwin.

Williams, Francis Edgar. [1939] 1977. Creed of a Government Anthropologist. In *"The Vailala Madness" and Other Essays*, ed. Erik Schwimmer, 396–418. Honolulu: University of Hawai'i Press.

Williams, Ronald Maslyn. 1958. New Guinea Patrol: Commentary. Australian Archives, Series A6895 Item 1958/86. Typescript (19 pp.).

———. 1964. *Stone Age Island: New Guinea Today*. Garden City, N.Y.: Doubleday.

————. 1966. Ethnographic Films Made in the Territory of Papua and New Guinea (including the Solomon Islands). Report presented to the Sydney (Australia) Round Table Meeting organized by UNESCO and the Australian National Advisory Committee for UNESCO, July 25–29.

————. 1967a. *The Far Side of the Sky*. New York: William Morrow.

————. 1967b. Oral History Interview, Hazel de Berg Recordings. Canberra: National Library of Australia.

Wiltshire, J. A. 1957–1958. Territory of Papua and New Guinea, Patrol Report No. 4, Kainantu. National Archives of Papua New Guinea.

Wise, Tigger. 1985. *The Self-Made Anthropologist: A Life of A. P. Elkin*. Sydney: George Allen and Unwin.

Wolf, Eric. 1982. *Europe and the People without History*. Berkeley: University of California Press.

Wolfers, Edward P. 1975. *Race Relations and Colonial Rule in Papua New Guinea*. Brookvale, NSW: Australia and New Zealand Book Co.

————. 1989. For the First "Generation With No Personal Recollection of Australian Rule"; Reflections on the Impact of Colonial Rule in Papua New Guinea. In *Papua New Guinea: A Century of Colonial Impact, 1884–1984*, ed. S. Latukefu, 417–444. Boroko, PNG: The National Research Institute and the University of Papua New Guinea.

Woollacott, Angela. 1997. "All this is the Empire, I told myself": Australian Women's Voyages "Home" and the Articulation of Colonial Whiteness. *American Historical Review* 102 (4): 1003–1029.

Wright, Malcolm. 1966. *The Gentle Savage*. Melbourne: Lansdowne Press.

Yoshihara, Tsutomu. 1955. Southern Cross: An Account of the Eastern New Guinea Campaign. Translated by Doris Heath. Canberra: Australian War Memorial, Class. No. 118.5.

Young, Michael. 1992. Gone Native in Isles of Illusion: In Search of Asterisk in Epi. In *History and Tradition in Melanesian Anthropology*, ed. James Carrier, 193–223. Berkeley: University of California Press.

————. 1998. *Malinowski's Kiriwina: Fieldwork Photography 1915–1918*. Chicago: University of Chicago Press.

Zanjani, Sally. 1997. *A Mine of Her Own: Women Prospectors in the American West, 1850–1950*. Lincoln: University of Nebraska Press.

Index

Abelam, 11, 13, 151–53, 156–62

Administration, 5–10, 17–18, 20, 22–26, 41, 45, 58–60, 68–70, 87, 90, 111–12, 114–18, 120–21, 149, 173, 175, 179–81, 183–86, 201*n4*, 202*n6*, 210*n8*, 217*n11*, 220*n5*; Australian, 2–4, 19, 32–33, 38, 47, 62, 71–72, 91–92, 113, 204*n22*, 207*n15*; Dutch, 32–33, 37

Administrative College, 190, 218*n13*

Administrative control, 22, 87, 96, 104, 114, 152–53

AFC. *See* Australian Film Commission

agency, 11, 13, 65, 127, 151–52, 162, 166, 171–72, 179, 192, 197, 215*n1*

ANGAU. *See* Australian New Guinea Administrative Unit

anthropologist, 12, 29, 45, 48–49, 52–54, 176, 183, 203*n13*, 216n3

anthropology: academic, 43; of colonialism, 27, 44, 46, 48, 62, 145, 195–98, 220*n6*; ethics, 41; history of, 46, 194

ANU. *See* Australian National University

Apulala, Moll, 12, 151–52, 154, 157–60

Asad, Talal, 27, 46, 145, 194–95

Asia Pacific Christian Mission, 176

ASOPA. *See* Australian School of Pacific Administration

Australian Film Commission, 208*n6*

Australian government film, 64, 74, 208*nn2, 5*

Australian national identity, 8, 64–65, 71, 73

Australian National University, 175, 186–87, 203*n3*

Australian New Guinea Administrative Unit, 19, 32, 54

Australian School of Pacific Administration, 7, 25, 50, 52–53, 55, 57, 59–61, 70, 198, 218*n3*

Bariai, 83, 99–100, 104, 201*n4*, 209*n2*

Bedamini, 175, 179–80, 217*n11*

Berndt, Ronald, 49, 55, 60

Bible, 12, 173, 176–77, 182–83, 192, 216*n3*, 217*n9*

big man, 9, 11, 112, 114, 151, 168

Bougainville, 10, 24, 37, 53, 111–13, 116–24, 207*n16*, 212*nn4–6, 8*

British New Guinea, 3, 17, 125–31, 138–39, 146, 149

Brown, George, 16

Brown, Paula, 2, 7, 15, 50–51, 60, 204*n22*

Brudo, Simone and Raphael, 131

Burns Philp, 128–29, 135, 138, 141–42, 210*n6*

cadet training. *See* patrols, training

cannibalism, 13, 18, 56, 147, 165, 173, 175, 177–83, 192

cargo cult, 39–40, 58, 60, 120, 124, 157, 198–99, 205*n24*, 207*n18*

Catholic Church, 30, 112, 123

census, 5–6, 12, 19, 22–23, 30, 54–55, 74, 90, 93, 129, 142, 147, 175, 184–85, 218*n16*

CFU. *See* Commonwealth Film Unit

Cheeseman, Evelyn, 138

Chinese. *See* traders

Chinnery: E. W. P., 25, 33, 47, 88, 90, 105, 197, 203*n9*; Sarah, 105, 107

Christianity, 123, 176, 182, 185, 193, 199

Cleland, Sir Donald, 20, 60, 69

Colonial studies, 195–96, 199–200

Colonial: administration, 3, 5, 9, 16, 18, 22, 32, 37, 47, 111, 149, 195; contact, 24, 27, 31, 34, 36, 39–42, 44, 145, 196; government, 3, 10, 26, 47, 111, 126, 128, 147, 151–52, 156, 207*n15*; policy, 50, 63

colonialism, 7, 46, 48, 92, 145–46, 171–73, 192–200, 210*n11*; masculinity and, 8, 128, 149; women and, 125

Commonwealth Film Unit, 65–68, 74–78, 208*n6*

ConZinc Riotinto Australia (CRA), 115–16, 118–19, 212*n4*

culture of colonialism, 26, 28, 177, 210*n11*

culture of contact, 25–26, 191–92

Daru, 142, 180
decolonization, 4, 7, 34, 41–42, 49, 68
didiman, 187–88; and chilies, 218*n18*
District Officer, 29–30, 58–59, 89, 92, 95–
97, 108, 160, 163–64, 173, 210*n8*, 211*n17*,
212*n5*
Downs, Ian, 8, 20–21, 24, 49, 51–52, 60–61,
204*n17*

education, 189, 218*n14*, 219*n19*
emancipation, 4, 28, 34, 41–42
ethnography: colonial, 45, 206*n1*
exchange, 11, 127, 132–38, 148, 178, 202*n1*,
206*n28*, 213*n4*

Far Side of the Sky, 79–80
Fenbury, D. M., 32, 48, 52, 211*n21*
first contact, 4, 12, 15–16, 22, 34–36, 38, 173,
204*n19*; first encounter, 21, 23, 73–74, 157
First Contact, 81
First World War, 18, 109, 130, 152
Foot Report, 49

Gebusi, 180, 217*n11*
German New Guinea, 16–18, 31, 129, 139, 198
Gofton, Flora, 127, 135, 139, 143–45, 148,
201*n5*, 214*n6*
gold: dust, 11, 129–30, 132–34, 136, 148;
mines, 133; mining, 151, 158; rush, 125,
129, 132, 137, 139, 142; goldfields, 139,
143–44, 153–54, 159
government anthropologist, 32, 60, 90,
202*n4*, 203*n8*; Charles Julius, 25; E. W. P.
Chinnery, 25, 33, 47, 88, 105, 197; F. E.
Williams, 25, 33, 47, 197; Walter Strong,
47
government film, 8, 64–66, 73–74, 76, 80–
81, 208*nn2, 5*
Grimshaw, Beatrice, 127, 133, 136–38, 148–
49, 201*n5*

Haddon, A. C., 47
Hasluck, Paul, 7–9, 20, 65–76, 79, 120, 179

Hiri Motu. *See* language
Hogbin, Ian, 48, 197
hotels, 130, 138–41, 150
household aggregation, 184

Indo-Europeans, 33, 202*n6*
Indonesia, 15, 20, 32–34, 42, 79, 209*n11*
inequality, 27–28, 34, 42
Irian Jaya, 4, 29, 33–34, 41–42, 44, 202*n5*,
204*n20*

Japanese, 11, 19, 113, 122, 145, 151, 154–56,
162, 164–68
Julius, Charles, 25, 59–60, 203*n8*

Kainantu Subdistrict, 45, 51, 54, 59
Kajizuki, Kikuo, 165–66
Kamoro, 29, 202*n4*
Kantoor voor Bevolkingszaken, 32
Kiap(s), 5–6, 9–10, 12, 22, 24–25, 35, 38, 45,
47, 51–60, 62, 88, 90–92, 94, 103, 106,
109–10, 114, 162, 179, 181–82, 184, 200,
205*n23*, 206*n6*, 211*n23*; indigenous, 13;
national officer, 190, 217*n10*; Papua New
Guinean, 61
Kirke, Hunter, 154, 162–63
kula, 132, 134–36

labor: indigenous, 38; recruitment, 20, 23,
152, 158; recruit native, 96; recruited for,
25; recruitment of, 6, 37
language: Hiri Motu, 191, 217*n12*; group, 24,
57; pidgin, 50, 53, 57, 89, 117, 125, 133,
145, 166, 213*nn1, 3*; Tok Pisin, 23, 57, 88–
89, 159, 168, 176, 187, 204*n16*, 213*n1*,
217*n12*
law and order, 23, 26, 70, 74, 96, 173
Lawes: Fanny, 130; William, 16
Lawrence, Peter, 50, 57, 60–61, 114, 157, 197–
98, 220*n7*
League of Nations, 3–4, 10, 19, 86, 99
Leahy, Michael, 19, 35–36, 51
linguistics, 55–57, 91, 180, 202*n5*, 215*n4*,
216*n3*, 217*n9*
literacy, 41, 206*n29*

London Missionary Society, 16, 130

MacGregor, William, 17–18, 132, 163
Mack, Margaret, 9, 85–86, 99, 102, 104,
 209nn3, 4
magistrate, 3, 132, 138, 142, 146–47, 190–91
Mahony: Elizabeth, 125–32, 136–37, 142–43,
 147–50, 170, 213n3; Frank, 135, 142; John,
 132–34
Malinowski, Bronislaw, 50, 126, 131, 134–35,
 137, 140, 142–45, 148, 213n2
mandated territory, 3, 19, 32, 197, 201n2; of
 New Guinea, 31, 33, 83–84, 86, 88, 142,
 144
Maprik, 54, 154–56, 158–62, 166–67
maritime frontier, 138, 145, 147
masculine, 8, 10, 148
McAuley, James, 48–53, 62
Mead, Margaret, 93, 138, 210n13
medical assistance, 188
medical assistant, 13–14, 72, 102, 154, 175,
 201n4
Melanesian Institute for Pastoral and Socio-
 Economic Service, 204n16
Mesiamo, 9–10, 13, 112–14, 122–23
Mimika, 12, 29–31
mining, 33, 96, 118–19, 123, 130, 139, 160,
 162, 212n4, 214n6
Misima Island, 130, 137
missionaries, 2, 10–11, 12, 15, 16, 18–24, 26,
 28–32, 34, 35, 37, 38, 51, 122, 126–27, 147,
 149, 173, 176–77, 182, 183, 197–98, 200,
 202n2, 204n22, 205n23, 217n9
missions: Anglican, 204n16; Asia Pacific
 Christian Mission, 176; Catholic, 16, 29–
 30, 38, 112, 122–23, 145, 203n10, 204n16;
 Methodist, 16, 122, 127; Protestant, 30,
 127; Seventh Day Adventist, 122
Mokolkols, 104, 211n21. See also Mukolkol
Mukolkol, 91
Murray: Sir Hubert, 18, 47–48, 126, 128, 130–
 31, 133, 136–38, 149, 201n5; J. K., 59

Nagovisi, 9–10, 111–12, 115–23
Nakanai, 92, 94–99, 103–4, 109–10

Native Affairs Bureau, 202n4
Netherlands New Guinea, 203n11
New Deal, 48, 52, 62
New Guinea Patrol, 65, 71–75, 77, 79
New Guinea Research Unit, 33
Nomad Patrol Post, 190
Nomad River, 172, 175–76, 186, 188, 190,
 216n6, 218n17

Pacific War, 31–32, 33, 37, 169, 204n21
pacification, 4, 17, 21–23, 28, 35, 37–38, 70,
 92, 111, 180
Paliau Movement, 39
Papua New Guinea, 2, 12–13, 24, 28, 34, 39,
 41–42, 44, 48–51, 56, 58, 61–63, 72, 111,
 116, 120, 122, 157–58, 165, 171, 173, 190–
 91, 196, 200, 201n2, 202nn2, 5–6,
 203nn12–14, 204n16, 206n3, 213n1, 217n9,
 219n19; Papua and New Guinea, 4, 7–8,
 10, 14–15, 19–20, 23, 25, 31–34, 47, 64–
 68, 70–71, 75, 79, 127–29, 145, 147, 156,
 204n21; administration, 33; National
 Archives, 45, 201n3
paranoia, 10, 24, 111–12, 118, 121, 208n6
Parer, Ray, 159–61
Parkinson, Phoebe, 17, 92–93, 210n13
paternalism, 10, 13, 24, 75, 86, 111–13, 115,
 156, 191
Patrol Officer, 5–11, 13–14, 20, 23, 25, 48, 50–
 51, 53, 57–58, 70, 72–74, 76, 82–84, 88–
 90, 94, 96–98, 102, 104, 107–9, 113–15,
 117–18, 120–21, 128, 136, 145, 154–57,
 162–64, 171, 173, 175, 183, 185, 193,
 210nn8, 10
patrol reports, 2, 5–6, 10, 45–46, 48, 53–62,
 72–73, 81, 83, 90, 99, 103–4, 111, 113–18,
 120–24, 156, 183, 186; as text, 7, 9, 180
patrols: cadet, 6, 50, 70, 88–89, 92, 94, 154;
 training, 6–7, 45–48, 50, 52, 57, 60–62,
 87–88, 118, 202n7, 203n13
Pax Neêrlandica, 37
pearl shell, 129–30, 133, 214n8
pearlers, 11, 127, 129, 138
Pidgin. See language
plantation(s), 1, 6–7, 11, 14–17, 20, 22, 33, 37,

99–100, 112, 120, 122, 124–27, 130, 136–
38, 141–43, 147, 149–52, 154, 158, 199,
210n13, 211n19, 212n6, 213n3, 214n5,
220n6
police, 19–21, 23–25, 72, 91–93, 95, 97–98,
100, 106, 108, 175, 179, 186, 190, 217n10;
indigenous, 51, 200; native constabulary,
5; native, 17, 79, 94, 96, 153, 163, 168
Port Moresby, 16, 18, 60, 68–69, 107, 127–
30, 138–41, 143–44, 147, 190, 214n6,
218n13
Pouwer, Jan, 12, 29, 31, 202n4
Powdermaker, Hortense, 139
progress, 5–6, 8, 10–11, 13, 20, 24, 68, 70, 72,
74, 78, 111, 116, 156–57
propaganda, 64–65, 74–75, 77, 208n6;
defined, 208n1
proselytization, 4, 35, 37–38
prospecting, 19–21, 94–95, 105, 118

Queen of Sudest. See Mahony, Elizabeth

Radcliffe-Brown, A. R., 6, 47–48, 50
raiding, 13, 175, 178–81, 216n4, 217n12
Read, Kenneth, 50, 52, 55–56
regional development, 177, 185
Rockefeller Foundation, 47
Rossel Island, 133, 135–36, 147

Salisbury, Richard, 55–56
Samarai, 127, 130–31, 135–36, 138–44, 147,
201n5, 213n3
Samo, 12–13, 171–73, 175–93
schools, 16, 26, 176, 189
Second World War, 151, 154, 167, 197
short-circuit reactions, 38
short-term ethnographic research, 41
SIL. See Summer Institute of Linguistics
Silas, Ellis, 131, 136, 140
Sinclair, James, 5, 18, 20–22, 51–52, 55, 72–
73, 79, 81, 205n23
Siwai, 112, 114, 116–17, 119
Stocking, George, 46, 62, 145, 194–95,
203n9, 206n2, 213n2
Stone Age Island, 78

Strong, Walter, 47
subaltern studies, 111, 121, 195, 200, 212n8
Sudest Island, 125, 129–30, 132–33, 135–36,
139, 142, 213nn1, 4
Summer Institute of Linguistics, 12, 176,
217n9
Sydney University, 34, 47–48, 50, 57, 203n13

taxation, 175, 186
Territory of Papua, 3, 70, 126, 128–29, 131,
149, 213n4
Thomas, Nicholas, 2, 15, 27, 46, 62–63, 81,
147, 169, 172, 192, 196, 198
Thurnwald, Richard, 35, 117, 152
time, notions of, 156
Tok Pisin. See language
Townsend, G. W. L., 24, 153–54, 160, 163
trade: Papuan, 134–35; goods, 18, 21, 23, 25,
133–35, 216n4; routes, 104, 134;
tradestores, 121, 129–30, 187, 189, 192
traders: Chinese, 20, 29, 33, 146; white, 125–
27, 130, 132–36, 147, 213n4
Trobriand Islands, 131, 134, 145
Tuzin, Donald, 54, 154, 207n7, 215n6

UN Trusteeship, 10, 71, 73
United Nations, 7–8, 10, 19–20, 32, 41, 49,
65, 67, 71–72, 124
unofficial whites, 13, 126–28, 147–48, 150

Vanatinai. See Sudest Island
village nucleation, 177, 183

Watson, James B., 40–41, 51, 56, 58, 106,
205n26, 206n6, 207n16, 211nn22, 23
Wedgwood, Camilla, 48, 50, 126, 196
West New Britain, 5–7, 82–83, 99, 157,
205n25, 209n2
West New Guinea, 20, 30, 31–34, 37, 41–42,
202nn5, 6, 203n12, 204nn15, 21
West Papua. See Irian Jaya
Western Province, 171, 186, 217n9, 219n19
Williams: F. E., 25, 33, 47, 197, 203n9;
Maslyn, 8–9, 13, 64–84, 208nn4–5, 7,
209nn10, 11

women: white, 11, 24, 125, 129, 142, 144, 149, 201$n5$, 214$n7$; European, 126–28, 139, 145, 148, 150

World War I, 9, 18, 83, 111, 138, 152

World War II, 7, 11, 18–19, 45, 47–48, 50, 54, 62, 64, 66, 111, 113–14, 120, 122, 125, 128, 145, 148, 151, 158, 197, 206$n1$, 212$n8$, 213$nn1$, 3

Wright, Malcolm, 47–48, 53

Yali, 58, 114, 157, 207$n18$

Yoshihara, Tsutomu, 155